NO COLLAR, NO SERVICE

A *Pooch Café* COLLECTION BY PAUL GILLIGAN

Andrews McMeel
Publishing

Kansas City

For information, write Andrews McMeel Publishing, an Andrews McMeel Universal company, 4520 Main Street, Kansas City, Missouri 64111.

05 06 07 08 09 BBG 10 9 8 7 6 5 4 3 2 1

ISBN: 0-7407-5003-8

Library of Congress Control Number: 2004112530

www.uComics.com

To Mom, for always making sure the peanut butter side was on top; to Dad, for building a Styrofoam fireplace so Santa could get into the house; and to all the dogs who passed through my life (you know who you are).

Foreword
by Sean Hayes

I have a dog. Her name is Madeline. She's an Australian shepherd. I've often wondered what she would sound like if she could speak. I think it would sound something like this: "Hi. I'm Madeline." Didn't think she'd have a slight drawl being an Aussie, but dogs always surprise. I guess that's why I love them. They're like infinite infants—an unending curiosity—constantly thinking and scheming about how to work any situation into their favor. I had never thought about what my dog does after I leave the house until I picked up *Pooch Café*. Now I'm left wondering if Maddy helps herself to the fridge, flips on the TV, or simply logs onto chat rooms for other pooches. Whatever she's doing, I just hope she finds time to kvetch about her owner in some local canine tavern, with a cast of characters as vibrant as those found in the magnificent world that Paul Gilligan has created with *Pooch Café*.

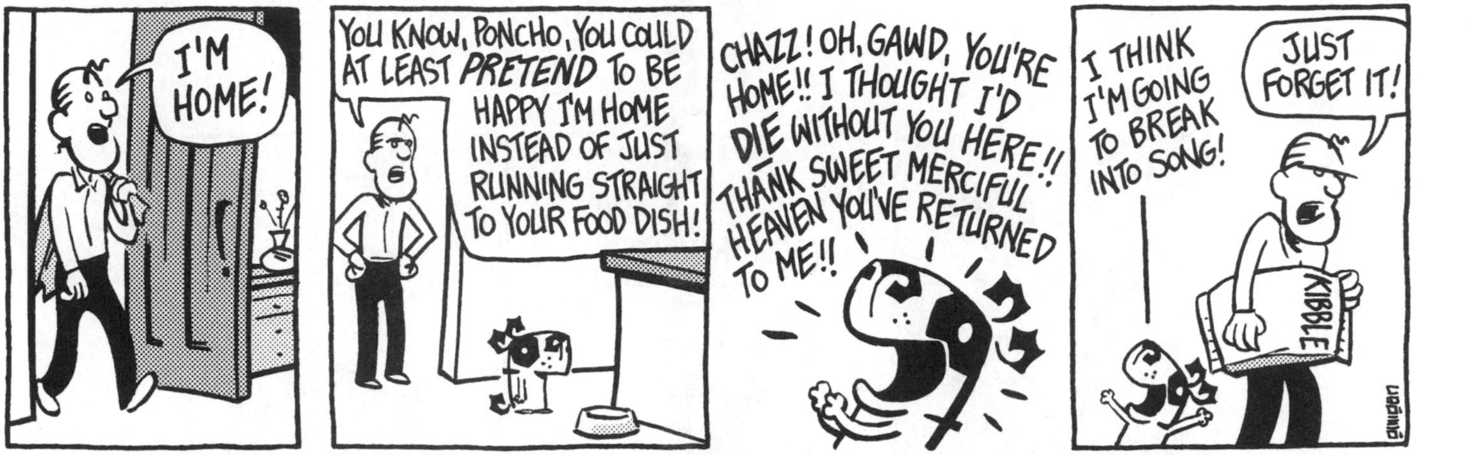
I'M HOME!
YOU KNOW, PONCHO, YOU COULD AT LEAST PRETEND TO BE HAPPY I'M HOME INSTEAD OF JUST RUNNING STRAIGHT TO YOUR FOOD DISH!
CHAZZ! OH, GAWD, YOU'RE HOME!! I THOUGHT I'D DIE WITHOUT YOU HERE!! THANK SWEET MERCIFUL HEAVEN YOU'VE RETURNED TO ME!!
I THINK I'M GOING TO BREAK INTO SONG!
JUST FORGET IT!
KIBBLE

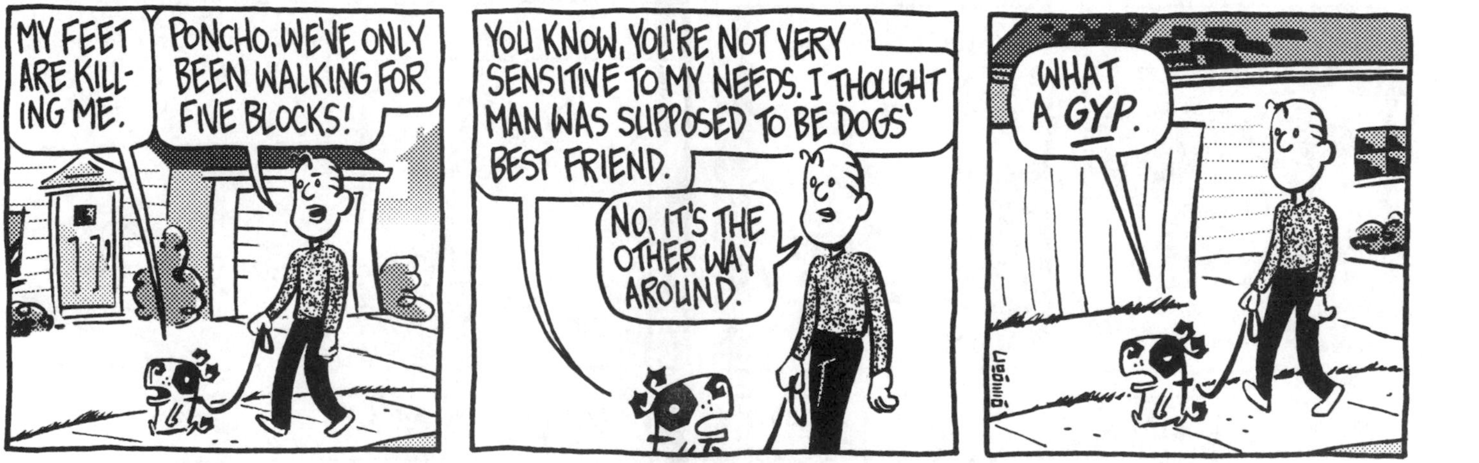
MY FEET ARE KILL-ING ME.
PONCHO, WE'VE ONLY BEEN WALKING FOR FIVE BLOCKS!
YOU KNOW, YOU'RE NOT VERY SENSITIVE TO MY NEEDS. I THOUGHT MAN WAS SUPPOSED TO BE DOGS' BEST FRIEND.
NO, IT'S THE OTHER WAY AROUND.
WHAT A GYP.

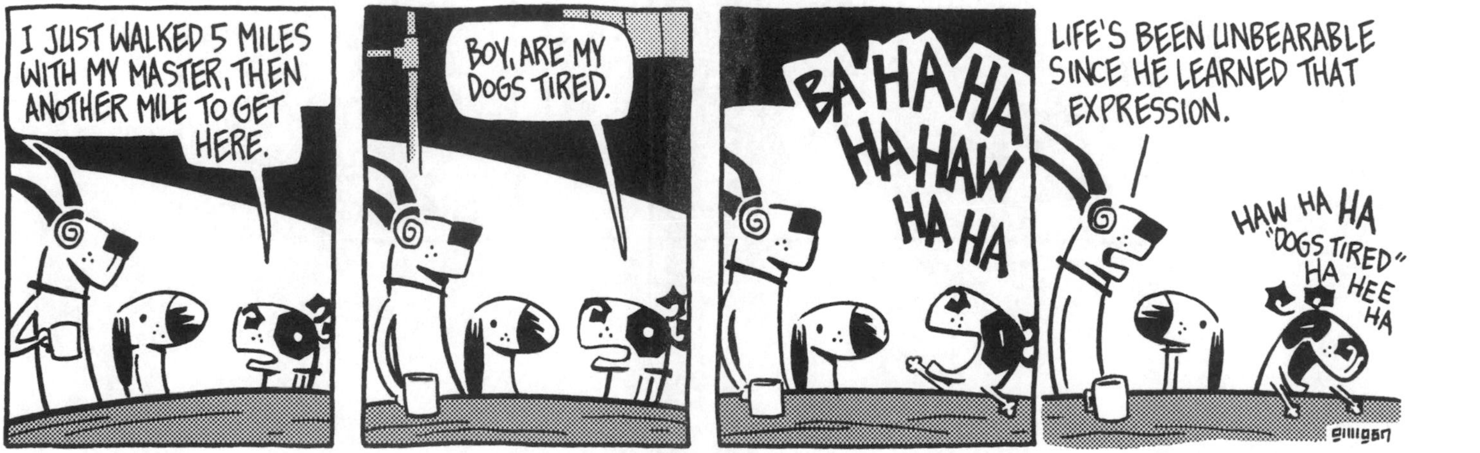
I JUST WALKED 5 MILES WITH MY MASTER, THEN ANOTHER MILE TO GET HERE.
BOY, ARE MY DOGS TIRED.
BA HA HA HA HA HAW HA HA
LIFE'S BEEN UNBEARABLE SINCE HE LEARNED THAT EXPRESSION.
HAW HA HA "DOGS TIRED" HA HEE HA

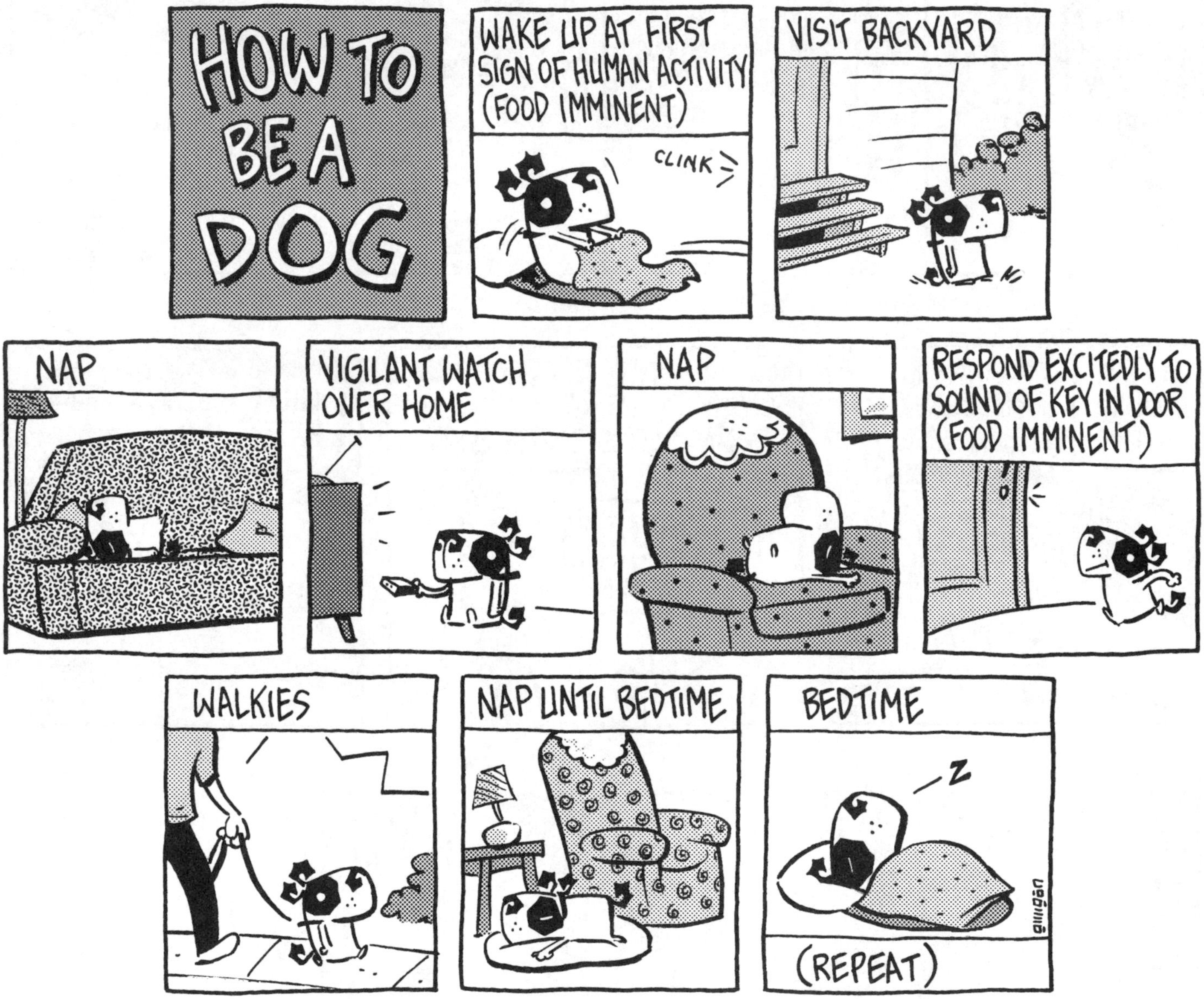
HOW TO BE A DOG
WAKE UP AT FIRST SIGN OF HUMAN ACTIVITY (FOOD IMMINENT)
CLINK
VISIT BACKYARD
NAP
VIGILANT WATCH OVER HOME
NAP
RESPOND EXCITEDLY TO SOUND OF KEY IN DOOR (FOOD IMMINENT)
WALKIES
NAP UNTIL BEDTIME
BEDTIME
Z
(REPEAT)
Gilligan

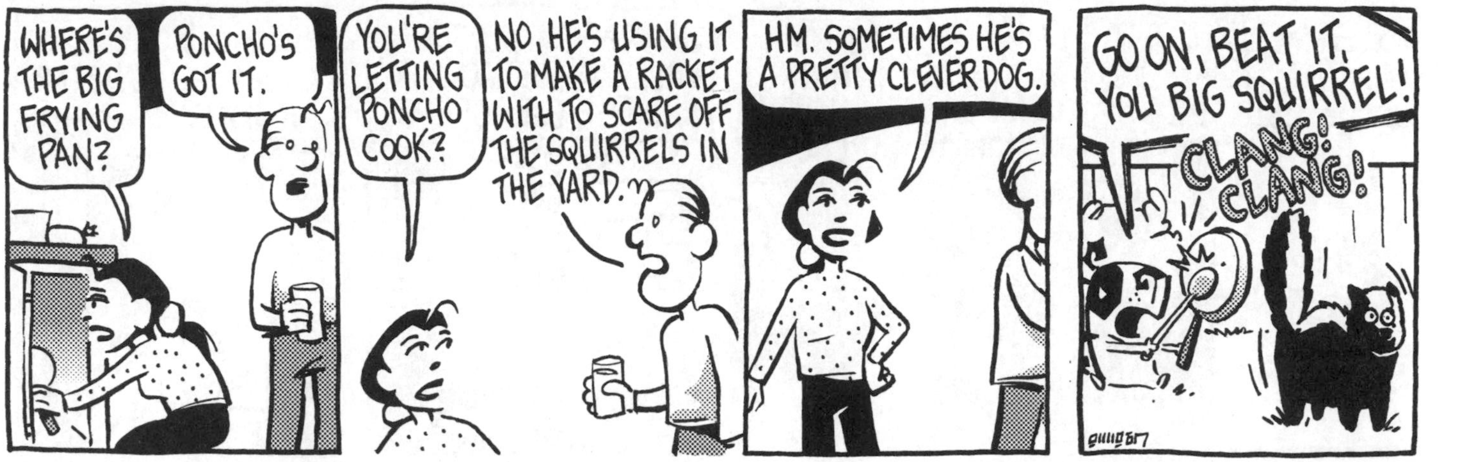
WHERE'S THE BIG FRYING PAN?
PONCHO'S GOT IT.
YOU'RE LETTING PONCHO COOK?
NO, HE'S USING IT TO MAKE A RACKET WITH TO SCARE OFF THE SQUIRRELS IN THE YARD.
HM. SOMETIMES HE'S A PRETTY CLEVER DOG.
GO ON, BEAT IT, YOU BIG SQUIRREL!
CLANG! CLANG!

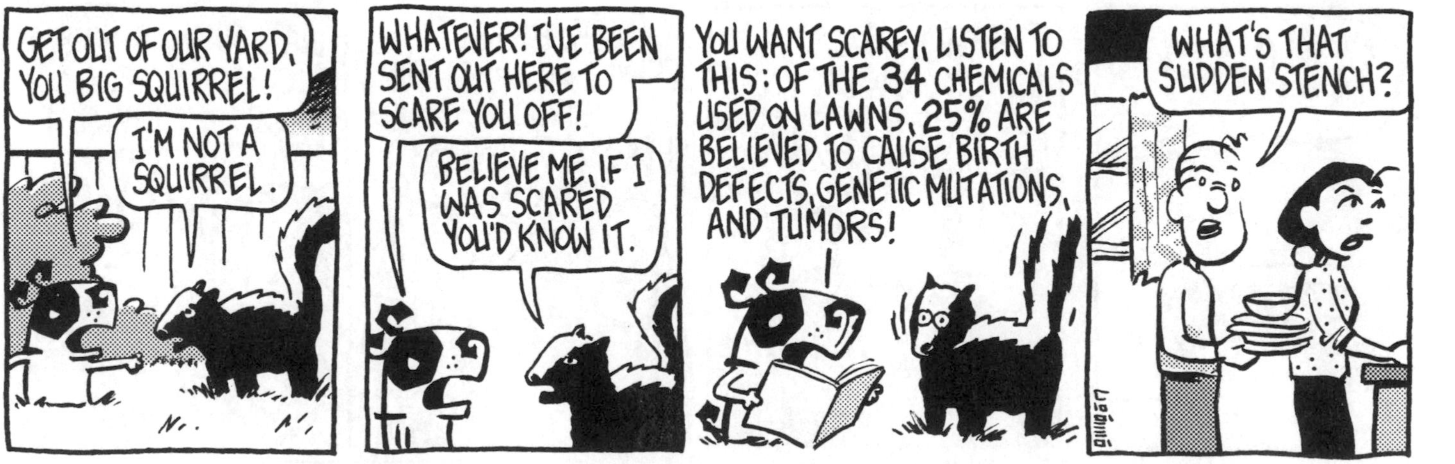
GET OUT OF OUR YARD, YOU BIG SQUIRREL!
I'M NOT A SQUIRREL.
WHATEVER! I'VE BEEN SENT OUT HERE TO SCARE YOU OFF!
BELIEVE ME, IF I WAS SCARED YOU'D KNOW IT.
YOU WANT SCAREY, LISTEN TO THIS: OF THE 34 CHEMICALS USED ON LAWNS, 25% ARE BELIEVED TO CAUSE BIRTH DEFECTS, GENETIC MUTATIONS, AND TUMORS!
WHAT'S THAT SUDDEN STENCH?

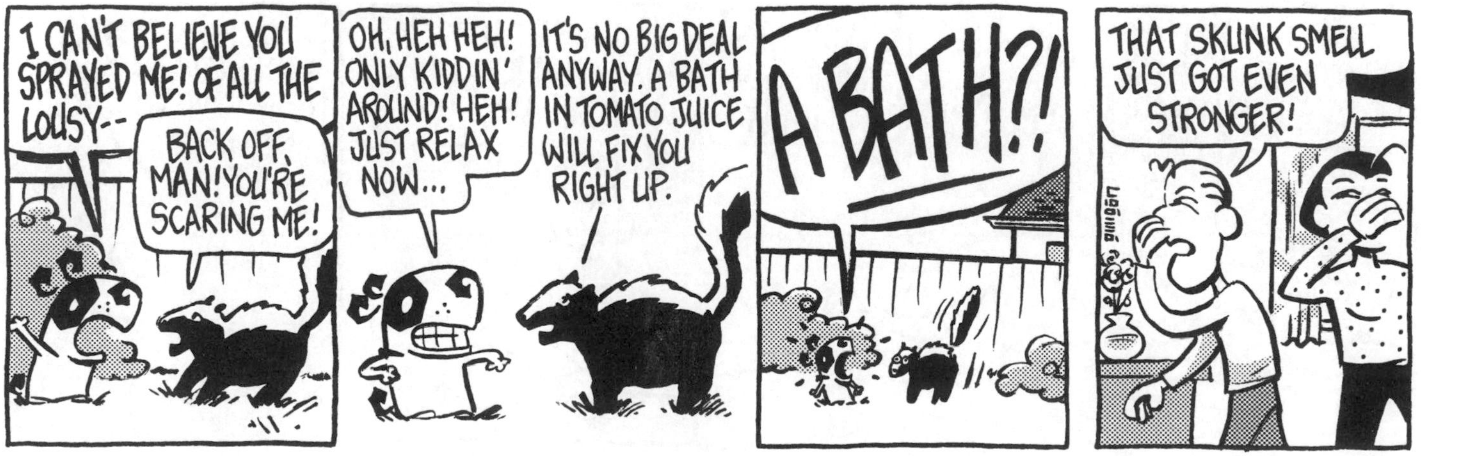
I CAN'T BELIEVE YOU SPRAYED ME! OF ALL THE LOUSY--
BACK OFF, MAN! YOU'RE SCARING ME!
OH, HEH HEH! ONLY KIDDIN' AROUND! HEH! JUST RELAX NOW...
IT'S NO BIG DEAL ANYWAY. A BATH IN TOMATO JUICE WILL FIX YOU RIGHT UP.
A BATH?!
THAT SKUNK SMELL JUST GOT EVEN STRONGER!

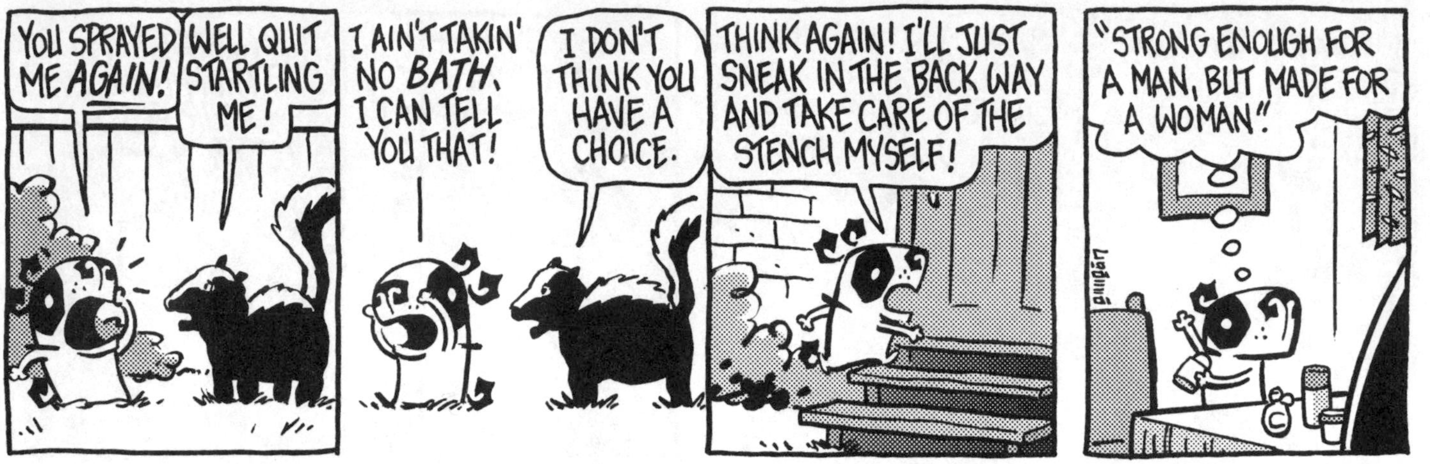
YOU SPRAYED ME *AGAIN*!
WELL QUIT STARTLING ME!
I AIN'T TAKIN' NO *BATH*. I CAN TELL YOU THAT!
I DON'T THINK YOU HAVE A CHOICE.
THINK AGAIN! I'LL JUST SNEAK IN THE BACK WAY AND TAKE CARE OF THE STENCH MYSELF!
"STRONG ENOUGH FOR A MAN, BUT MADE FOR A WOMAN."

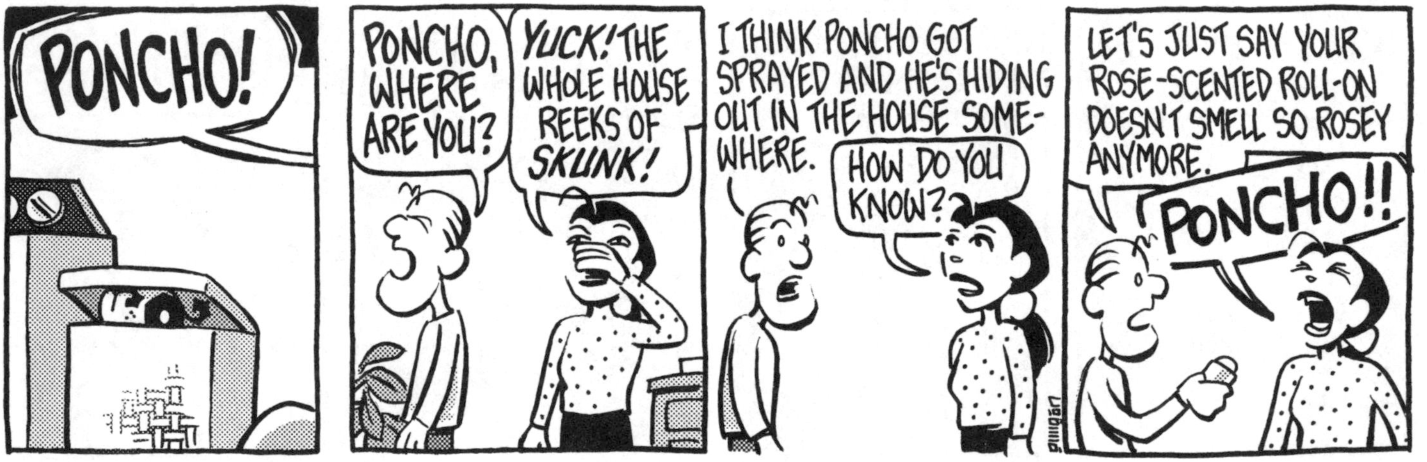
PONCHO!
PONCHO, WHERE ARE YOU?
YUCK! THE WHOLE HOUSE REEKS OF *SKUNK*!
I THINK PONCHO GOT SPRAYED AND HE'S HIDING OUT IN THE HOUSE SOMEWHERE.
HOW DO YOU KNOW?
LET'S JUST SAY YOUR ROSE-SCENTED ROLL-ON DOESN'T SMELL SO ROSEY ANYMORE.
PONCHO!!

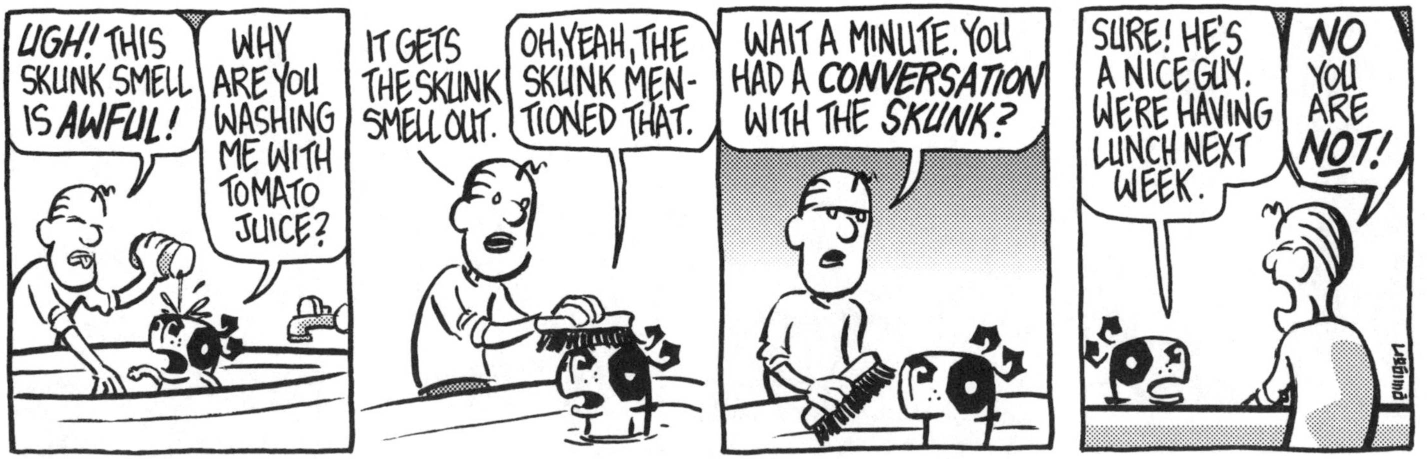
UGH! THIS SKUNK SMELL IS *AWFUL*!
WHY ARE YOU WASHING ME WITH TOMATO JUICE?
IT GETS THE SKUNK SMELL OUT.
OH, YEAH, THE SKUNK MENTIONED THAT.
WAIT A MINUTE. YOU HAD A *CONVERSATION* WITH THE *SKUNK*?
SURE! HE'S A NICE GUY. WE'RE HAVING LUNCH NEXT WEEK.
NO YOU ARE *NOT*!

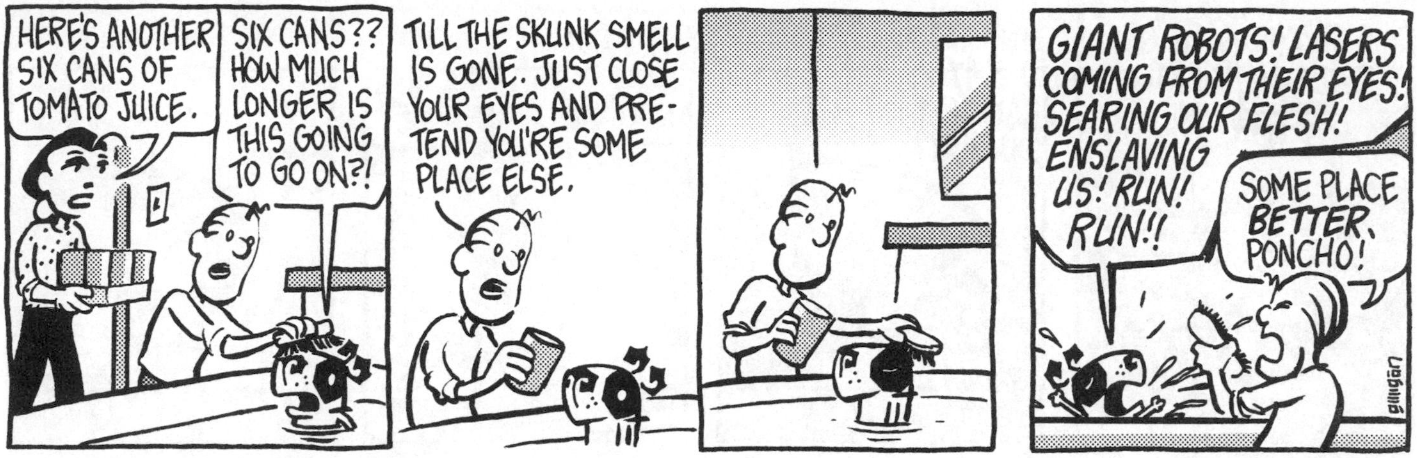
HERE'S ANOTHER SIX CANS OF TOMATO JUICE.
SIX CANS?? HOW MUCH LONGER IS THIS GOING TO GO ON?!
TILL THE SKUNK SMELL IS GONE. JUST CLOSE YOUR EYES AND PRE-TEND YOU'RE SOME PLACE ELSE.
GIANT ROBOTS! LASERS COMING FROM THEIR EYES! SEARING OUR FLESH! ENSLAVING US! RUN! RUN!!
SOME PLACE BETTER, PONCHO!

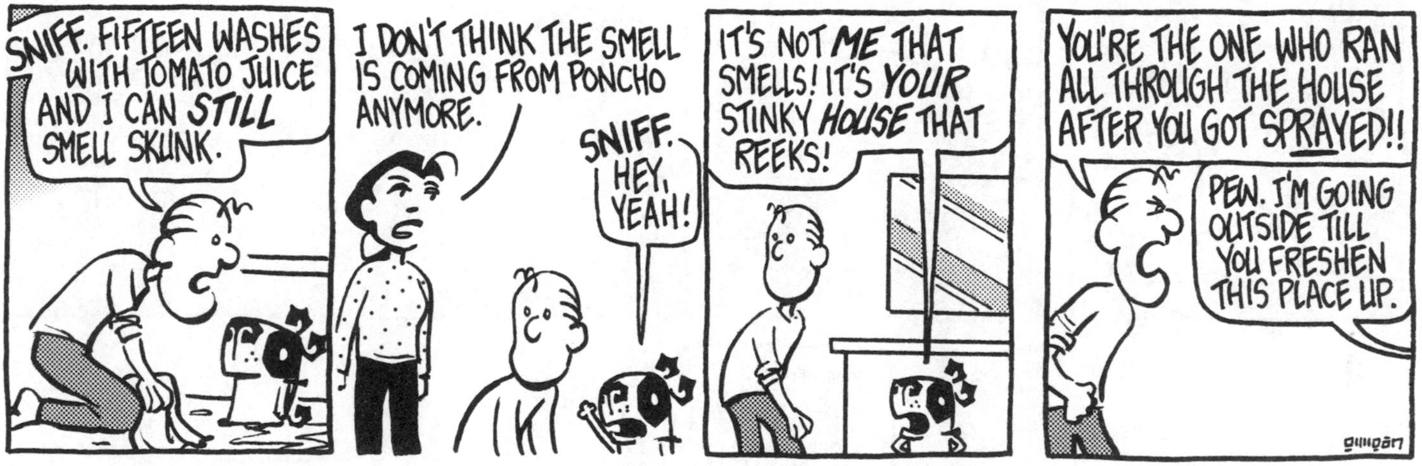
SNIFF. FIFTEEN WASHES WITH TOMATO JUICE AND I CAN STILL SMELL SKUNK.
I DON'T THINK THE SMELL IS COMING FROM PONCHO ANYMORE.
SNIFF. HEY, YEAH!
IT'S NOT ME THAT SMELLS! IT'S YOUR STINKY HOUSE THAT REEKS!
YOU'RE THE ONE WHO RAN ALL THROUGH THE HOUSE AFTER YOU GOT SPRAYED!!
PEW. I'M GOING OUTSIDE TILL YOU FRESHEN THIS PLACE UP.

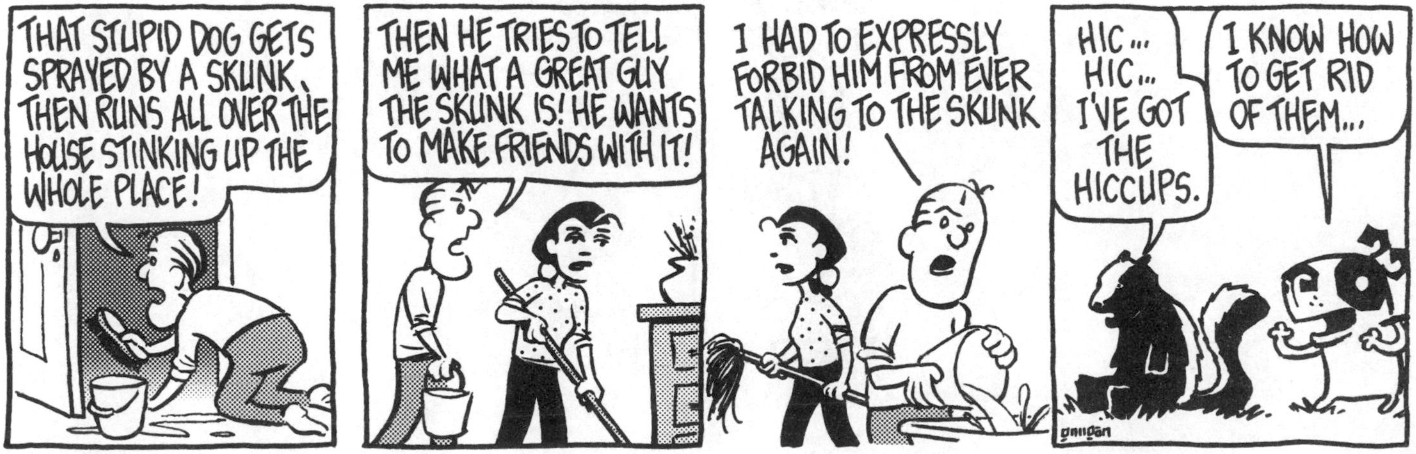
THAT STUPID DOG GETS SPRAYED BY A SKUNK, THEN RUNS ALL OVER THE HOUSE STINKING UP THE WHOLE PLACE!
THEN HE TRIES TO TELL ME WHAT A GREAT GUY THE SKUNK IS! HE WANTS TO MAKE FRIENDS WITH IT!
I HAD TO EXPRESSLY FORBID HIM FROM EVER TALKING TO THE SKUNK AGAIN!
HIC... HIC... I'VE GOT THE HICCUPS.
I KNOW HOW TO GET RID OF THEM...

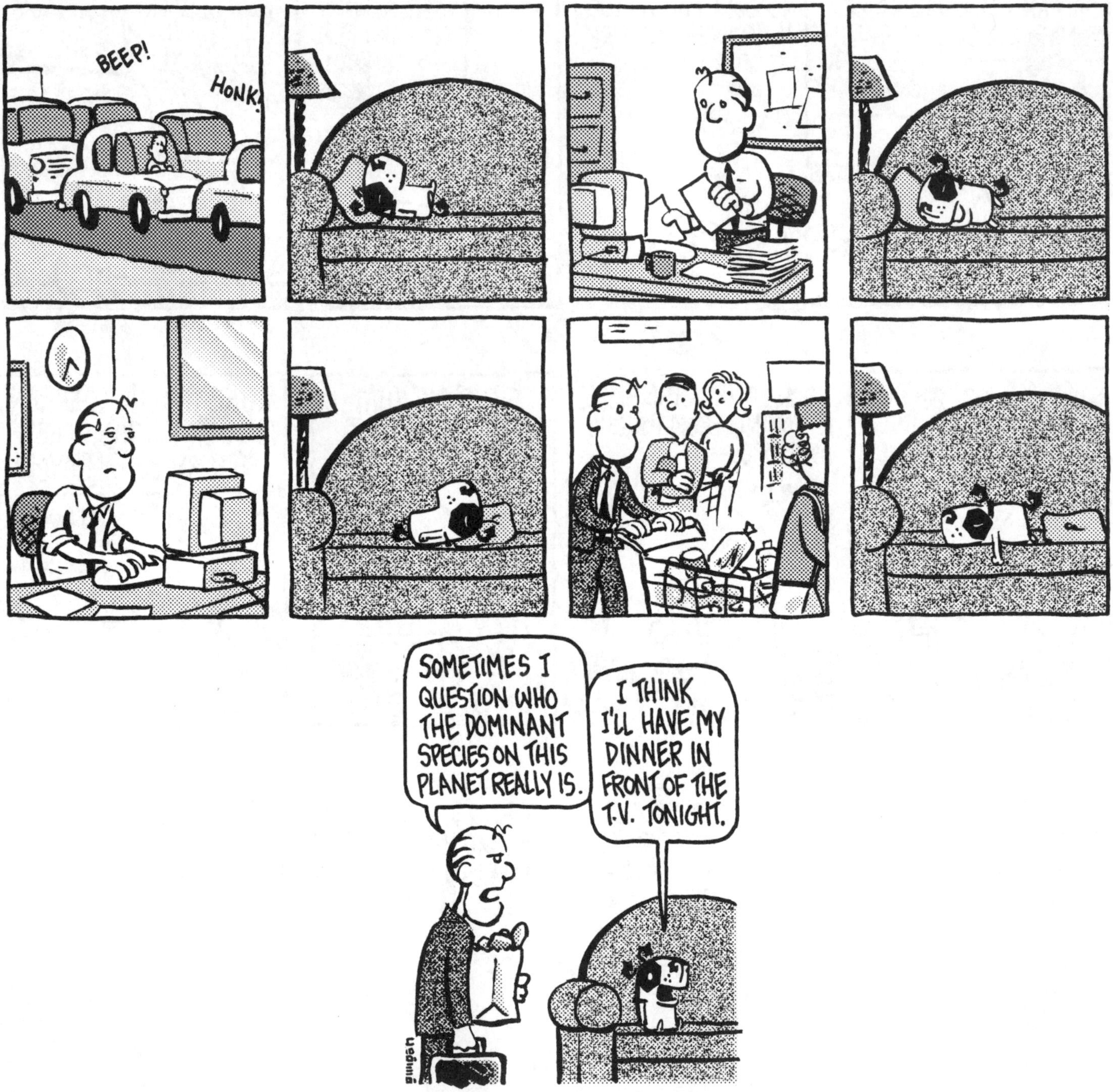
BEEP!
HONK!
SOMETIMES I QUESTION WHO THE DOMINANT SPECIES ON THIS PLANET REALLY IS.
I THINK I'LL HAVE MY DINNER IN FRONT OF THE T.V. TONIGHT.

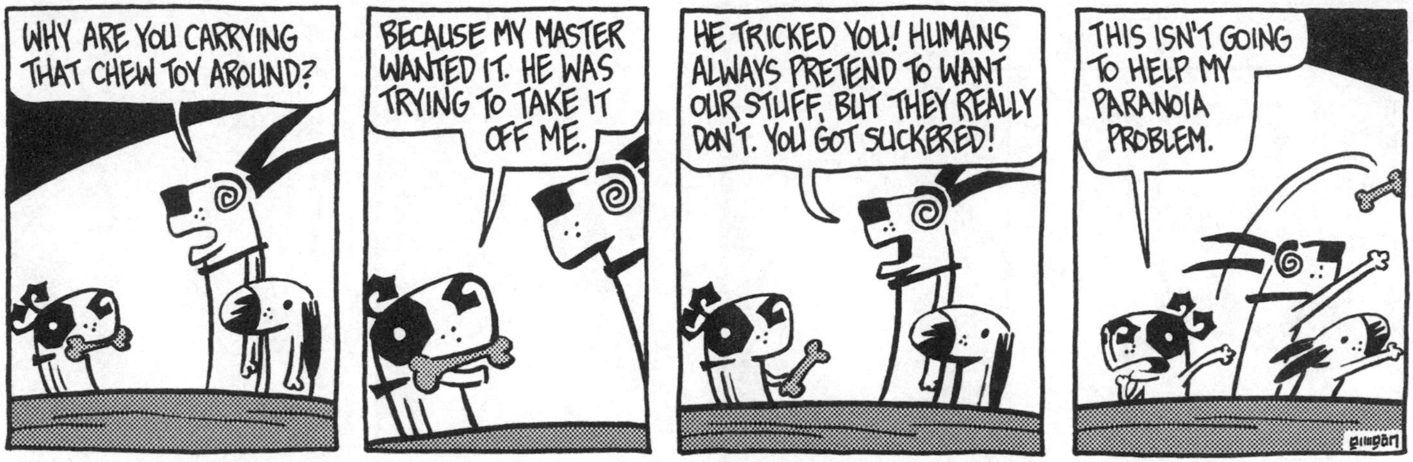
WHY ARE YOU CARRYING THAT CHEW TOY AROUND?
BECAUSE MY MASTER WANTED IT. HE WAS TRYING TO TAKE IT OFF ME.
HE TRICKED YOU! HUMANS ALWAYS PRETEND TO WANT OUR STUFF, BUT THEY REALLY DON'T. YOU GOT SUCKERED!
THIS ISN'T GOING TO HELP MY PARANOIA PROBLEM.

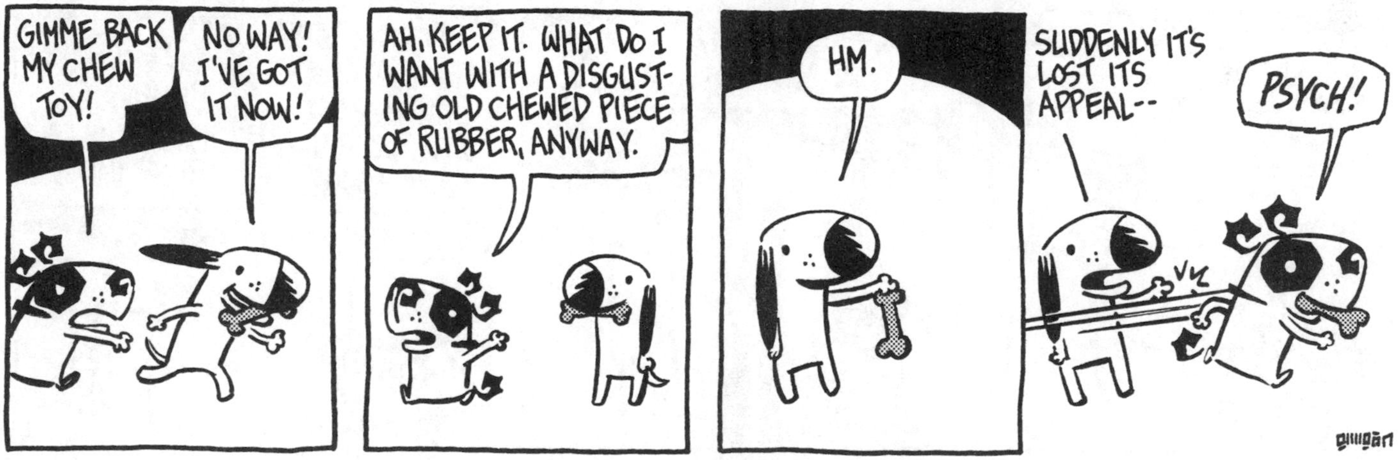
GIMME BACK MY CHEW TOY!
NO WAY! I'VE GOT IT NOW!
AH, KEEP IT. WHAT DO I WANT WITH A DISGUSTING OLD CHEWED PIECE OF RUBBER, ANYWAY.
HM.
SUDDENLY IT'S LOST ITS APPEAL--
PSYCH!

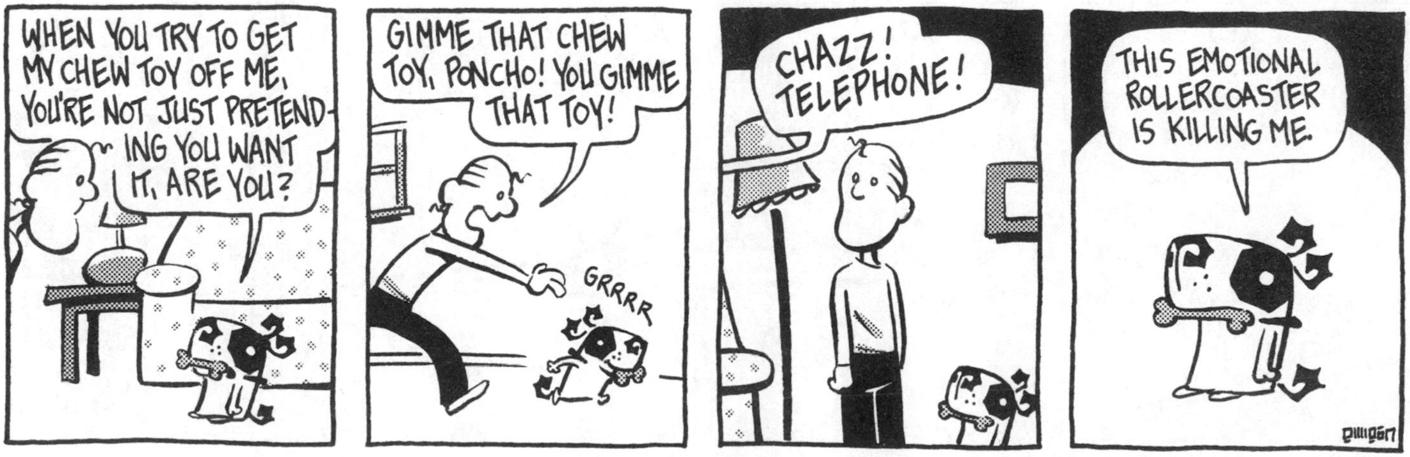
WHEN YOU TRY TO GET MY CHEW TOY OFF ME, YOU'RE NOT JUST PRETENDING YOU WANT IT, ARE YOU?
GIMME THAT CHEW TOY, PONCHO! YOU GIMME THAT TOY!
GRRRR
CHAZZ! TELEPHONE!
THIS EMOTIONAL ROLLERCOASTER IS KILLING ME.

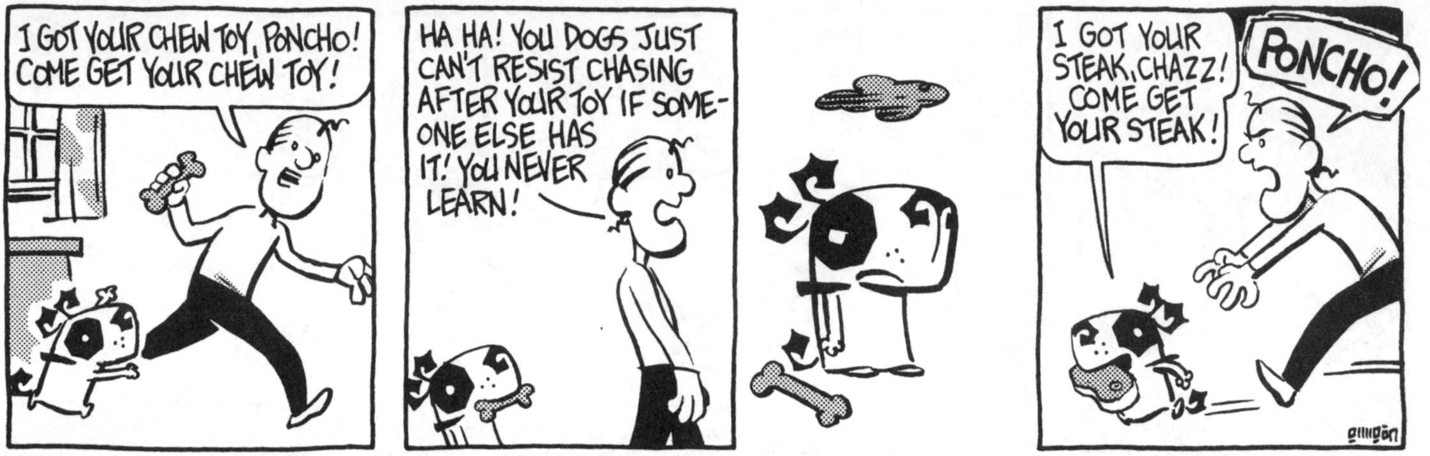
I GOT YOUR CHEW TOY, PONCHO! COME GET YOUR CHEW TOY!
HA HA! YOU DOGS JUST CAN'T RESIST CHASING AFTER YOUR TOY IF SOME-ONE ELSE HAS IT! YOU NEVER LEARN!
I GOT YOUR STEAK, CHAZZ! COME GET YOUR STEAK!
PONCHO!

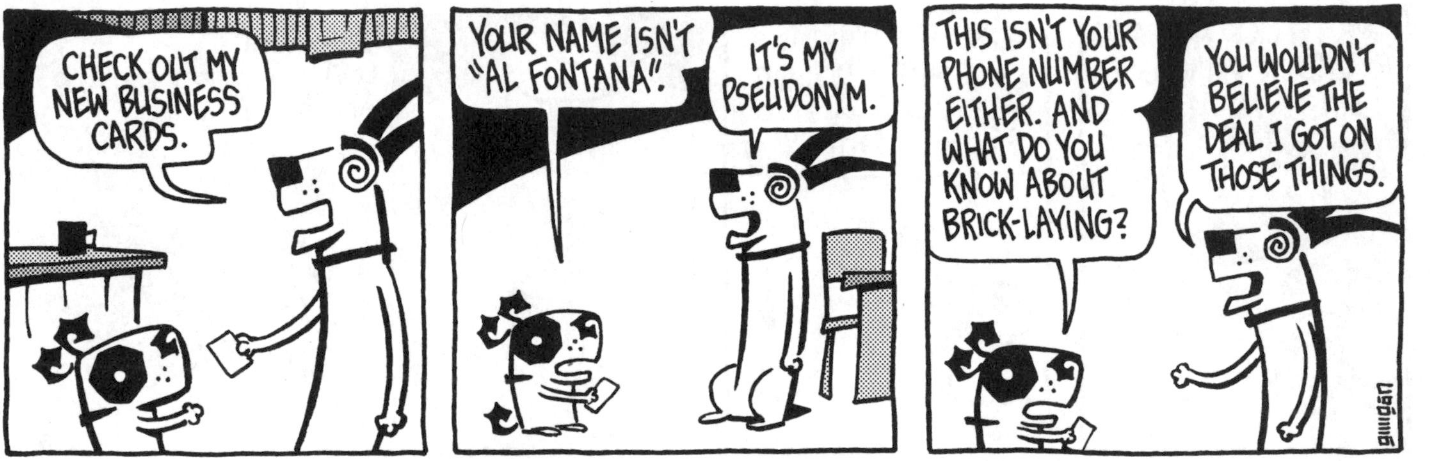
CHECK OUT MY NEW BUSINESS CARDS.
YOUR NAME ISN'T "AL FONTANA".
IT'S MY PSEUDONYM.
THIS ISN'T YOUR PHONE NUMBER EITHER. AND WHAT DO YOU KNOW ABOUT BRICK-LAYING?
YOU WOULDN'T BELIEVE THE DEAL I GOT ON THOSE THINGS.

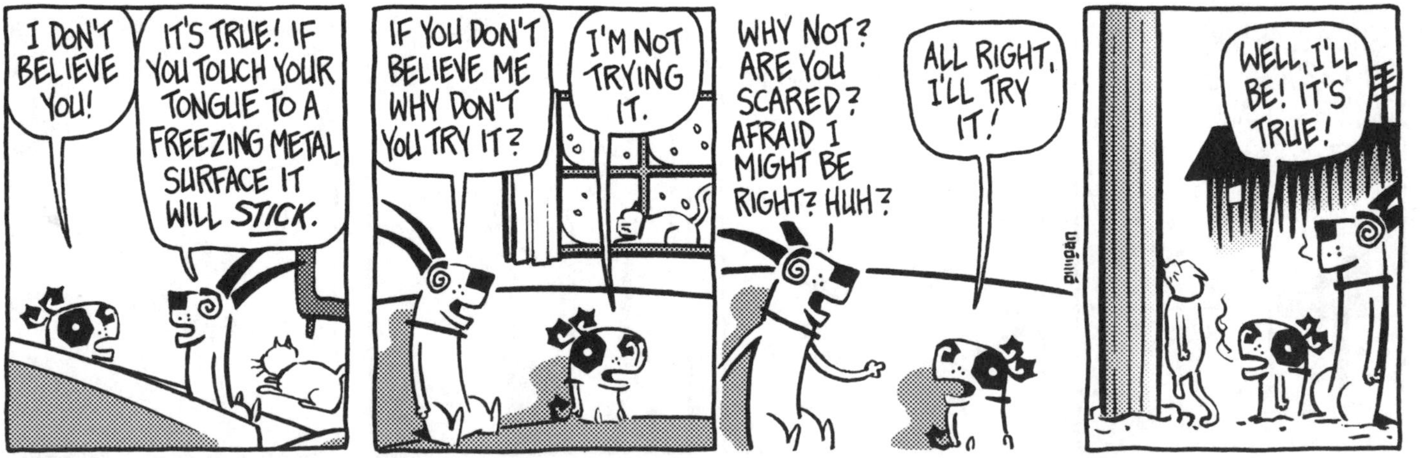
I DON'T BELIEVE YOU!
IT'S TRUE! IF YOU TOUCH YOUR TONGUE TO A FREEZING METAL SURFACE IT WILL STICK.
IF YOU DON'T BELIEVE ME WHY DON'T YOU TRY IT?
I'M NOT TRYING IT.
WHY NOT? ARE YOU SCARED? AFRAID I MIGHT BE RIGHT? HUH?
ALL RIGHT, I'LL TRY IT!
WELL, I'LL BE! IT'S TRUE!

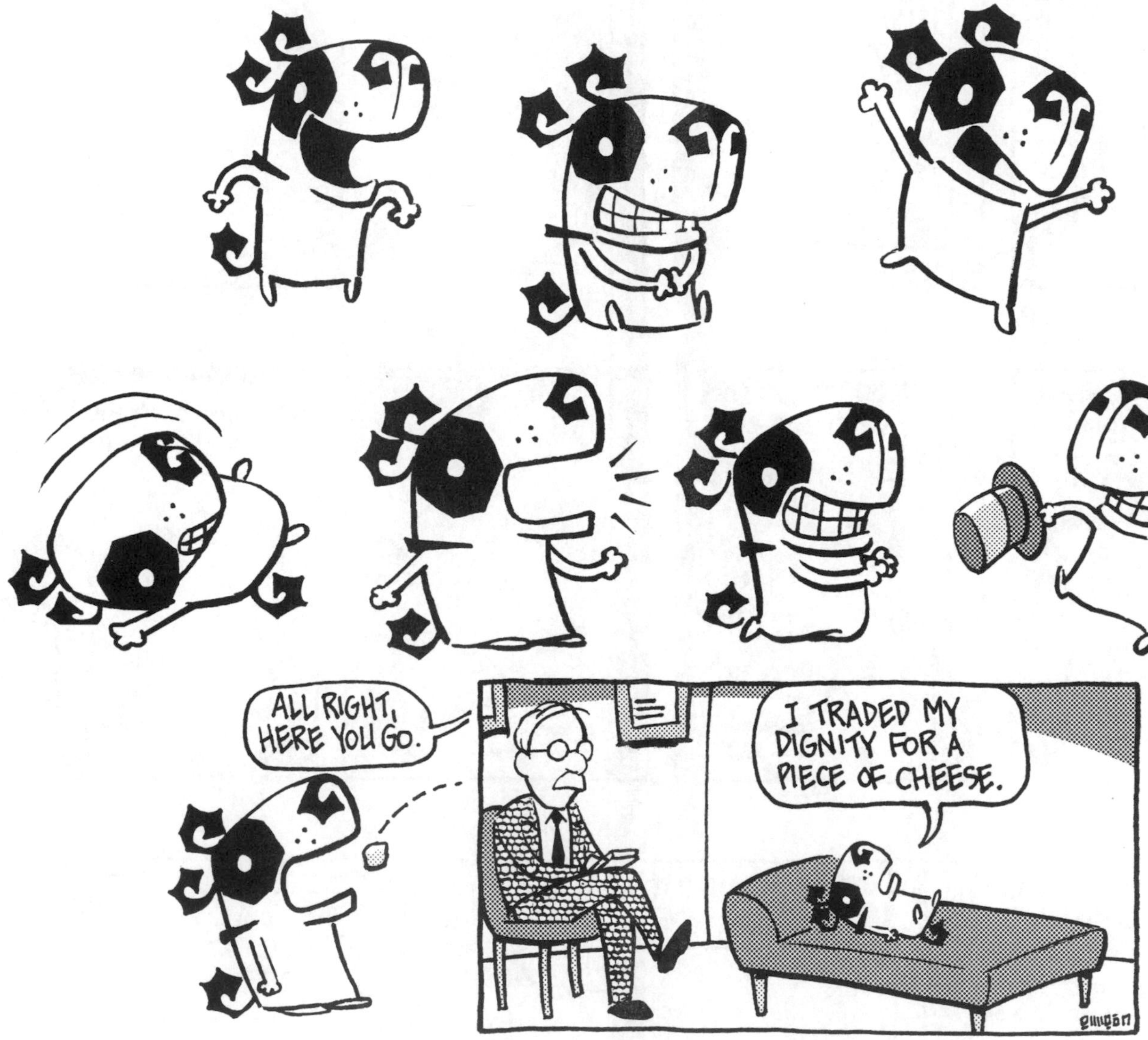
ALL RIGHT, HERE YOU GO.
I TRADED MY DIGNITY FOR A PIECE OF CHEESE.

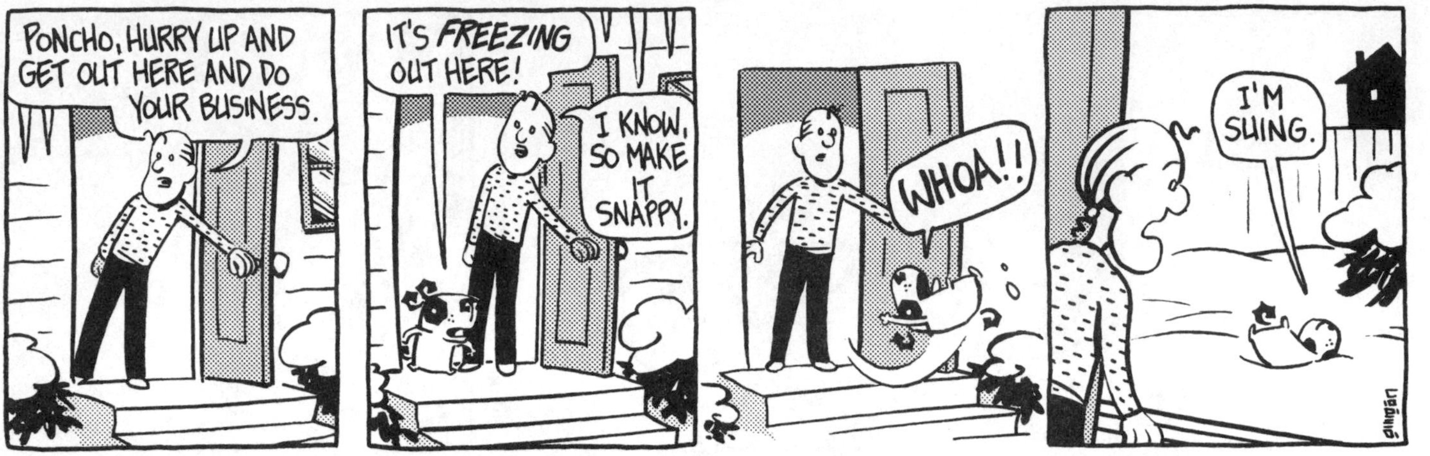
PONCHO, HURRY UP AND GET OUT HERE AND DO YOUR BUSINESS.
IT'S FREEZING OUT HERE!
I KNOW, SO MAKE IT SNAPPY.
WHOA!!
I'M SUING.

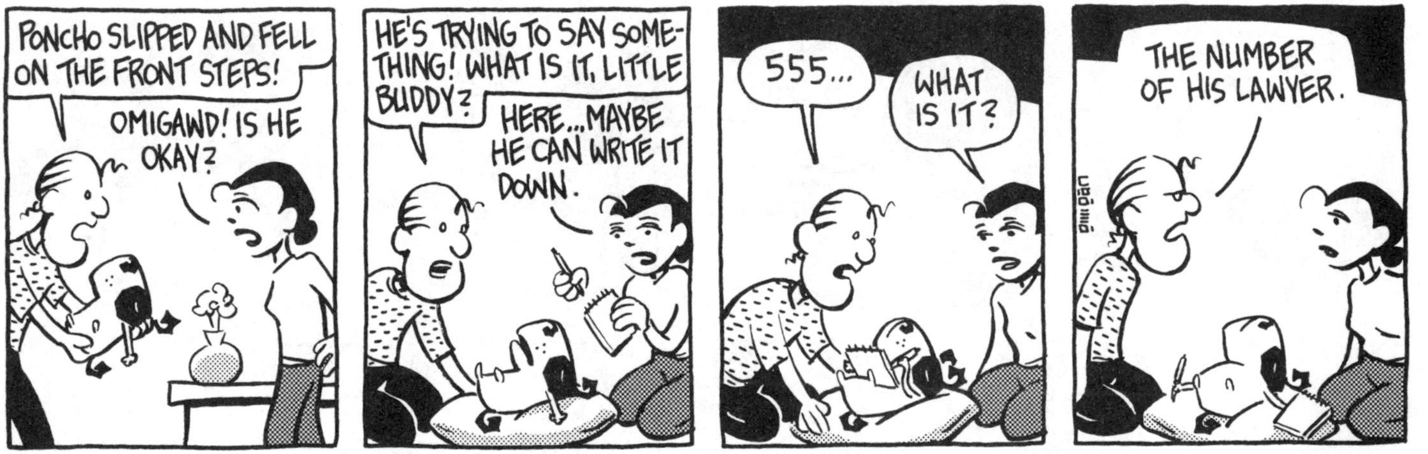
PONCHO SLIPPED AND FELL ON THE FRONT STEPS!
OMIGAWD! IS HE OKAY?
HE'S TRYING TO SAY SOMETHING! WHAT IS IT, LITTLE BUDDY?
HERE...MAYBE HE CAN WRITE IT DOWN.
555...
WHAT IS IT?
THE NUMBER OF HIS LAWYER.

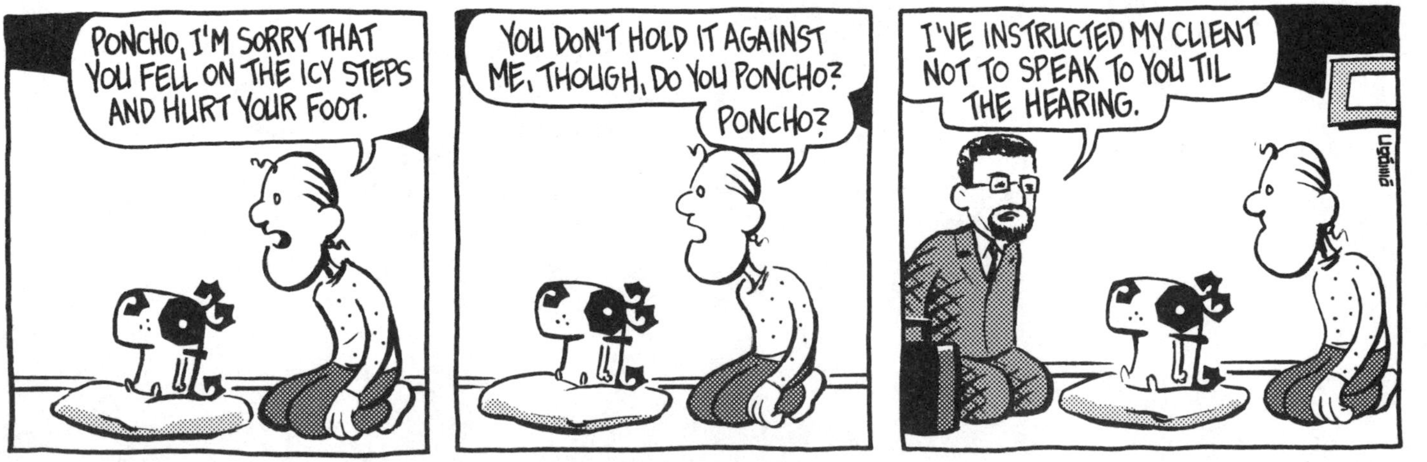
PONCHO, I'M SORRY THAT YOU FELL ON THE ICY STEPS AND HURT YOUR FOOT.
YOU DON'T HOLD IT AGAINST ME, THOUGH, DO YOU PONCHO?
PONCHO?
I'VE INSTRUCTED MY CLIENT NOT TO SPEAK TO YOU TIL THE HEARING.

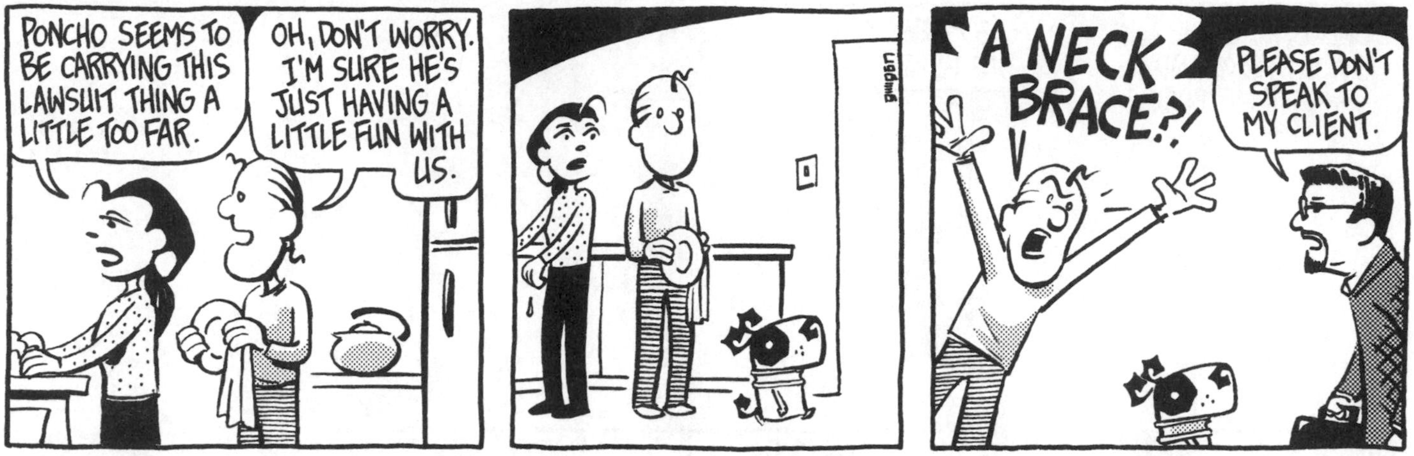
PONCHO SEEMS TO BE CARRYING THIS LAWSUIT THING A LITTLE TOO FAR.
OH, DON'T WORRY. I'M SURE HE'S JUST HAVING A LITTLE FUN WITH US.
A NECK BRACE?!
PLEASE DON'T SPEAK TO MY CLIENT.

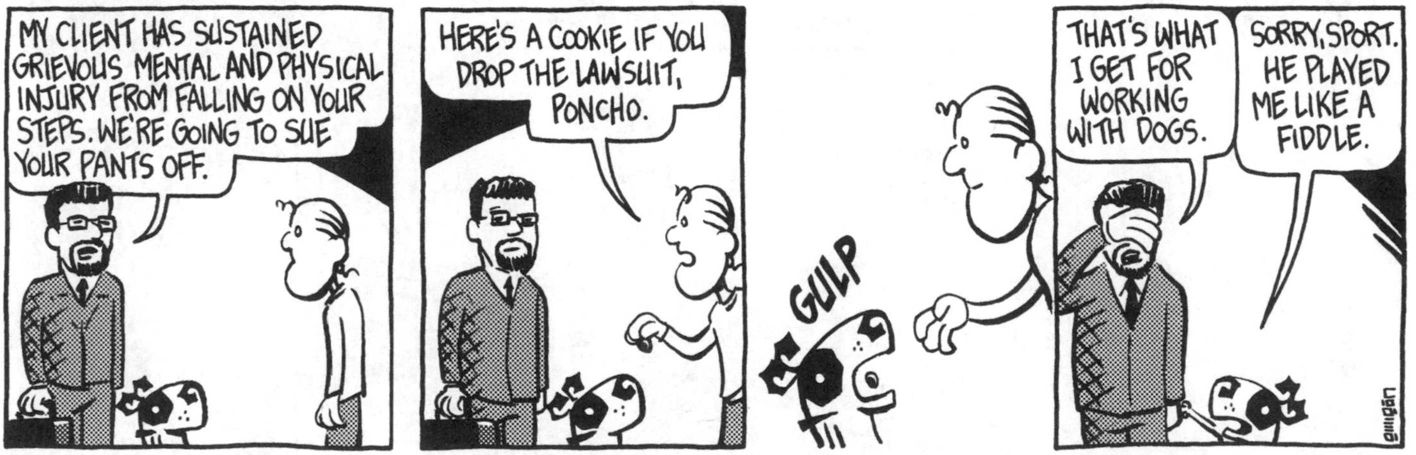
MY CLIENT HAS SUSTAINED GRIEVOUS MENTAL AND PHYSICAL INJURY FROM FALLING ON YOUR STEPS. WE'RE GOING TO SUE YOUR PANTS OFF.
HERE'S A COOKIE IF YOU DROP THE LAWSUIT, PONCHO.
GULP
THAT'S WHAT I GET FOR WORKING WITH DOGS.
SORRY, SPORT. HE PLAYED ME LIKE A FIDDLE.

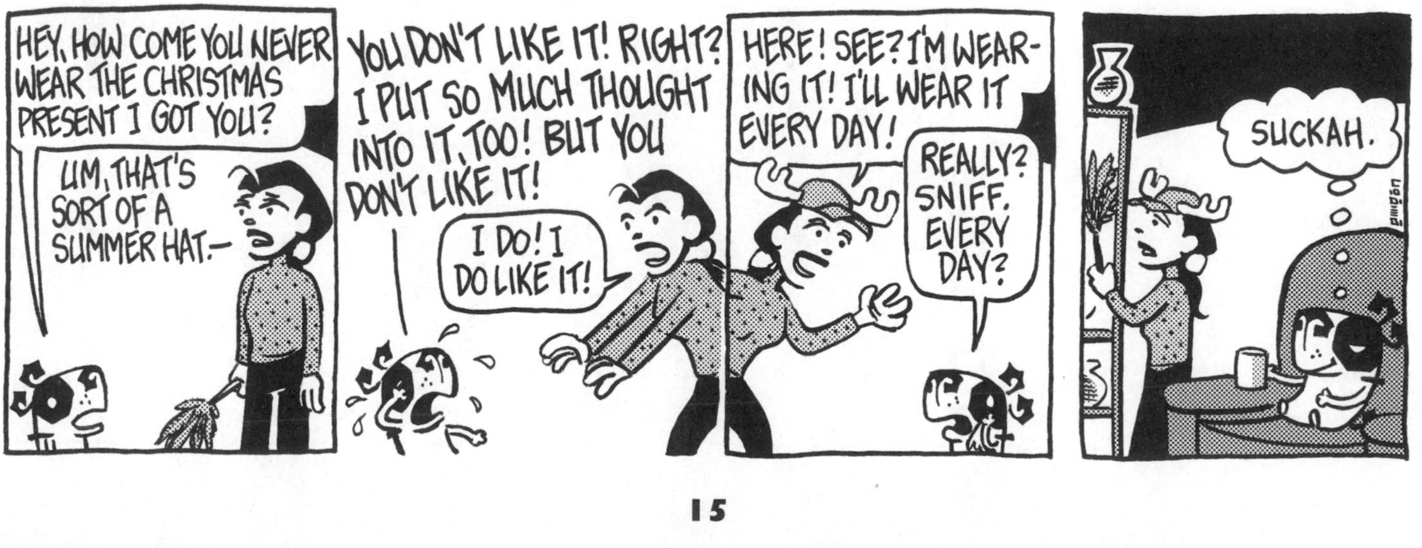
HEY, HOW COME YOU NEVER WEAR THE CHRISTMAS PRESENT I GOT YOU?
UM, THAT'S SORT OF A SUMMER HAT.–
YOU DON'T LIKE IT! RIGHT? I PUT SO MUCH THOUGHT INTO IT, TOO! BUT YOU DON'T LIKE IT!
I DO! I DO LIKE IT!
HERE! SEE? I'M WEARING IT! I'LL WEAR IT EVERY DAY!
REALLY? SNIFF. EVERY DAY?
SUCKAH.

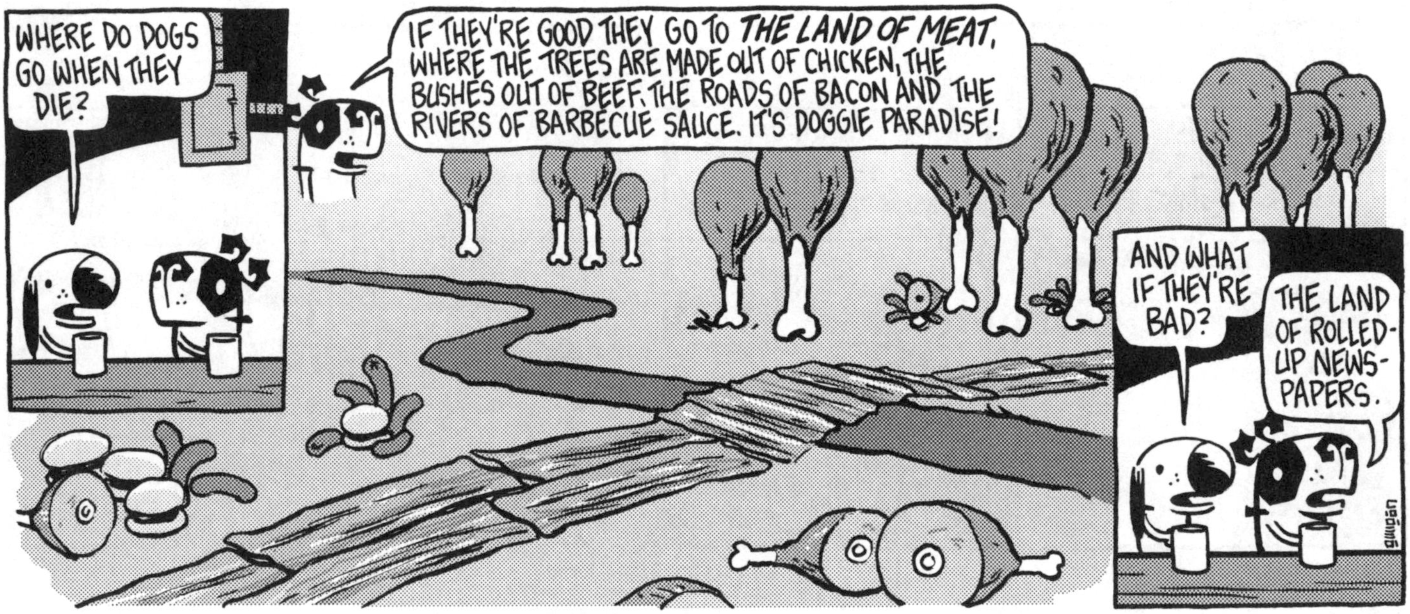
WHERE DO DOGS GO WHEN THEY DIE?
IF THEY'RE GOOD THEY GO TO *THE LAND OF MEAT*, WHERE THE TREES ARE MADE OUT OF CHICKEN, THE BUSHES OUT OF BEEF, THE ROADS OF BACON AND THE RIVERS OF BARBECUE SAUCE. IT'S DOGGIE PARADISE!
AND WHAT IF THEY'RE BAD?
THE LAND OF ROLLED-UP NEWS-PAPERS.
gilligan

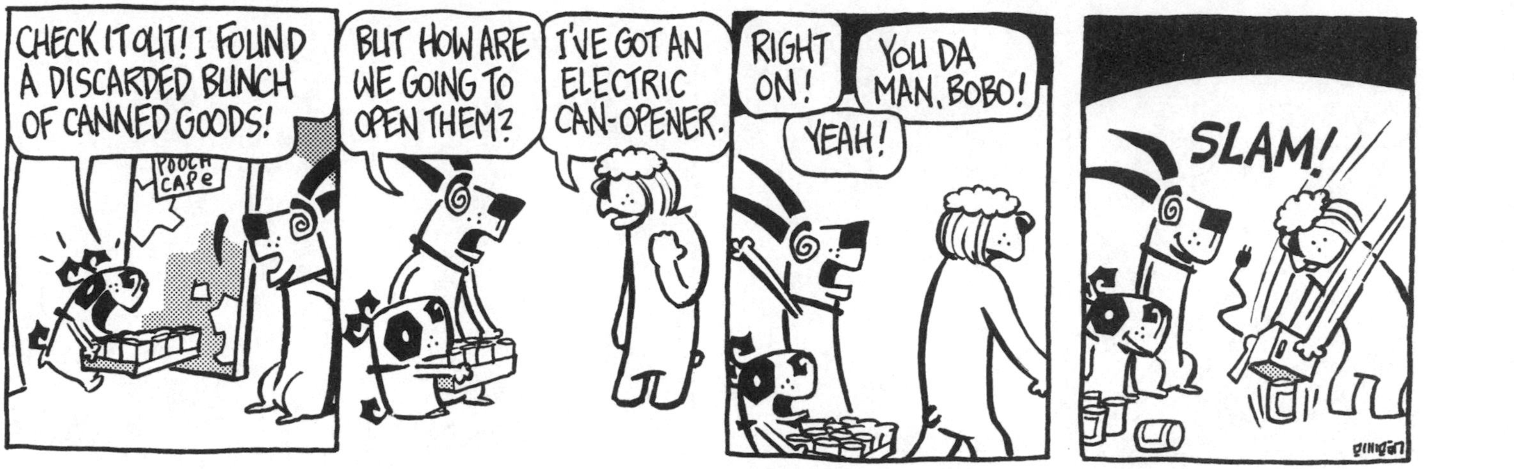
CHECK IT OUT! I FOUND A DISCARDED BUNCH OF CANNED GOODS!
POOCH CAFE
BUT HOW ARE WE GOING TO OPEN THEM?
I'VE GOT AN ELECTRIC CAN-OPENER.
RIGHT ON!
YOU DA MAN, BOBO!
YEAH!
SLAM!

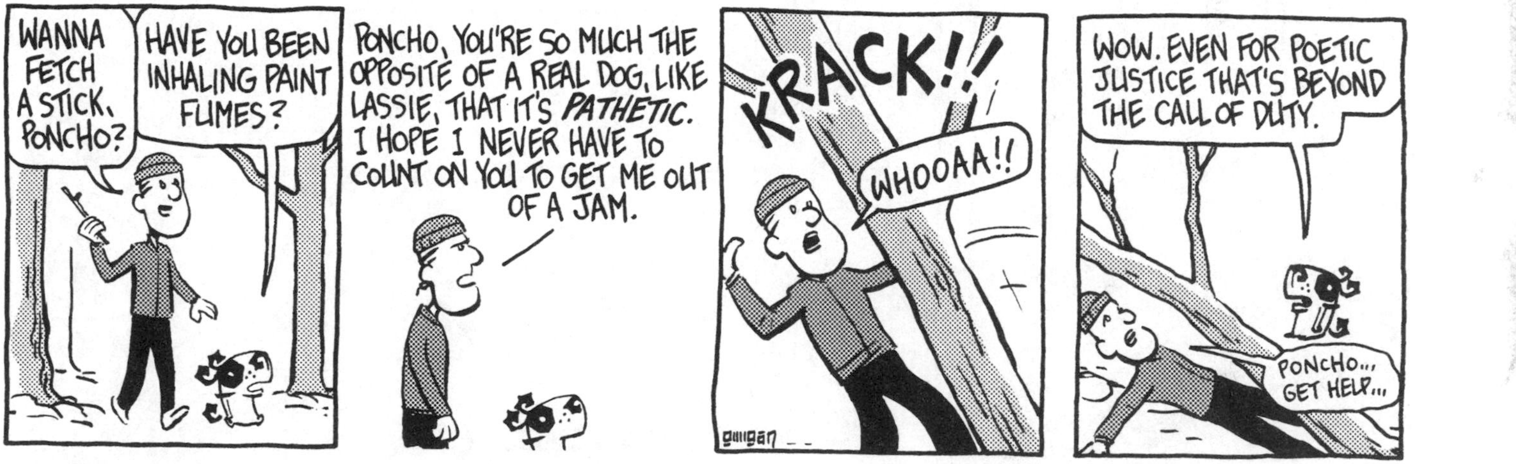
WANNA FETCH A STICK, PONCHO?
HAVE YOU BEEN INHALING PAINT FUMES?
PONCHO, YOU'RE SO MUCH THE OPPOSITE OF A REAL DOG, LIKE LASSIE, THAT IT'S PATHETIC. I HOPE I NEVER HAVE TO COUNT ON YOU TO GET ME OUT OF A JAM.
KRACK!!!
WHOOAA!!
WOW. EVEN FOR POETIC JUSTICE THAT'S BEYOND THE CALL OF DUTY.
PONCHO... GET HELP...

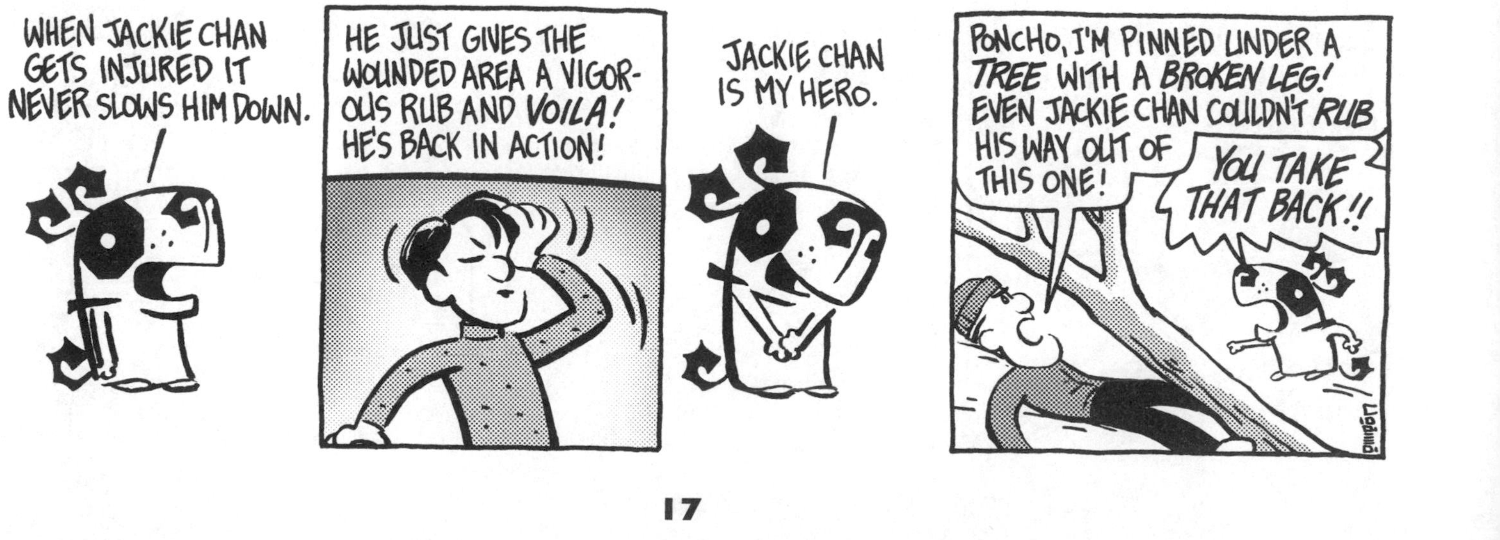
WHEN JACKIE CHAN GETS INJURED IT NEVER SLOWS HIM DOWN.
HE JUST GIVES THE WOUNDED AREA A VIGOROUS RUB AND VOILA! HE'S BACK IN ACTION!
JACKIE CHAN IS MY HERO.
PONCHO, I'M PINNED UNDER A TREE WITH A BROKEN LEG! EVEN JACKIE CHAN COULDN'T RUB HIS WAY OUT OF THIS ONE!
YOU TAKE THAT BACK!!

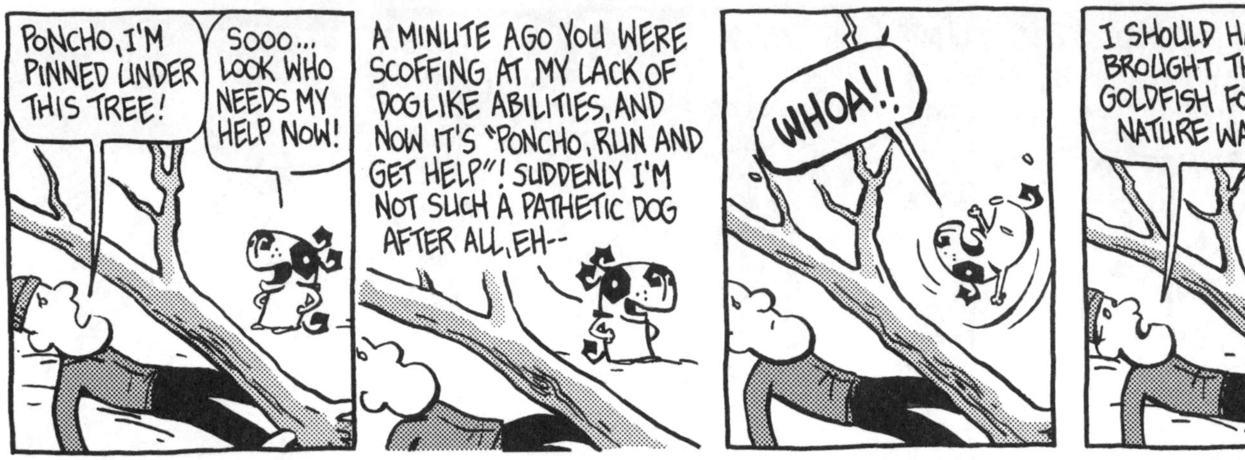
PONCHO, I'M PINNED UNDER THIS TREE!
SOOO... LOOK WHO NEEDS MY HELP NOW!
A MINUTE AGO YOU WERE SCOFFING AT MY LACK OF DOGLIKE ABILITIES, AND NOW IT'S "PONCHO, RUN AND GET HELP"! SUDDENLY I'M NOT SUCH A PATHETIC DOG AFTER ALL, EH--
WHOA!!
I SHOULD HAVE BROUGHT THE GOLDFISH FOR A NATURE WALK.
OW.

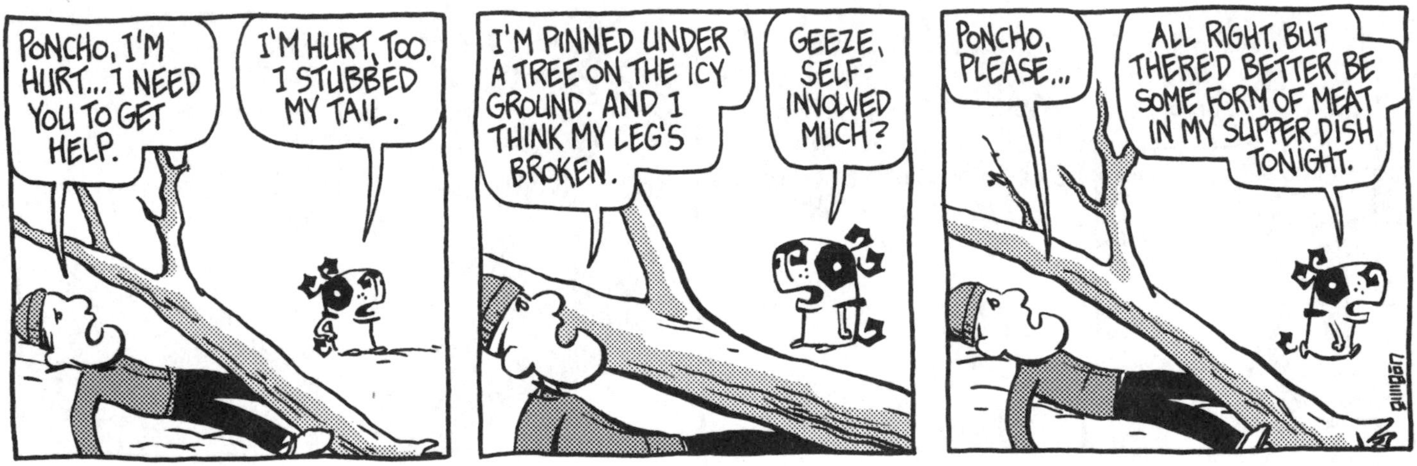
PONCHO, I'M HURT... I NEED YOU TO GET HELP.
I'M HURT, TOO. I STUBBED MY TAIL.
I'M PINNED UNDER A TREE ON THE ICY GROUND. AND I THINK MY LEG'S BROKEN.
GEEZE, SELF-INVOLVED MUCH?
PONCHO, PLEASE...
ALL RIGHT, BUT THERE'D BETTER BE SOME FORM OF MEAT IN MY SUPPER DISH TONIGHT.

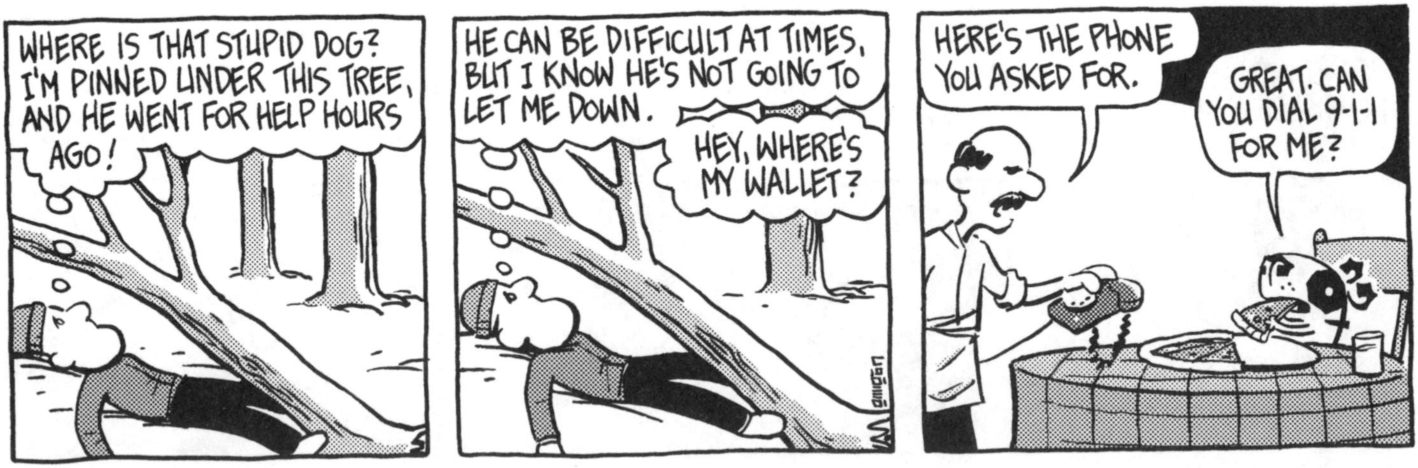
WHERE IS THAT STUPID DOG? I'M PINNED UNDER THIS TREE, AND HE WENT FOR HELP HOURS AGO!
HE CAN BE DIFFICULT AT TIMES, BUT I KNOW HE'S NOT GOING TO LET ME DOWN.
HEY, WHERE'S MY WALLET?
HERE'S THE PHONE YOU ASKED FOR.
GREAT. CAN YOU DIAL 9-1-1 FOR ME?

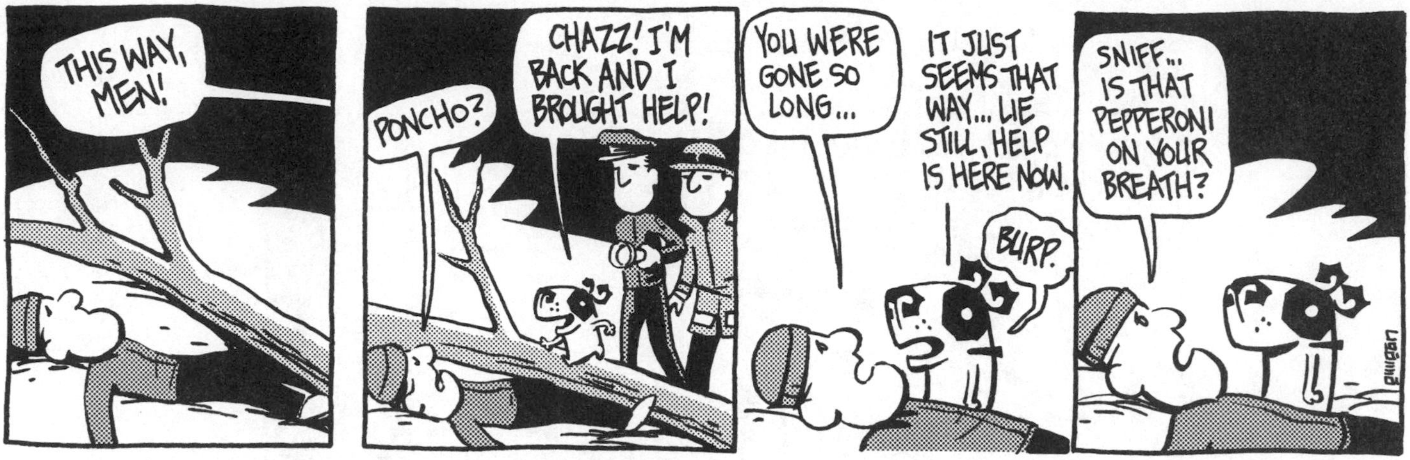
THIS WAY, MEN!
PONCHO?
CHAZZ! I'M BACK AND I BROUGHT HELP!
YOU WERE GONE SO LONG...
IT JUST SEEMS THAT WAY... LIE STILL, HELP IS HERE NOW.
BURP.
SNIFF... IS THAT PEPPERONI ON YOUR BREATH?

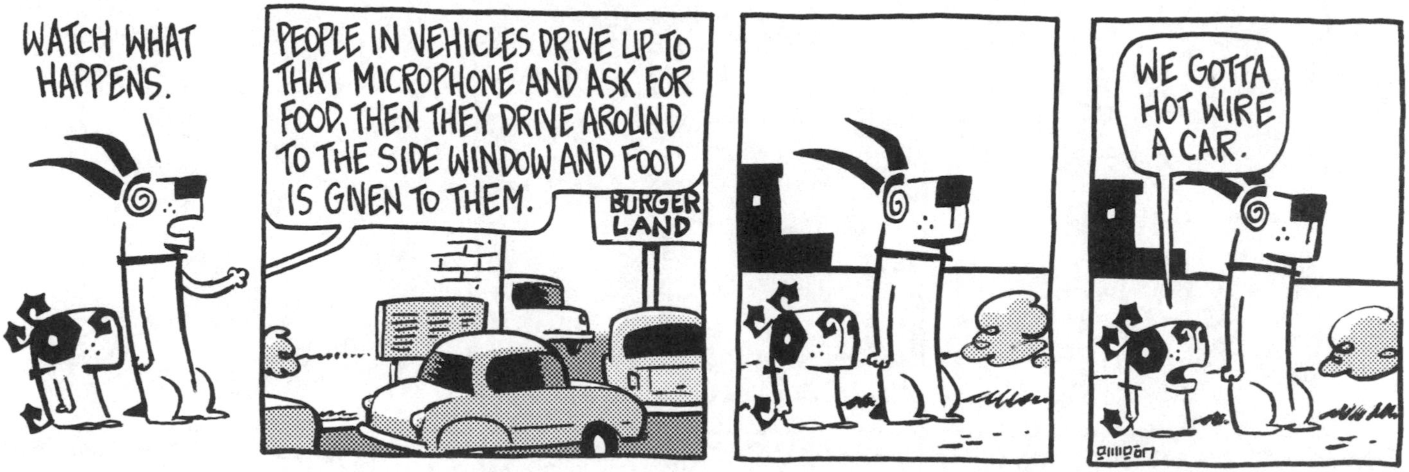
WATCH WHAT HAPPENS.
PEOPLE IN VEHICLES DRIVE UP TO THAT MICROPHONE AND ASK FOR FOOD, THEN THEY DRIVE AROUND TO THE SIDE WINDOW AND FOOD IS GIVEN TO THEM.
BURGER LAND
WE GOTTA HOT WIRE A CAR.

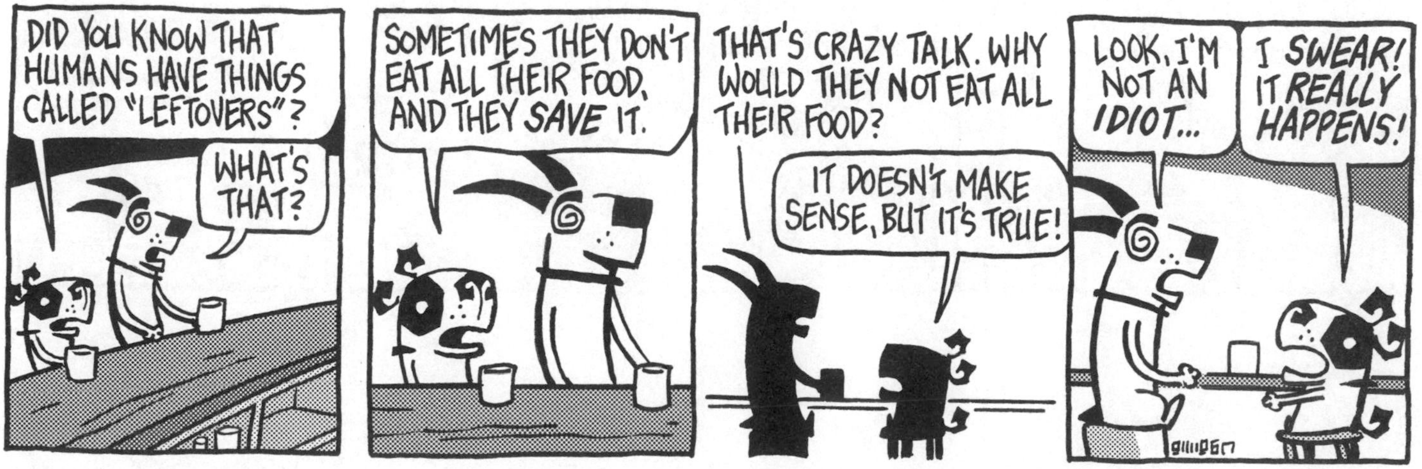
DID YOU KNOW THAT HUMANS HAVE THINGS CALLED "LEFTOVERS"?
WHAT'S THAT?
SOMETIMES THEY DON'T EAT ALL THEIR FOOD, AND THEY *SAVE* IT.
THAT'S CRAZY TALK. WHY WOULD THEY NOT EAT ALL THEIR FOOD?
IT DOESN'T MAKE SENSE, BUT IT'S TRUE!
LOOK, I'M NOT AN *IDIOT*...
I *SWEAR!* IT *REALLY HAPPENS!*

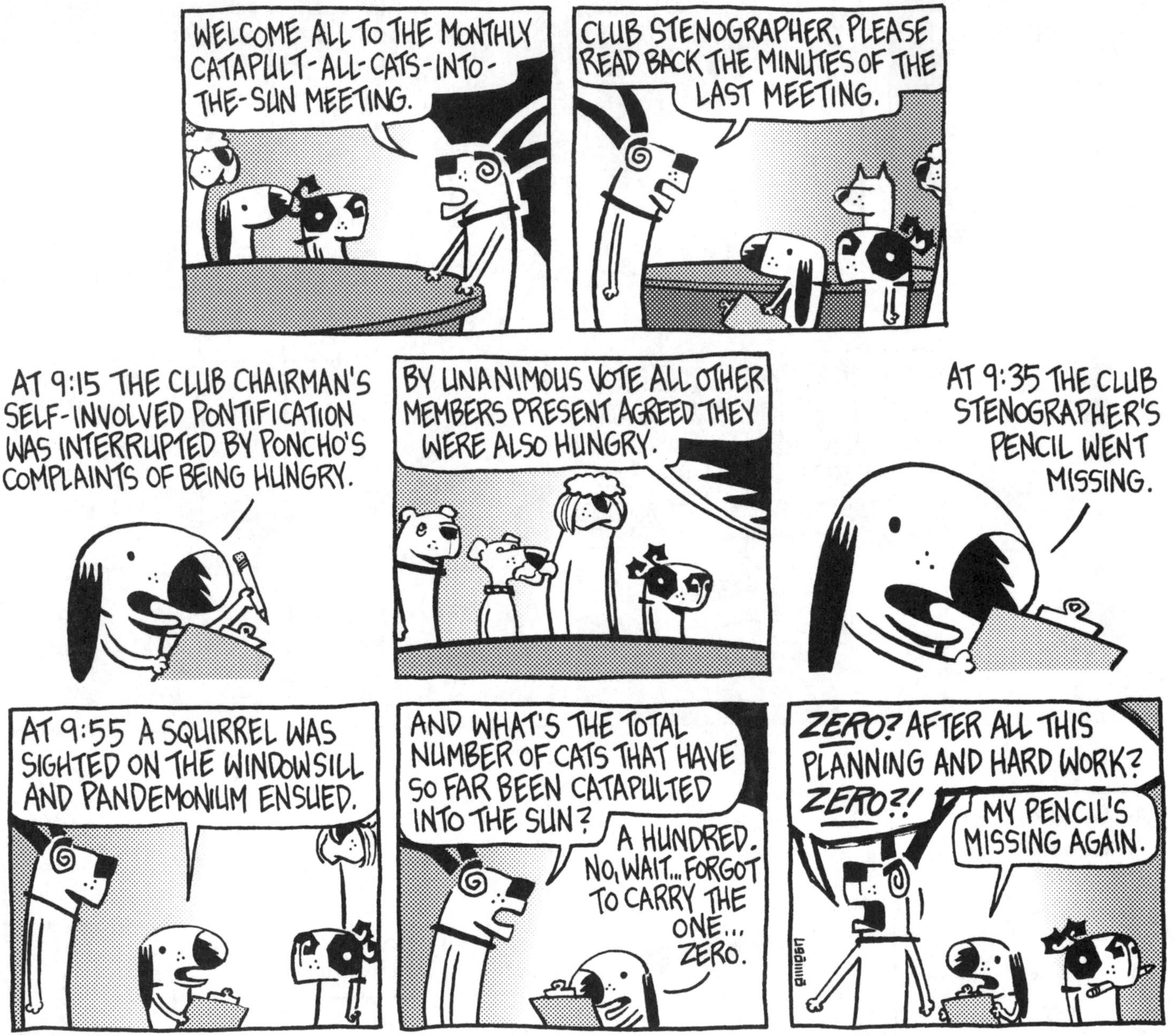
WELCOME ALL TO THE MONTHLY CATAPULT-ALL-CATS-INTO-THE-SUN MEETING.
CLUB STENOGRAPHER, PLEASE READ BACK THE MINUTES OF THE LAST MEETING.
AT 9:15 THE CLUB CHAIRMAN'S SELF-INVOLVED PONTIFICATION WAS INTERRUPTED BY PONCHO'S COMPLAINTS OF BEING HUNGRY.
BY UNANIMOUS VOTE ALL OTHER MEMBERS PRESENT AGREED THEY WERE ALSO HUNGRY.
AT 9:35 THE CLUB STENOGRAPHER'S PENCIL WENT MISSING.
AT 9:55 A SQUIRREL WAS SIGHTED ON THE WINDOWSILL AND PANDEMONIUM ENSUED.
AND WHAT'S THE TOTAL NUMBER OF CATS THAT HAVE SO FAR BEEN CATAPULTED INTO THE SUN?
A HUNDRED. NO, WAIT... FORGOT TO CARRY THE ONE... ZERO.
ZERO? AFTER ALL THIS PLANNING AND HARD WORK? ZERO?!
MY PENCIL'S MISSING AGAIN.

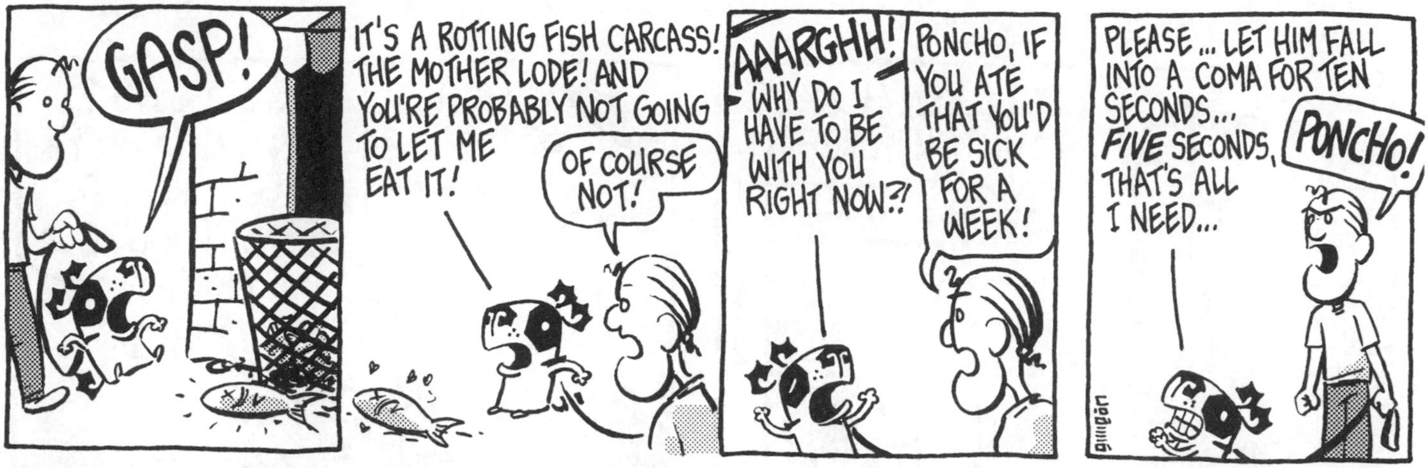
GASP!
IT'S A ROTTING FISH CARCASS! THE MOTHER LODE! AND YOU'RE PROBABLY NOT GOING TO LET ME EAT IT!
OF COURSE NOT!
AAARGHH!
WHY DO I HAVE TO BE WITH YOU RIGHT NOW?!
PONCHO, IF YOU ATE THAT YOU'D BE SICK FOR A WEEK!
PLEASE... LET HIM FALL INTO A COMA FOR TEN SECONDS... ***FIVE*** SECONDS, THAT'S ALL I NEED...
PONCHO!

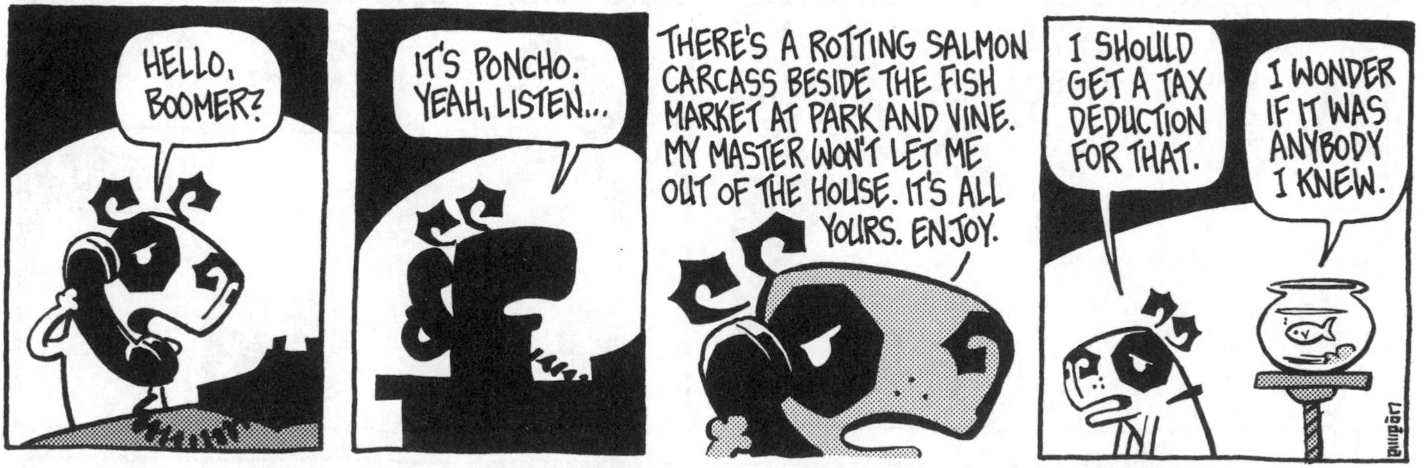
HELLO, BOOMER?
IT'S PONCHO. YEAH, LISTEN...
THERE'S A ROTTING SALMON CARCASS BESIDE THE FISH MARKET AT PARK AND VINE. MY MASTER WON'T LET ME OUT OF THE HOUSE. IT'S ALL YOURS. ENJOY.
I SHOULD GET A TAX DEDUCTION FOR THAT.
I WONDER IF IT WAS ANYBODY I KNEW.

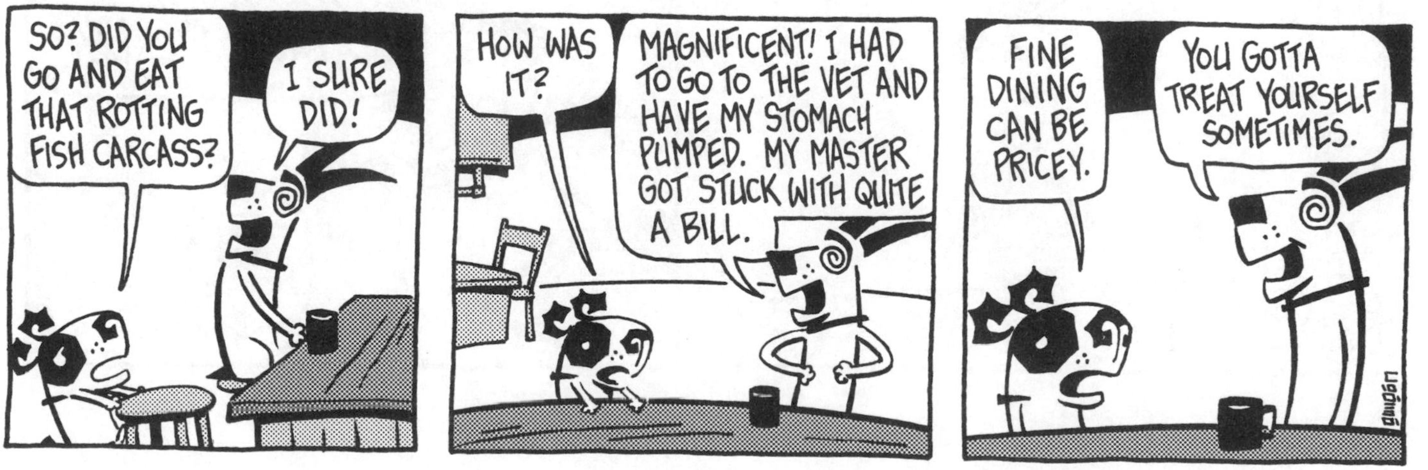
SO? DID YOU GO AND EAT THAT ROTTING FISH CARCASS?
I SURE DID!
HOW WAS IT?
MAGNIFICENT! I HAD TO GO TO THE VET AND HAVE MY STOMACH PUMPED. MY MASTER GOT STUCK WITH QUITE A BILL.
FINE DINING CAN BE PRICEY.
YOU GOTTA TREAT YOURSELF SOMETIMES.

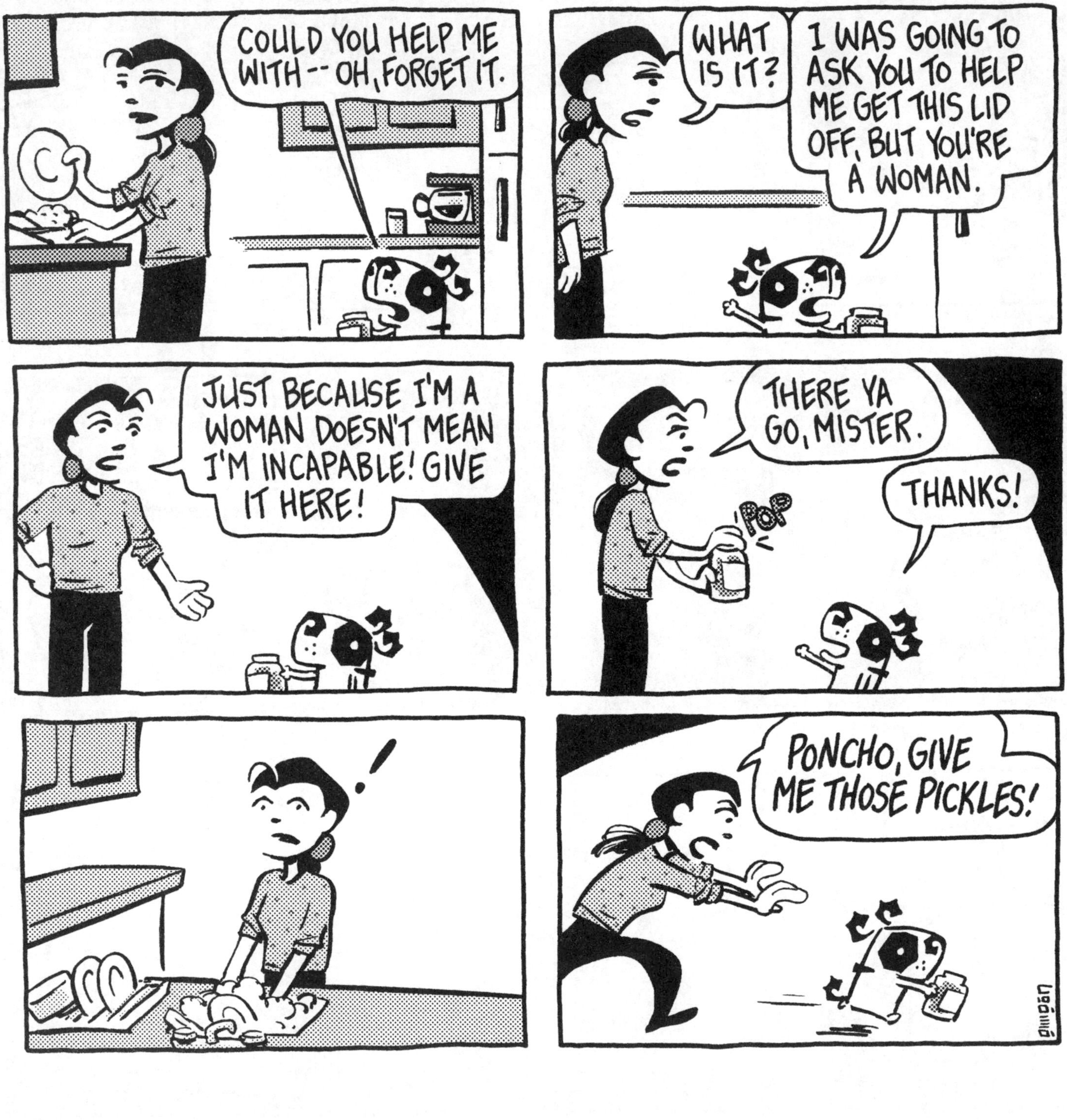
COULD YOU HELP ME WITH -- OH, FORGET IT.
WHAT IS IT?
I WAS GOING TO ASK YOU TO HELP ME GET THIS LID OFF, BUT YOU'RE A WOMAN.
JUST BECAUSE I'M A WOMAN DOESN'T MEAN I'M INCAPABLE! GIVE IT HERE!
THERE YA GO, MISTER.
POP
THANKS!
!
PONCHO, GIVE ME THOSE PICKLES!
gilligan

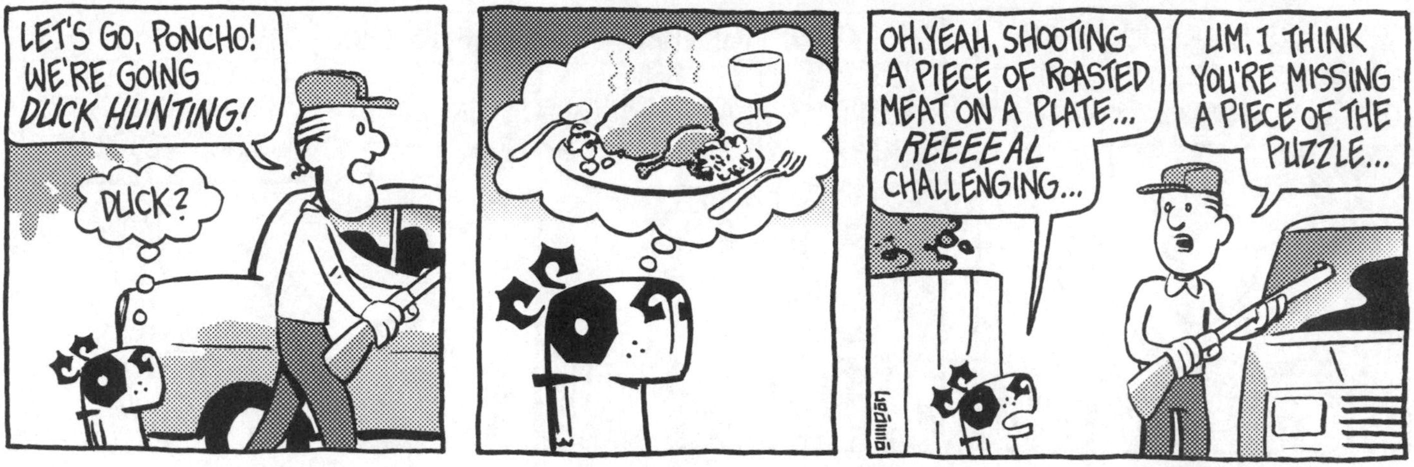
LET'S GO, PONCHO! WE'RE GOING *DUCK HUNTING!*
DUCK?
OH, YEAH, SHOOTING A PIECE OF ROASTED MEAT ON A PLATE... *REEEEAL* CHALLENGING...
UM, I THINK YOU'RE MISSING A PIECE OF THE PUZZLE...
gilligan

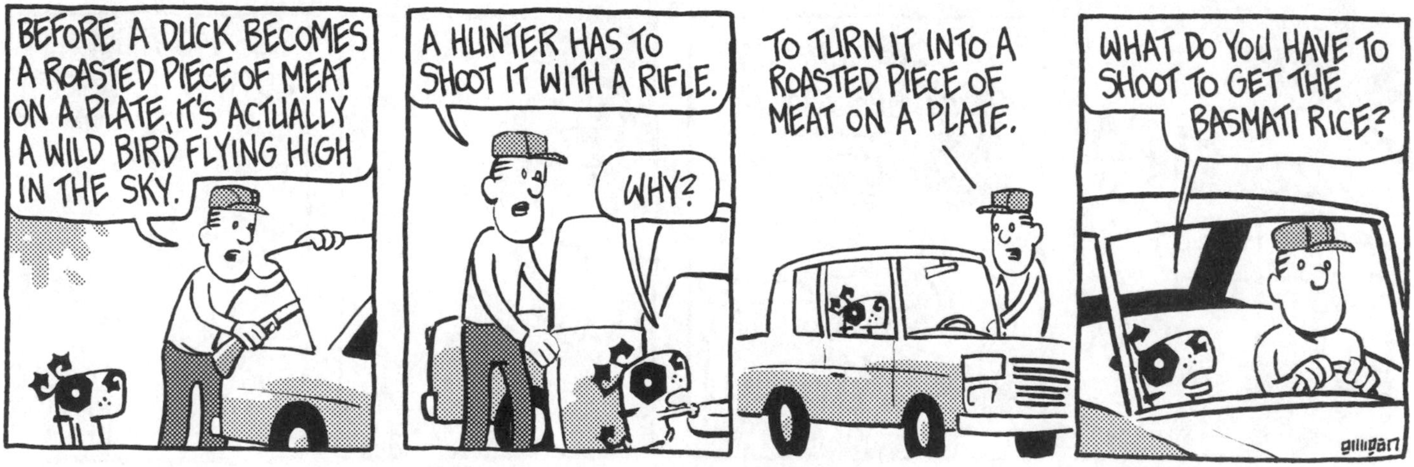
BEFORE A DUCK BECOMES A ROASTED PIECE OF MEAT ON A PLATE, IT'S ACTUALLY A WILD BIRD FLYING HIGH IN THE SKY.
A HUNTER HAS TO SHOOT IT WITH A RIFLE.
WHY?
TO TURN IT INTO A ROASTED PIECE OF MEAT ON A PLATE.
WHAT DO YOU HAVE TO SHOOT TO GET THE BASMATI RICE?
gilligan

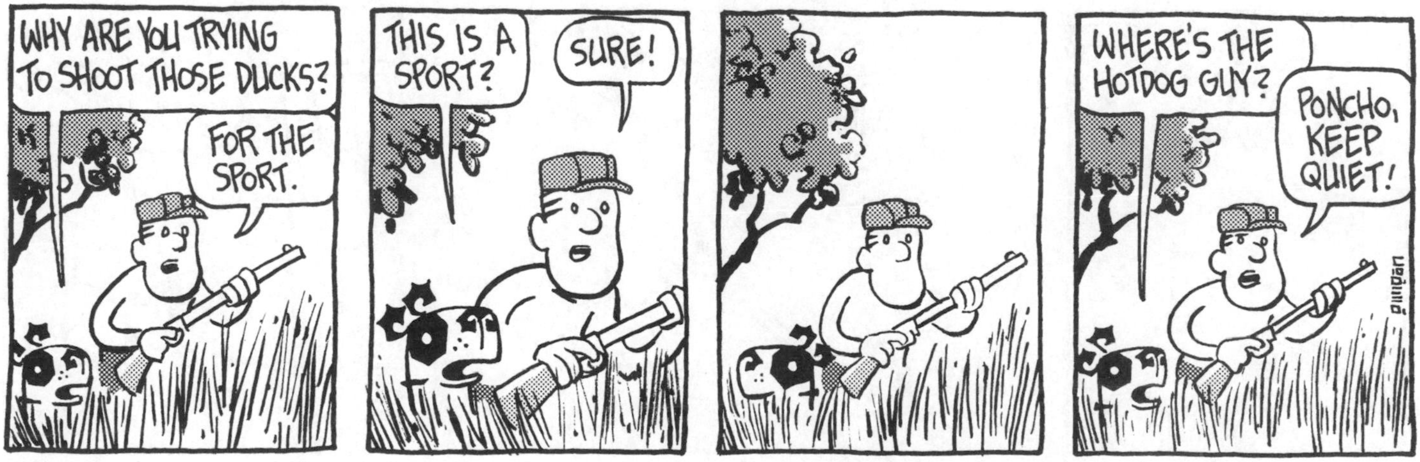
WHY ARE YOU TRYING TO SHOOT THOSE DUCKS?
FOR THE SPORT.
THIS IS A SPORT?
SURE!
WHERE'S THE HOTDOG GUY?
PONCHO, KEEP QUIET!
gilligan

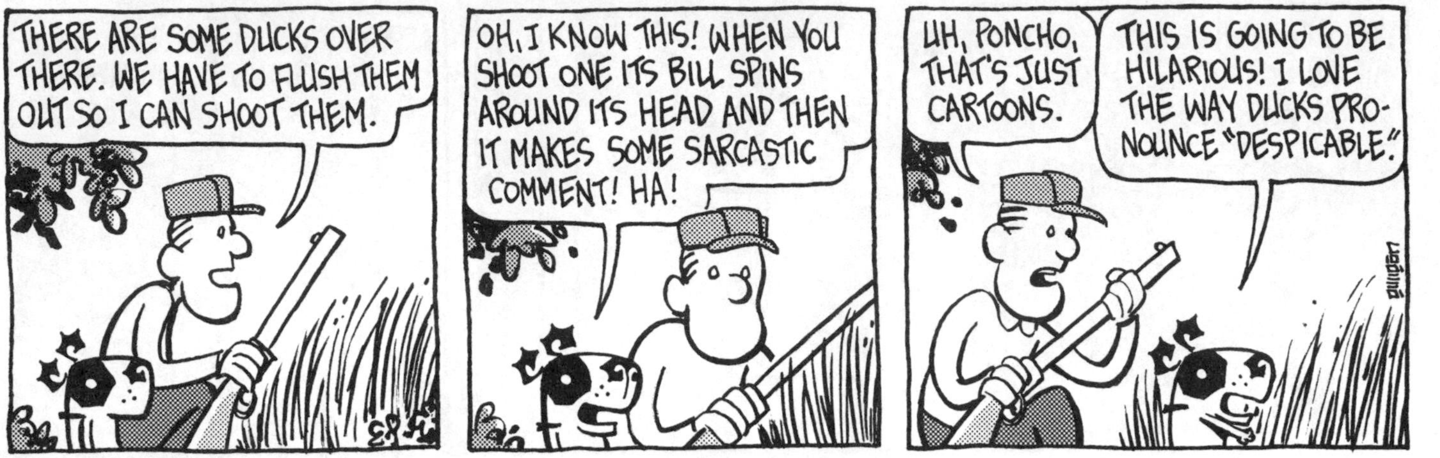
THERE ARE SOME DUCKS OVER THERE. WE HAVE TO FLUSH THEM OUT SO I CAN SHOOT THEM.
OH, I KNOW THIS! WHEN YOU SHOOT ONE ITS BILL SPINS AROUND ITS HEAD AND THEN IT MAKES SOME SARCASTIC COMMENT! HA!
UH, PONCHO, THAT'S JUST CARTOONS.
THIS IS GOING TO BE HILARIOUS! I LOVE THE WAY DUCKS PRONOUNCE "DESPICABLE."
gilligan

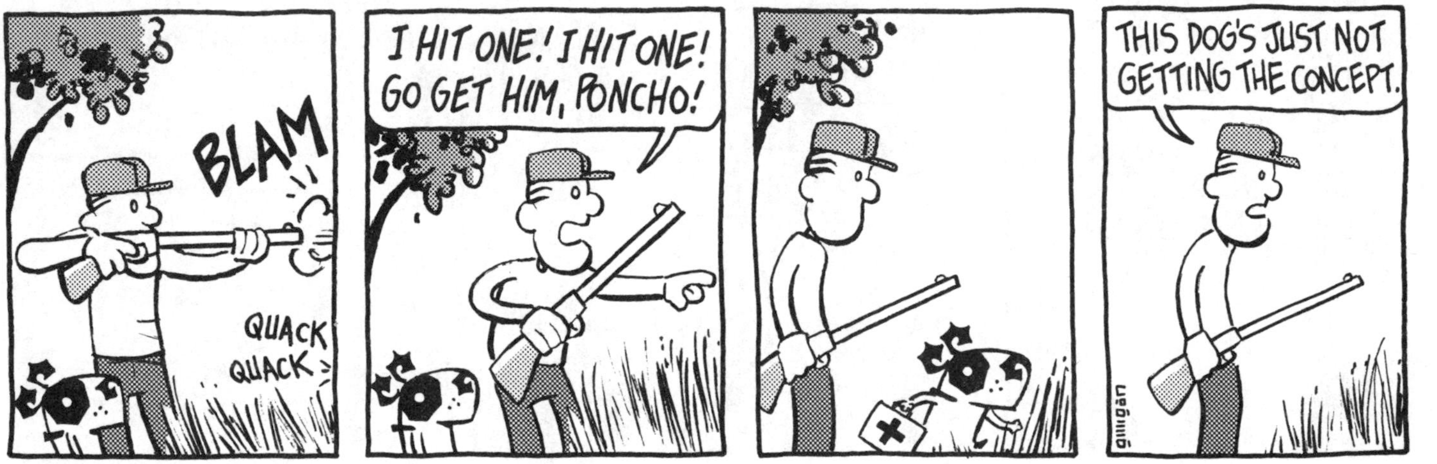
BLAM
QUACK
QUACK
I HIT ONE! I HIT ONE! GO GET HIM, PONCHO!
THIS DOG'S JUST NOT GETTING THE CONCEPT.
gilligan

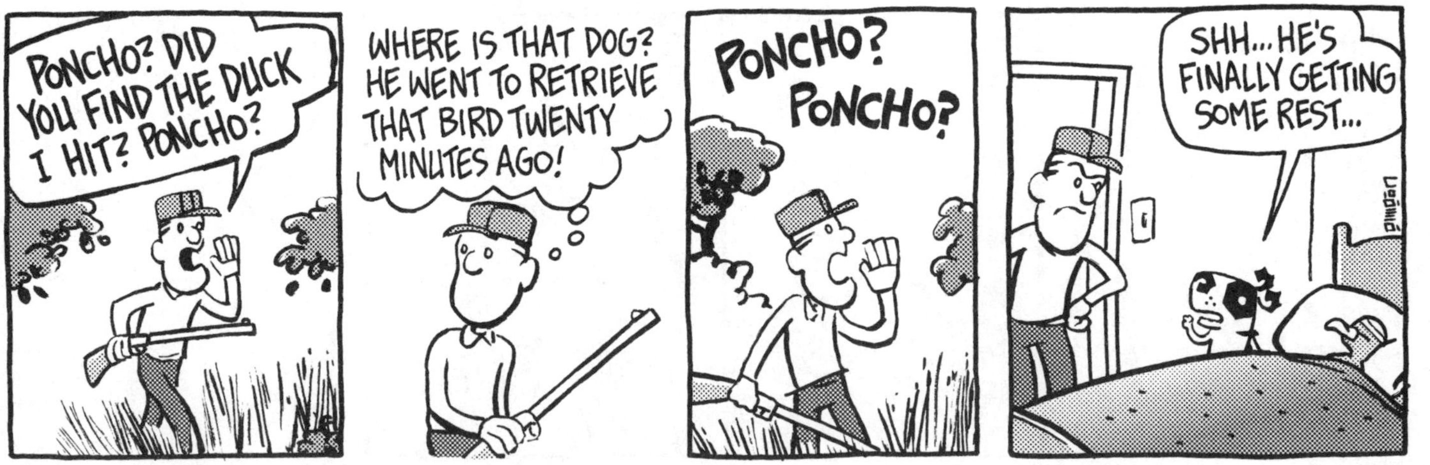
PONCHO? DID YOU FIND THE DUCK I HIT? PONCHO?
WHERE IS THAT DOG? HE WENT TO RETRIEVE THAT BIRD TWENTY MINUTES AGO!
PONCHO?
PONCHO?
SHH... HE'S FINALLY GETTING SOME REST...
gilligan

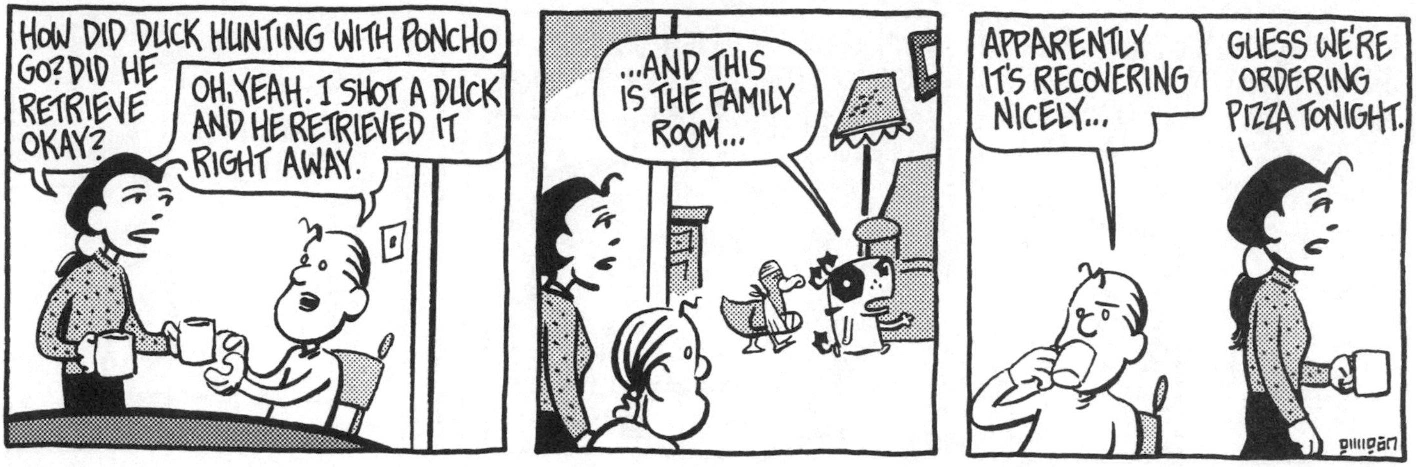
HOW DID DUCK HUNTING WITH PONCHO GO? DID HE RETRIEVE OKAY?
OH, YEAH. I SHOT A DUCK AND HE RETRIEVED IT RIGHT AWAY.
...AND THIS IS THE FAMILY ROOM...
APPARENTLY IT'S RECOVERING NICELY...
GUESS WE'RE ORDERING PIZZA TONIGHT.

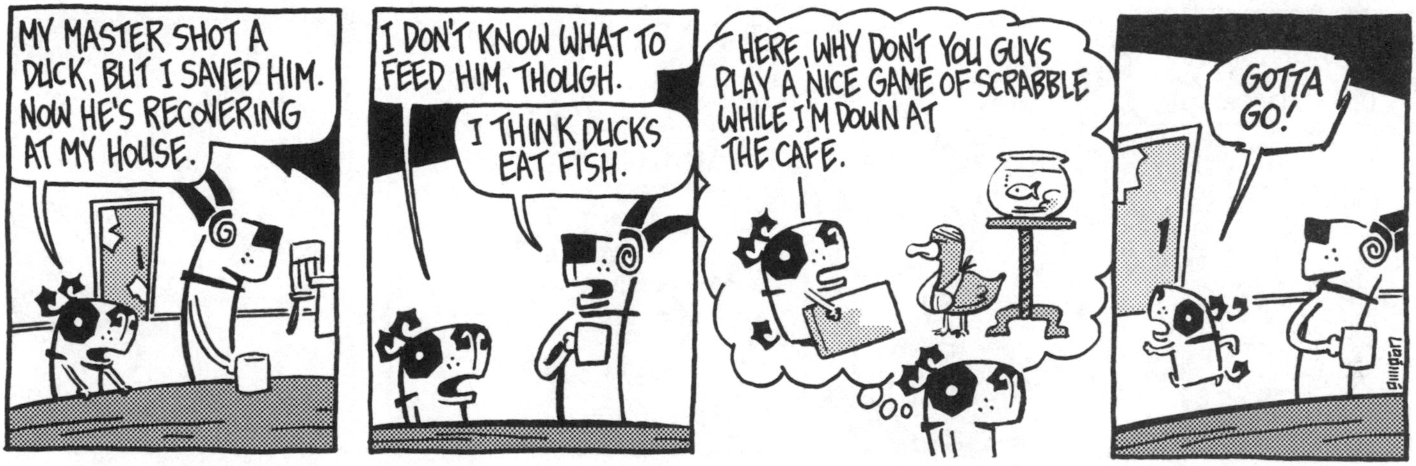
MY MASTER SHOT A DUCK, BUT I SAVED HIM. NOW HE'S RECOVERING AT MY HOUSE.
I DON'T KNOW WHAT TO FEED HIM, THOUGH.
I THINK DUCKS EAT FISH.
HERE, WHY DON'T YOU GUYS PLAY A NICE GAME OF SCRABBLE WHILE I'M DOWN AT THE CAFE.
GOTTA GO!

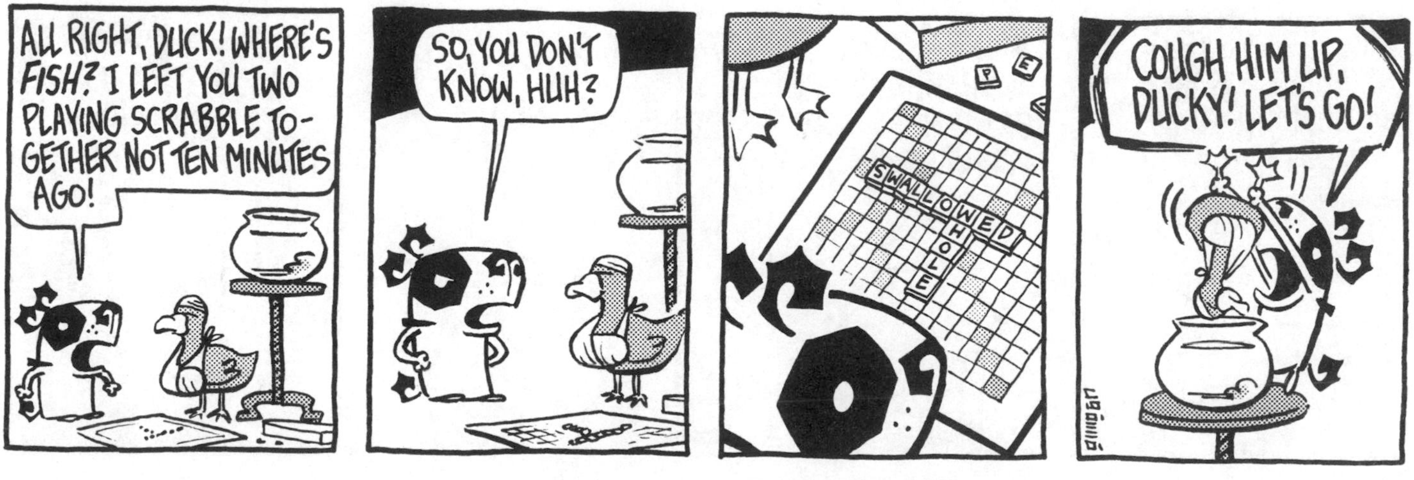
ALL RIGHT, DUCK! WHERE'S *FISH*? I LEFT YOU TWO PLAYING SCRABBLE TOGETHER NOT TEN MINUTES AGO!
SO, YOU DON'T KNOW, HUH?
SWALLOWED
WHOLE
COUGH HIM UP, DUCKY! LET'S GO!

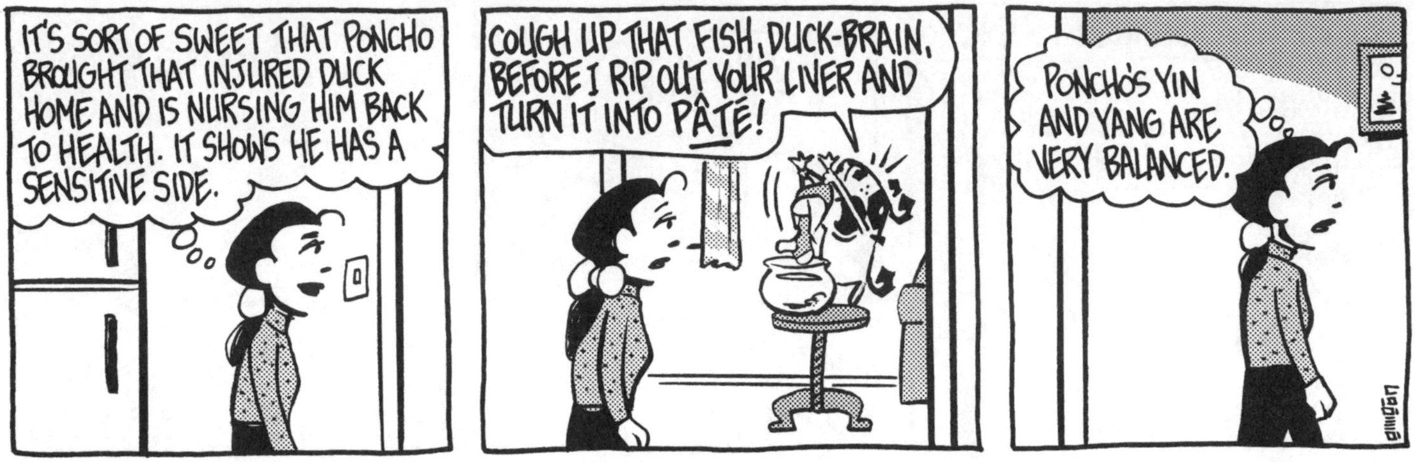
IT'S SORT OF SWEET THAT PONCHO BROUGHT THAT INJURED DUCK HOME AND IS NURSING HIM BACK TO HEALTH. IT SHOWS HE HAS A SENSITIVE SIDE.
COUGH UP THAT FISH, DUCK-BRAIN, BEFORE I RIP OUT YOUR LIVER AND TURN IT INTO PÂTÉ!
PONCHO'S YIN AND YANG ARE VERY BALANCED.

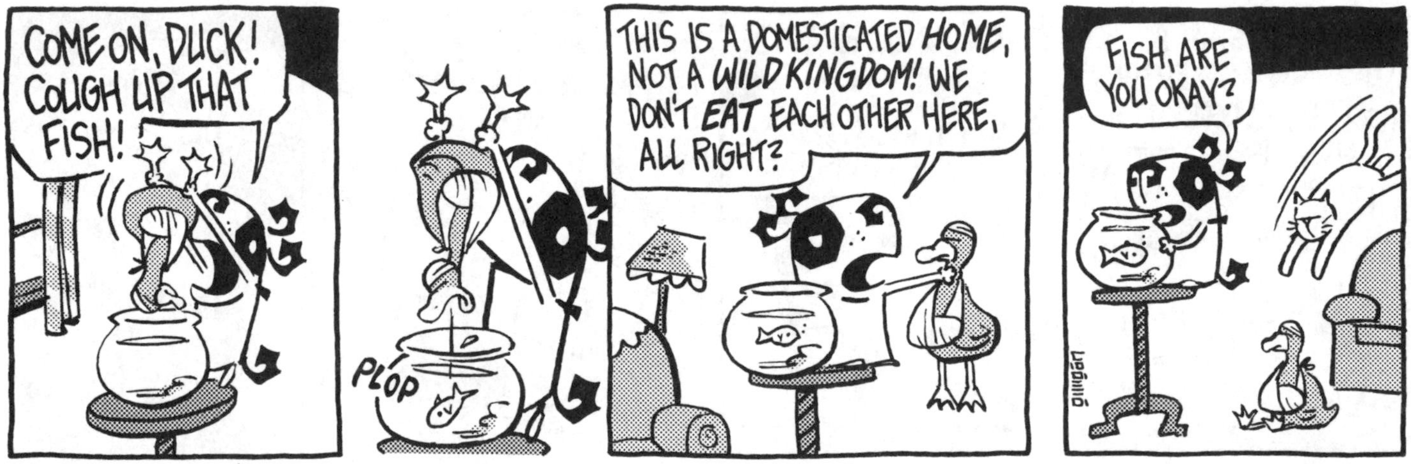
COME ON, DUCK! COUGH UP THAT FISH!
PLOP
THIS IS A DOMESTICATED HOME, NOT A WILD KINGDOM! WE DON'T EAT EACH OTHER HERE, ALL RIGHT?
FISH, ARE YOU OKAY?

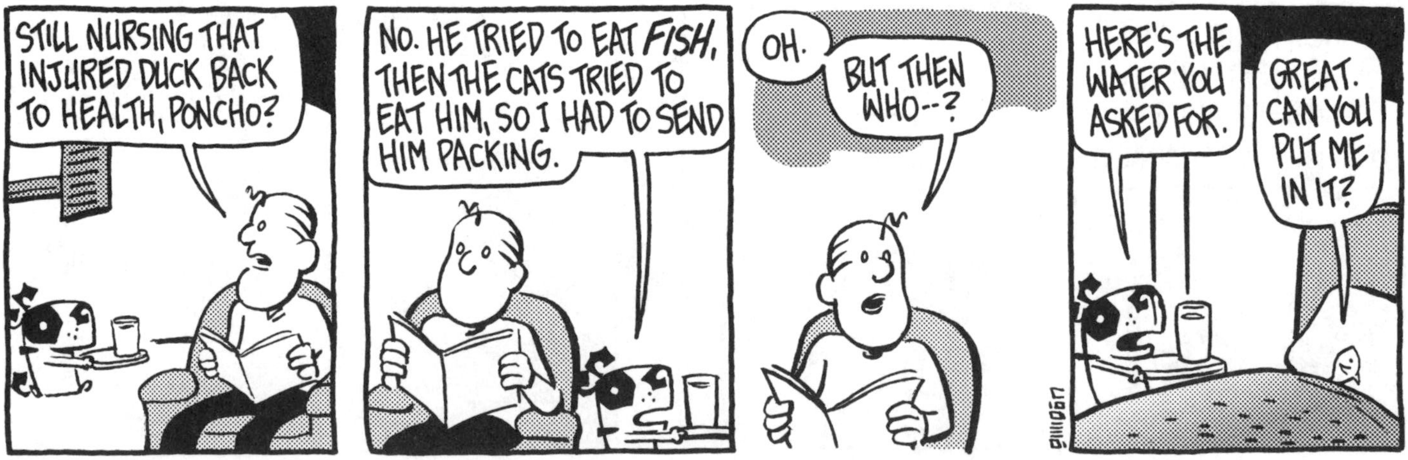
STILL NURSING THAT INJURED DUCK BACK TO HEALTH, PONCHO?
NO. HE TRIED TO EAT FISH, THEN THE CATS TRIED TO EAT HIM, SO I HAD TO SEND HIM PACKING.
OH.
BUT THEN WHO--?
HERE'S THE WATER YOU ASKED FOR.
GREAT. CAN YOU PUT ME IN IT?

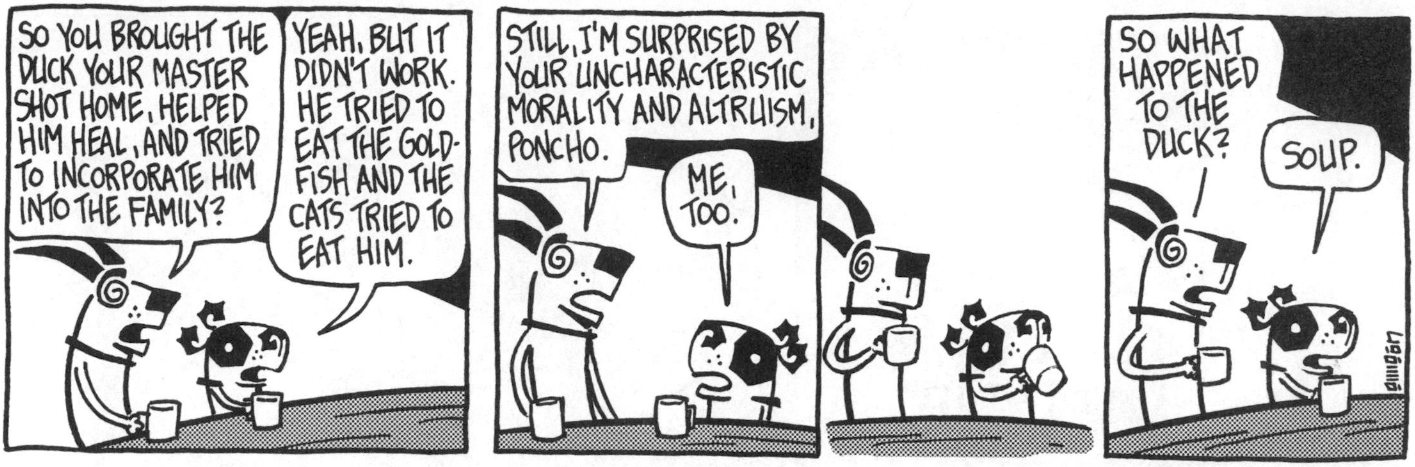
SO YOU BROUGHT THE DUCK YOUR MASTER SHOT HOME, HELPED HIM HEAL, AND TRIED TO INCORPORATE HIM INTO THE FAMILY?
YEAH, BUT IT DIDN'T WORK. HE TRIED TO EAT THE GOLD-FISH AND THE CATS TRIED TO EAT HIM.
STILL, I'M SURPRISED BY YOUR UNCHARACTERISTIC MORALITY AND ALTRUISM, PONCHO.
ME, TOO.
SO WHAT HAPPENED TO THE DUCK?
SOUP.

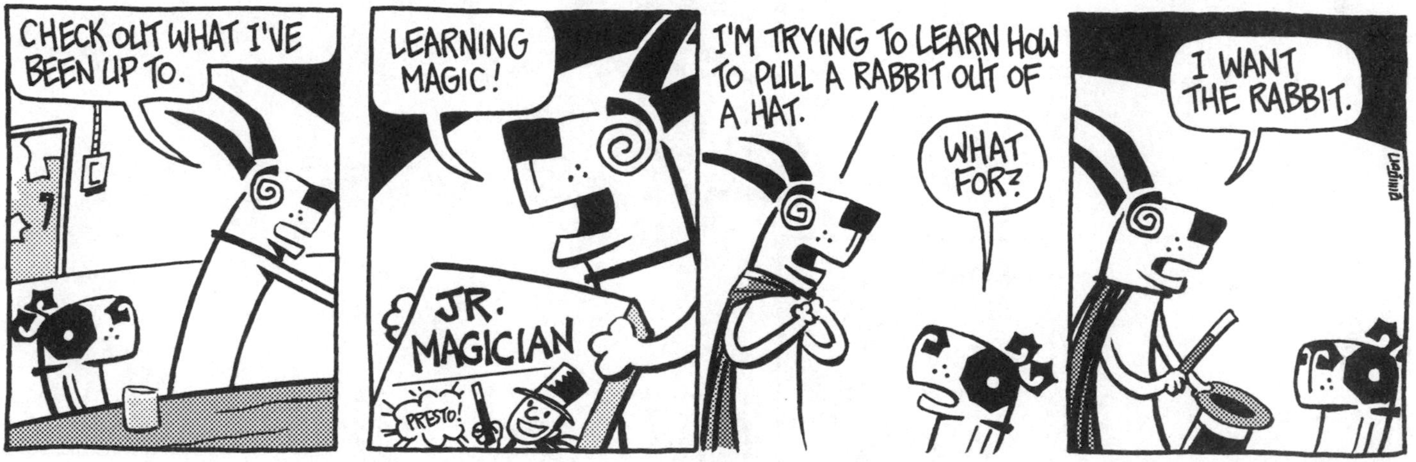
CHECK OUT WHAT I'VE BEEN UP TO.
LEARNING MAGIC!
JR. MAGICIAN
PRESTO!
I'M TRYING TO LEARN HOW TO PULL A RABBIT OUT OF A HAT.
WHAT FOR?
I WANT THE RABBIT.

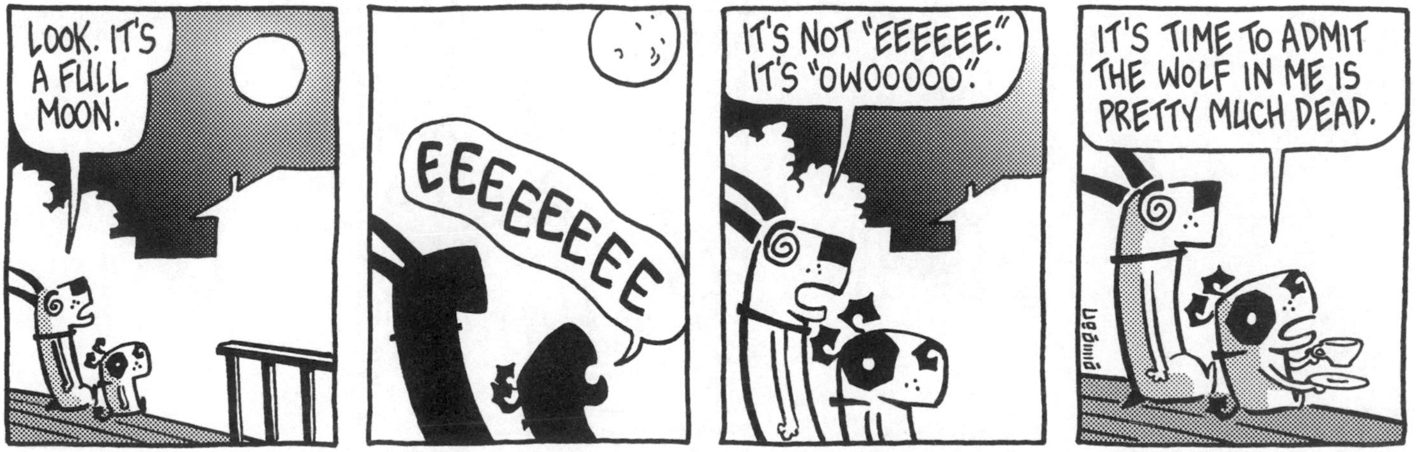
LOOK. IT'S A FULL MOON.
EEEEEEEEE
IT'S NOT "EEEEEE." IT'S "OWOOOOO."
IT'S TIME TO ADMIT THE WOLF IN ME IS PRETTY MUCH DEAD.

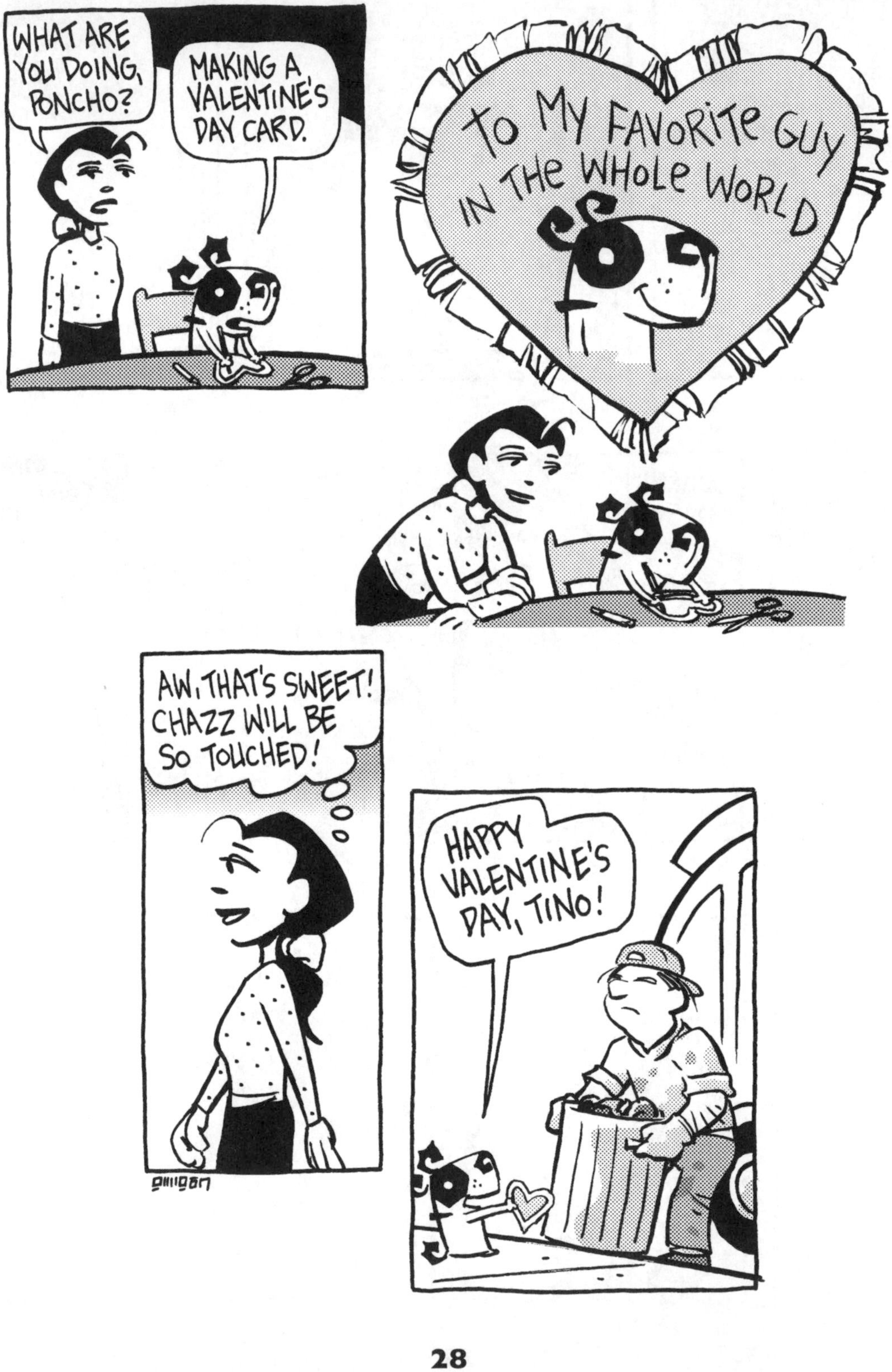
WHAT ARE YOU DOING, PONCHO?
MAKING A VALENTINE'S DAY CARD.
TO MY FAVORITE GUY IN THE WHOLE WORLD
AW, THAT'S SWEET! CHAZZ WILL BE SO TOUCHED!
HAPPY VALENTINE'S DAY, TINO!

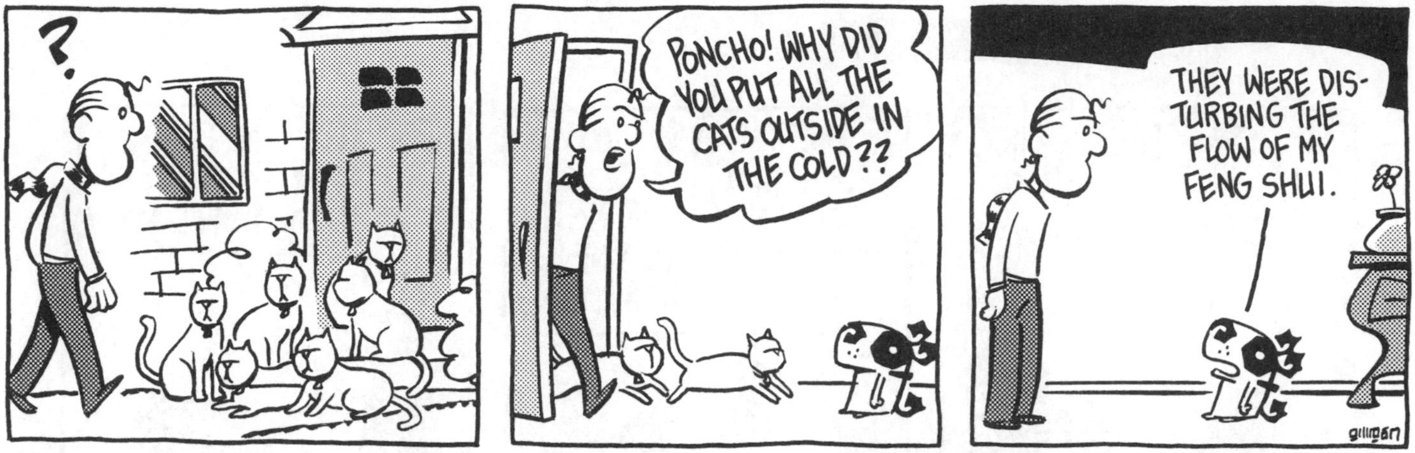
?
PONCHO! WHY DID YOU PUT ALL THE CATS OUTSIDE IN THE COLD??
THEY WERE DISTURBING THE FLOW OF MY FENG SHUI.

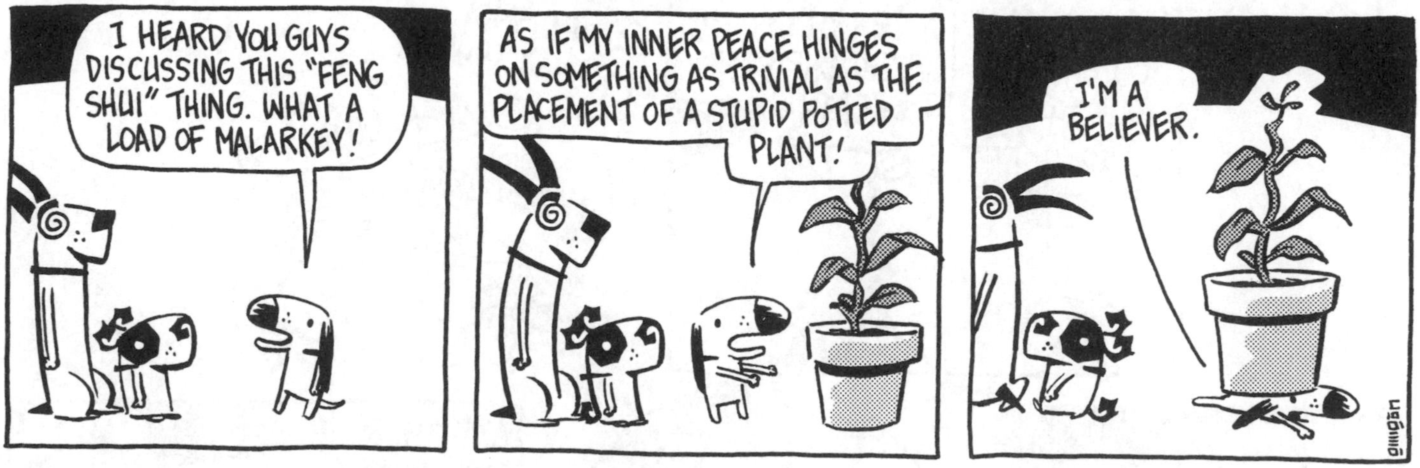
I HEARD YOU GUYS DISCUSSING THIS "FENG SHUI" THING. WHAT A LOAD OF MALARKEY!
AS IF MY INNER PEACE HINGES ON SOMETHING AS TRIVIAL AS THE PLACEMENT OF A STUPID POTTED PLANT!
I'M A BELIEVER.

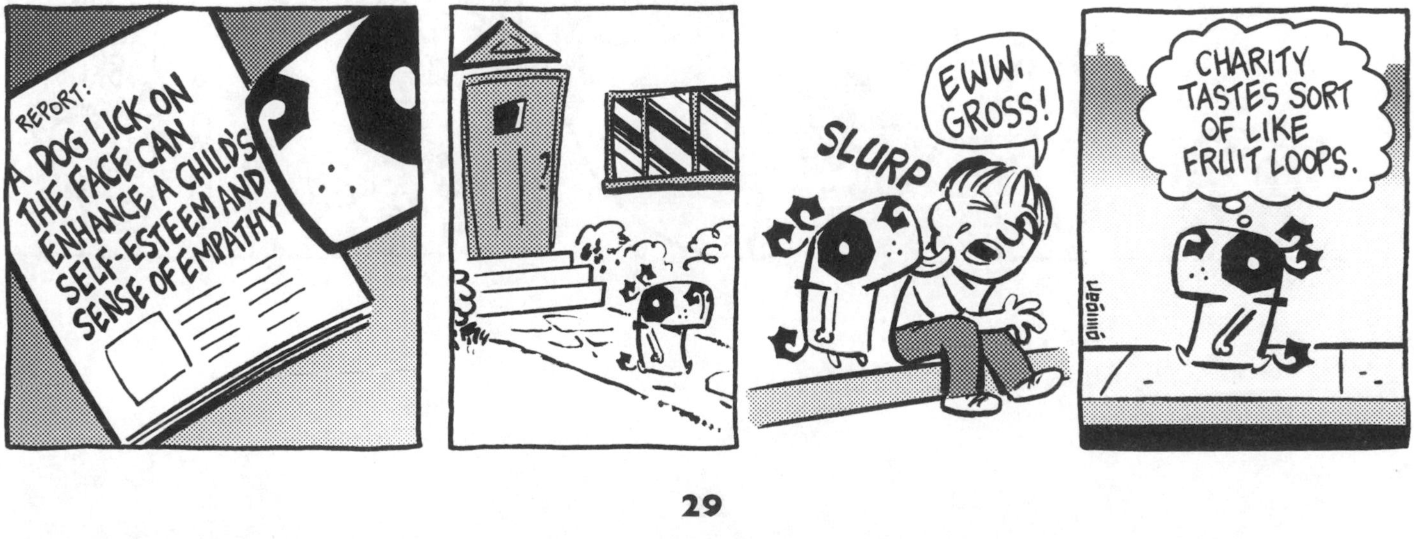
REPORT:
A DOG LICK ON THE FACE CAN ENHANCE A CHILD'S SELF-ESTEEM AND SENSE OF EMPATHY
SLURP
EWW. GROSS!
CHARITY TASTES SORT OF LIKE FRUIT LOOPS.

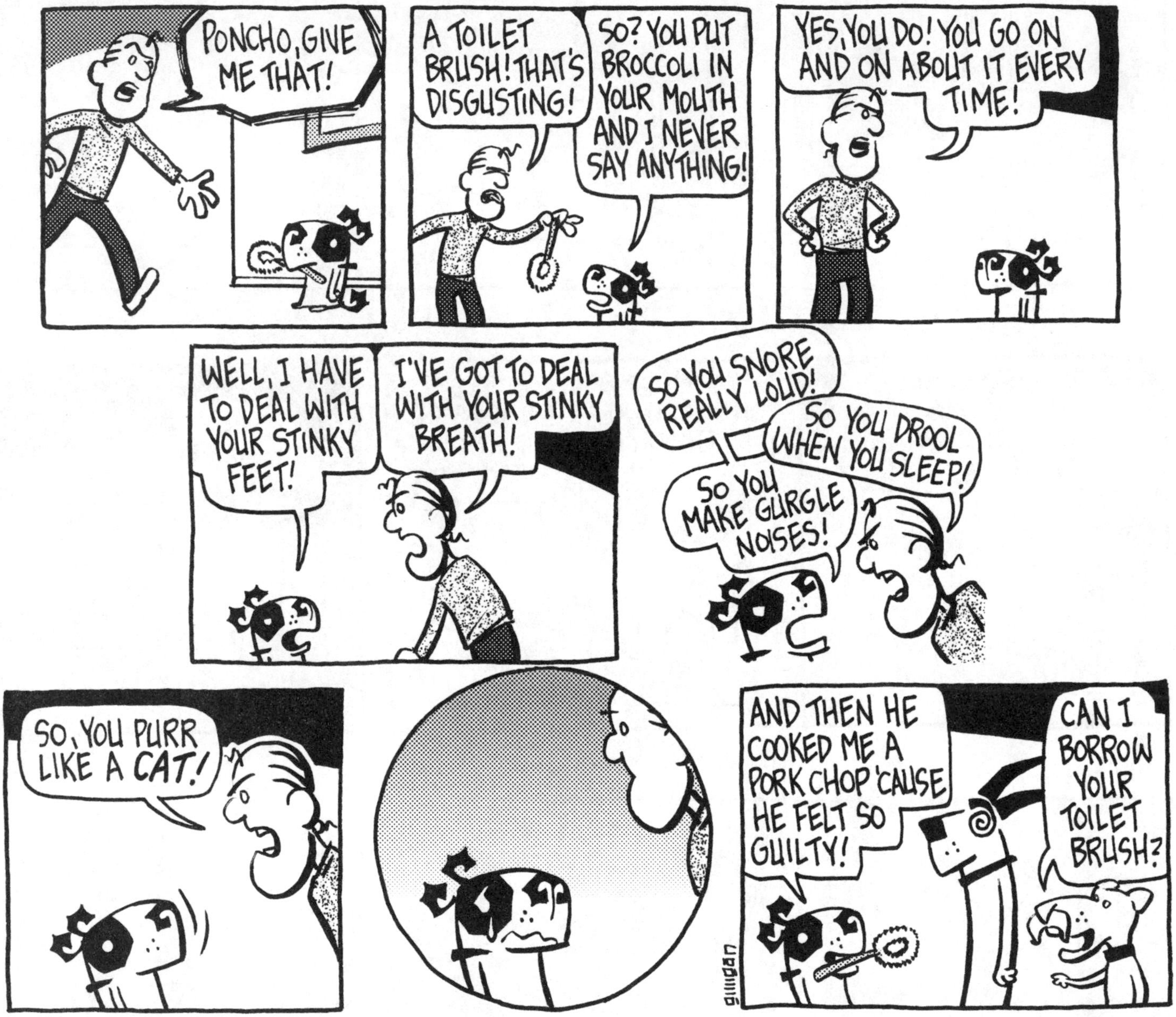
PONCHO, GIVE ME THAT!
A TOILET BRUSH! THAT'S DISGUSTING!
SO? YOU PUT BROCCOLI IN YOUR MOUTH AND I NEVER SAY ANYTHING!
YES, YOU DO! YOU GO ON AND ON ABOUT IT EVERY TIME!
WELL, I HAVE TO DEAL WITH YOUR STINKY FEET!
I'VE GOT TO DEAL WITH YOUR STINKY BREATH!
SO YOU SNORE REALLY LOUD!
SO YOU DROOL WHEN YOU SLEEP!
SO YOU MAKE GURGLE NOISES!
SO, YOU PURR LIKE A CAT!
AND THEN HE COOKED ME A PORK CHOP 'CAUSE HE FELT SO GUILTY!
CAN I BORROW YOUR TOILET BRUSH?
gilligan

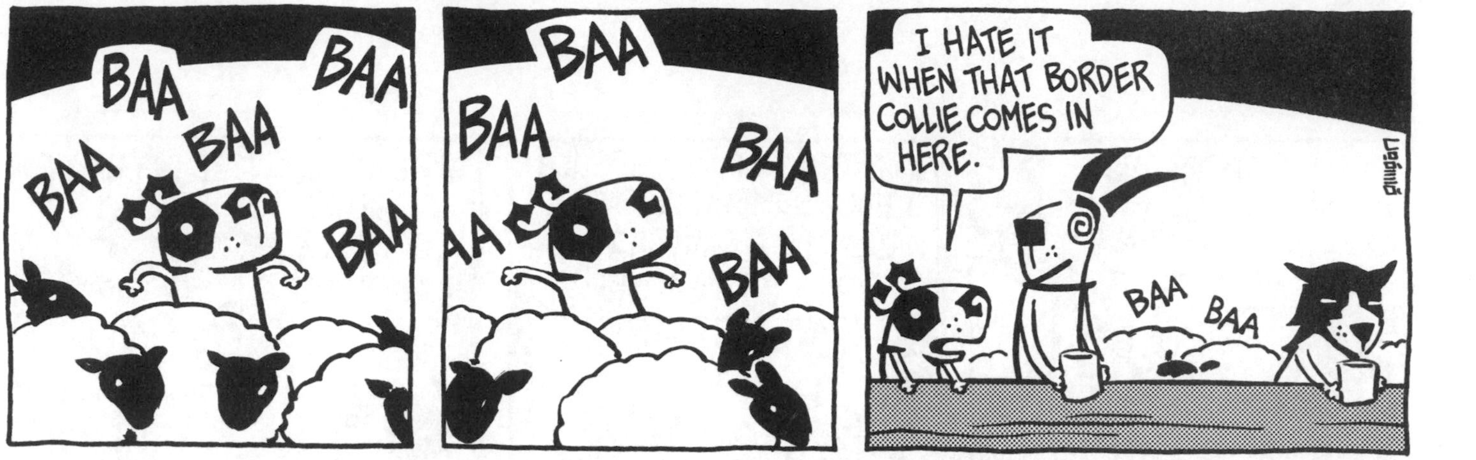
BAA BAA BAA BAA BAA
BAA BAA BAA BAA BAA AA
I HATE IT WHEN THAT BORDER COLLIE COMES IN HERE.
BAA BAA

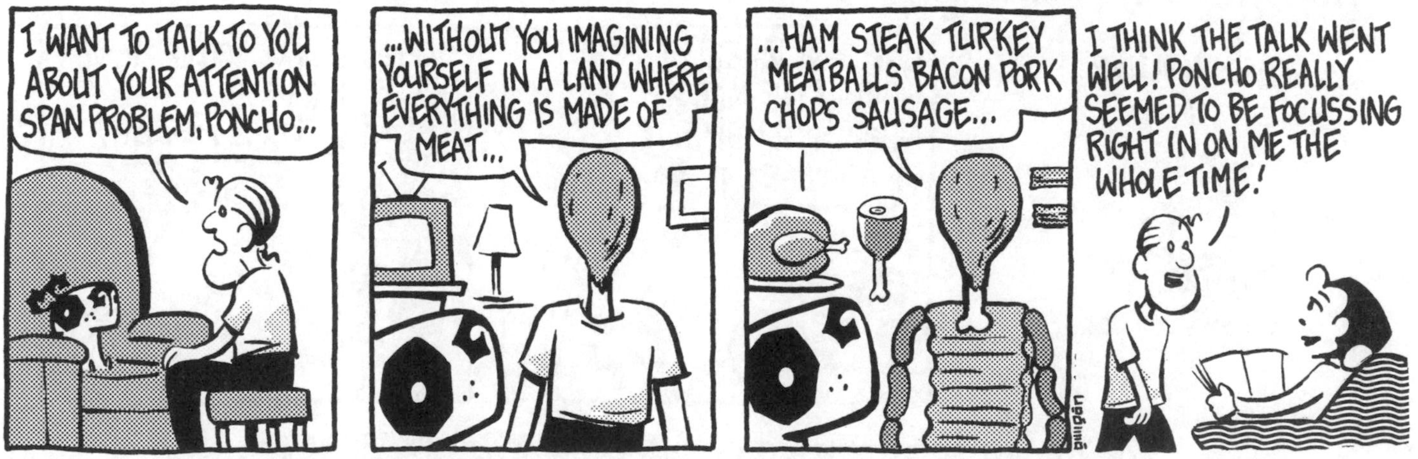
I WANT TO TALK TO YOU ABOUT YOUR ATTENTION SPAN PROBLEM, PONCHO...
...WITHOUT YOU IMAGINING YOURSELF IN A LAND WHERE EVERYTHING IS MADE OF MEAT...
...HAM STEAK TURKEY MEATBALLS BACON PORK CHOPS SAUSAGE...
I THINK THE TALK WENT WELL! PONCHO REALLY SEEMED TO BE FOCUSSING RIGHT IN ON ME THE WHOLE TIME!

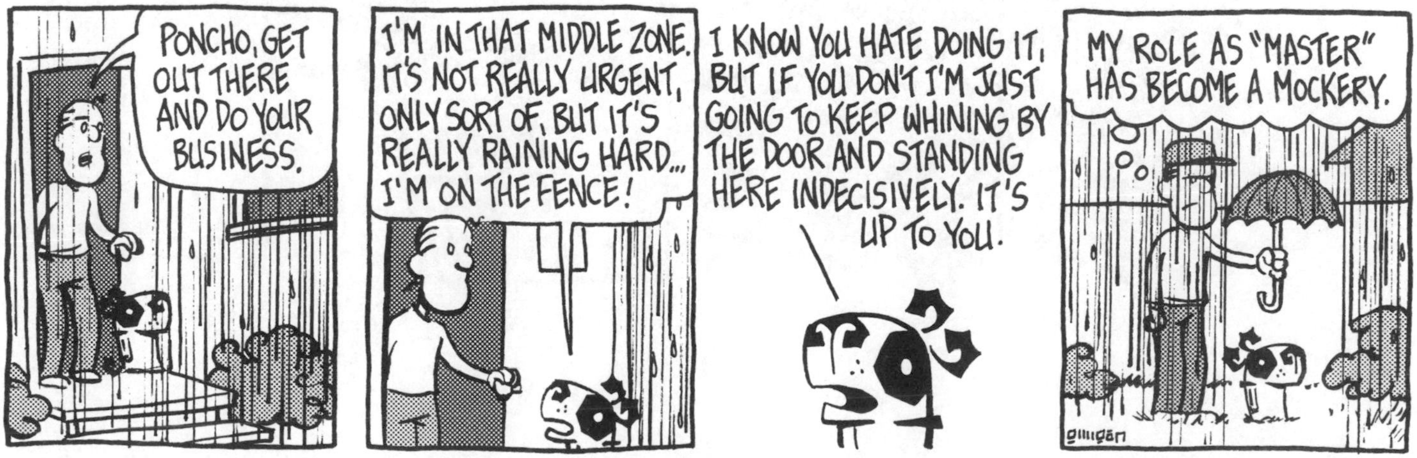
PONCHO, GET OUT THERE AND DO YOUR BUSINESS.
I'M IN THAT MIDDLE ZONE. IT'S NOT REALLY URGENT, ONLY SORT OF, BUT IT'S REALLY RAINING HARD... I'M ON THE FENCE!
I KNOW YOU HATE DOING IT, BUT IF YOU DON'T I'M JUST GOING TO KEEP WHINING BY THE DOOR AND STANDING HERE INDECISIVELY. IT'S UP TO YOU.
MY ROLE AS "MASTER" HAS BECOME A MOCKERY.

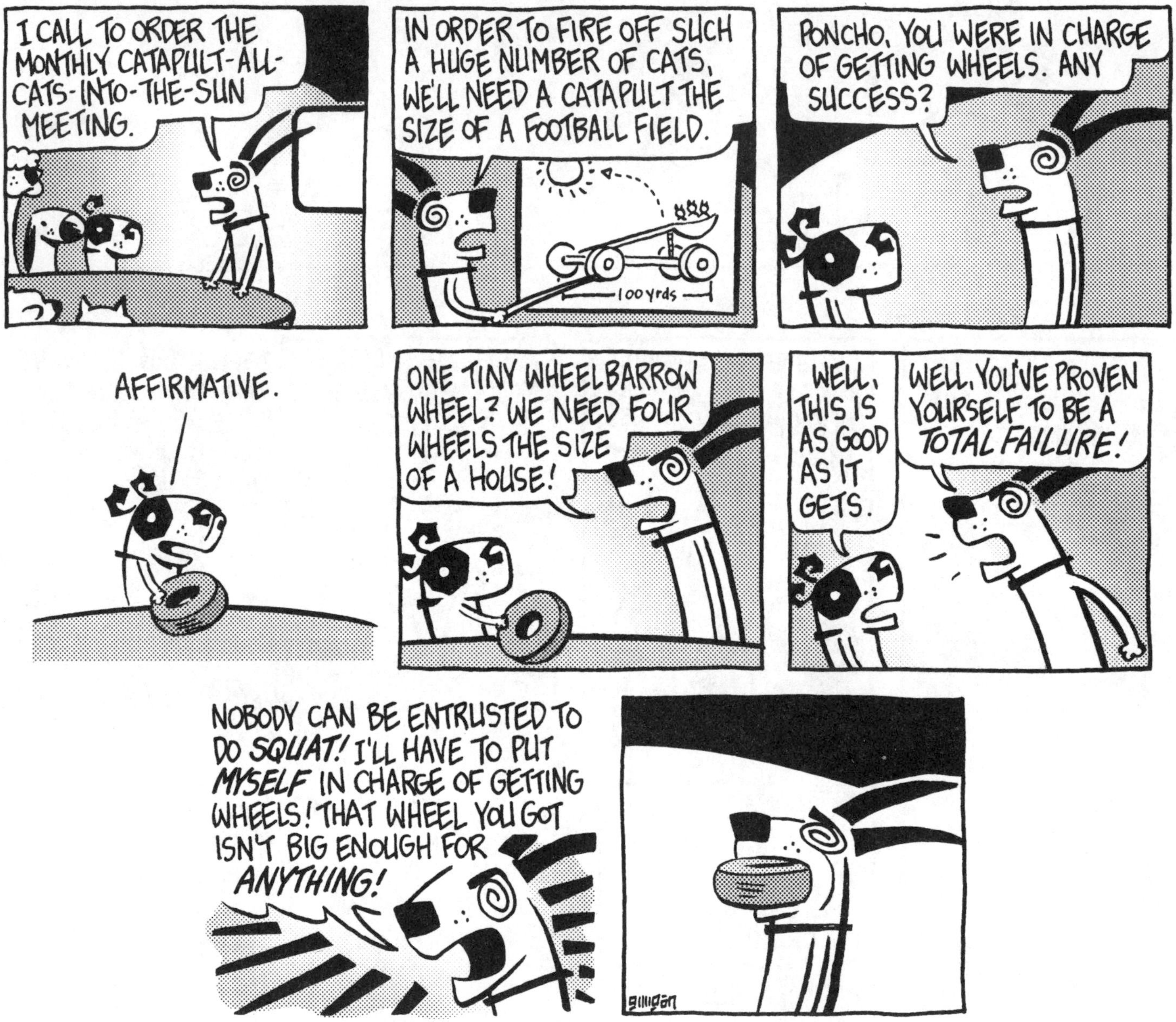
I CALL TO ORDER THE MONTHLY CATAPULT-ALL-CATS-INTO-THE-SUN MEETING.
IN ORDER TO FIRE OFF SUCH A HUGE NUMBER OF CATS, WE'LL NEED A CATAPULT THE SIZE OF A FOOTBALL FIELD.
100 yrds
PONCHO, YOU WERE IN CHARGE OF GETTING WHEELS. ANY SUCCESS?
AFFIRMATIVE.
ONE TINY WHEELBARROW WHEEL? WE NEED FOUR WHEELS THE SIZE OF A HOUSE!
WELL, THIS IS AS GOOD AS IT GETS.
WELL, YOU'VE PROVEN YOURSELF TO BE A *TOTAL FAILURE!*
NOBODY CAN BE ENTRUSTED TO DO *SQUAT!* I'LL HAVE TO PUT *MYSELF* IN CHARGE OF GETTING WHEELS! THAT WHEEL YOU GOT ISN'T BIG ENOUGH FOR *ANYTHING!*
gilligan

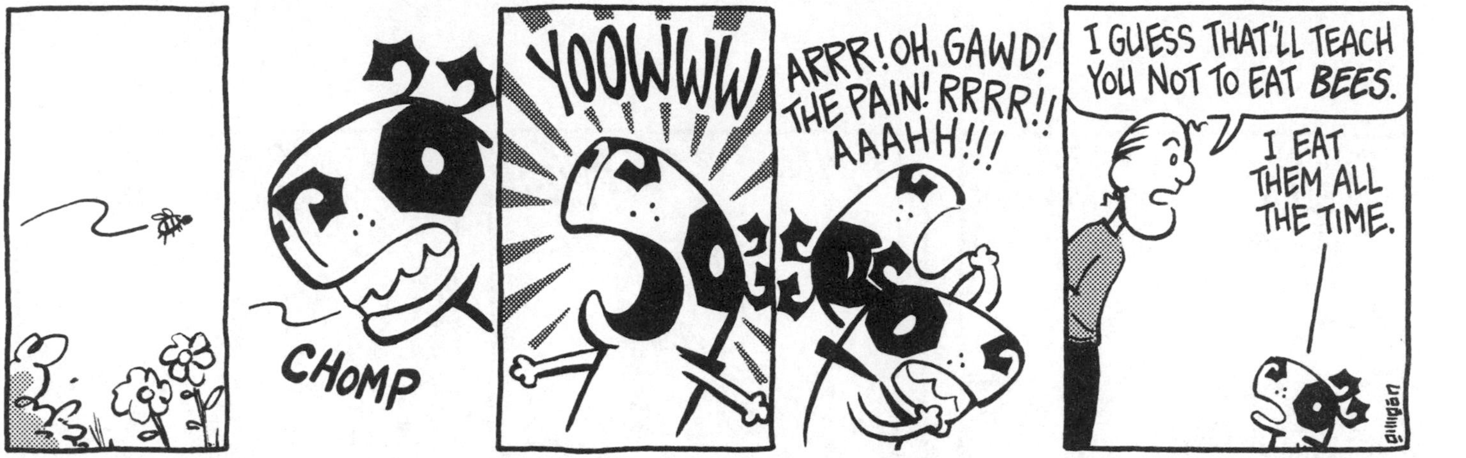
CHOMP
YOOWWW
ARRR! OH, GAWD! THE PAIN! RRRR!! AAAHH!!!
I GUESS THAT'LL TEACH YOU NOT TO EAT BEES.
I EAT THEM ALL THE TIME.

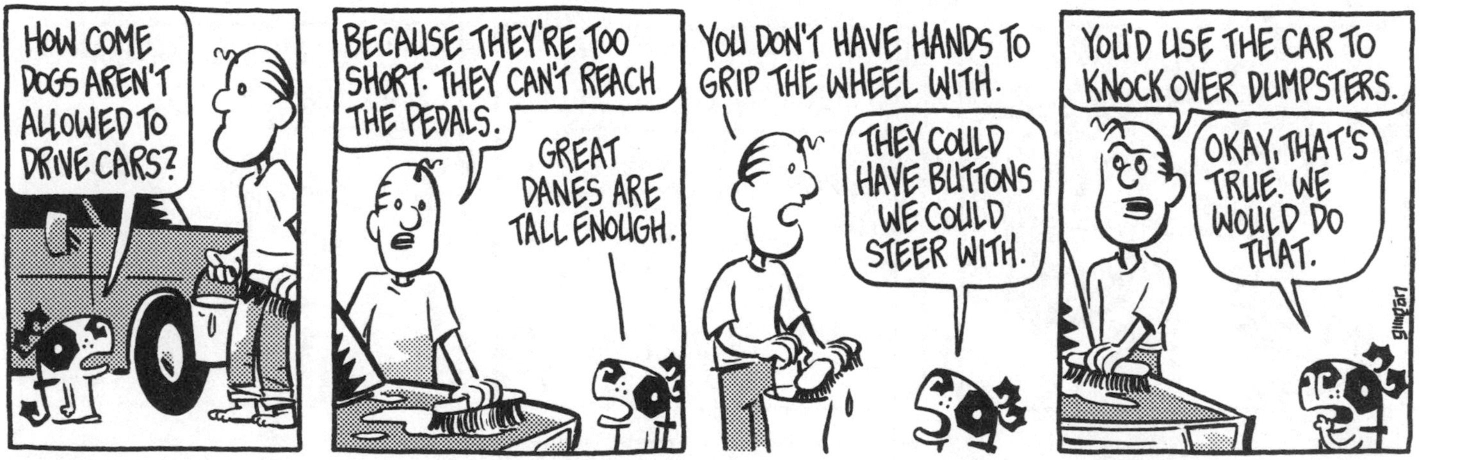
HOW COME DOGS AREN'T ALLOWED TO DRIVE CARS?
BECAUSE THEY'RE TOO SHORT. THEY CAN'T REACH THE PEDALS.
GREAT DANES ARE TALL ENOUGH.
YOU DON'T HAVE HANDS TO GRIP THE WHEEL WITH.
THEY COULD HAVE BUTTONS WE COULD STEER WITH.
YOU'D USE THE CAR TO KNOCK OVER DUMPSTERS.
OKAY, THAT'S TRUE. WE WOULD DO THAT.

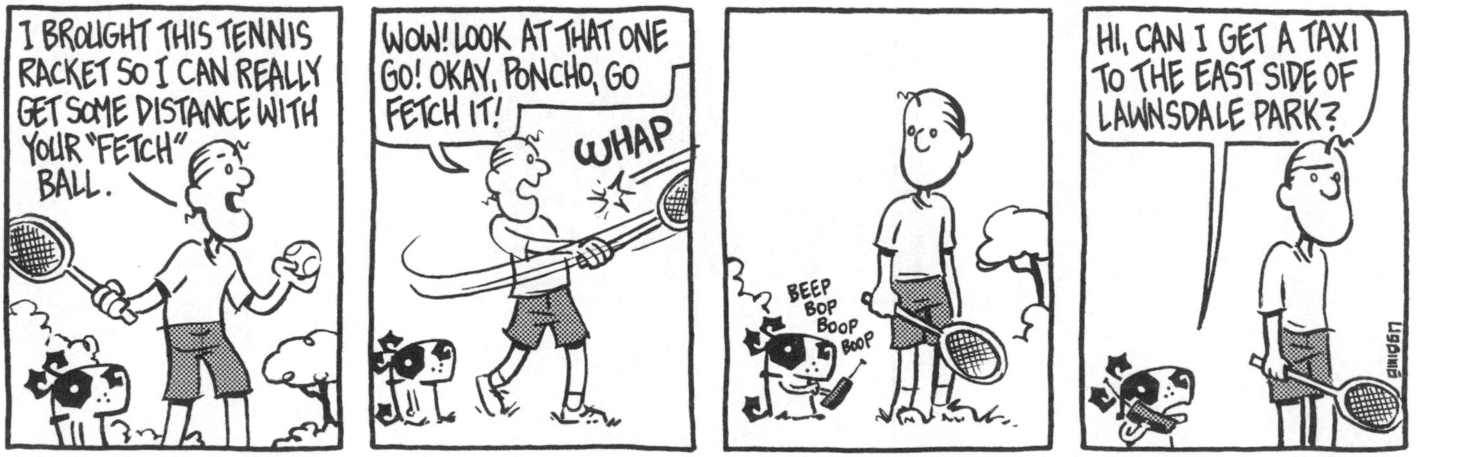
I BROUGHT THIS TENNIS RACKET SO I CAN REALLY GET SOME DISTANCE WITH YOUR "FETCH" BALL.
WOW! LOOK AT THAT ONE GO! OKAY, PONCHO, GO FETCH IT!
WHAP
BEEP BOP BOOP BOOP
HI, CAN I GET A TAXI TO THE EAST SIDE OF LAWNSDALE PARK?

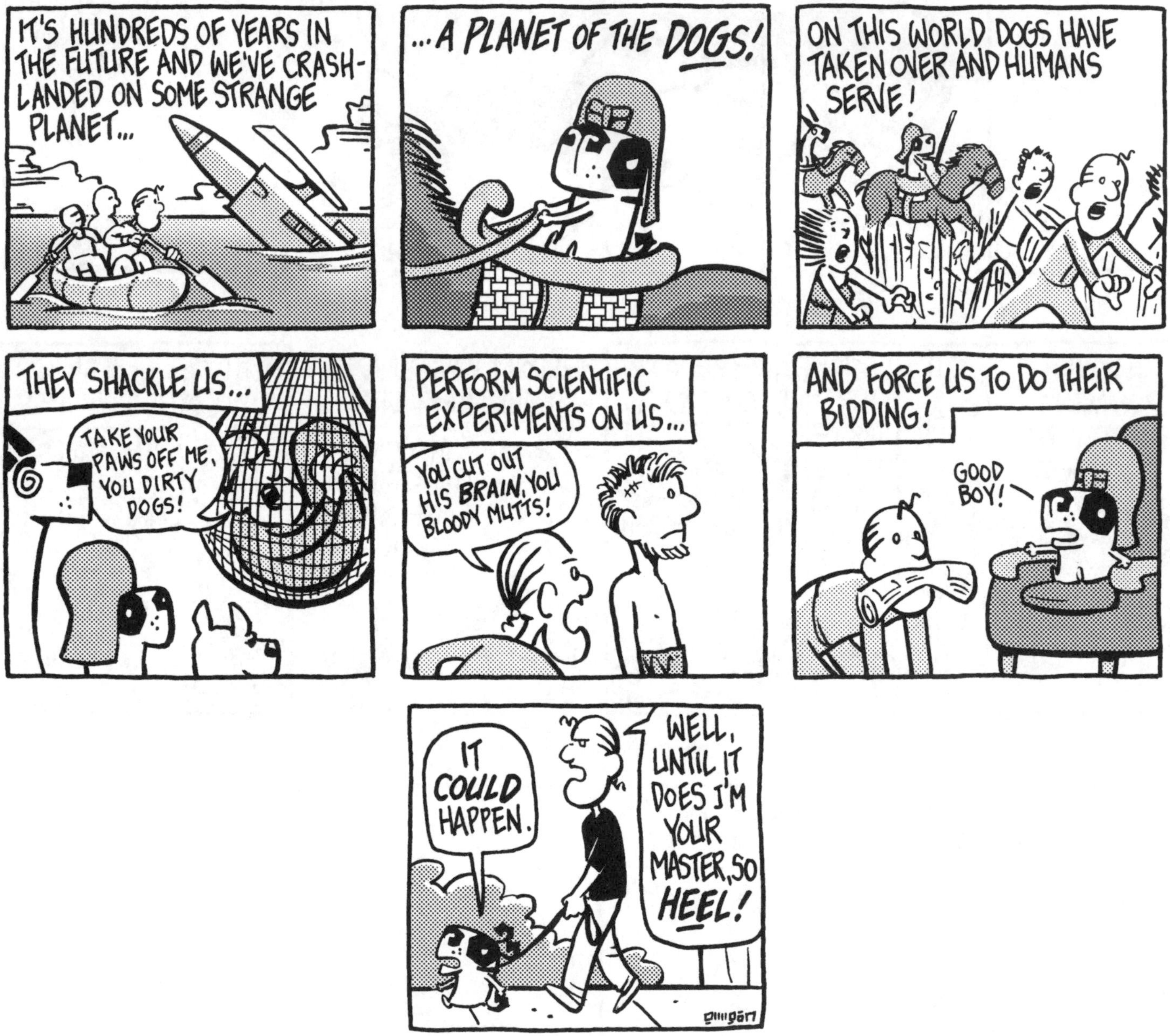
IT'S HUNDREDS OF YEARS IN THE FUTURE AND WE'VE CRASH-LANDED ON SOME STRANGE PLANET...
...A PLANET OF THE DOGS!
ON THIS WORLD DOGS HAVE TAKEN OVER AND HUMANS SERVE!
THEY SHACKLE US...
TAKE YOUR PAWS OFF ME, YOU DIRTY DOGS!
PERFORM SCIENTIFIC EXPERIMENTS ON US...
YOU CUT OUT HIS BRAIN, YOU BLOODY MUTTS!
AND FORCE US TO DO THEIR BIDDING!
GOOD BOY!
IT COULD HAPPEN.
WELL, UNTIL IT DOES I'M YOUR MASTER, SO HEEL!

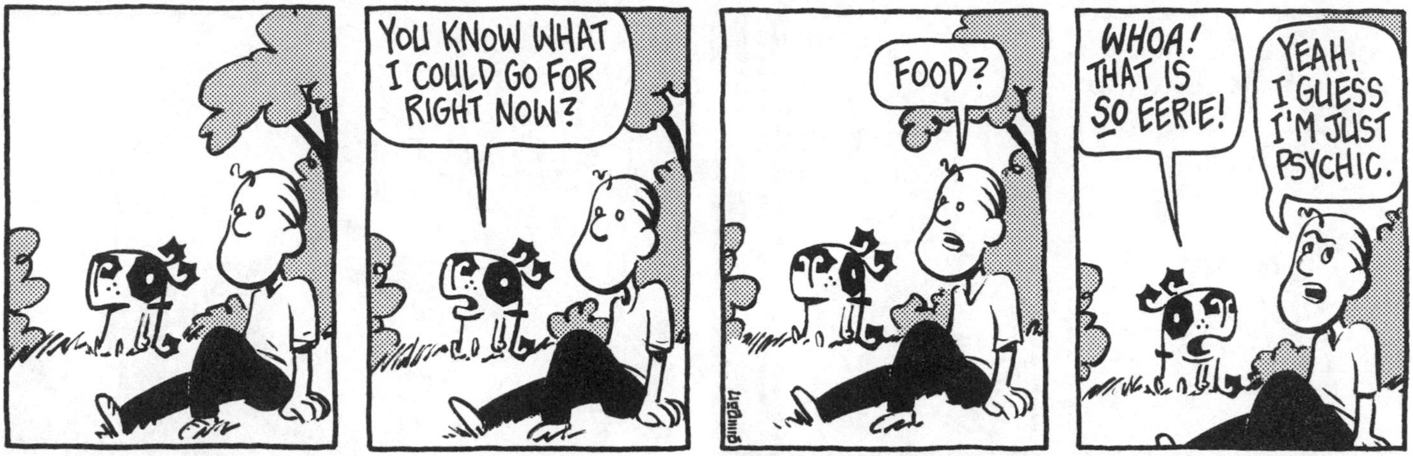
YOU KNOW WHAT I COULD GO FOR RIGHT NOW?
FOOD?
WHOA! THAT IS SO EERIE!
YEAH, I GUESS I'M JUST PSYCHIC.

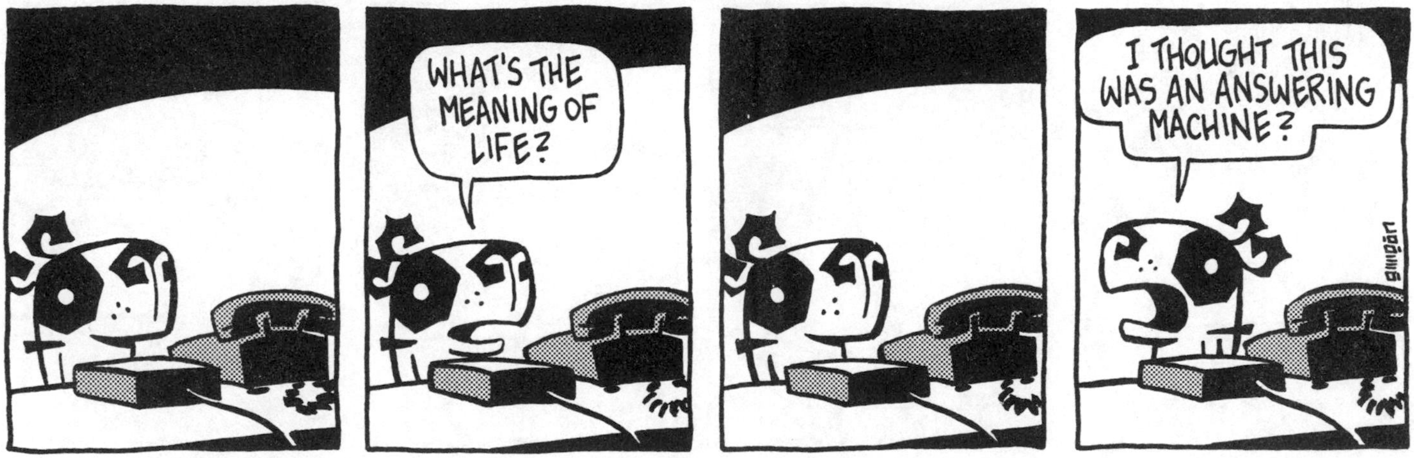
WHAT'S THE MEANING OF LIFE?
I THOUGHT THIS WAS AN ANSWERING MACHINE?

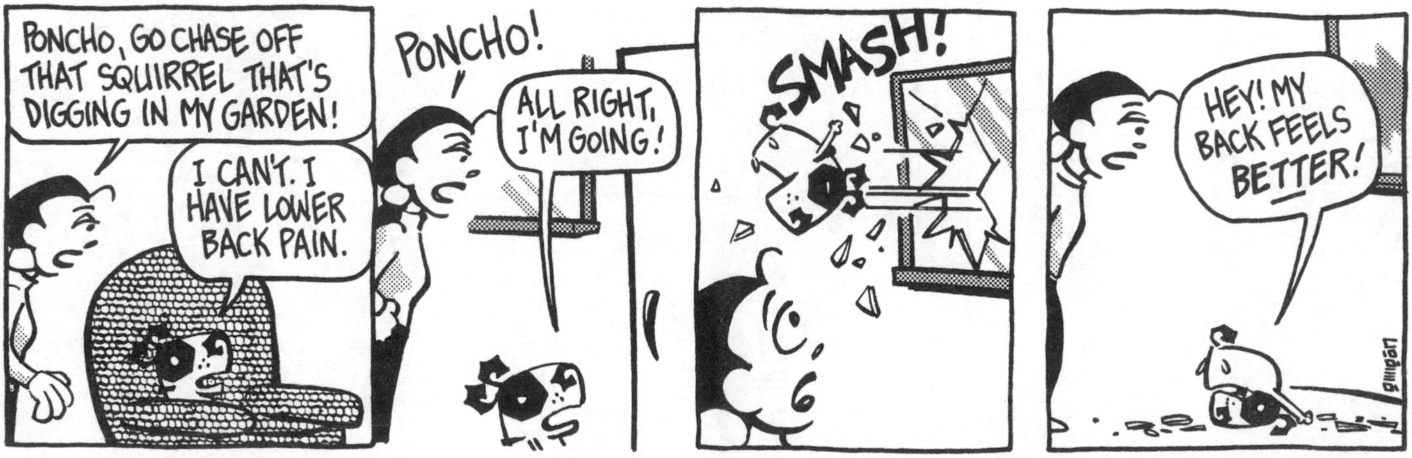
PONCHO, GO CHASE OFF THAT SQUIRREL THAT'S DIGGING IN MY GARDEN!
I CAN'T. I HAVE LOWER BACK PAIN.
PONCHO!
ALL RIGHT, I'M GOING!
SMASH!
HEY! MY BACK FEELS BETTER!

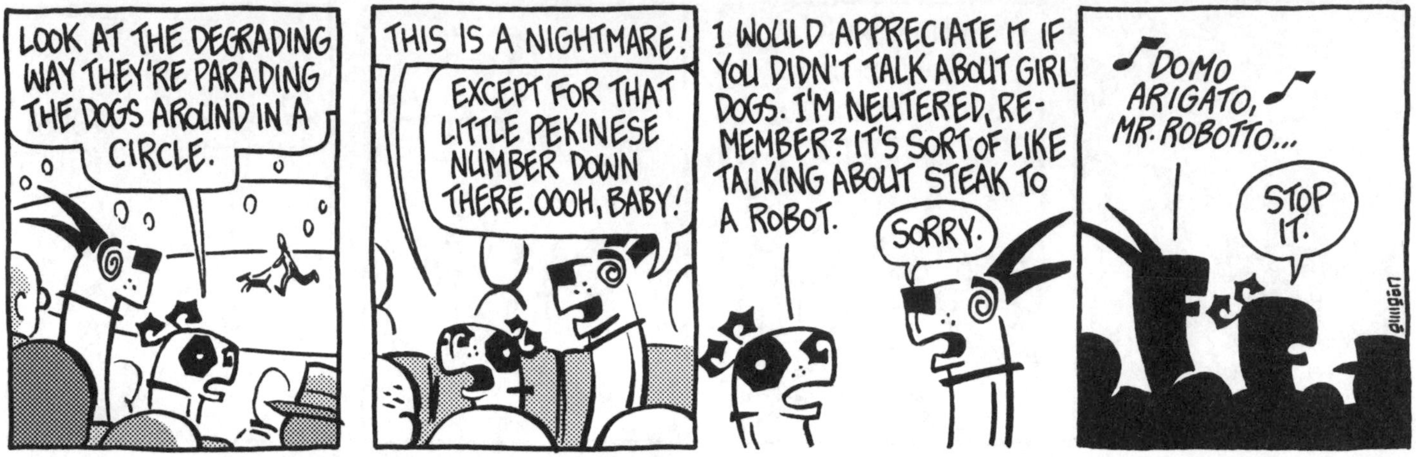
LOOK AT THE DEGRADING WAY THEY'RE PARADING THE DOGS AROUND IN A CIRCLE.
THIS IS A NIGHTMARE!
EXCEPT FOR THAT LITTLE PEKINESE NUMBER DOWN THERE. OOOH, BABY!
I WOULD APPRECIATE IT IF YOU DIDN'T TALK ABOUT GIRL DOGS. I'M NEUTERED, REMEMBER? IT'S SORT OF LIKE TALKING ABOUT STEAK TO A ROBOT.
SORRY.
♪DOMO ARIGATO, MR. ROBOTTO...♪
STOP IT.

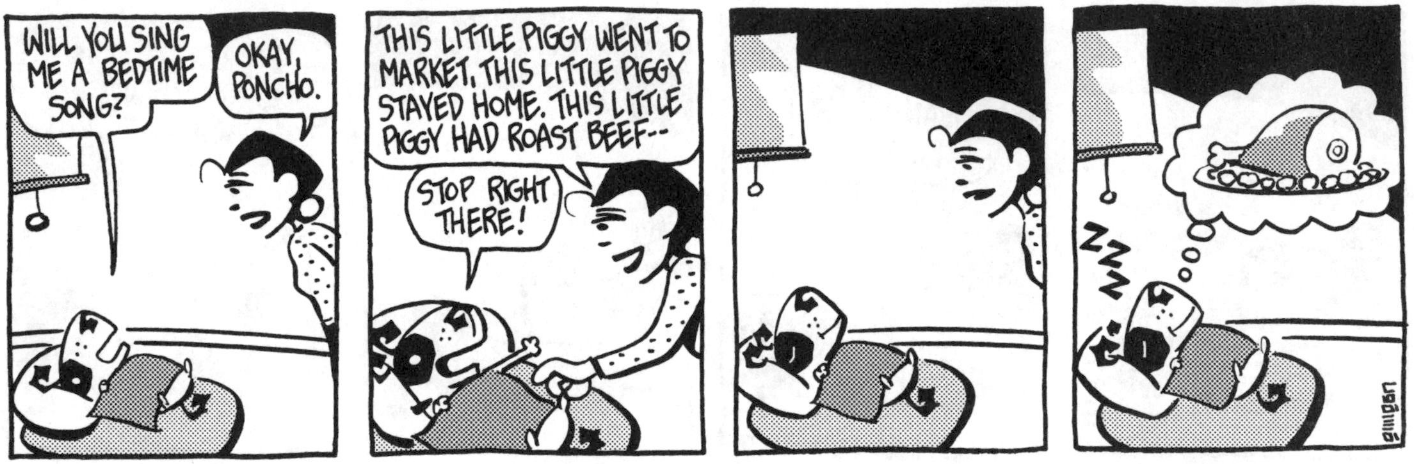
WILL YOU SING ME A BEDTIME SONG?
OKAY, PONCHO.
THIS LITTLE PIGGY WENT TO MARKET, THIS LITTLE PIGGY STAYED HOME. THIS LITTLE PIGGY HAD ROAST BEEF--
STOP RIGHT THERE!
ZZZ

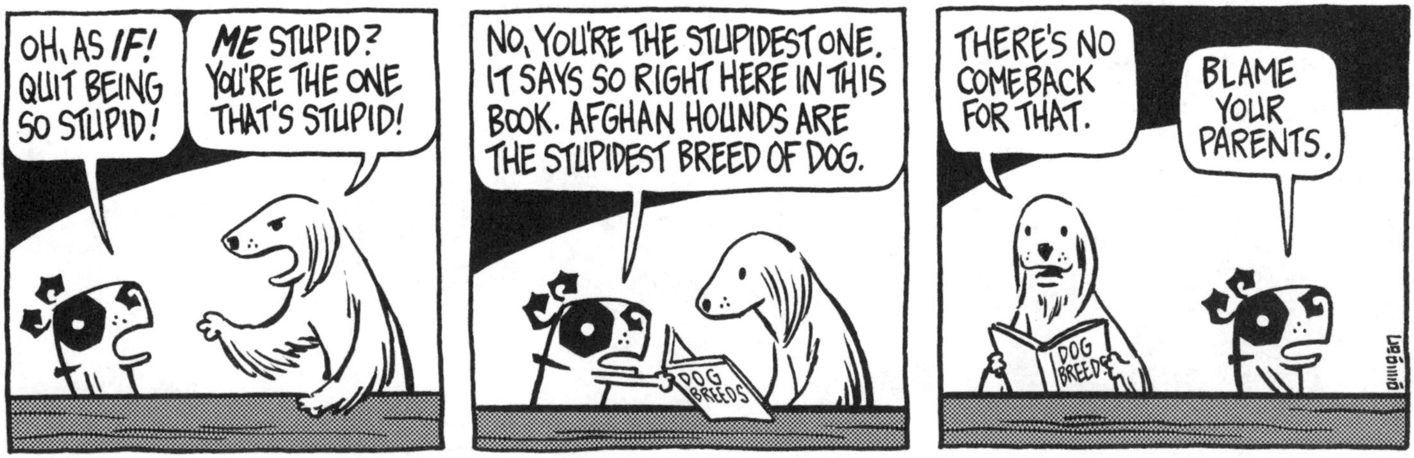
OH, AS *IF*! QUIT BEING SO STUPID!
ME STUPID? YOU'RE THE ONE THAT'S STUPID!
NO, YOU'RE THE STUPIDEST ONE. IT SAYS SO RIGHT HERE IN THIS BOOK. AFGHAN HOUNDS ARE THE STUPIDEST BREED OF DOG.
DOG BREEDS
THERE'S NO COMEBACK FOR THAT.
BLAME YOUR PARENTS.
DOG BREEDS

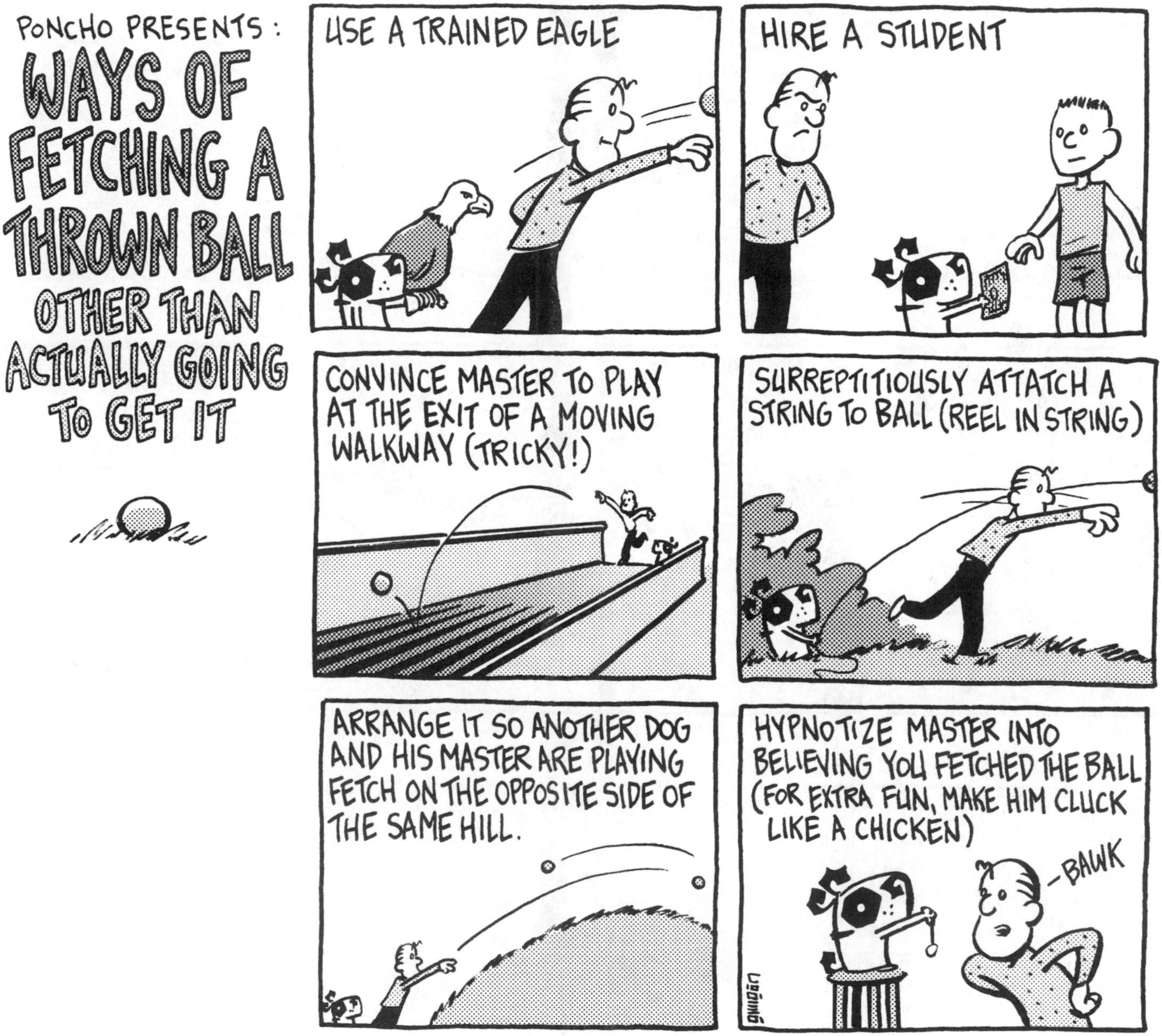
PONCHO PRESENTS:
WAYS OF FETCHING A THROWN BALL OTHER THAN ACTUALLY GOING TO GET IT
USE A TRAINED EAGLE
HIRE A STUDENT
CONVINCE MASTER TO PLAY AT THE EXIT OF A MOVING WALKWAY (TRICKY!)
SURREPTITIOUSLY ATTATCH A STRING TO BALL (REEL IN STRING)
ARRANGE IT SO ANOTHER DOG AND HIS MASTER ARE PLAYING FETCH ON THE OPPOSITE SIDE OF THE SAME HILL.
HYPNOTIZE MASTER INTO BELIEVING YOU FETCHED THE BALL (FOR EXTRA FUN, MAKE HIM CLUCK LIKE A CHICKEN)
-BAWK

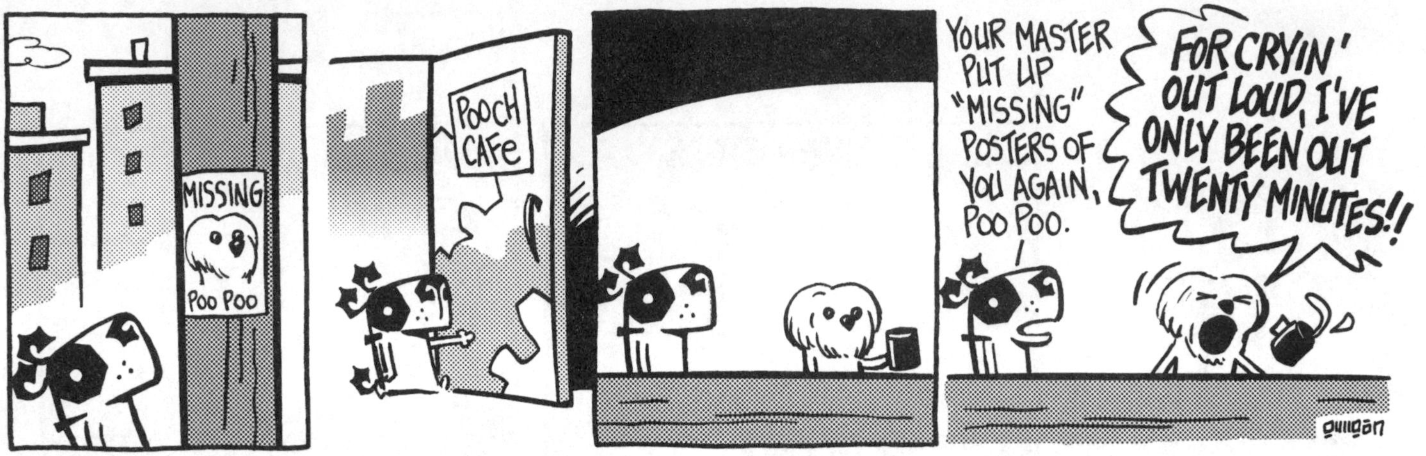
MISSING
POO POO
POOCH CAFE
YOUR MASTER PUT UP "MISSING" POSTERS OF YOU AGAIN, POO POO.
FOR CRYIN' OUT LOUD, I'VE ONLY BEEN OUT TWENTY MINUTES!!

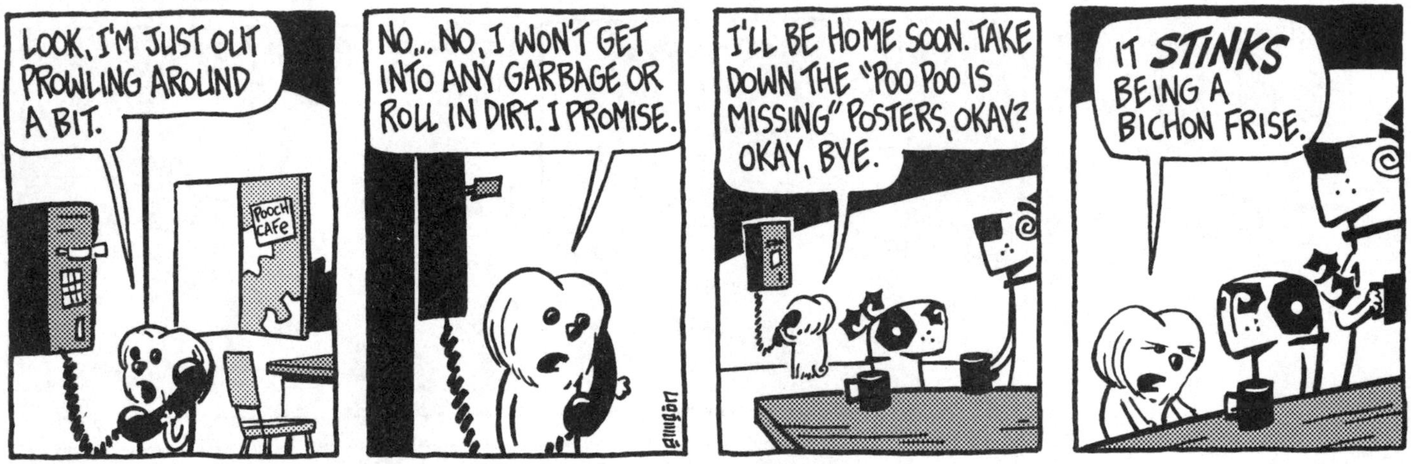
LOOK, I'M JUST OUT PROWLING AROUND A BIT.
POOCH CAFE
NO... NO, I WON'T GET INTO ANY GARBAGE OR ROLL IN DIRT. I PROMISE.
I'LL BE HOME SOON. TAKE DOWN THE "POO POO IS MISSING" POSTERS, OKAY? OKAY, BYE.
IT STINKS BEING A BICHON FRISE.

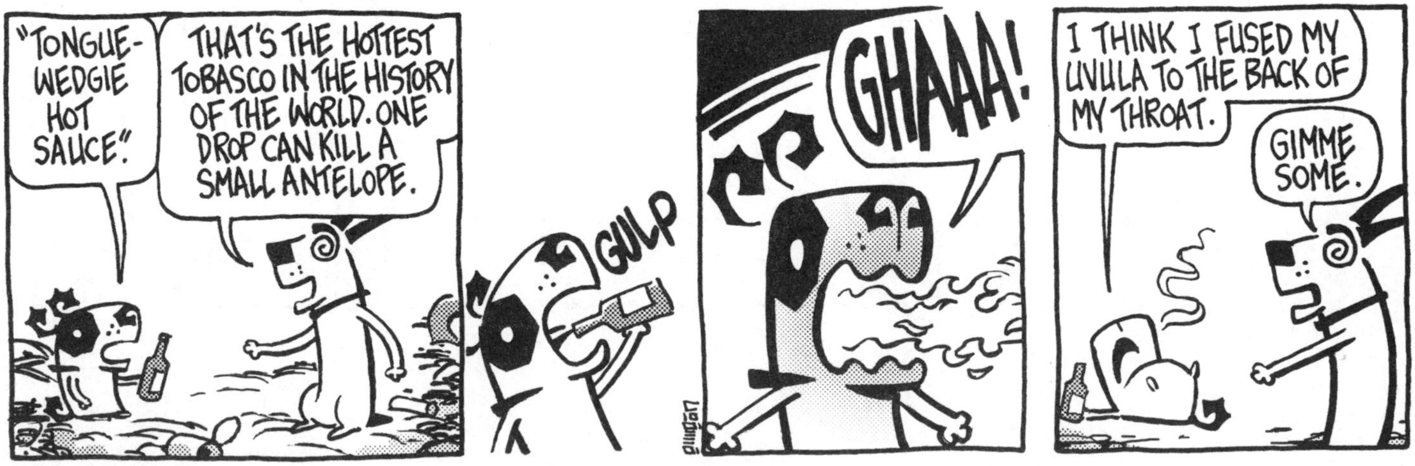
"TONGUE-WEDGIE HOT SAUCE".
THAT'S THE HOTTEST TOBASCO IN THE HISTORY OF THE WORLD. ONE DROP CAN KILL A SMALL ANTELOPE.
GULP
GHAAA!
I THINK I FUSED MY UVULA TO THE BACK OF MY THROAT.
GIMME SOME.

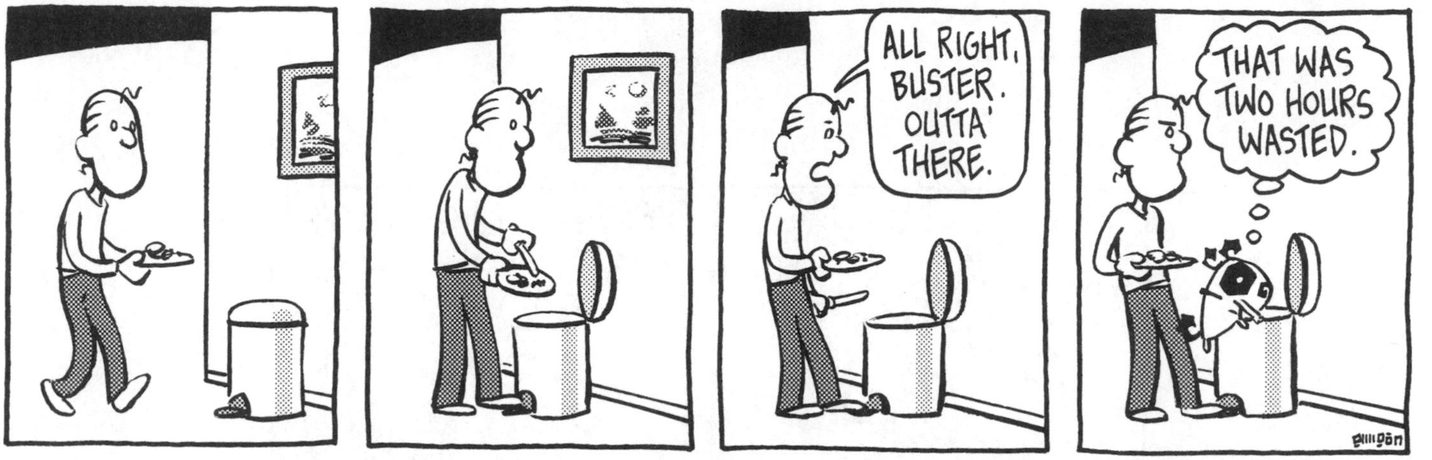
ALL RIGHT, BUSTER. OUTTA' THERE.
THAT WAS TWO HOURS WASTED.

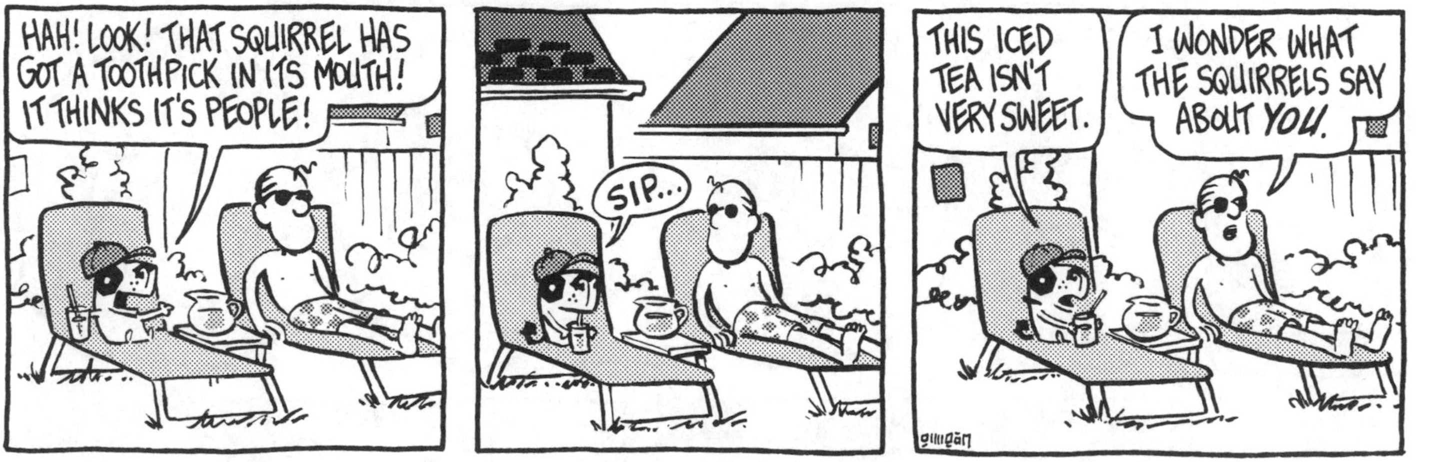
HAH! LOOK! THAT SQUIRREL HAS GOT A TOOTHPICK IN ITS MOUTH! IT THINKS IT'S PEOPLE!
SIP...
THIS ICED TEA ISN'T VERY SWEET.
I WONDER WHAT THE SQUIRRELS SAY ABOUT *YOU*.

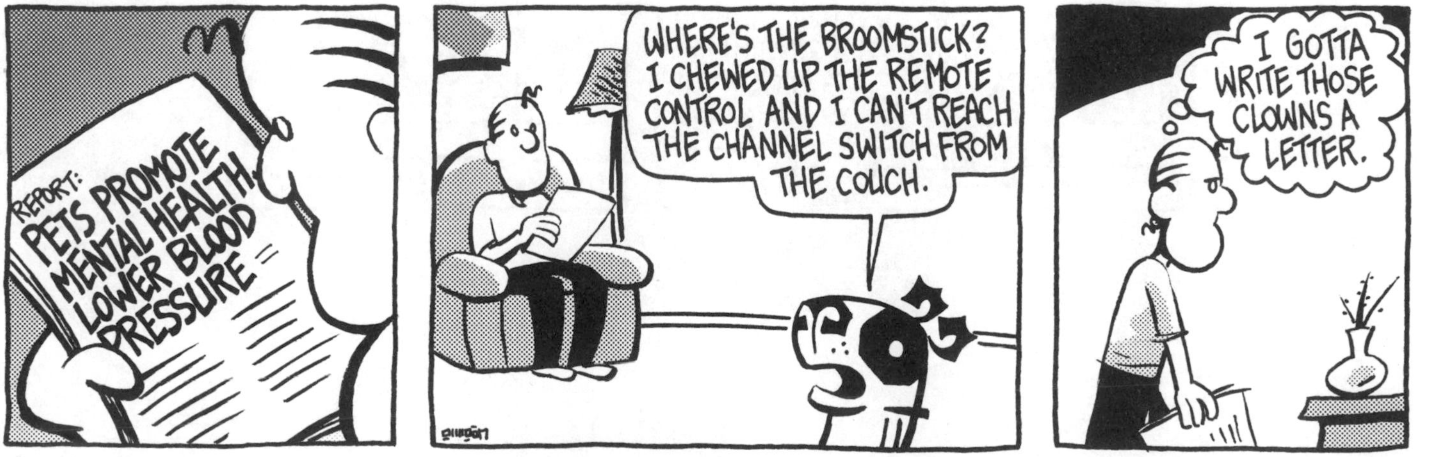
REPORT:
PETS PROMOTE MENTAL HEALTH, LOWER BLOOD PRESSURE
WHERE'S THE BROOMSTICK? I CHEWED UP THE REMOTE CONTROL AND I CAN'T REACH THE CHANNEL SWITCH FROM THE COUCH.
I GOTTA WRITE THOSE CLOWNS A LETTER.

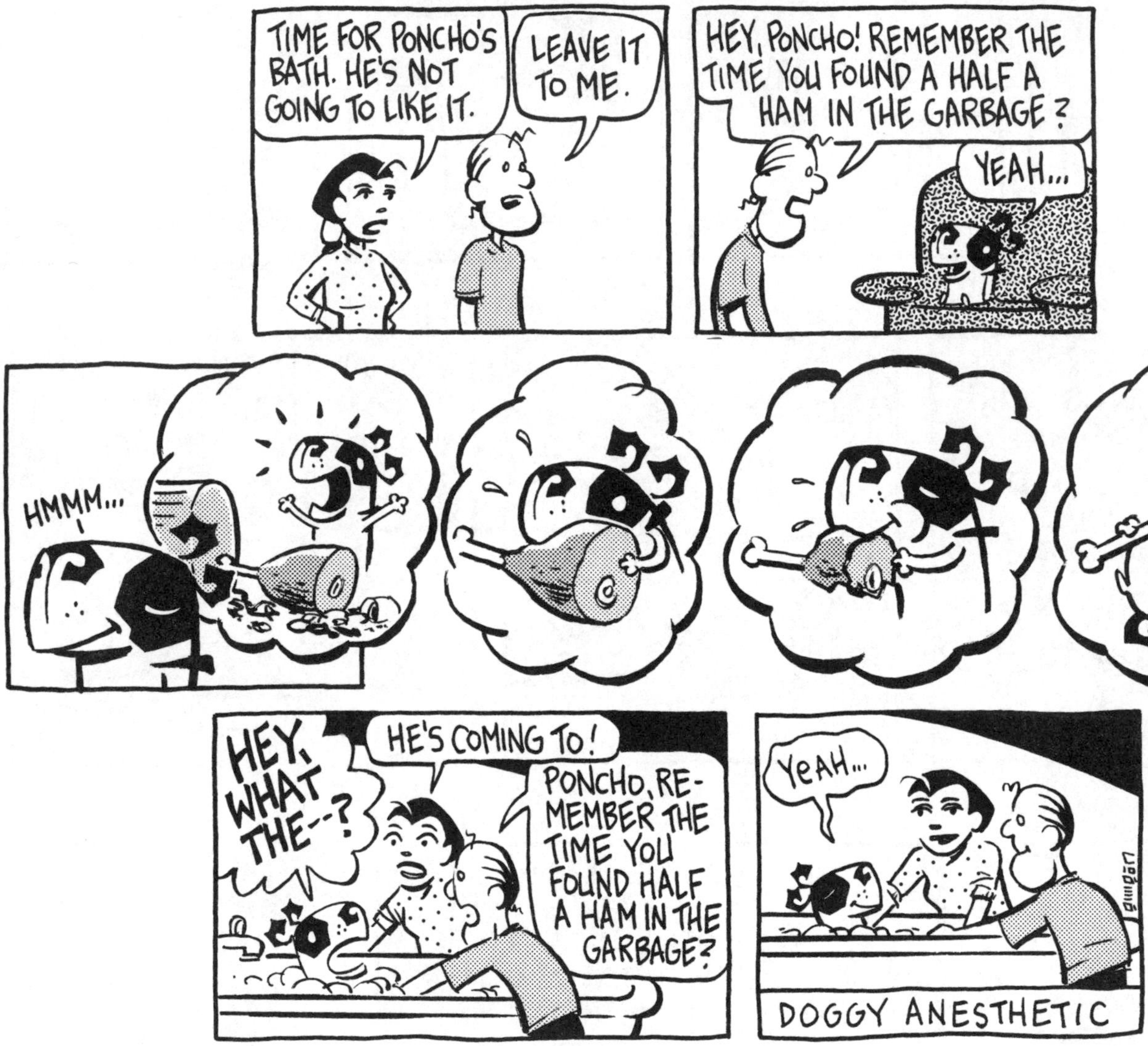
TIME FOR PONCHO'S BATH. HE'S NOT GOING TO LIKE IT.
LEAVE IT TO ME.
HEY, PONCHO! REMEMBER THE TIME YOU FOUND A HALF A HAM IN THE GARBAGE?
YEAH...
HMMM...
HEY, WHAT THE--?
HE'S COMING TO!
PONCHO, REMEMBER THE TIME YOU FOUND HALF A HAM IN THE GARBAGE?
YeAH...
DOGGY ANESTHETIC

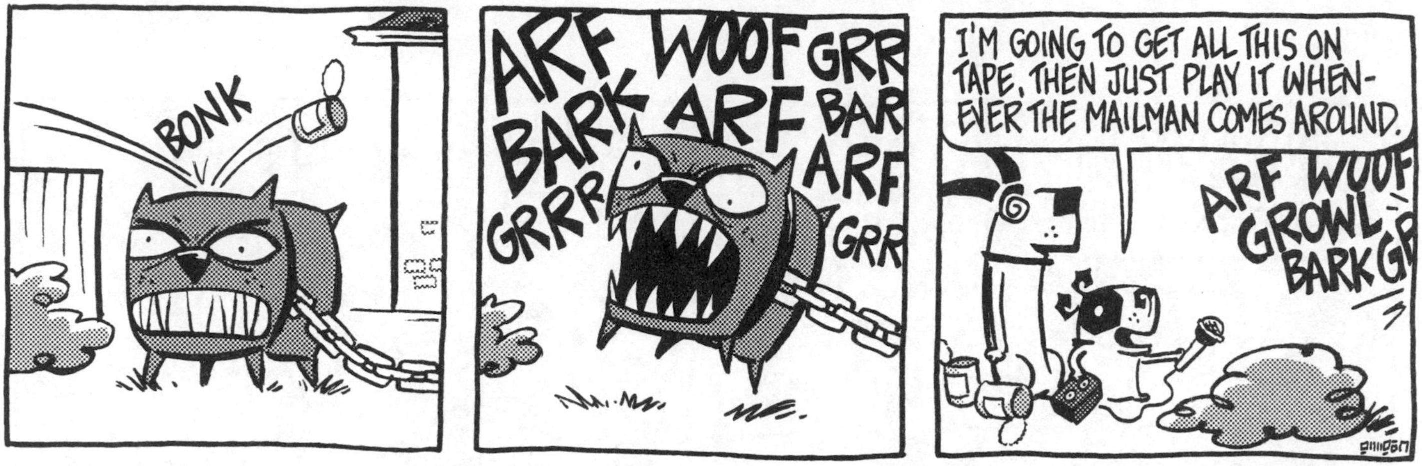
BONK
ARF WOOF GRR
BARK ARF BAR
GRRR ARF
GRR
I'M GOING TO GET ALL THIS ON TAPE, THEN JUST PLAY IT WHENEVER THE MAILMAN COMES AROUND.
ARF WOOF
GROWL
BARK

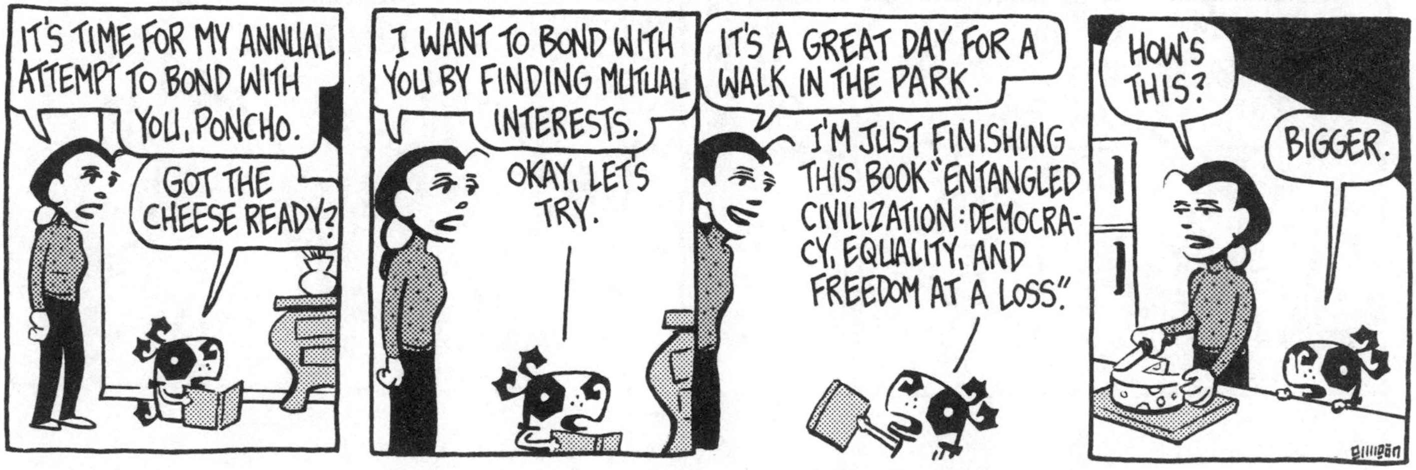
IT'S TIME FOR MY ANNUAL ATTEMPT TO BOND WITH YOU, PONCHO.
GOT THE CHEESE READY?
I WANT TO BOND WITH YOU BY FINDING MUTUAL INTERESTS.
OKAY, LET'S TRY.
IT'S A GREAT DAY FOR A WALK IN THE PARK.
I'M JUST FINISHING THIS BOOK "ENTANGLED CIVILIZATION: DEMOCRACY, EQUALITY, AND FREEDOM AT A LOSS."
HOW'S THIS?
BIGGER.

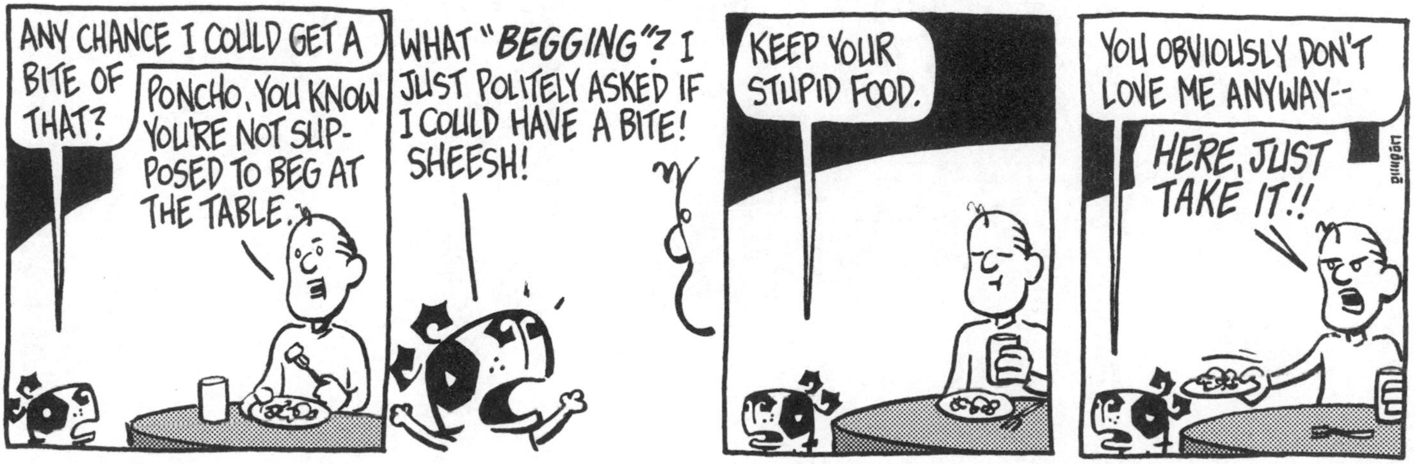
ANY CHANCE I COULD GET A BITE OF THAT?
PONCHO, YOU KNOW YOU'RE NOT SUPPOSED TO BEG AT THE TABLE.
WHAT "BEGGING"? I JUST POLITELY ASKED IF I COULD HAVE A BITE! SHEESH!
KEEP YOUR STUPID FOOD.
YOU OBVIOUSLY DON'T LOVE ME ANYWAY--
HERE, JUST TAKE IT!!

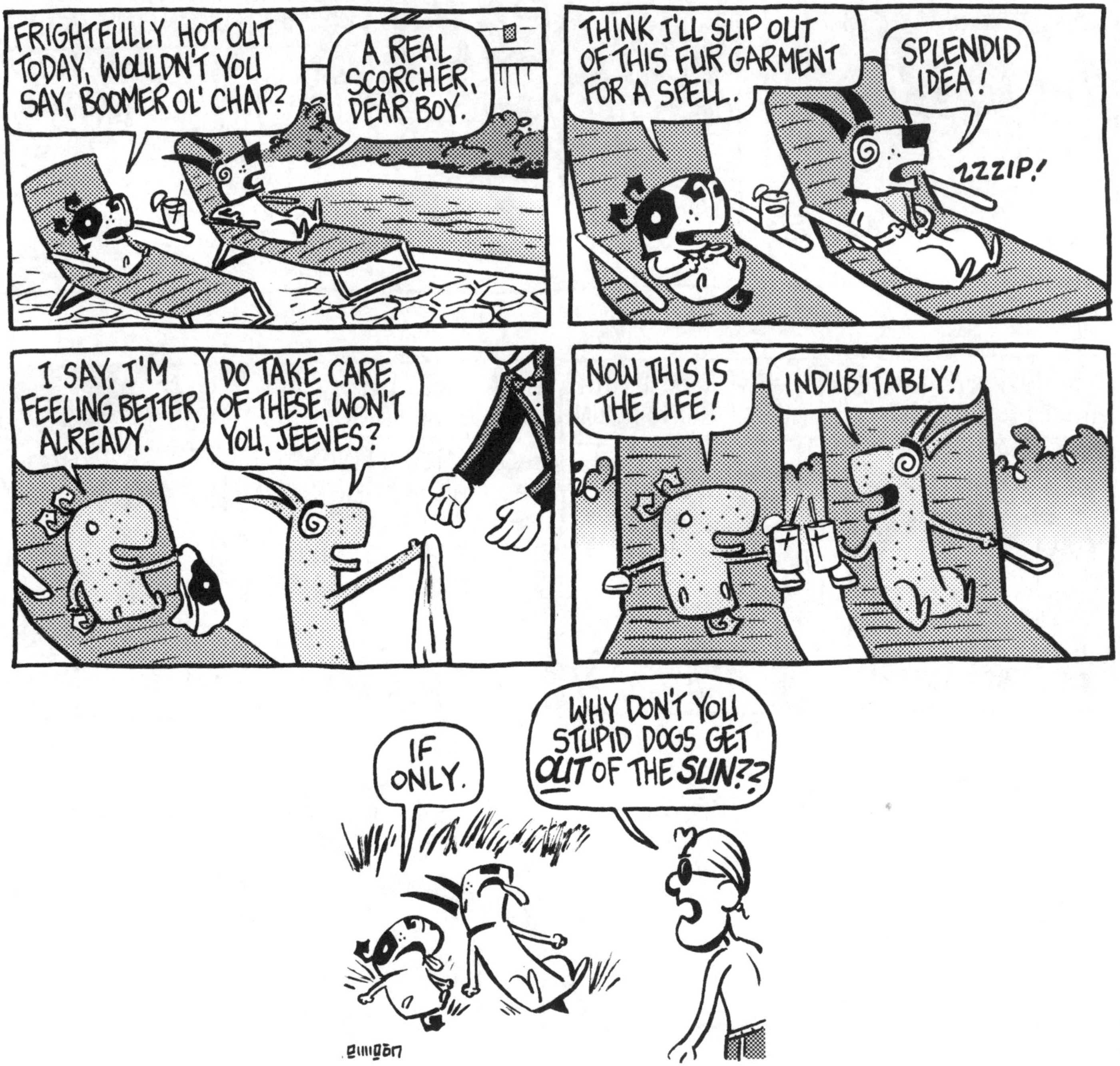
FRIGHTFULLY HOT OUT TODAY, WOULDN'T YOU SAY, BOOMER OL' CHAP?
A REAL SCORCHER, DEAR BOY.
THINK I'LL SLIP OUT OF THIS FUR GARMENT FOR A SPELL.
SPLENDID IDEA!
ZZZIP!
I SAY, I'M FEELING BETTER ALREADY.
DO TAKE CARE OF THESE, WON'T YOU, JEEVES?
NOW THIS IS THE LIFE!
INDUBITABLY!
IF ONLY.
WHY DON'T YOU STUPID DOGS GET OUT OF THE SUN??

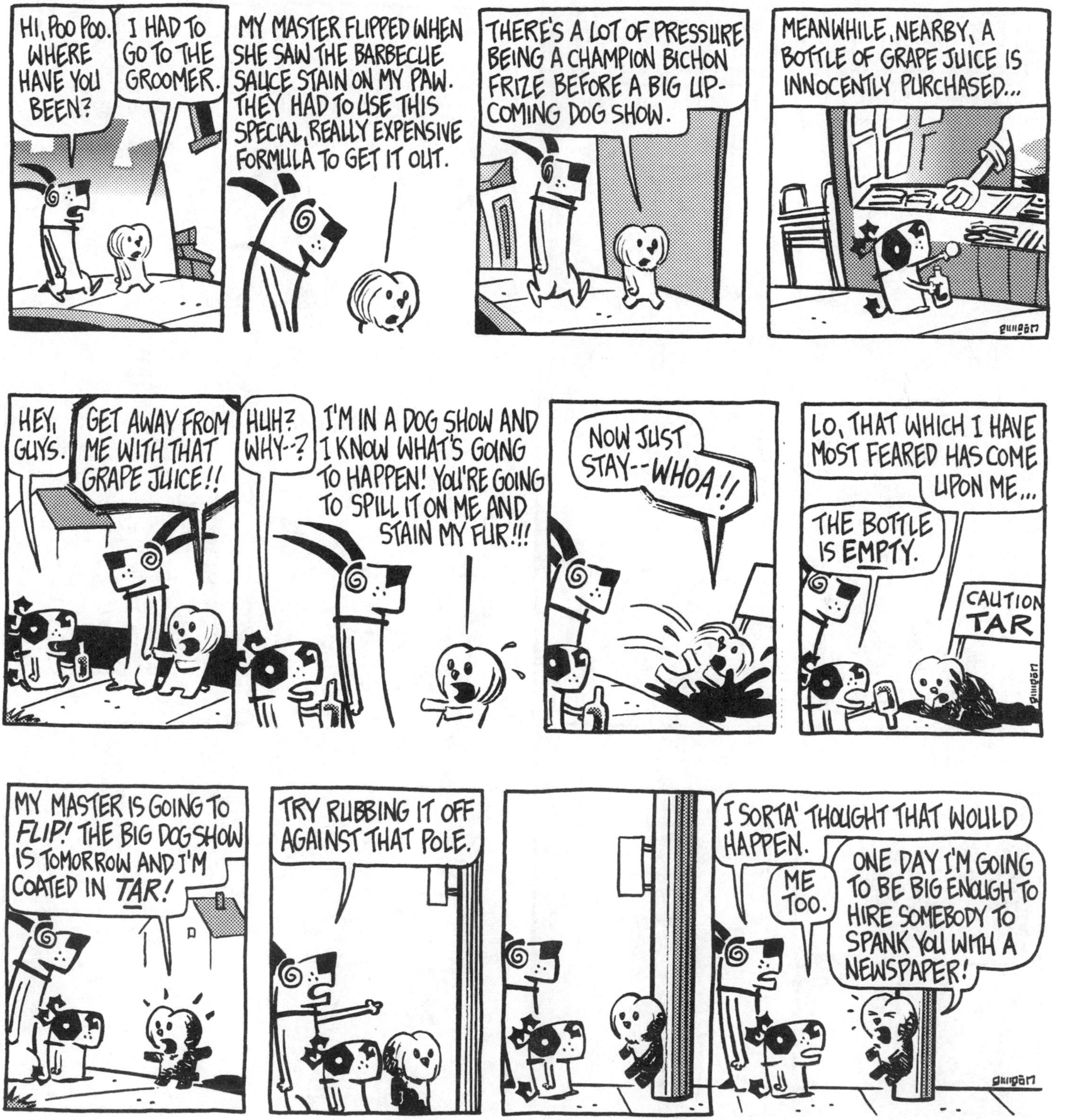
HI, POO POO. WHERE HAVE YOU BEEN?
I HAD TO GO TO THE GROOMER.
MY MASTER FLIPPED WHEN SHE SAW THE BARBECUE SAUCE STAIN ON MY PAW. THEY HAD TO USE THIS SPECIAL, REALLY EXPENSIVE FORMULA TO GET IT OUT.
THERE'S A LOT OF PRESSURE BEING A CHAMPION BICHON FRIZE BEFORE A BIG UPCOMING DOG SHOW.
MEANWHILE, NEARBY, A BOTTLE OF GRAPE JUICE IS INNOCENTLY PURCHASED...
HEY, GUYS.
GET AWAY FROM ME WITH THAT GRAPE JUICE!!
HUH? WHY--?
I'M IN A DOG SHOW AND I KNOW WHAT'S GOING TO HAPPEN! YOU'RE GOING TO SPILL IT ON ME AND STAIN MY FUR!!!
NOW JUST STAY--WHOA!!
LO, THAT WHICH I HAVE MOST FEARED HAS COME UPON ME...
THE BOTTLE IS EMPTY.
CAUTION TAR
MY MASTER IS GOING TO FLIP! THE BIG DOG SHOW IS TOMORROW AND I'M COATED IN TAR!
TRY RUBBING IT OFF AGAINST THAT POLE.
I SORTA' THOUGHT THAT WOULD HAPPEN.
ME TOO.
ONE DAY I'M GOING TO BE BIG ENOUGH TO HIRE SOMEBODY TO SPANK YOU WITH A NEWSPAPER!

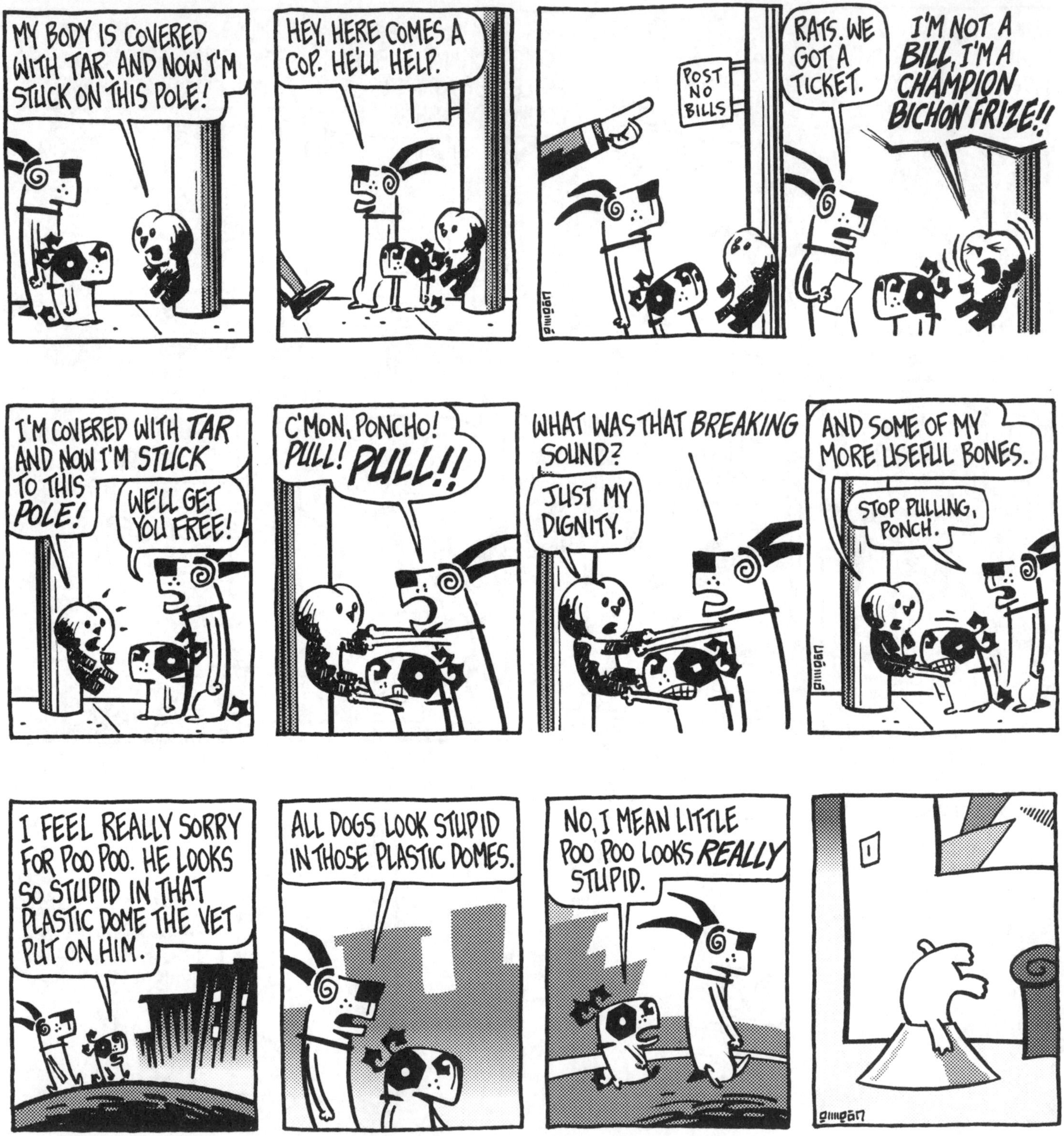
MY BODY IS COVERED WITH TAR, AND NOW I'M STUCK ON THIS POLE!
HEY, HERE COMES A COP. HE'LL HELP.
POST NO BILLS
RATS. WE GOT A TICKET.
I'M NOT A BILL, I'M A CHAMPION BICHON FRIZE!!
I'M COVERED WITH TAR AND NOW I'M STUCK TO THIS POLE!
WE'LL GET YOU FREE!
C'MON, PONCHO! PULL! PULL!!
WHAT WAS THAT BREAKING SOUND?
JUST MY DIGNITY.
AND SOME OF MY MORE USEFUL BONES.
STOP PULLING, PONCH.
I FEEL REALLY SORRY FOR POO POO. HE LOOKS SO STUPID IN THAT PLASTIC DOME THE VET PUT ON HIM.
ALL DOGS LOOK STUPID IN THOSE PLASTIC DOMES.
NO, I MEAN LITTLE POO POO LOOKS REALLY STUPID.

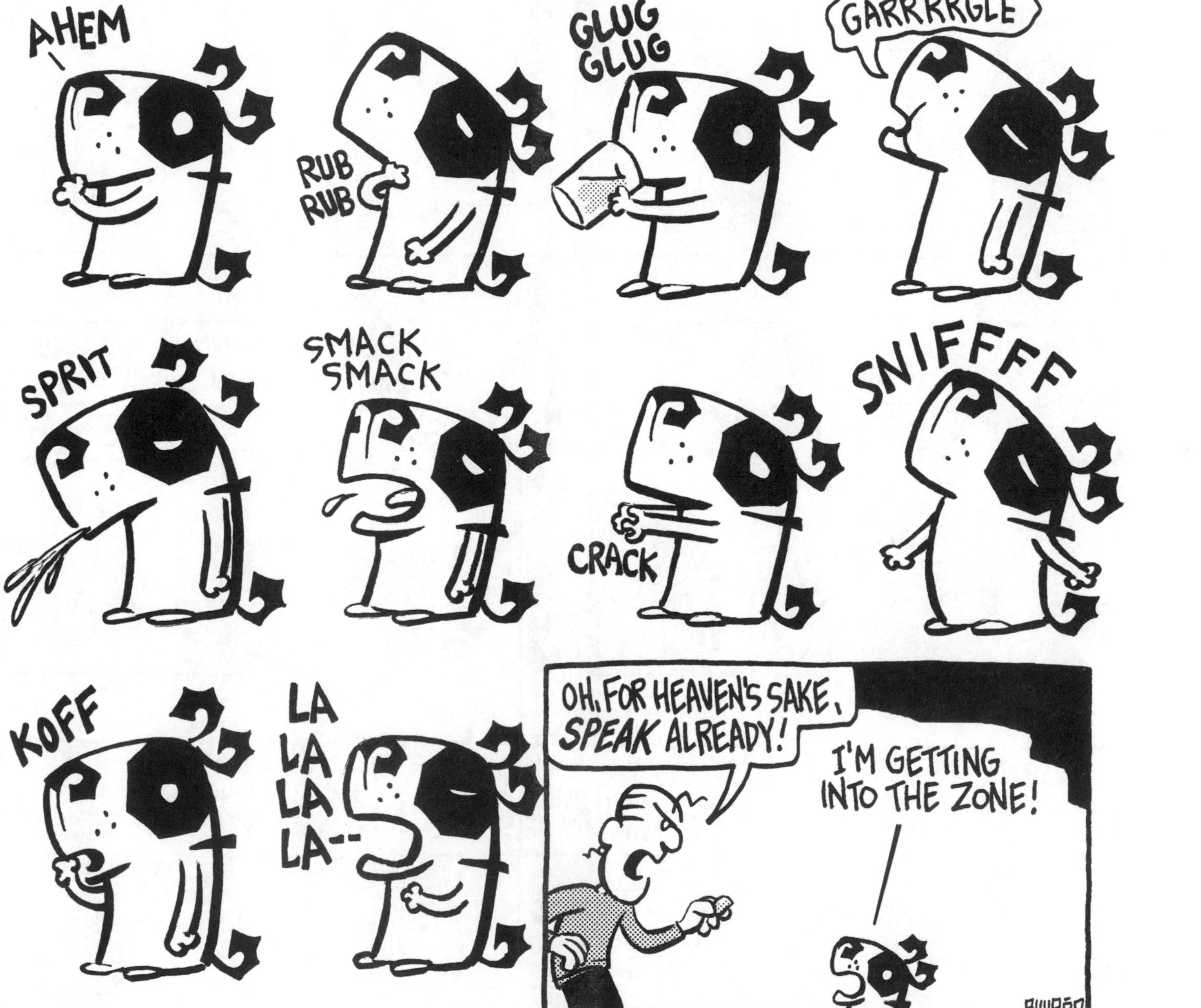
AHEM
RUB RUB
GLUG GLUG
GARRRRGLE
SPRIT
SMACK SMACK
CRACK
SNIFFFFF
KOFF
LA LA LA LA LA--
OH, FOR HEAVEN'S SAKE, SPEAK ALREADY!
I'M GETTING INTO THE ZONE!
QUIGAN

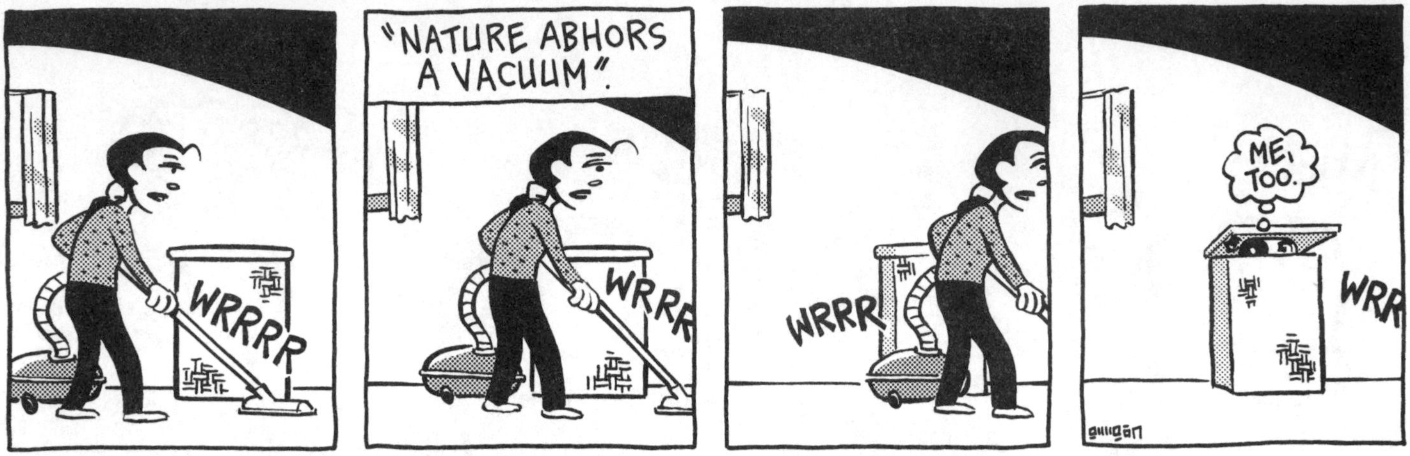
WRRRRR
"NATURE ABHORS A VACUUM".
WRRR
WRRR
ME, TOO.
WRR

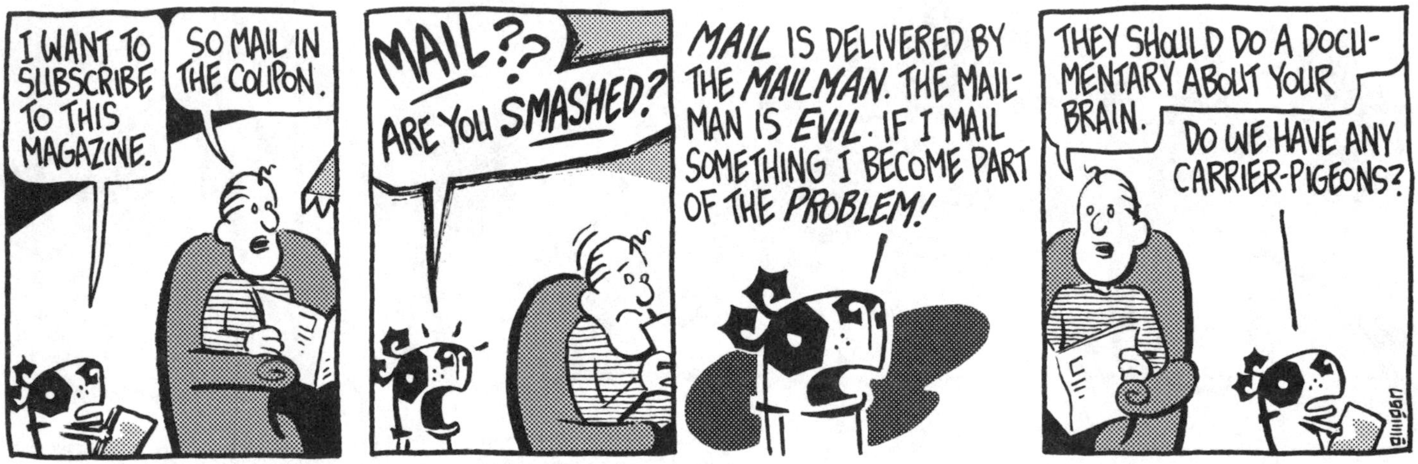
I WANT TO SUBSCRIBE TO THIS MAGAZINE.
SO MAIL IN THE COUPON.
MAIL??
ARE YOU SMASHED?
MAIL IS DELIVERED BY THE MAILMAN. THE MAILMAN IS EVIL. IF I MAIL SOMETHING I BECOME PART OF THE PROBLEM!
THEY SHOULD DO A DOCUMENTARY ABOUT YOUR BRAIN.
DO WE HAVE ANY CARRIER-PIGEONS?

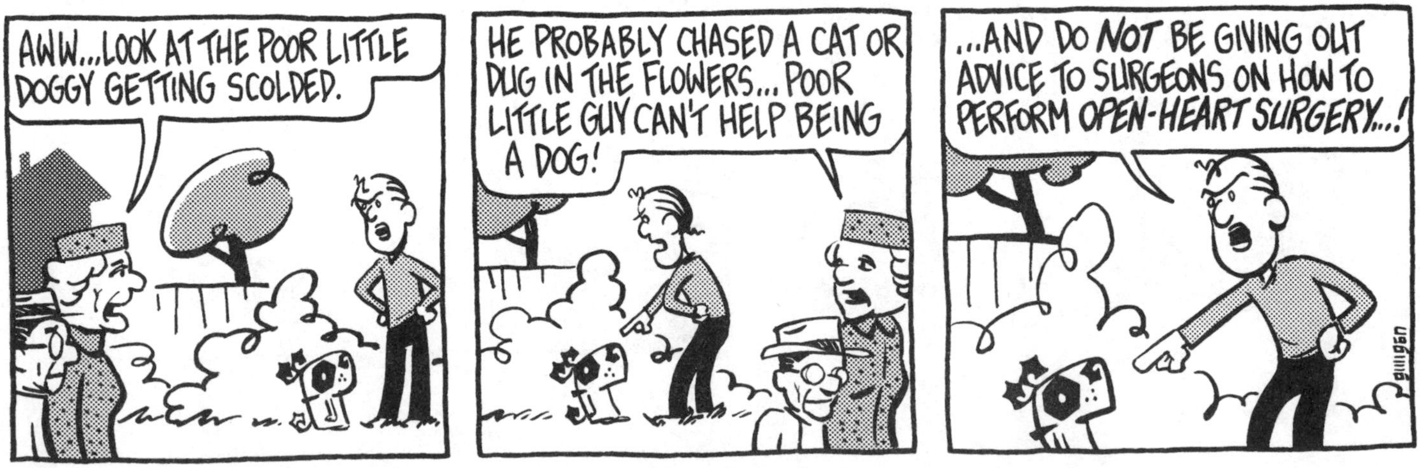
AWW...LOOK AT THE POOR LITTLE DOGGY GETTING SCOLDED.
HE PROBABLY CHASED A CAT OR DUG IN THE FLOWERS... POOR LITTLE GUY CAN'T HELP BEING A DOG!
...AND DO NOT BE GIVING OUT ADVICE TO SURGEONS ON HOW TO PERFORM OPEN-HEART SURGERY...!

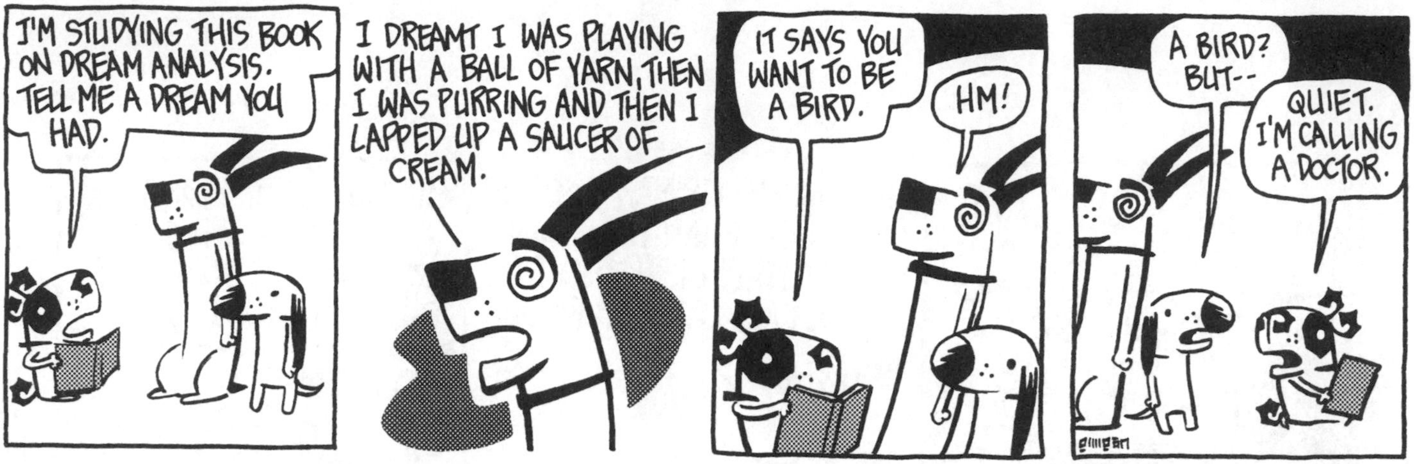
I'M STUDYING THIS BOOK ON DREAM ANALYSIS. TELL ME A DREAM YOU HAD.
I DREAMT I WAS PLAYING WITH A BALL OF YARN, THEN I WAS PURRING AND THEN I LAPPED UP A SAUCER OF CREAM.
IT SAYS YOU WANT TO BE A BIRD.
HM!
A BIRD? BUT--
QUIET. I'M CALLING A DOCTOR.

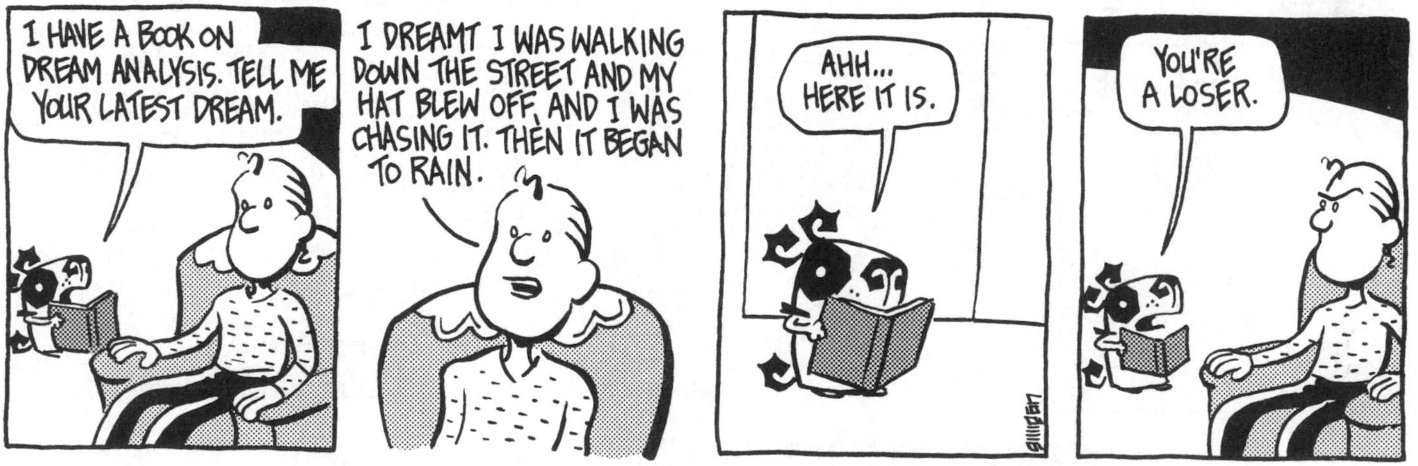
I HAVE A BOOK ON DREAM ANALYSIS. TELL ME YOUR LATEST DREAM.
I DREAMT I WAS WALKING DOWN THE STREET AND MY HAT BLEW OFF, AND I WAS CHASING IT. THEN IT BEGAN TO RAIN.
AHH... HERE IT IS.
YOU'RE A LOSER.

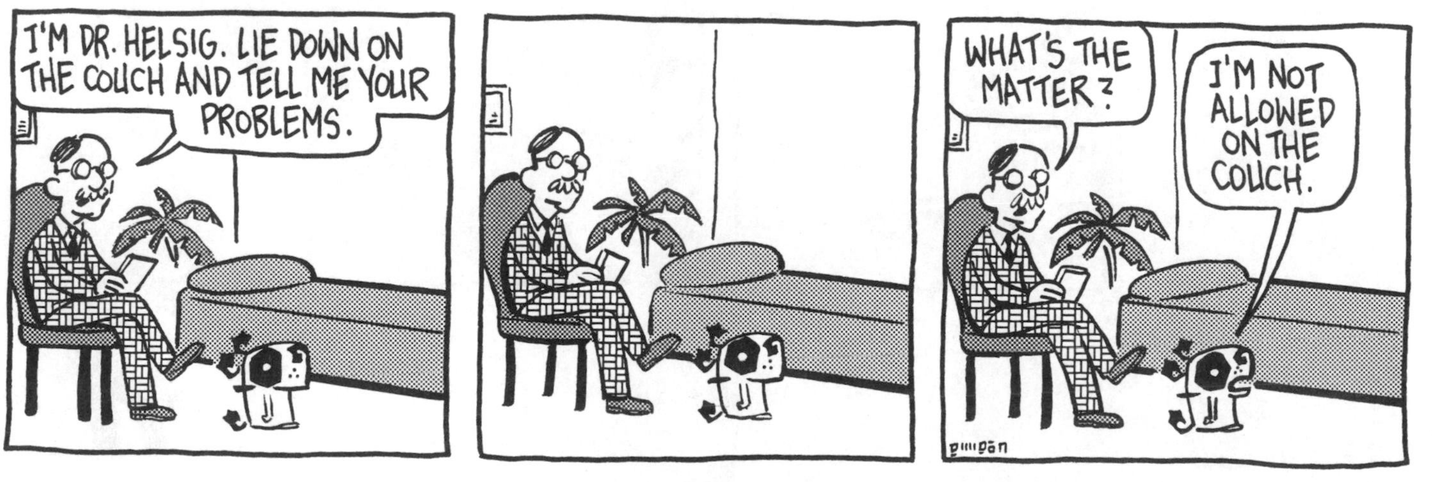
I'M DR. HELSIG. LIE DOWN ON THE COUCH AND TELL ME YOUR PROBLEMS.
WHAT'S THE MATTER?
I'M NOT ALLOWED ON THE COUCH.

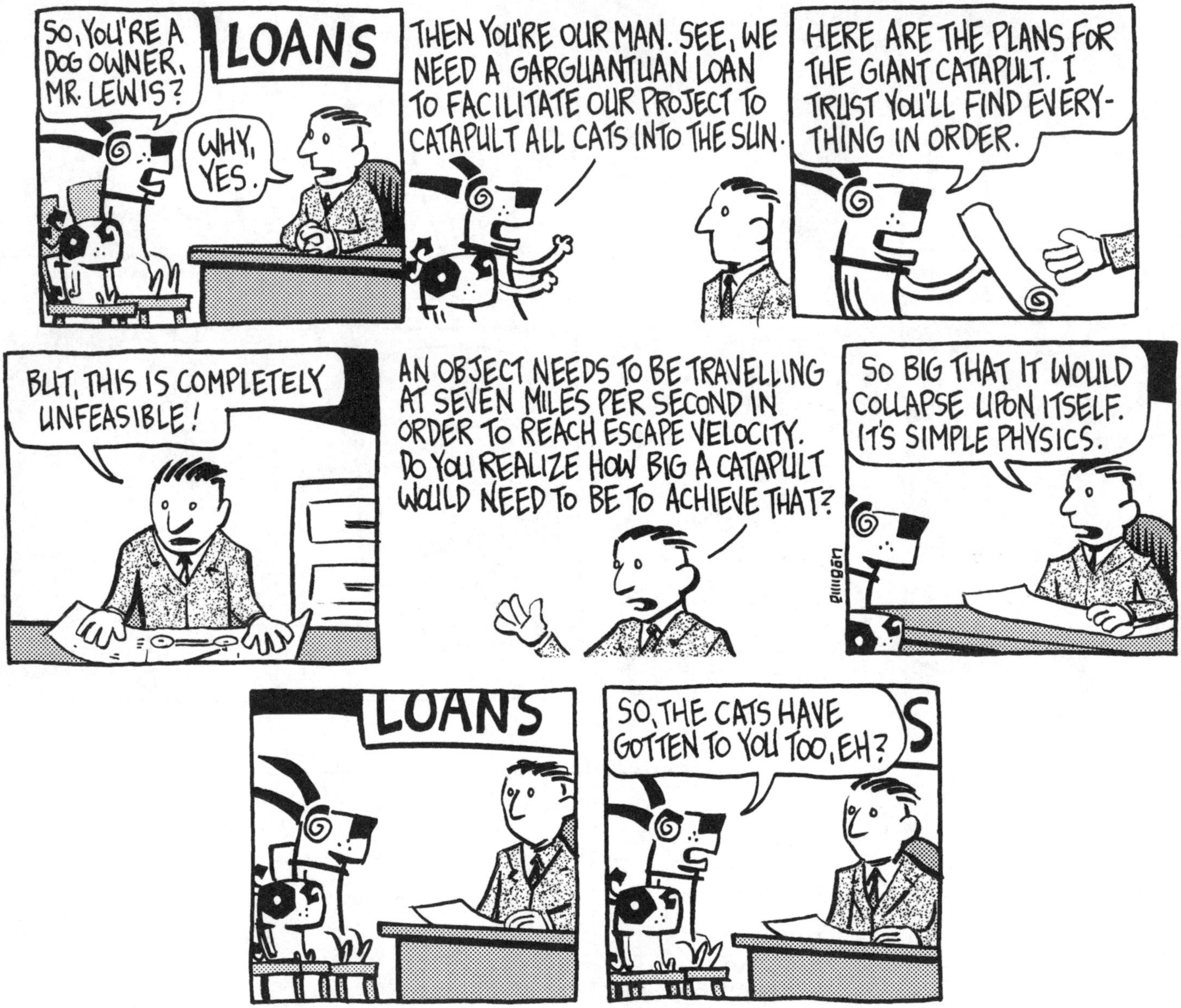
SO, YOU'RE A DOG OWNER, MR. LEWIS?
LOANS
WHY, YES.
THEN YOU'RE OUR MAN. SEE, WE NEED A GARGUANTUAN LOAN TO FACILITATE OUR PROJECT TO CATAPULT ALL CATS INTO THE SUN.
HERE ARE THE PLANS FOR THE GIANT CATAPULT. I TRUST YOU'LL FIND EVERYTHING IN ORDER.
BUT, THIS IS COMPLETELY UNFEASIBLE!
AN OBJECT NEEDS TO BE TRAVELLING AT SEVEN MILES PER SECOND IN ORDER TO REACH ESCAPE VELOCITY. DO YOU REALIZE HOW BIG A CATAPULT WOULD NEED TO BE TO ACHIEVE THAT?
SO BIG THAT IT WOULD COLLAPSE UPON ITSELF. IT'S SIMPLE PHYSICS.
LOANS
SO, THE CATS HAVE GOTTEN TO YOU TOO, EH?

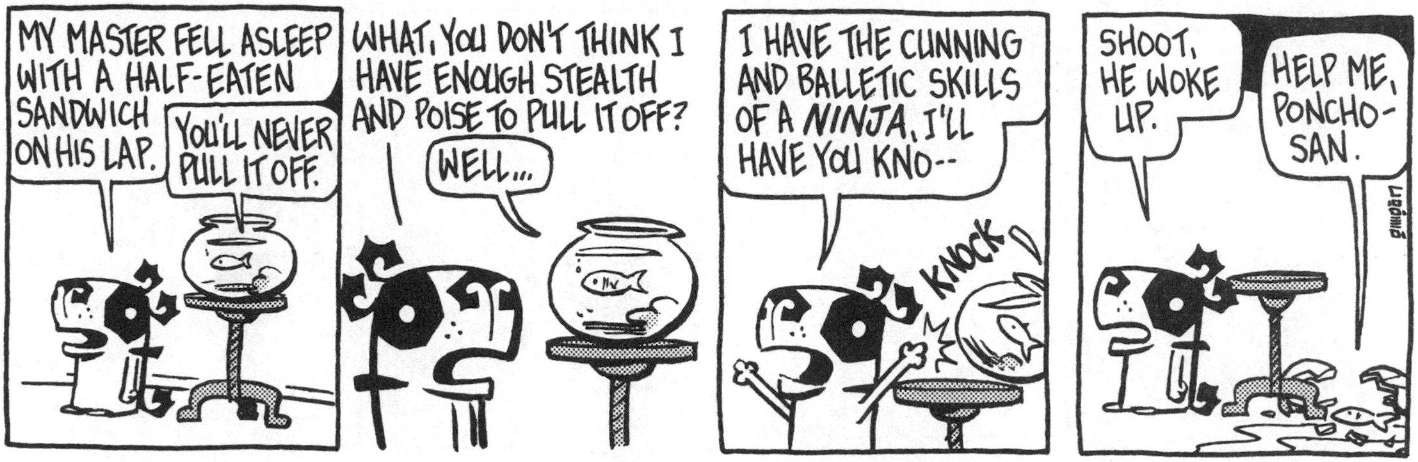
MY MASTER FELL ASLEEP WITH A HALF-EATEN SANDWICH ON HIS LAP.
YOU'LL NEVER PULL IT OFF.
WHAT, YOU DON'T THINK I HAVE ENOUGH STEALTH AND POISE TO PULL IT OFF?
WELL...
I HAVE THE CUNNING AND BALLETIC SKILLS OF A *NINJA*, I'LL HAVE YOU KNO--
KNOCK
SHOOT, HE WOKE UP.
HELP ME, PONCHO-SAN.

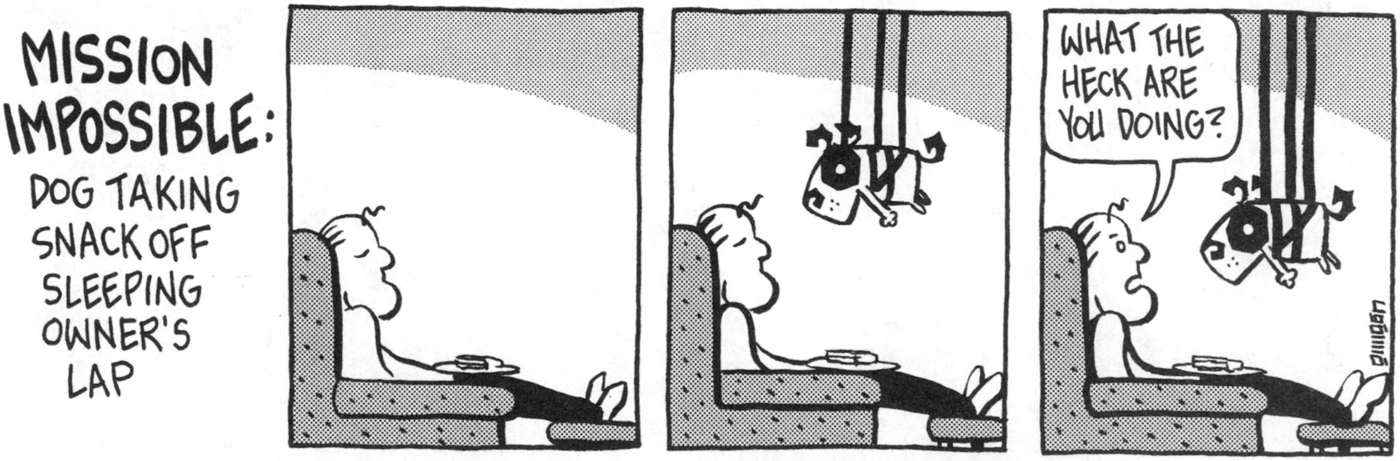
MISSION IMPOSSIBLE:
DOG TAKING SNACK OFF SLEEPING OWNER'S LAP
WHAT THE HECK ARE YOU DOING?

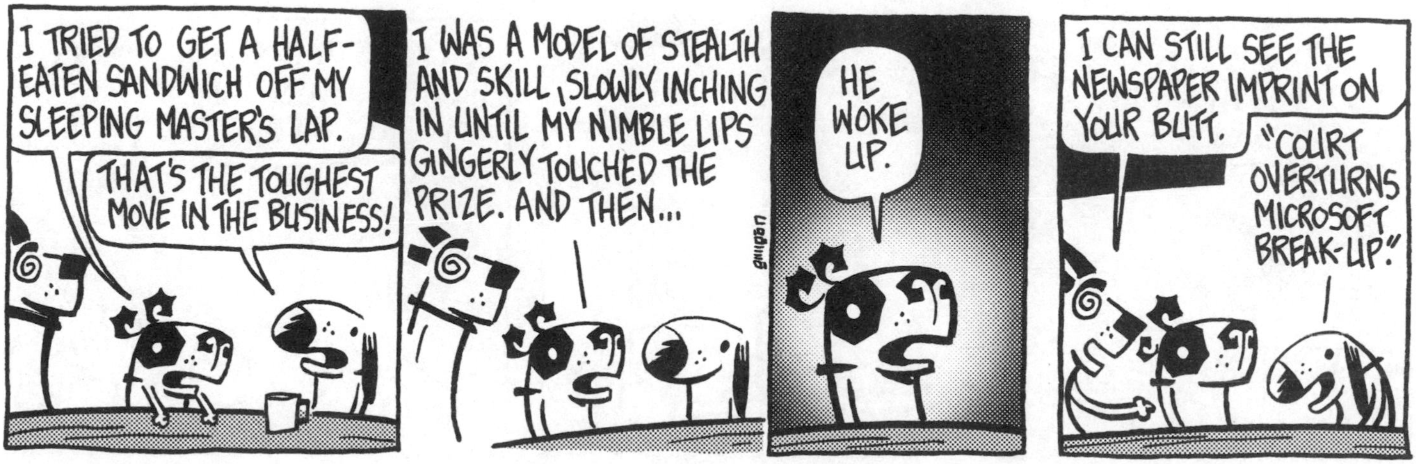
I TRIED TO GET A HALF-EATEN SANDWICH OFF MY SLEEPING MASTER'S LAP.
THAT'S THE TOUGHEST MOVE IN THE BUSINESS!
I WAS A MODEL OF STEALTH AND SKILL, SLOWLY INCHING IN UNTIL MY NIMBLE LIPS GINGERLY TOUCHED THE PRIZE. AND THEN...
HE WOKE UP.
I CAN STILL SEE THE NEWSPAPER IMPRINT ON YOUR BUTT.
"COURT OVERTURNS MICROSOFT BREAK-UP!"

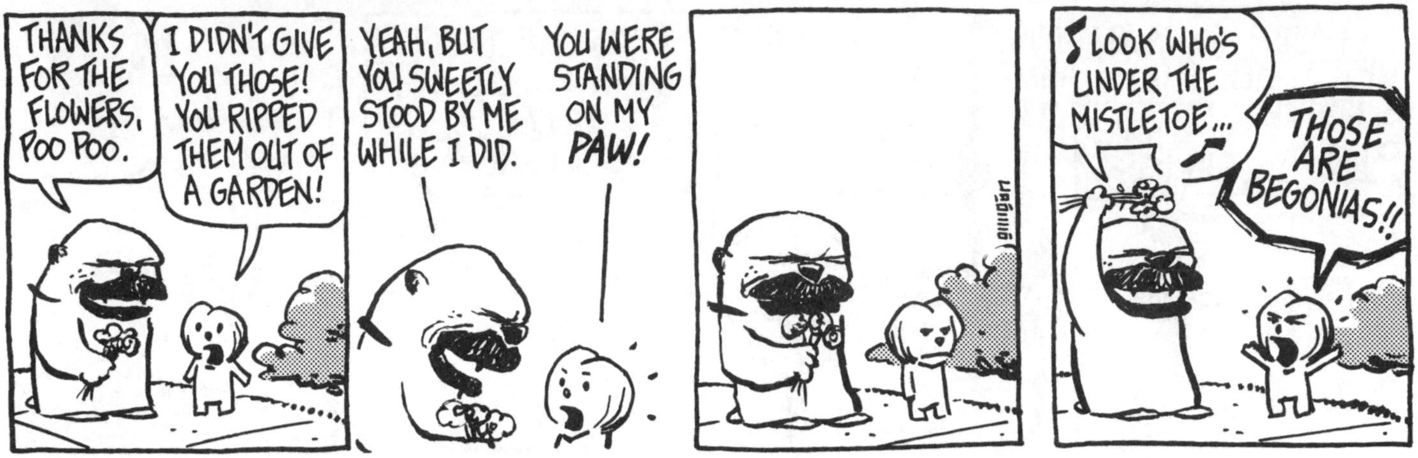
THANKS FOR THE FLOWERS, POO POO.
I DIDN'T GIVE YOU THOSE! YOU RIPPED THEM OUT OF A GARDEN!
YEAH, BUT YOU SWEETLY STOOD BY ME WHILE I DID.
YOU WERE STANDING ON MY PAW!
LOOK WHO'S UNDER THE MISTLETOE...
THOSE ARE BEGONIAS!!

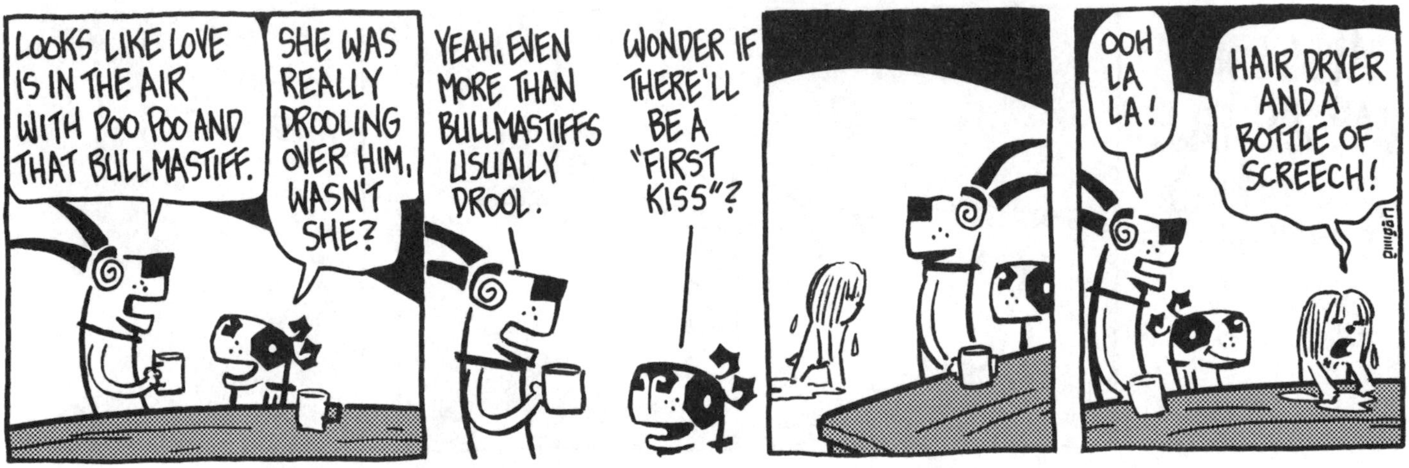
LOOKS LIKE LOVE IS IN THE AIR WITH POO POO AND THAT BULLMASTIFF.
SHE WAS REALLY DROOLING OVER HIM, WASN'T SHE?
YEAH, EVEN MORE THAN BULLMASTIFFS USUALLY DROOL.
WONDER IF THERE'LL BE A "FIRST KISS"?
OOH LA LA!
HAIR DRYER AND A BOTTLE OF SCREECH!

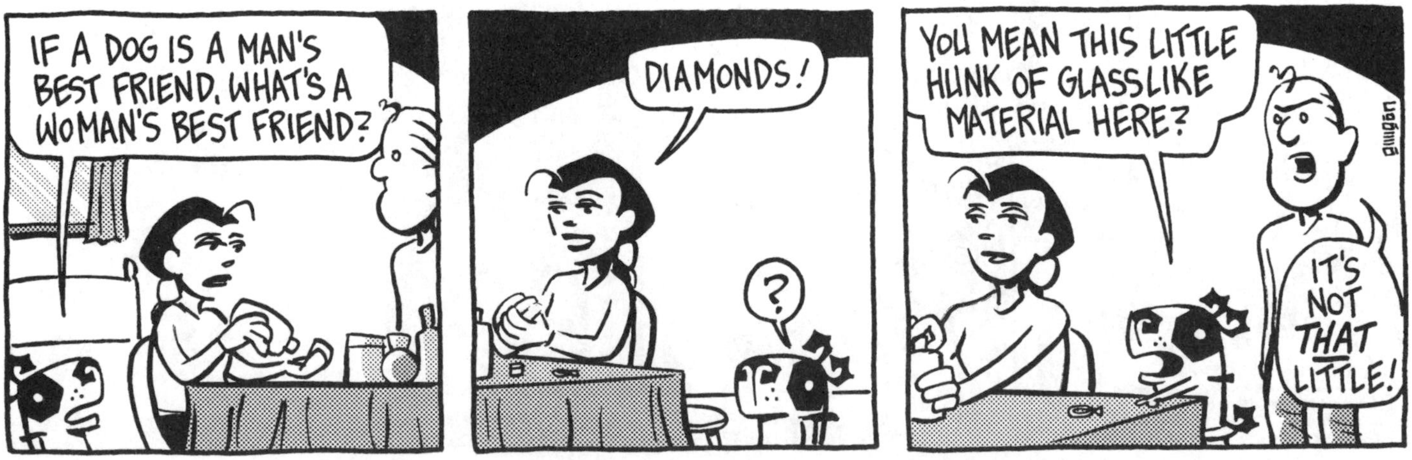
IF A DOG IS A MAN'S BEST FRIEND, WHAT'S A WOMAN'S BEST FRIEND?
DIAMONDS!
?
YOU MEAN THIS LITTLE HUNK OF GLASSLIKE MATERIAL HERE?
IT'S NOT THAT LITTLE!

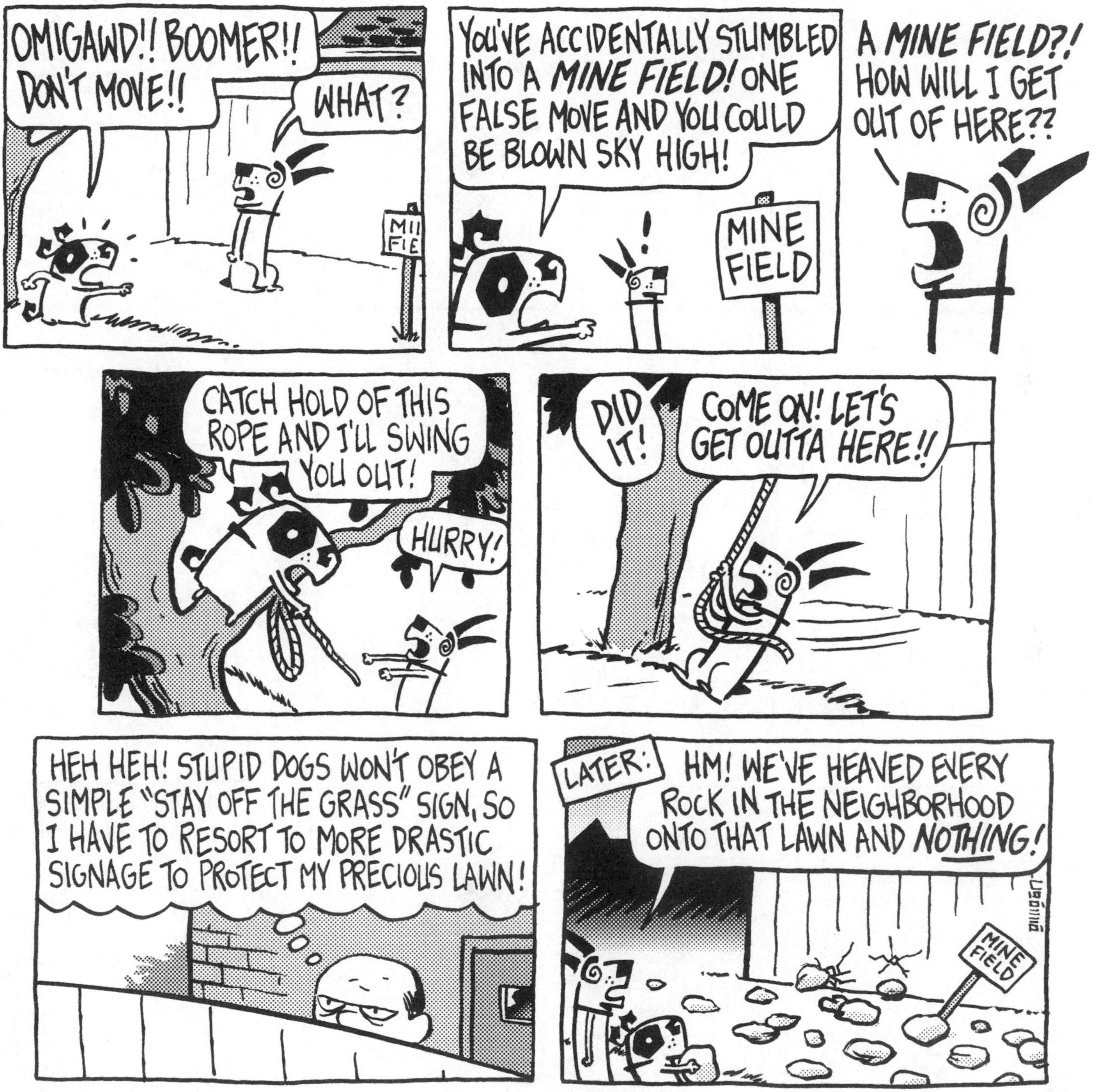
OMIGAWD!! BOOMER!! DON'T MOVE!!
WHAT?
YOU'VE ACCIDENTALLY STUMBLED INTO A *MINE FIELD!* ONE FALSE MOVE AND YOU COULD BE BLOWN SKY HIGH!
!
MINE FIELD
A *MINE FIELD?!* HOW WILL I GET OUT OF HERE??
CATCH HOLD OF THIS ROPE AND I'LL SWING YOU OUT!
HURRY!
DID IT!
COME ON! LET'S GET OUTTA HERE!!
HEH HEH! STUPID DOGS WON'T OBEY A SIMPLE "STAY OFF THE GRASS" SIGN, SO I HAVE TO RESORT TO MORE DRASTIC SIGNAGE TO PROTECT MY PRECIOUS LAWN!
LATER:
HM! WE'VE HEAVED EVERY ROCK IN THE NEIGHBORHOOD ONTO THAT LAWN AND NOTHING!
MINE FIELD

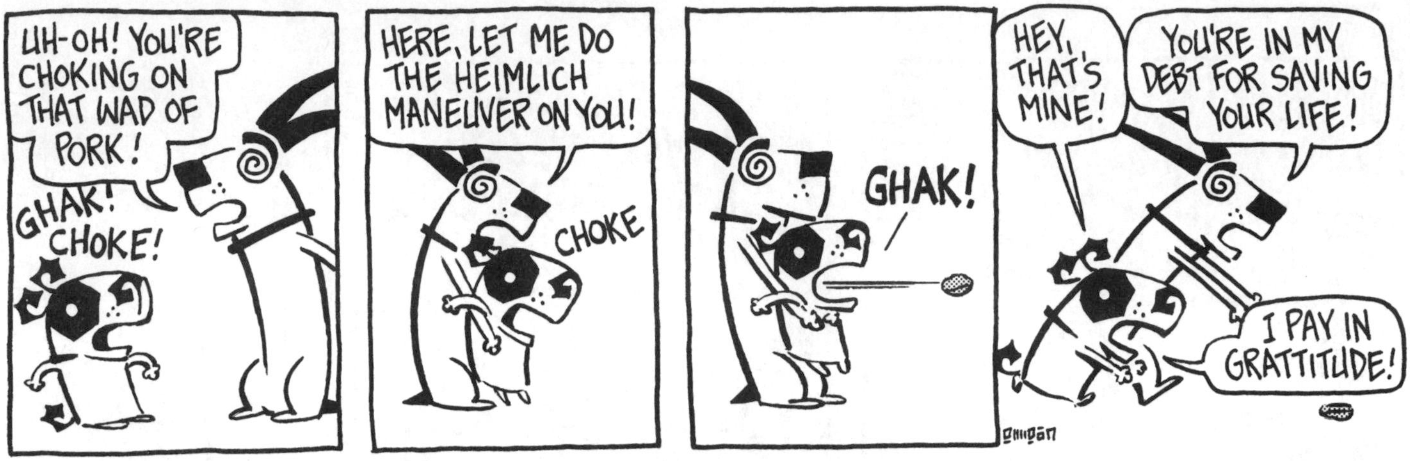
UH-OH! YOU'RE CHOKING ON THAT WAD OF PORK!
GHAK! CHOKE!
HERE, LET ME DO THE HEIMLICH MANEUVER ON YOU!
CHOKE
GHAK!
HEY, THAT'S MINE!
YOU'RE IN MY DEBT FOR SAVING YOUR LIFE!
I PAY IN GRATTITUDE!

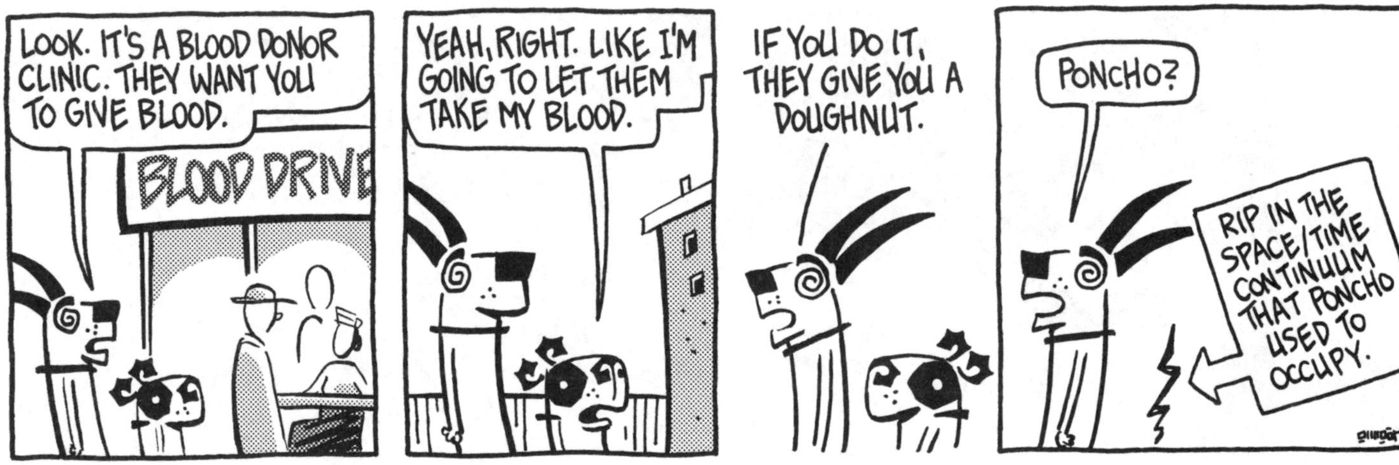
LOOK. IT'S A BLOOD DONOR CLINIC. THEY WANT YOU TO GIVE BLOOD.
BLOOD DRIVE
YEAH, RIGHT. LIKE I'M GOING TO LET THEM TAKE MY BLOOD.
IF YOU DO IT, THEY GIVE YOU A DOUGHNUT.
PONCHO?
RIP IN THE SPACE/TIME CONTINUUM THAT PONCHO USED TO OCCUPY.

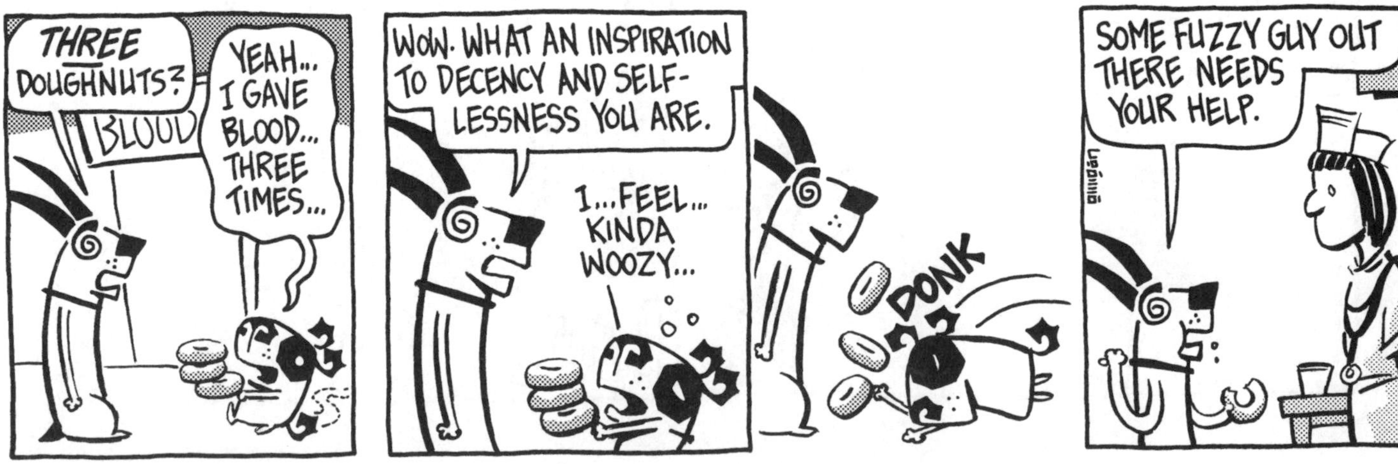
THREE DOUGHNUTS?
YEAH... I GAVE BLOOD... THREE TIMES...
BLOOD
WOW. WHAT AN INSPIRATION TO DECENCY AND SELF-LESSNESS YOU ARE.
I...FEEL... KINDA WOOZY...
DONK
SOME FUZZY GUY OUT THERE NEEDS YOUR HELP.

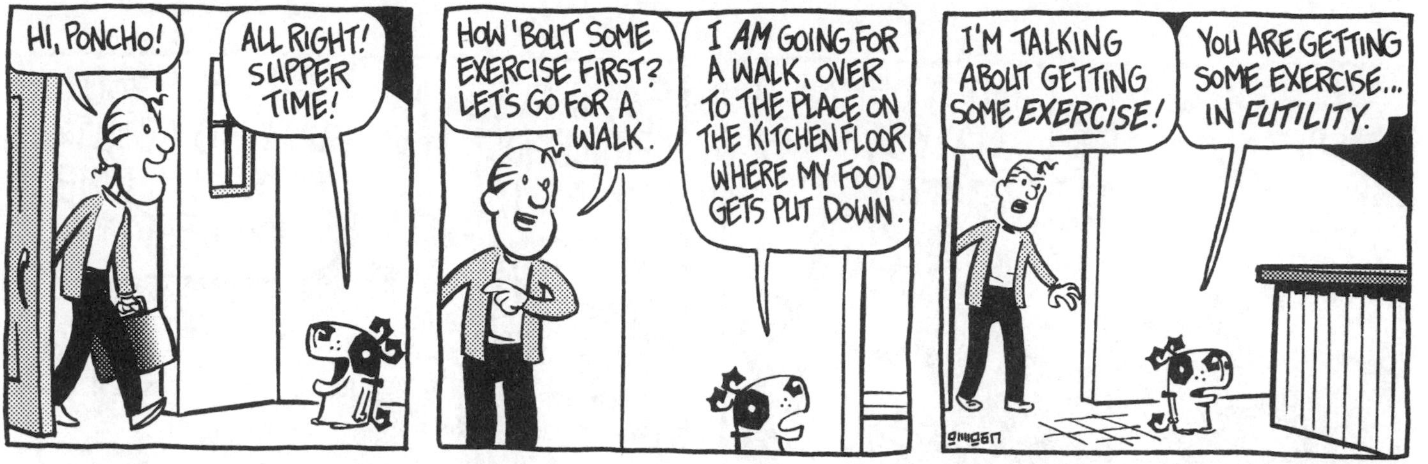
HI, PONCHO!
ALL RIGHT! SUPPER TIME!
HOW 'BOUT SOME EXERCISE FIRST? LET'S GO FOR A WALK.
I *AM* GOING FOR A WALK, OVER TO THE PLACE ON THE KITCHEN FLOOR WHERE MY FOOD GETS PUT DOWN.
I'M TALKING ABOUT GETTING SOME *EXERCISE!*
YOU ARE GETTING SOME EXERCISE... IN *FUTILITY*.

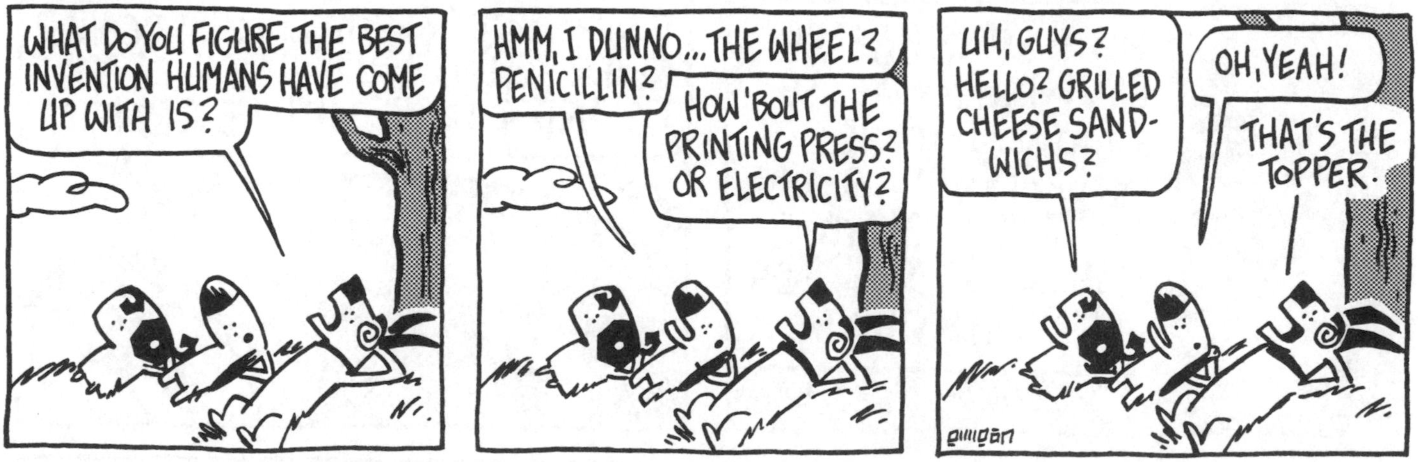
WHAT DO YOU FIGURE THE BEST INVENTION HUMANS HAVE COME UP WITH IS?
HMM, I DUNNO... THE WHEEL? PENICILLIN?
HOW 'BOUT THE PRINTING PRESS? OR ELECTRICITY?
UH, GUYS? HELLO? GRILLED CHEESE SAND-WICHS?
OH, YEAH!
THAT'S THE TOPPER.

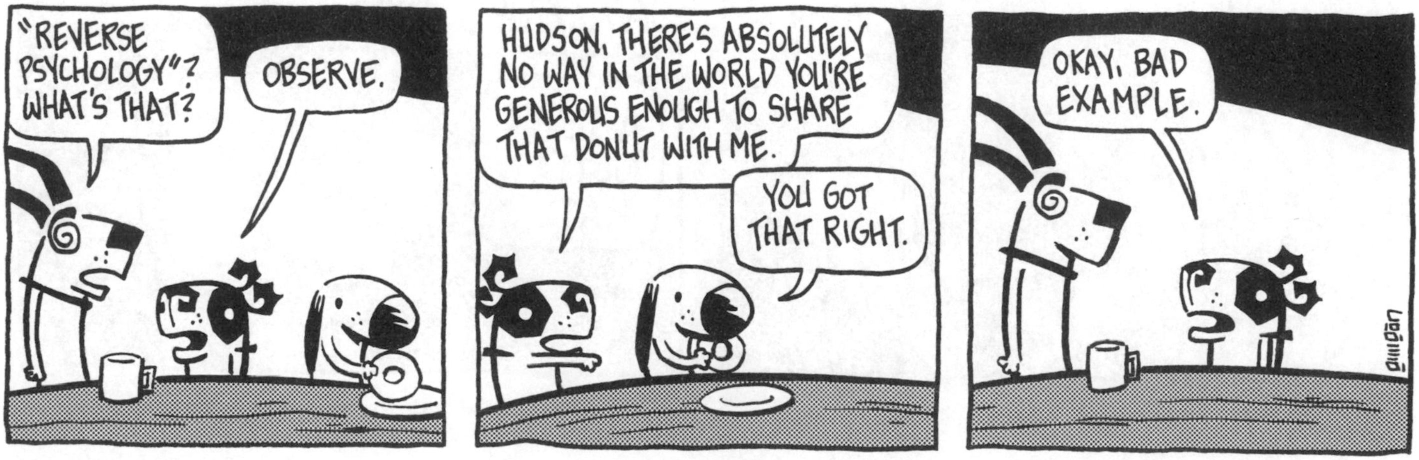
"REVERSE PSYCHOLOGY"? WHAT'S THAT?
OBSERVE.
HUDSON, THERE'S ABSOLUTELY NO WAY IN THE WORLD YOU'RE GENEROUS ENOUGH TO SHARE THAT DONUT WITH ME.
YOU GOT THAT RIGHT.
OKAY, BAD EXAMPLE.

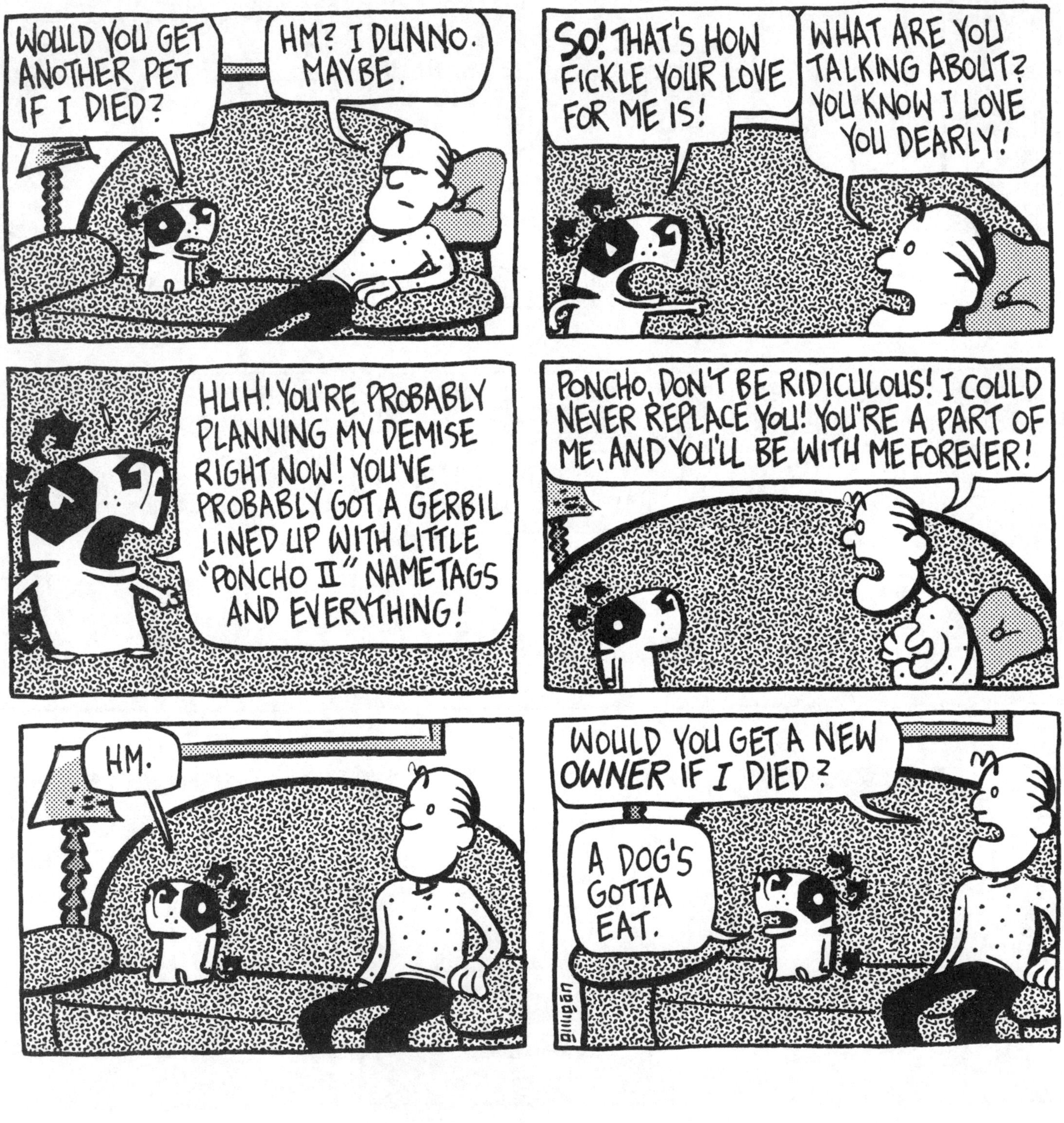
WOULD YOU GET ANOTHER PET IF I DIED?
HM? I DUNNO. MAYBE.
SO! THAT'S HOW FICKLE YOUR LOVE FOR ME IS!
WHAT ARE YOU TALKING ABOUT? YOU KNOW I LOVE YOU DEARLY!
HUH! YOU'RE PROBABLY PLANNING MY DEMISE RIGHT NOW! YOU'VE PROBABLY GOT A GERBIL LINED UP WITH LITTLE "PONCHO II" NAMETAGS AND EVERYTHING!
PONCHO, DON'T BE RIDICULOUS! I COULD NEVER REPLACE YOU! YOU'RE A PART OF ME, AND YOU'LL BE WITH ME FOREVER!
HM.
WOULD YOU GET A NEW OWNER IF I DIED?
A DOG'S GOTTA EAT.
Gilligan

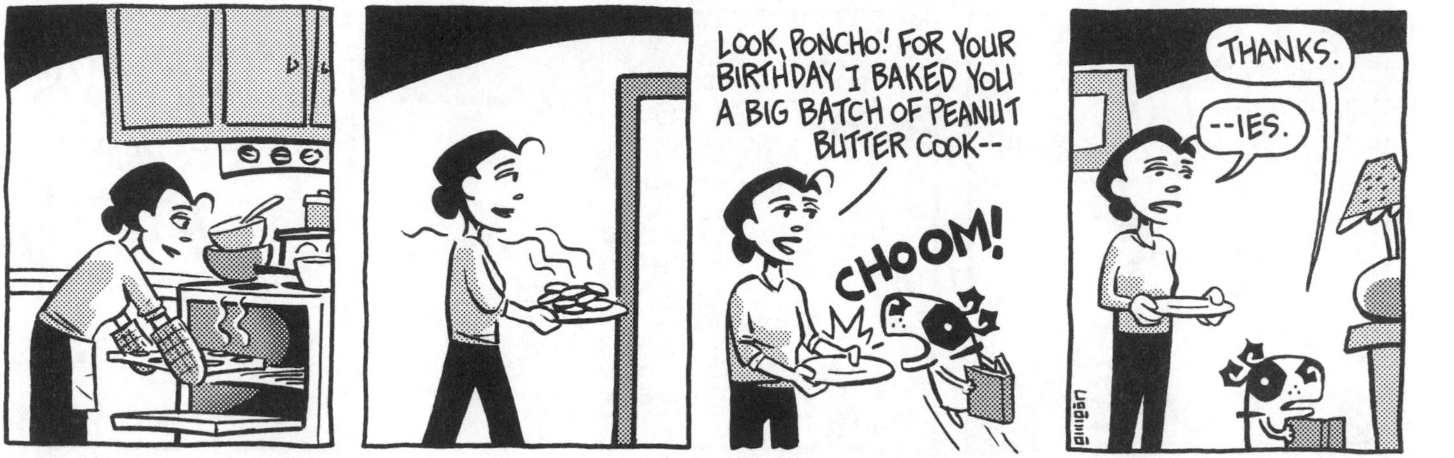
LOOK, PONCHO! FOR YOUR BIRTHDAY I BAKED YOU A BIG BATCH OF PEANUT BUTTER COOK--
CHOOM!
THANKS.
--IES.

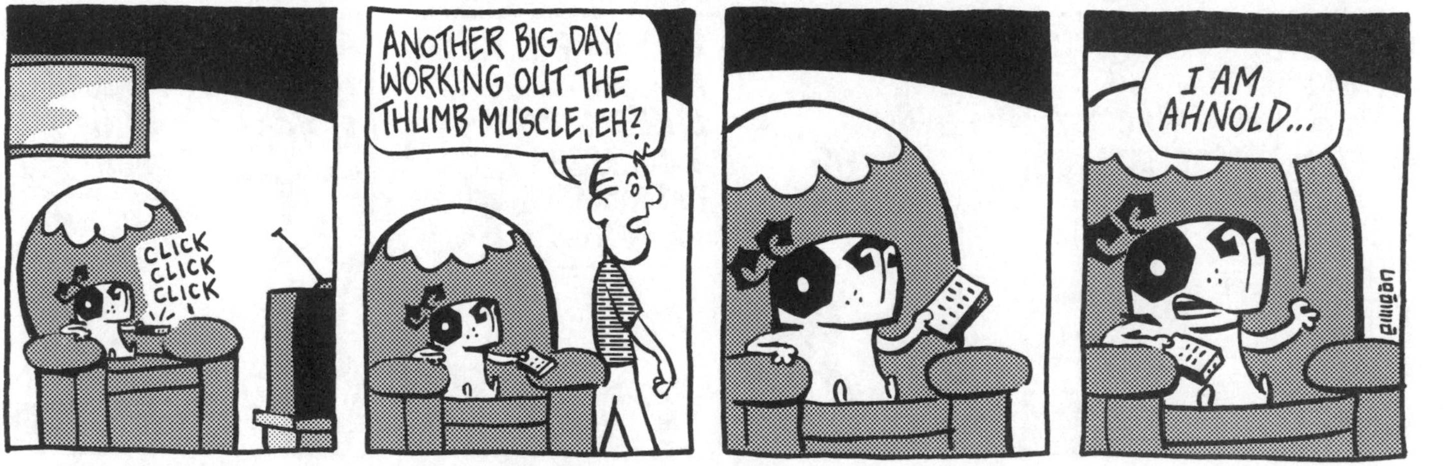
CLICK CLICK CLICK
ANOTHER BIG DAY WORKING OUT THE THUMB MUSCLE, EH?
I AM AHNOLD...

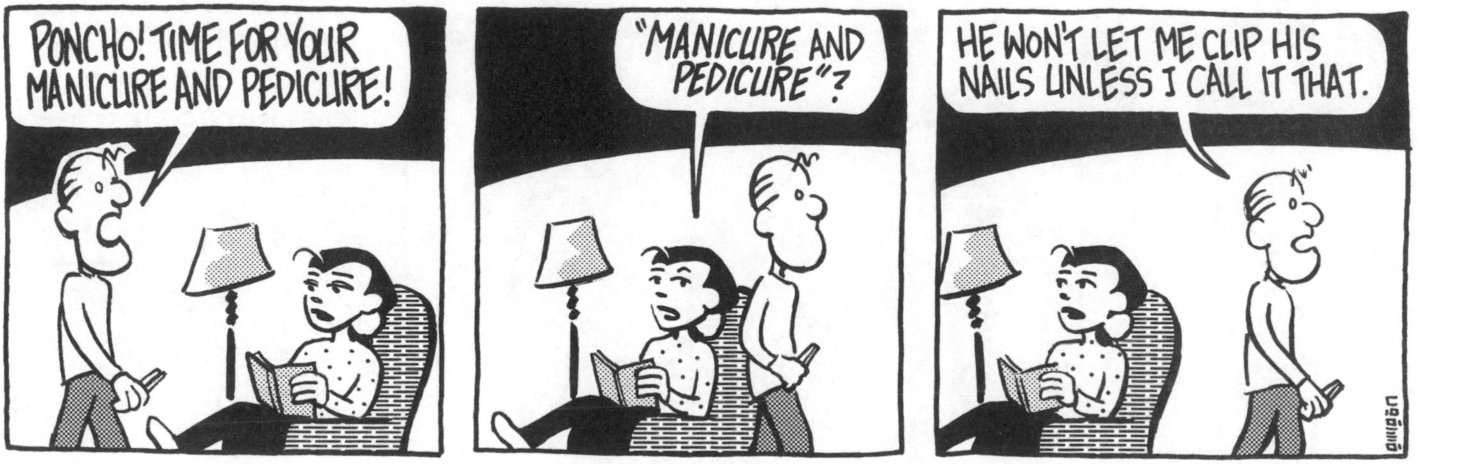
PONCHO! TIME FOR YOUR MANICURE AND PEDICURE!
"MANICURE AND PEDICURE"?
HE WON'T LET ME CLIP HIS NAILS UNLESS I CALL IT THAT.

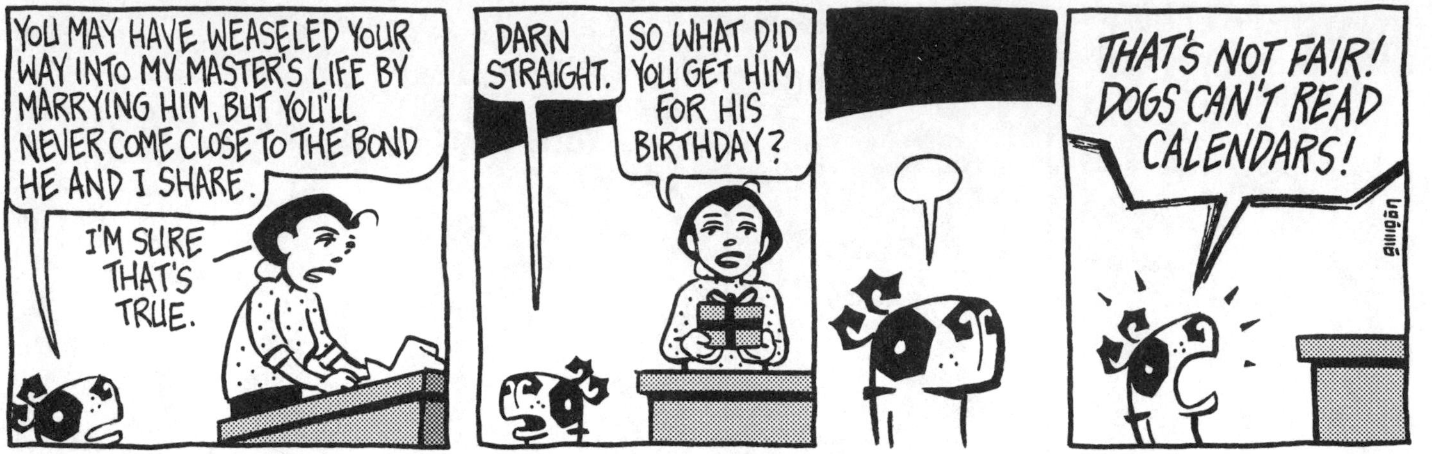
YOU MAY HAVE WEASELED YOUR WAY INTO MY MASTER'S LIFE BY MARRYING HIM, BUT YOU'LL NEVER COME CLOSE TO THE BOND HE AND I SHARE.
I'M SURE THAT'S TRUE.
DARN STRAIGHT.
SO WHAT DID YOU GET HIM FOR HIS BIRTHDAY?
THAT'S NOT FAIR! DOGS CAN'T READ CALENDARS!

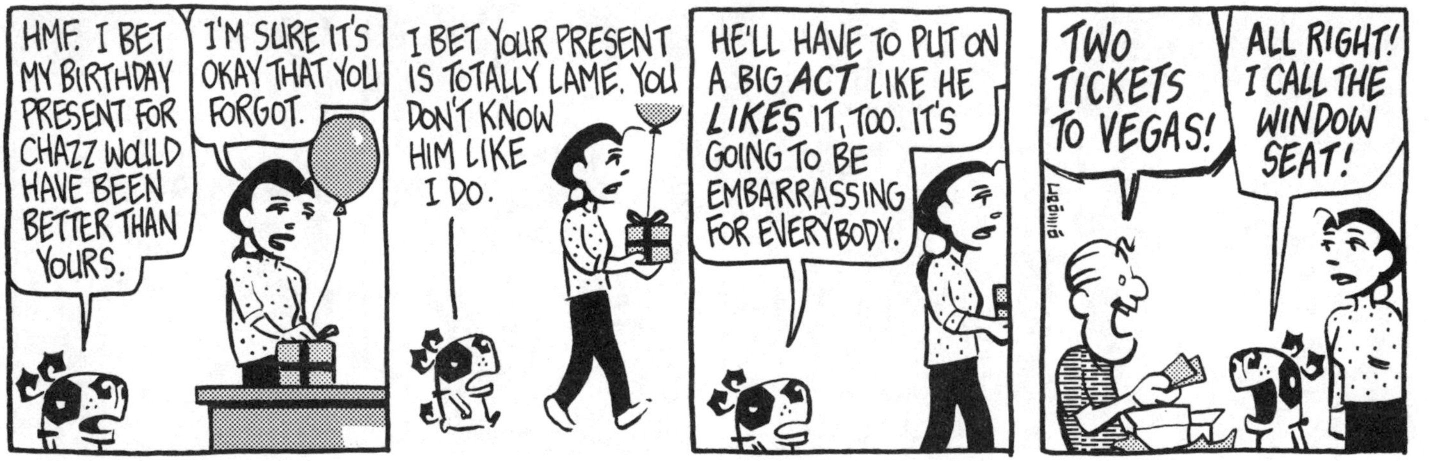
HMF. I BET MY BIRTHDAY PRESENT FOR CHAZZ WOULD HAVE BEEN BETTER THAN YOURS.
I'M SURE IT'S OKAY THAT YOU FORGOT.
I BET YOUR PRESENT IS TOTALLY LAME. YOU DON'T KNOW HIM LIKE I DO.
HE'LL HAVE TO PUT ON A BIG ACT LIKE HE LIKES IT, TOO. IT'S GOING TO BE EMBARRASSING FOR EVERYBODY.
TWO TICKETS TO VEGAS!
ALL RIGHT! I CALL THE WINDOW SEAT!

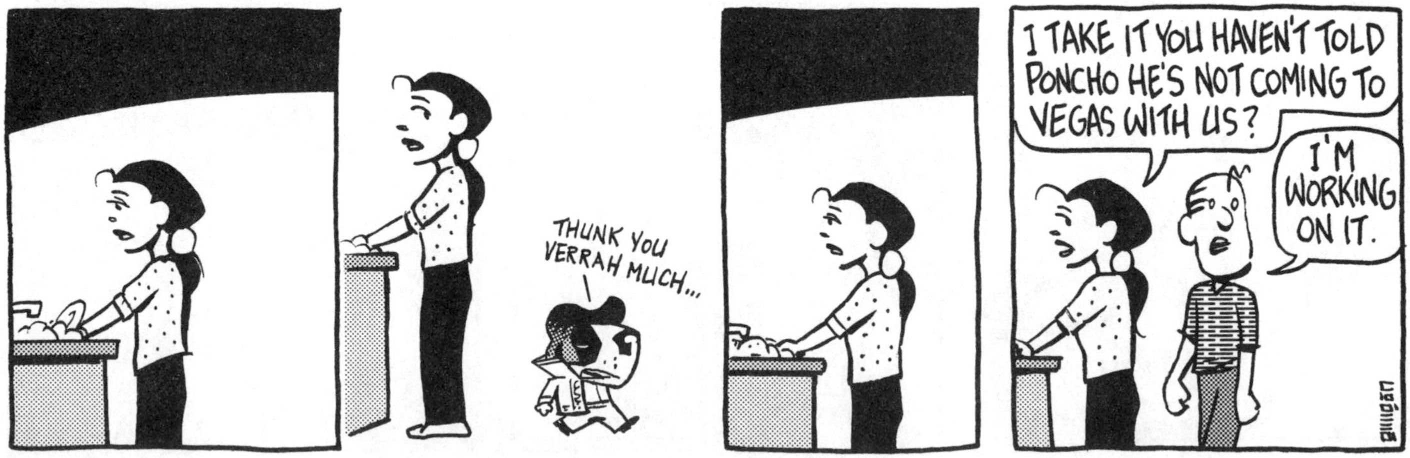
THUNK YOU VERRAH MUCH...
I TAKE IT YOU HAVEN'T TOLD PONCHO HE'S NOT COMING TO VEGAS WITH US?
I'M WORKING ON IT.

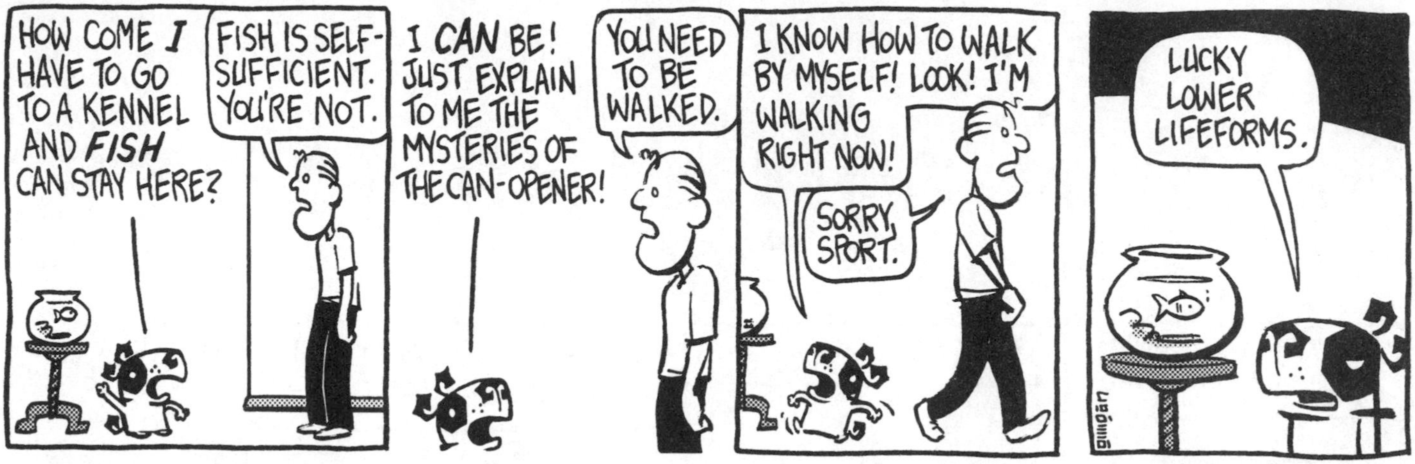
HOW COME I HAVE TO GO TO A KENNEL AND FISH CAN STAY HERE?
FISH IS SELF-SUFFICIENT. YOU'RE NOT.
I CAN BE! JUST EXPLAIN TO ME THE MYSTERIES OF THE CAN-OPENER!
YOU NEED TO BE WALKED.
I KNOW HOW TO WALK BY MYSELF! LOOK! I'M WALKING RIGHT NOW!
SORRY, SPORT.
LUCKY LOWER LIFEFORMS.

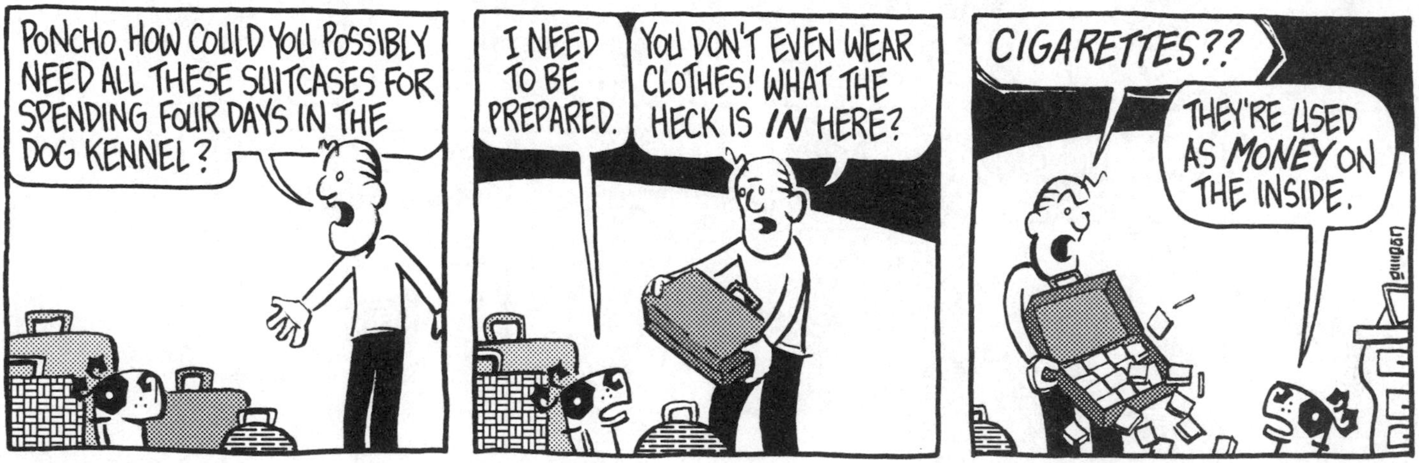
PONCHO, HOW COULD YOU POSSIBLY NEED ALL THESE SUITCASES FOR SPENDING FOUR DAYS IN THE DOG KENNEL?
I NEED TO BE PREPARED.
YOU DON'T EVEN WEAR CLOTHES! WHAT THE HECK IS IN HERE?
CIGARETTES??
THEY'RE USED AS MONEY ON THE INSIDE.

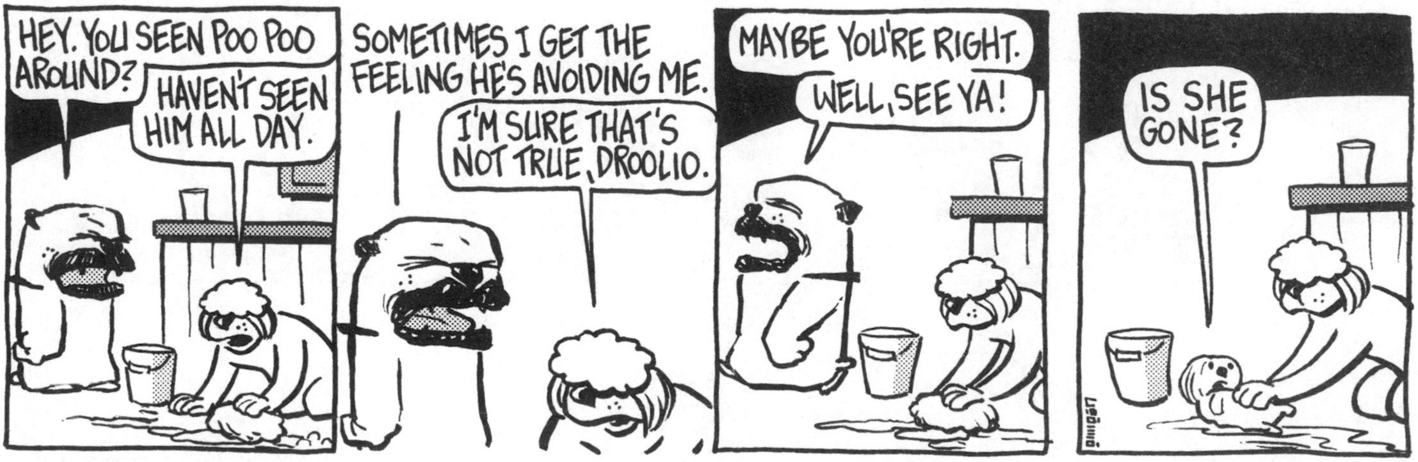
HEY. YOU SEEN POO POO AROUND?
HAVEN'T SEEN HIM ALL DAY.
SOMETIMES I GET THE FEELING HE'S AVOIDING ME.
I'M SURE THAT'S NOT TRUE, DROOLIO.
MAYBE YOU'RE RIGHT.
WELL, SEE YA!
IS SHE GONE?

THE TEN COMMANDMENTS OF DOGS

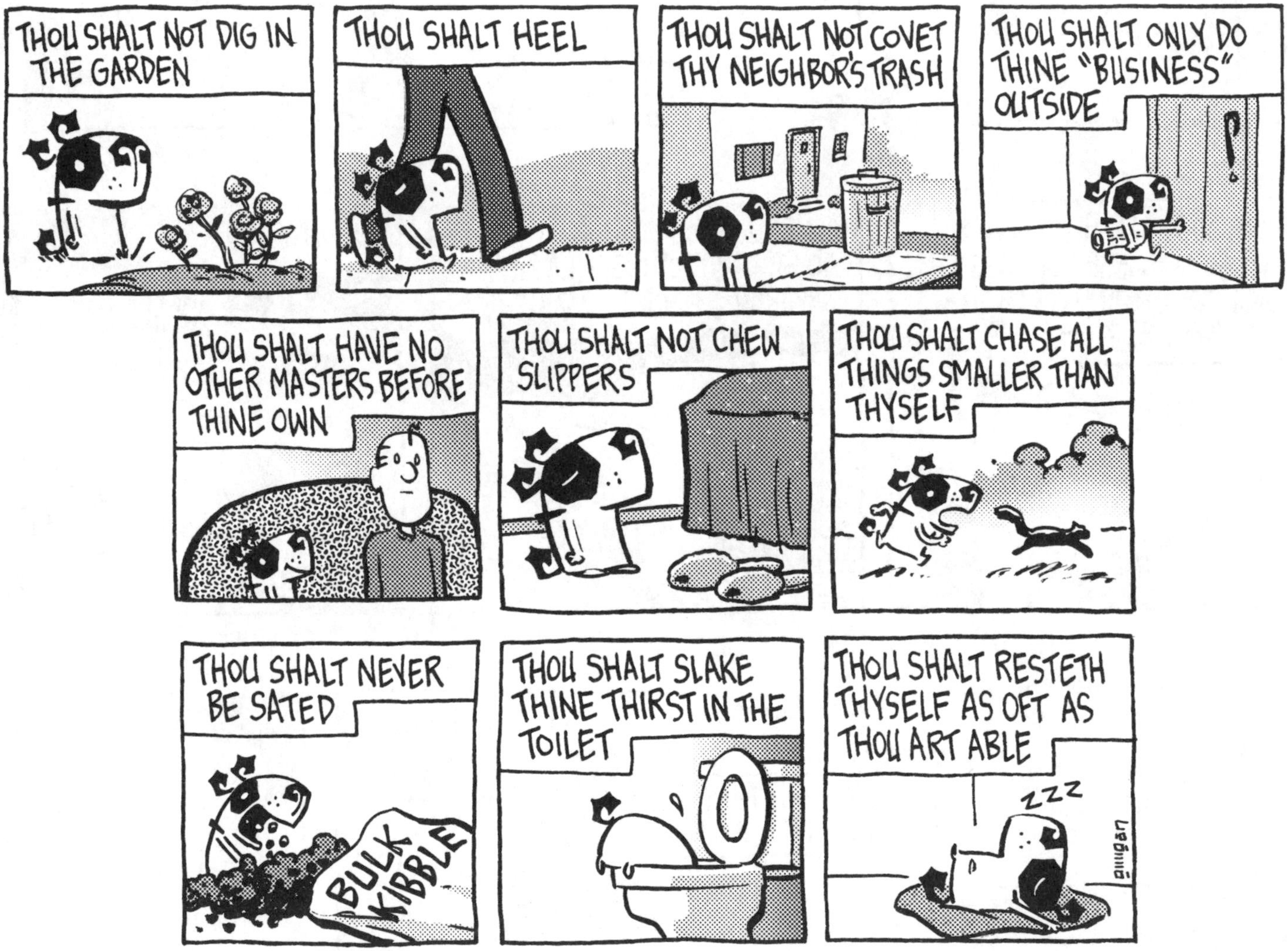
THOU SHALT NOT DIG IN THE GARDEN
THOU SHALT HEEL
THOU SHALT NOT COVET THY NEIGHBOR'S TRASH
THOU SHALT ONLY DO THINE "BUSINESS" OUTSIDE
THOU SHALT HAVE NO OTHER MASTERS BEFORE THINE OWN
THOU SHALT NOT CHEW SLIPPERS
THOU SHALT CHASE ALL THINGS SMALLER THAN THYSELF
THOU SHALT NEVER BE SATED
BULK KIBBLE
THOU SHALT SLAKE THINE THIRST IN THE TOILET
THOU SHALT RESTETH THYSELF AS OFT AS THOU ART ABLE
ZZZ

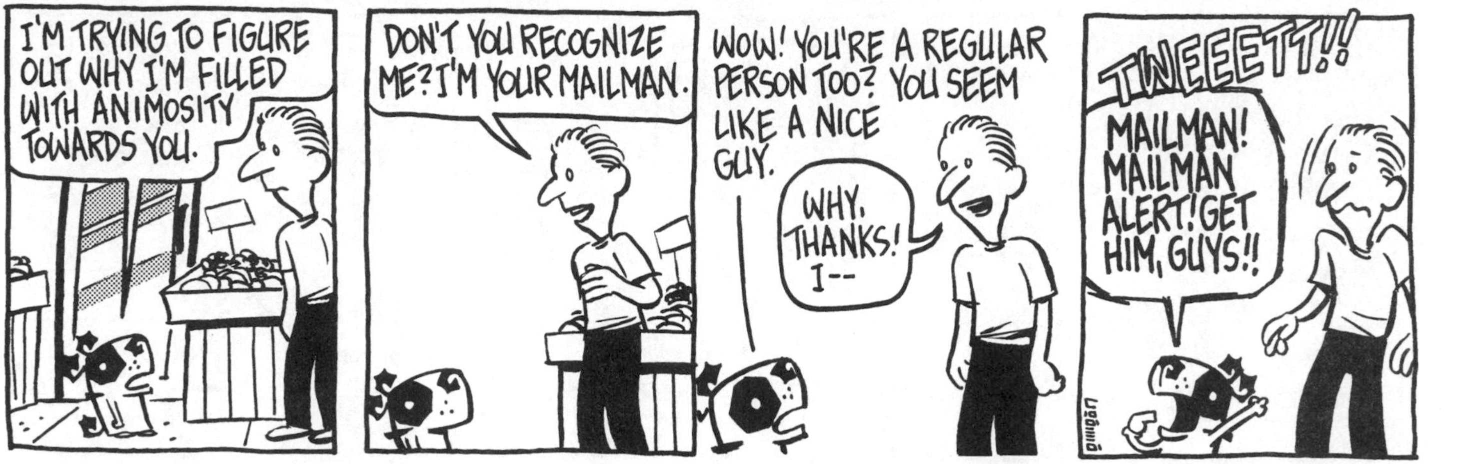
I'M TRYING TO FIGURE OUT WHY I'M FILLED WITH ANIMOSITY TOWARDS YOU.
DON'T YOU RECOGNIZE ME? I'M YOUR MAILMAN.
WOW! YOU'RE A REGULAR PERSON TOO? YOU SEEM LIKE A NICE GUY.
WHY, THANKS! I--
TWEEEETT!!
MAILMAN! MAILMAN ALERT! GET HIM, GUYS!!

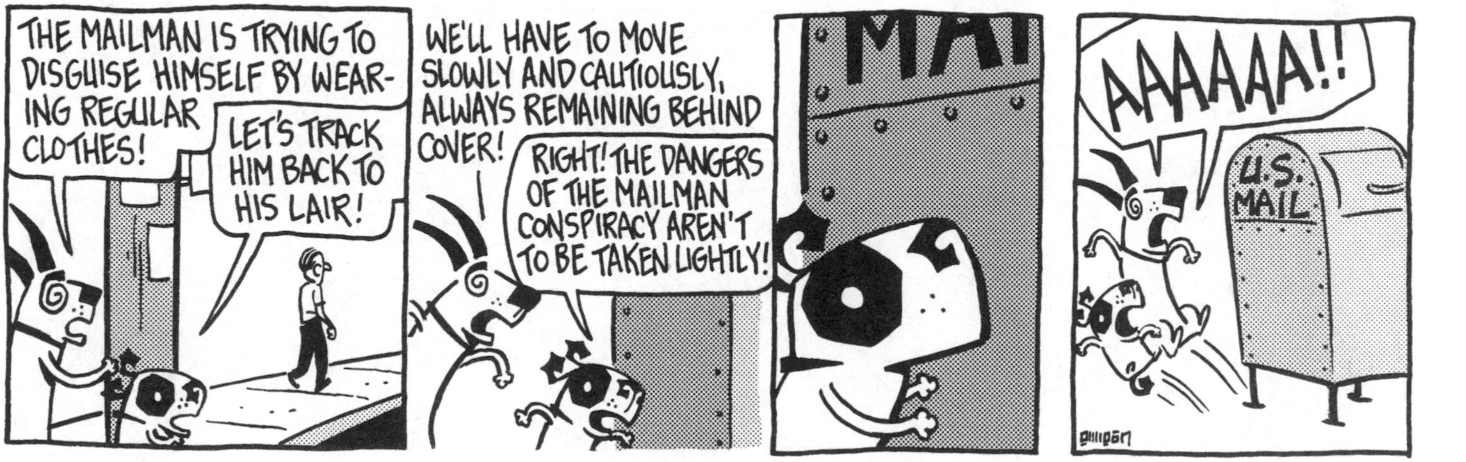
THE MAILMAN IS TRYING TO DISGUISE HIMSELF BY WEARING REGULAR CLOTHES!
LET'S TRACK HIM BACK TO HIS LAIR!
WE'LL HAVE TO MOVE SLOWLY AND CAUTIOUSLY, ALWAYS REMAINING BEHIND COVER!
RIGHT! THE DANGERS OF THE MAILMAN CONSPIRACY AREN'T TO BE TAKEN LIGHTLY!
MAI
AAAAAA!!
U.S. MAIL

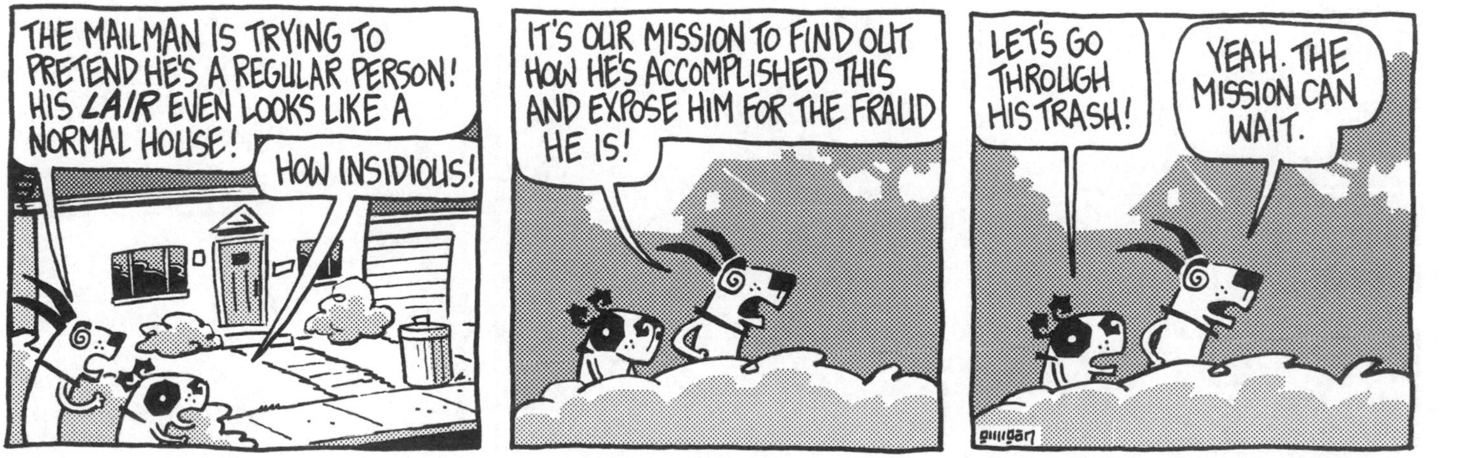
THE MAILMAN IS TRYING TO PRETEND HE'S A REGULAR PERSON! HIS LAIR EVEN LOOKS LIKE A NORMAL HOUSE!
HOW INSIDIOUS!
IT'S OUR MISSION TO FIND OUT HOW HE'S ACCOMPLISHED THIS AND EXPOSE HIM FOR THE FRAUD HE IS!
LET'S GO THROUGH HIS TRASH!
YEAH. THE MISSION CAN WAIT.

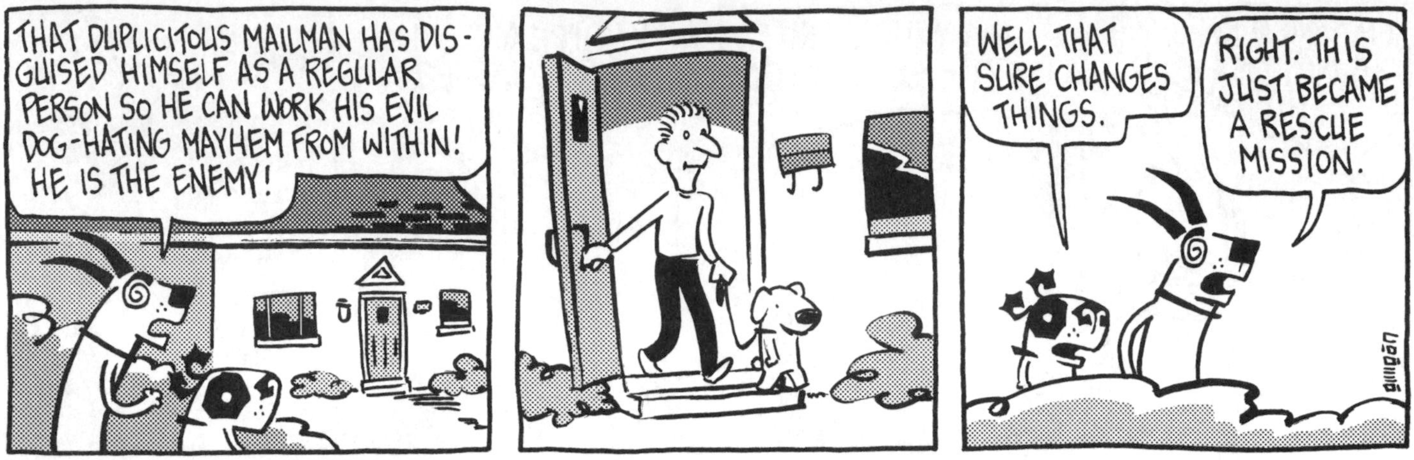
THAT DUPLICITOUS MAILMAN HAS DISGUISED HIMSELF AS A REGULAR PERSON SO HE CAN WORK HIS EVIL DOG-HATING MAYHEM FROM WITHIN! HE IS THE ENEMY!
WELL, THAT SURE CHANGES THINGS.
RIGHT. THIS JUST BECAME A RESCUE MISSION.

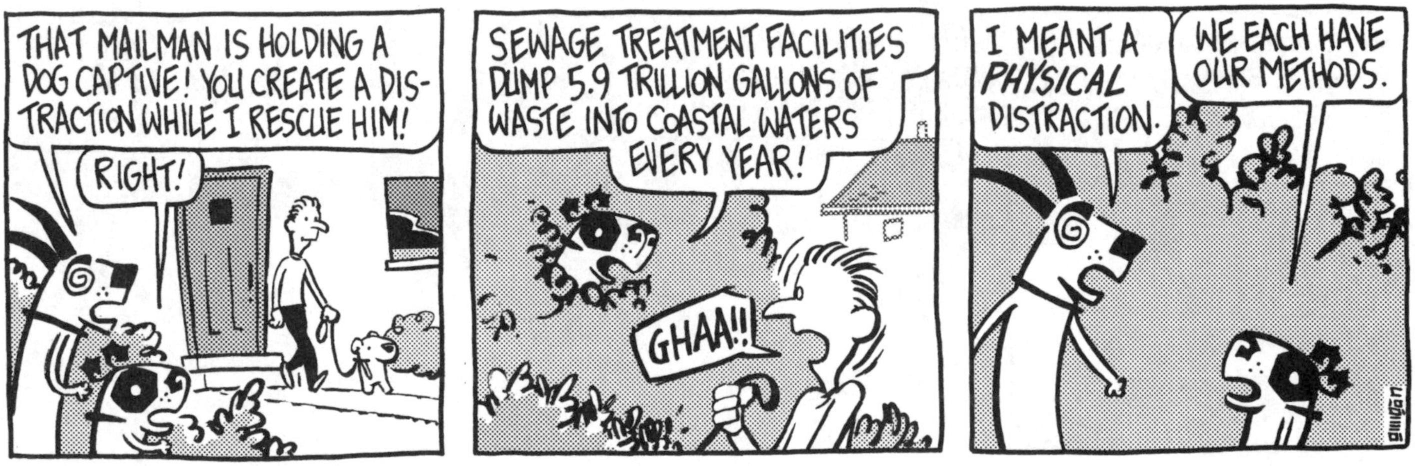
THAT MAILMAN IS HOLDING A DOG CAPTIVE! YOU CREATE A DISTRACTION WHILE I RESCUE HIM!
RIGHT!
SEWAGE TREATMENT FACILITIES DUMP 5.9 TRILLION GALLONS OF WASTE INTO COASTAL WATERS EVERY YEAR!
GHAA!!
I MEANT A *PHYSICAL* DISTRACTION.
WE EACH HAVE OUR METHODS.

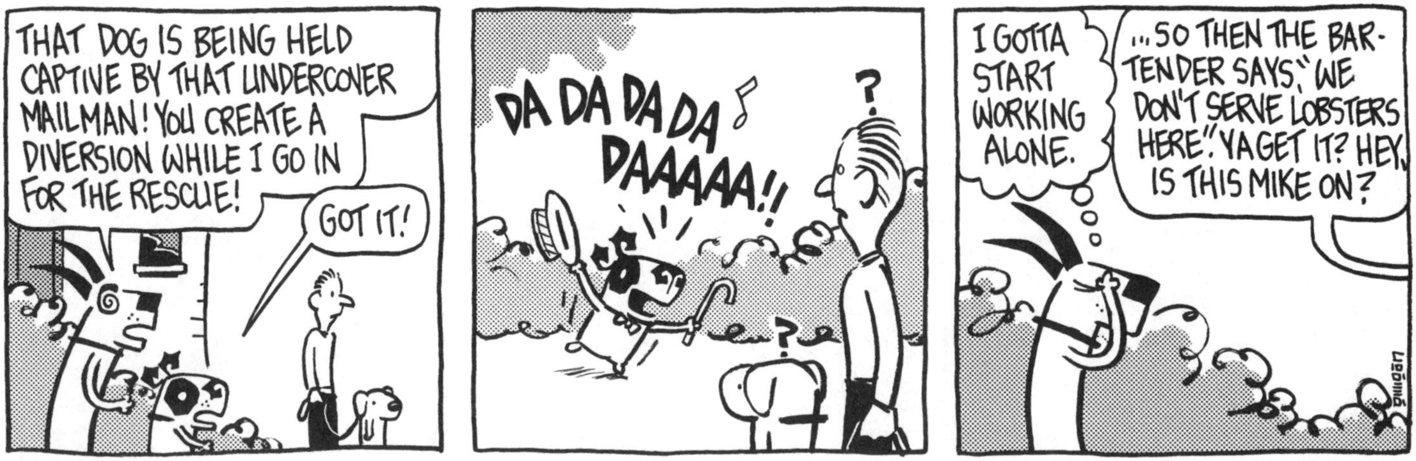
THAT DOG IS BEING HELD CAPTIVE BY THAT UNDERCOVER MAILMAN! YOU CREATE A DIVERSION WHILE I GO IN FOR THE RESCUE!
GOT IT!
DA DA DA DA DAAAAA!!
?
?
I GOTTA START WORKING ALONE.
...SO THEN THE BARTENDER SAYS, "WE DON'T SERVE LOBSTERS HERE." YA GET IT? HEY, IS THIS MIKE ON?

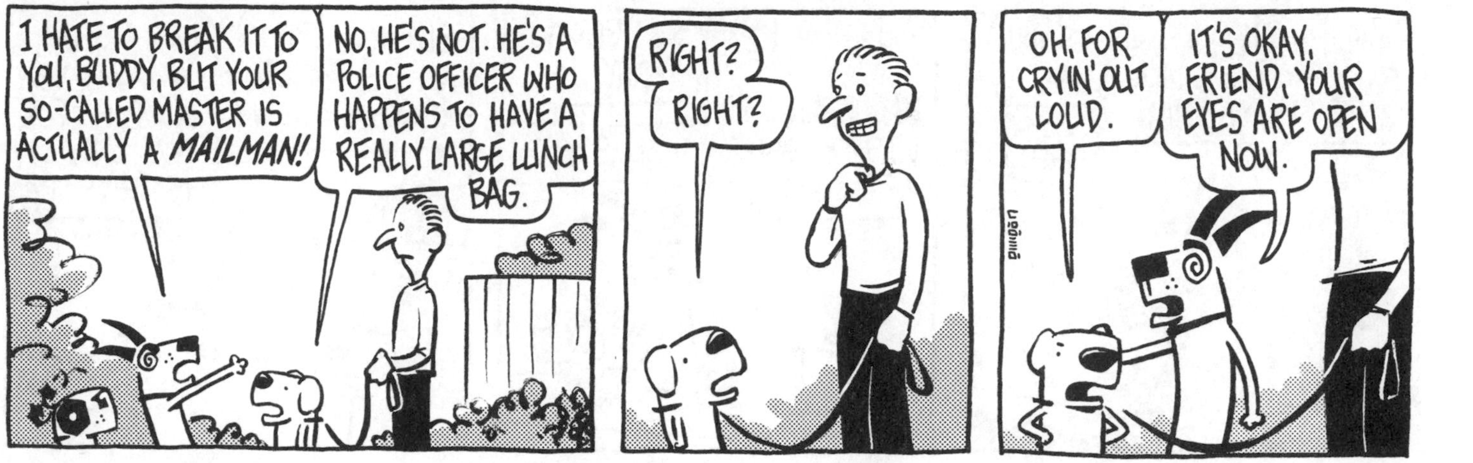
I HATE TO BREAK IT TO YOU, BUDDY, BUT YOUR SO-CALLED MASTER IS ACTUALLY A *MAILMAN*!
NO, HE'S NOT. HE'S A POLICE OFFICER WHO HAPPENS TO HAVE A REALLY LARGE LUNCH BAG.
RIGHT?
RIGHT?
OH, FOR CRYIN' OUT LOUD.
IT'S OKAY, FRIEND, YOUR EYES ARE OPEN NOW.

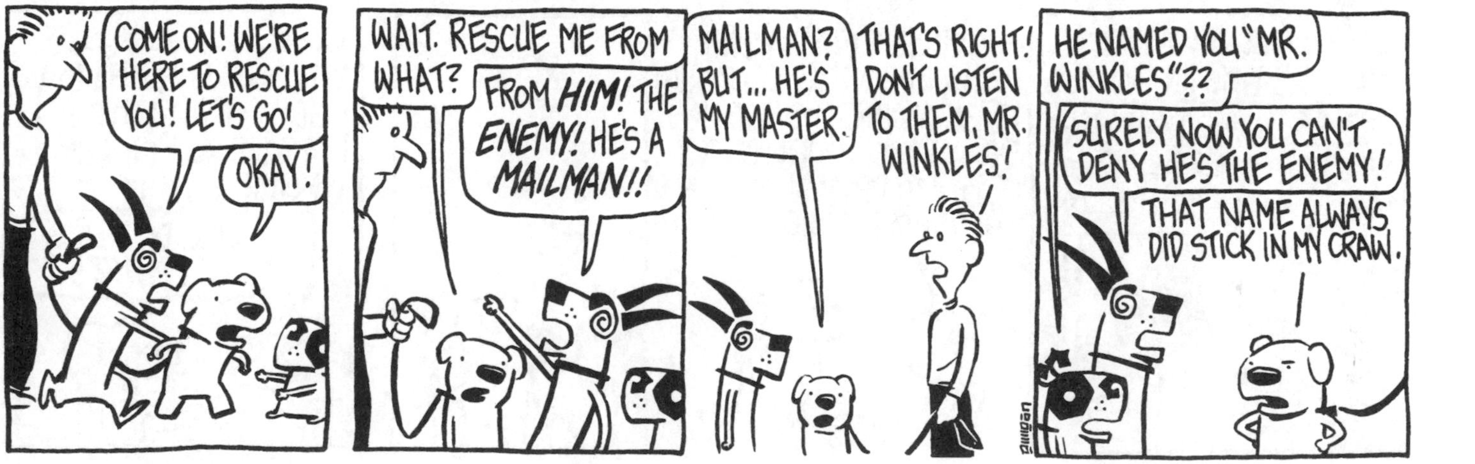
COME ON! WE'RE HERE TO RESCUE YOU! LET'S GO!
OKAY!
WAIT. RESCUE ME FROM WHAT?
FROM *HIM*! THE *ENEMY*! HE'S A *MAILMAN*!!
MAILMAN? BUT... HE'S MY MASTER.
THAT'S RIGHT! DON'T LISTEN TO THEM, MR. WINKLES!
HE NAMED YOU "MR. WINKLES"??
SURELY NOW YOU CAN'T DENY HE'S THE ENEMY!
THAT NAME ALWAYS DID STICK IN MY CRAW.

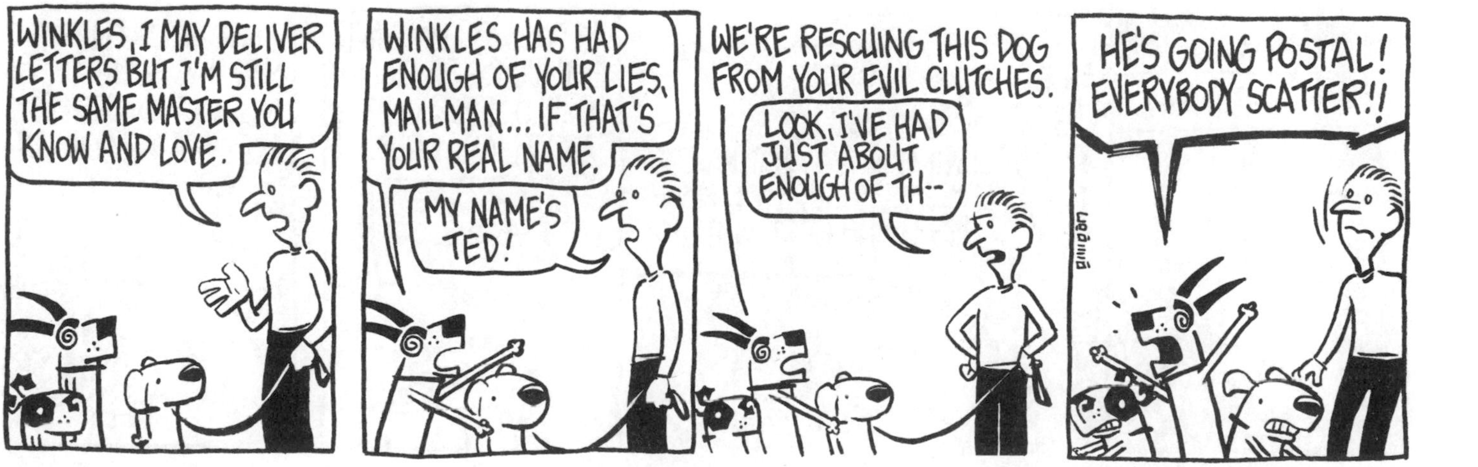
WINKLES, I MAY DELIVER LETTERS BUT I'M STILL THE SAME MASTER YOU KNOW AND LOVE.
WINKLES HAS HAD ENOUGH OF YOUR LIES, MAILMAN... IF THAT'S YOUR REAL NAME.
MY NAME'S TED!
WE'RE RESCUING THIS DOG FROM YOUR EVIL CLUTCHES.
LOOK, I'VE HAD JUST ABOUT ENOUGH OF TH--
HE'S GOING POSTAL! EVERYBODY SCATTER!!

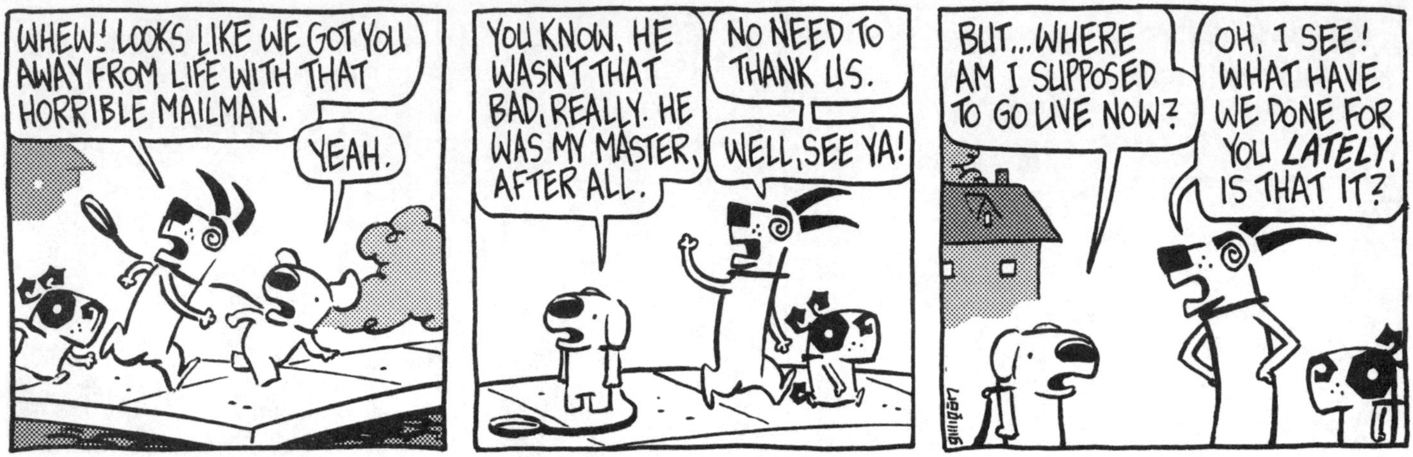
WHEW! LOOKS LIKE WE GOT YOU AWAY FROM LIFE WITH THAT HORRIBLE MAILMAN.
YEAH.
YOU KNOW, HE WASN'T THAT BAD, REALLY. HE WAS MY MASTER, AFTER ALL.
NO NEED TO THANK US.
WELL, SEE YA!
BUT... WHERE AM I SUPPOSED TO GO LIVE NOW?
OH, I SEE! WHAT HAVE WE DONE FOR YOU *LATELY*, IS THAT IT?

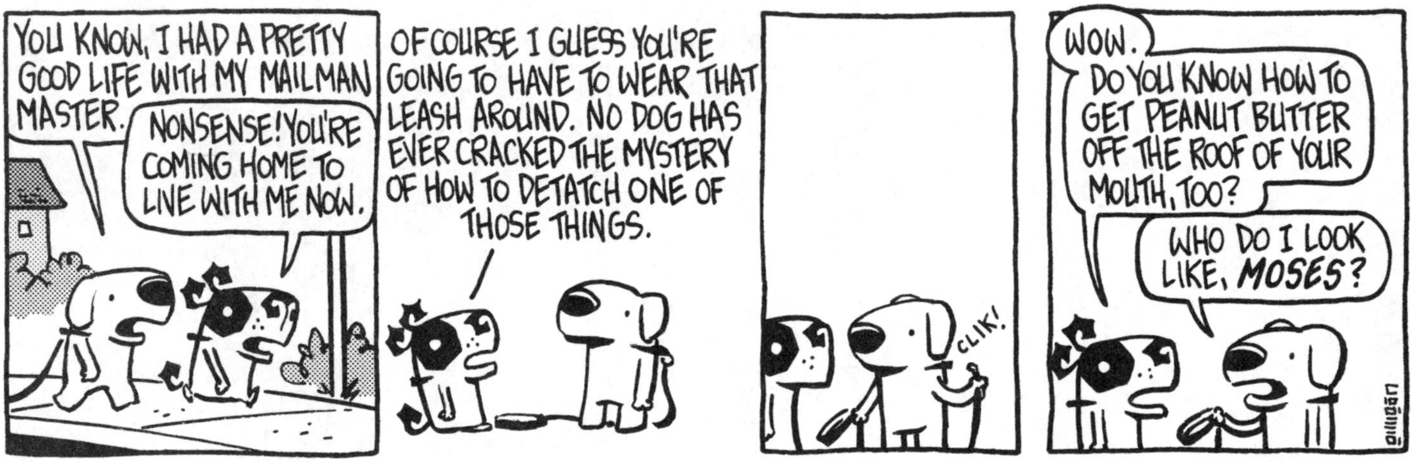
YOU KNOW, I HAD A PRETTY GOOD LIFE WITH MY MAILMAN MASTER.
NONSENSE! YOU'RE COMING HOME TO LIVE WITH ME NOW.
OF COURSE I GUESS YOU'RE GOING TO HAVE TO WEAR THAT LEASH AROUND. NO DOG HAS EVER CRACKED THE MYSTERY OF HOW TO DETATCH ONE OF THOSE THINGS.
CLIK!
WOW.
DO YOU KNOW HOW TO GET PEANUT BUTTER OFF THE ROOF OF YOUR MOUTH, TOO?
WHO DO I LOOK LIKE, ***MOSES***?

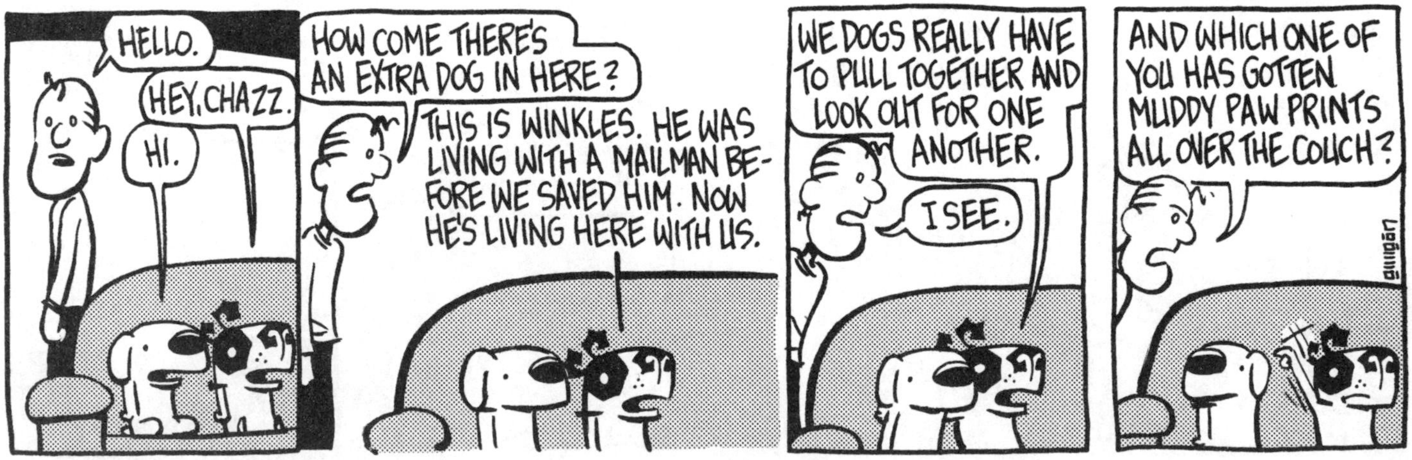
HELLO.
HEY, CHAZZ.
HI.
HOW COME THERE'S AN EXTRA DOG IN HERE?
THIS IS WINKLES. HE WAS LIVING WITH A MAILMAN BEFORE WE SAVED HIM. NOW HE'S LIVING HERE WITH US.
WE DOGS REALLY HAVE TO PULL TOGETHER AND LOOK OUT FOR ONE ANOTHER.
I SEE.
AND WHICH ONE OF YOU HAS GOTTEN MUDDY PAW PRINTS ALL OVER THE COUCH?

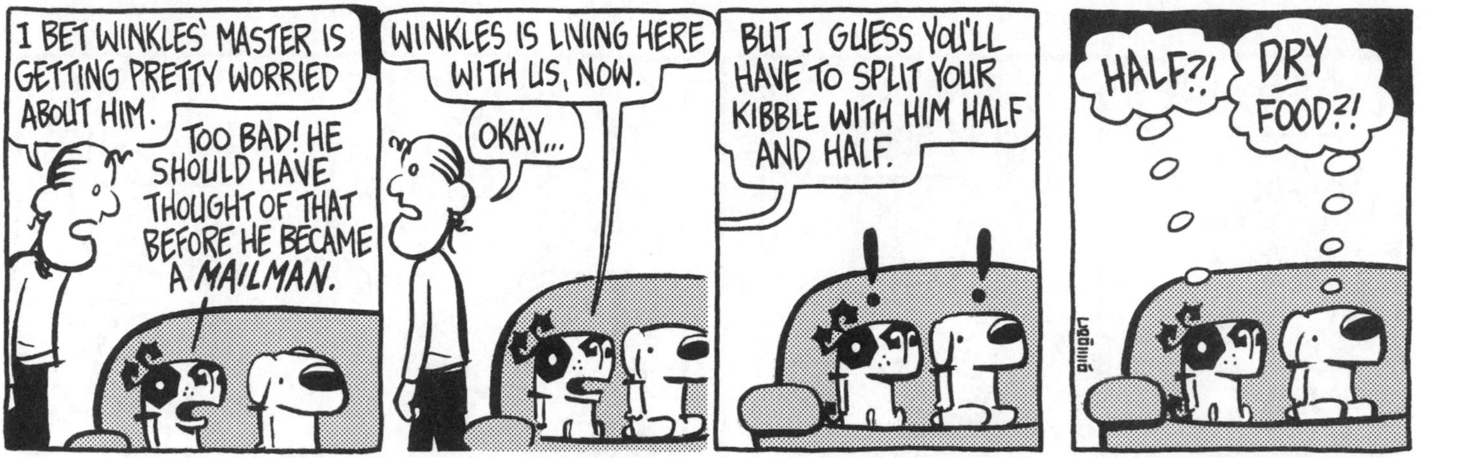
I BET WINKLES' MASTER IS GETTING PRETTY WORRIED ABOUT HIM.
TOO BAD! HE SHOULD HAVE THOUGHT OF THAT BEFORE HE BECAME A *MAILMAN*.
WINKLES IS LIVING HERE WITH US, NOW.
OKAY...
BUT I GUESS YOU'LL HAVE TO SPLIT YOUR KIBBLE WITH HIM HALF AND HALF.
HALF?!
DRY FOOD?!

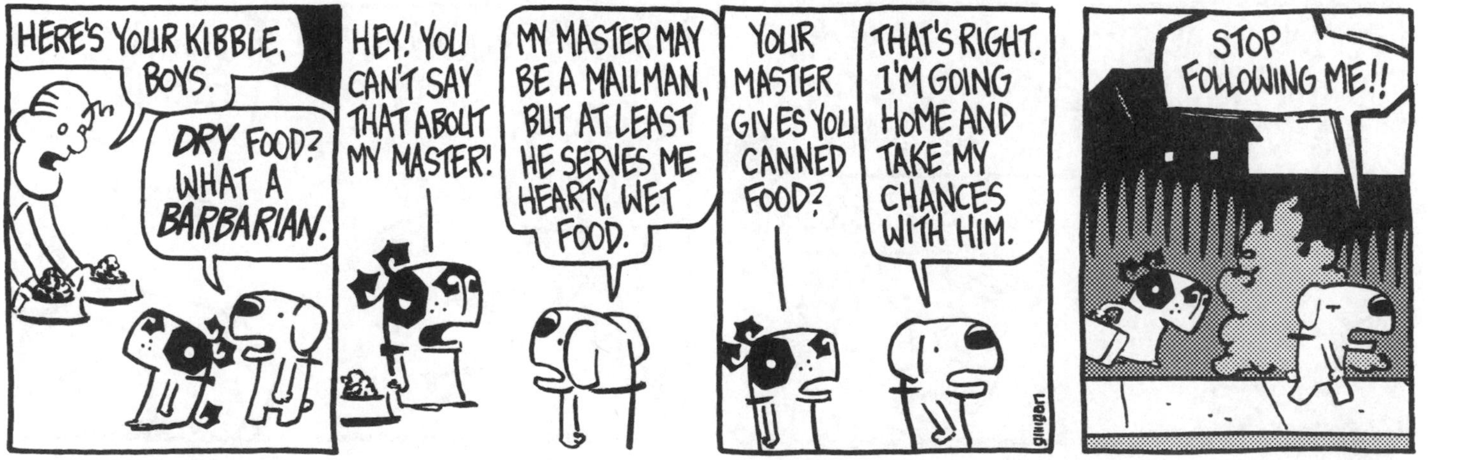
HERE'S YOUR KIBBLE, BOYS.
DRY FOOD? WHAT A *BARBARIAN*.
HEY! YOU CAN'T SAY THAT ABOUT MY MASTER!
MY MASTER MAY BE A MAILMAN, BUT AT LEAST HE SERVES ME HEARTY, WET FOOD.
YOUR MASTER GIVES YOU CANNED FOOD?
THAT'S RIGHT. I'M GOING HOME AND TAKE MY CHANCES WITH HIM.
STOP FOLLOWING ME!!

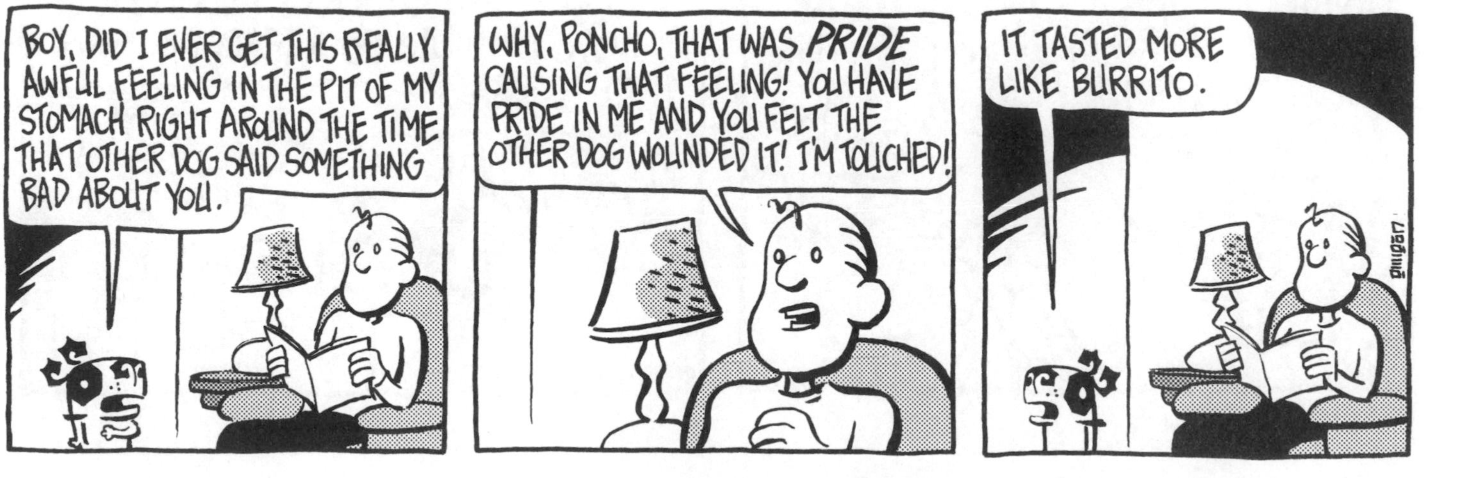
BOY, DID I EVER GET THIS REALLY AWFUL FEELING IN THE PIT OF MY STOMACH RIGHT AROUND THE TIME THAT OTHER DOG SAID SOMETHING BAD ABOUT YOU.
WHY, PONCHO, THAT WAS *PRIDE* CAUSING THAT FEELING! YOU HAVE PRIDE IN ME AND YOU FELT THE OTHER DOG WOUNDED IT! I'M TOUCHED!
IT TASTED MORE LIKE BURRITO.

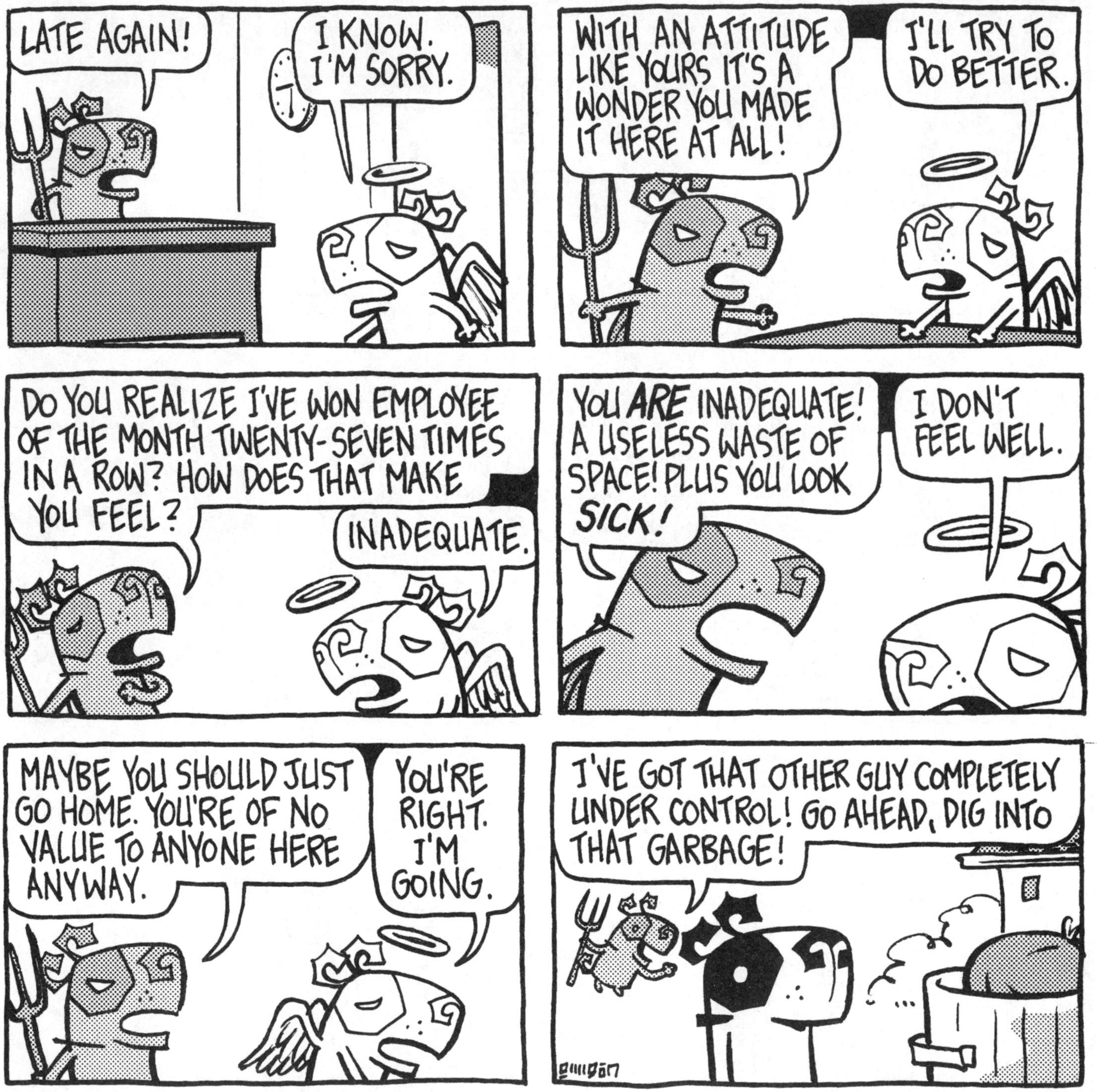
LATE AGAIN!
I KNOW. I'M SORRY.
WITH AN ATTITUDE LIKE YOURS IT'S A WONDER YOU MADE IT HERE AT ALL!
I'LL TRY TO DO BETTER.
DO YOU REALIZE I'VE WON EMPLOYEE OF THE MONTH TWENTY-SEVEN TIMES IN A ROW? HOW DOES THAT MAKE YOU FEEL?
INADEQUATE.
YOU ARE INADEQUATE! A USELESS WASTE OF SPACE! PLUS YOU LOOK SICK!
I DON'T FEEL WELL.
MAYBE YOU SHOULD JUST GO HOME. YOU'RE OF NO VALUE TO ANYONE HERE ANYWAY.
YOU'RE RIGHT. I'M GOING.
I'VE GOT THAT OTHER GUY COMPLETELY UNDER CONTROL! GO AHEAD, DIG INTO THAT GARBAGE!
...

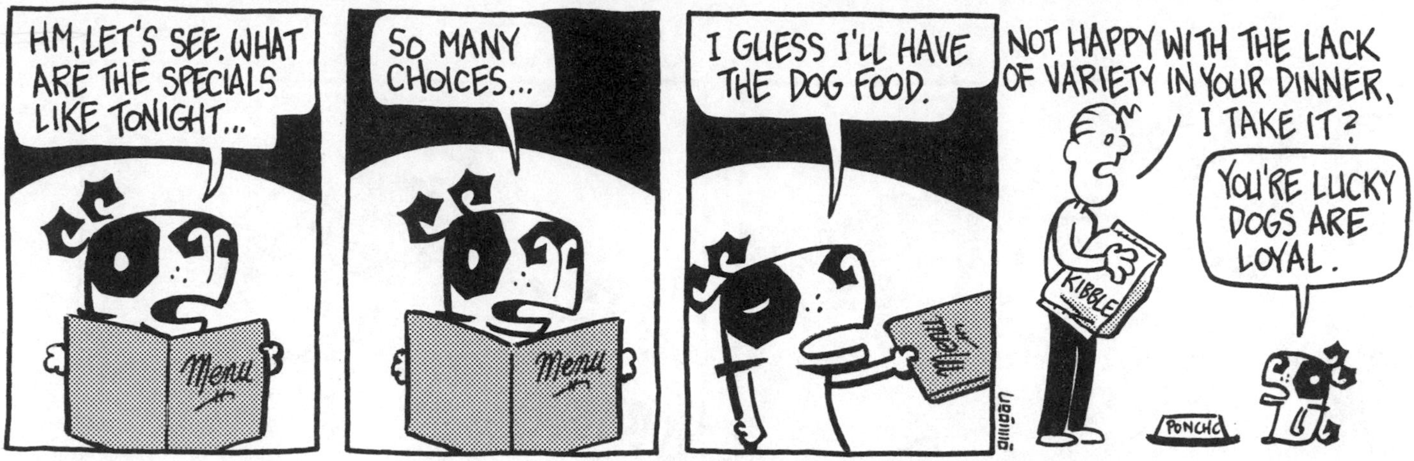
HM, LET'S SEE. WHAT ARE THE SPECIALS LIKE TONIGHT...
Menu
SO MANY CHOICES...
Menu
I GUESS I'LL HAVE THE DOG FOOD.
NOT HAPPY WITH THE LACK OF VARIETY IN YOUR DINNER, I TAKE IT?
YOU'RE LUCKY DOGS ARE LOYAL.
KIBBLE
PONCHO

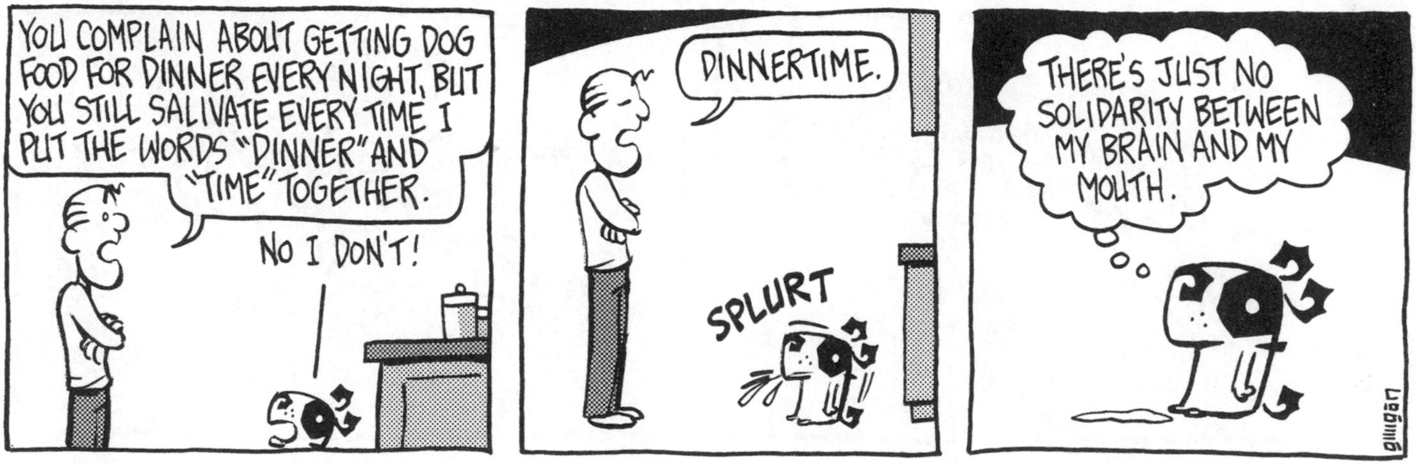
YOU COMPLAIN ABOUT GETTING DOG FOOD FOR DINNER EVERY NIGHT, BUT YOU STILL SALIVATE EVERY TIME I PUT THE WORDS "DINNER" AND "TIME" TOGETHER.
NO I DON'T!
DINNERTIME.
SPLURT
THERE'S JUST NO SOLIDARITY BETWEEN MY BRAIN AND MY MOUTH.

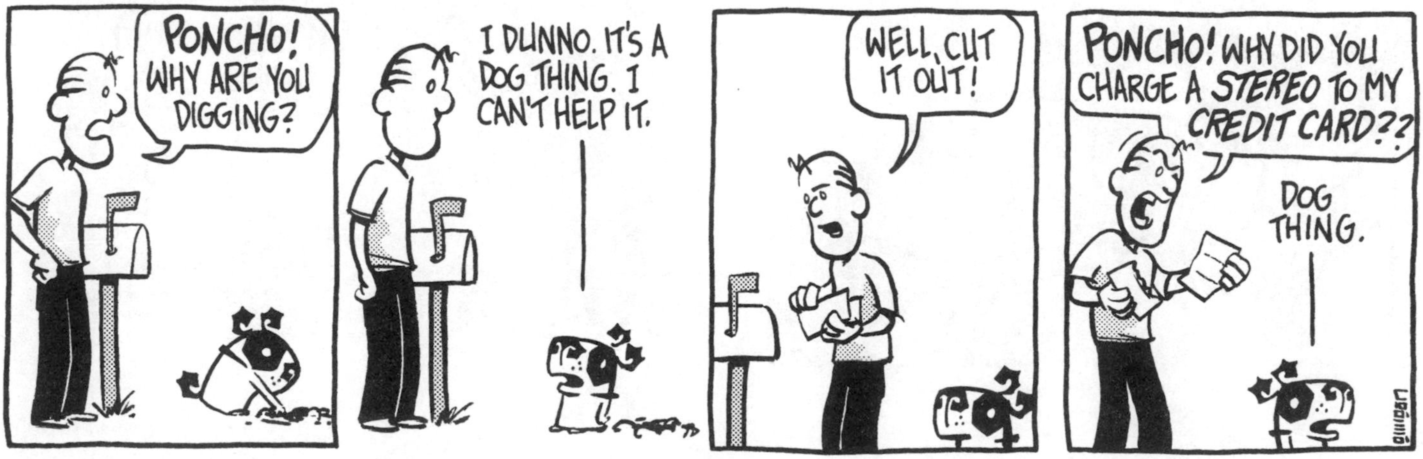
PONCHO! WHY ARE YOU DIGGING?
I DUNNO. IT'S A DOG THING. I CAN'T HELP IT.
WELL, CUT IT OUT!
PONCHO! WHY DID YOU CHARGE A STEREO TO MY CREDIT CARD??
DOG THING.

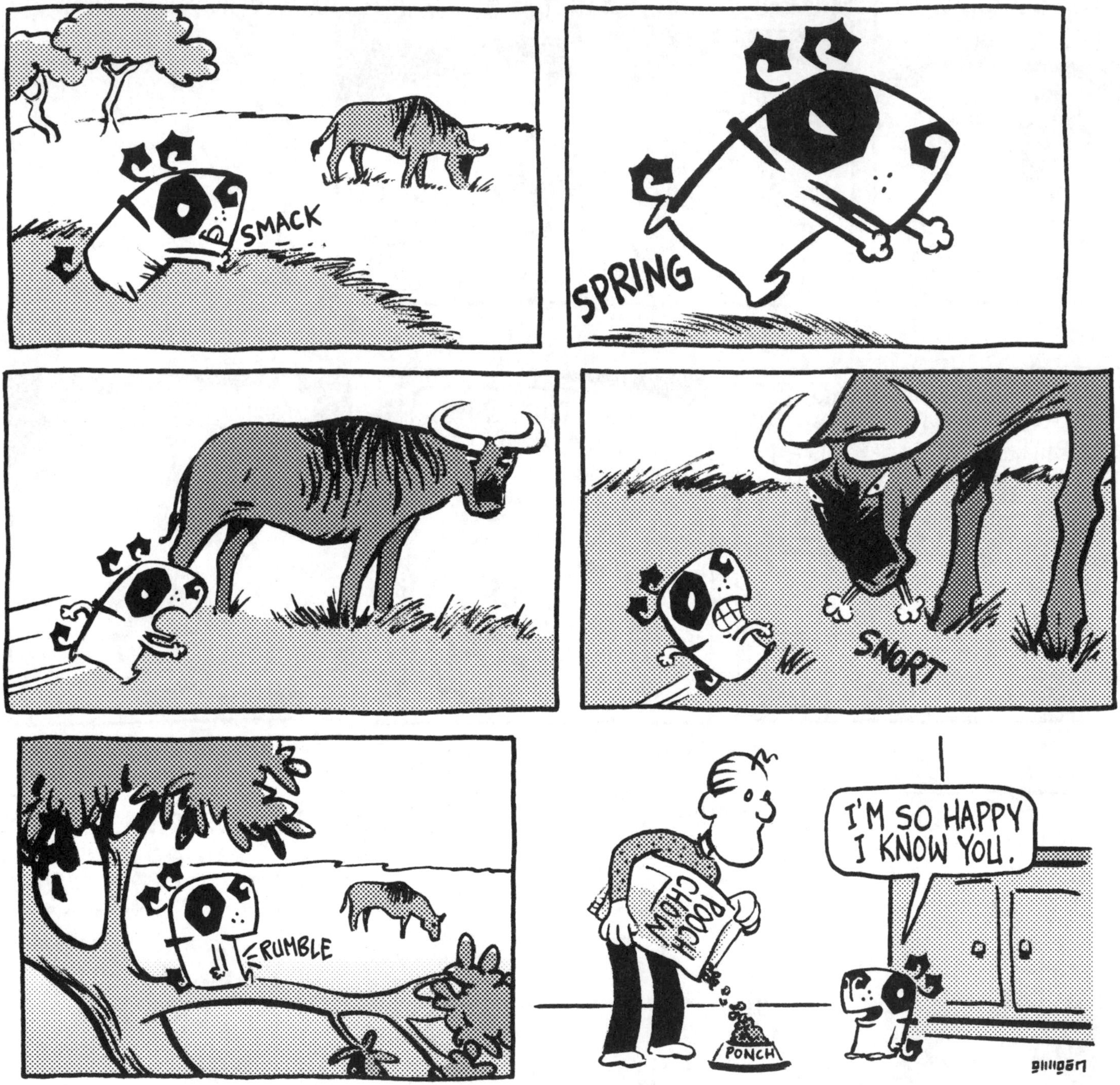
SMACK
SPRING
SNORT
RUMBLE
POOCH CHOW
PONCH
I'M SO HAPPY I KNOW YOU.
gilligan

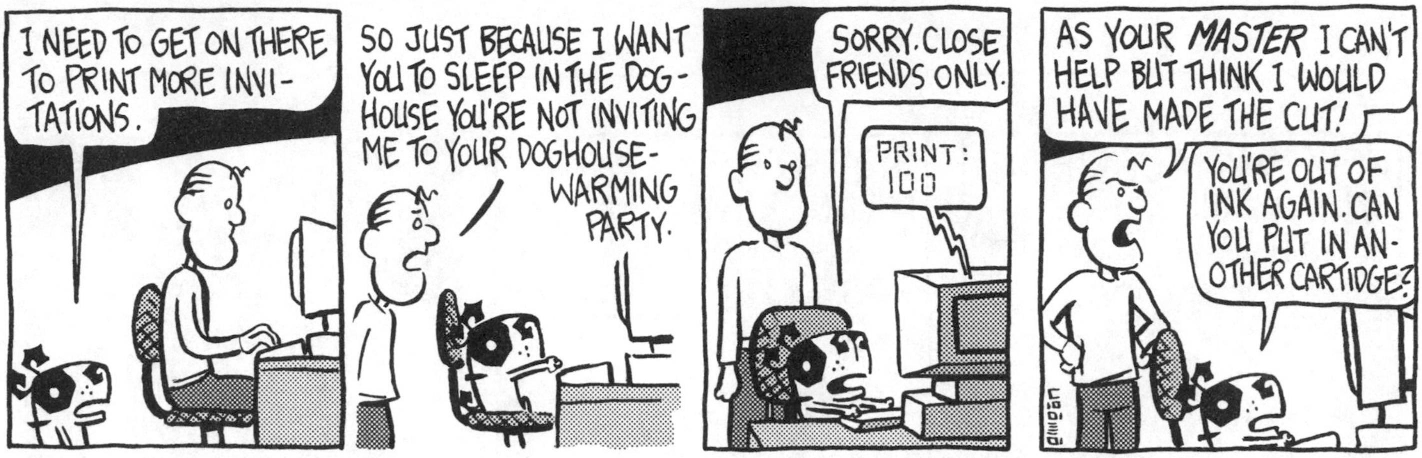
I NEED TO GET ON THERE TO PRINT MORE INVITATIONS.
SO JUST BECAUSE I WANT YOU TO SLEEP IN THE DOGHOUSE YOU'RE NOT INVITING ME TO YOUR DOGHOUSE-WARMING PARTY.
SORRY. CLOSE FRIENDS ONLY.
PRINT: 100
AS YOUR MASTER I CAN'T HELP BUT THINK I WOULD HAVE MADE THE CUT!
YOU'RE OUT OF INK AGAIN. CAN YOU PUT IN ANOTHER CARTIDGE?

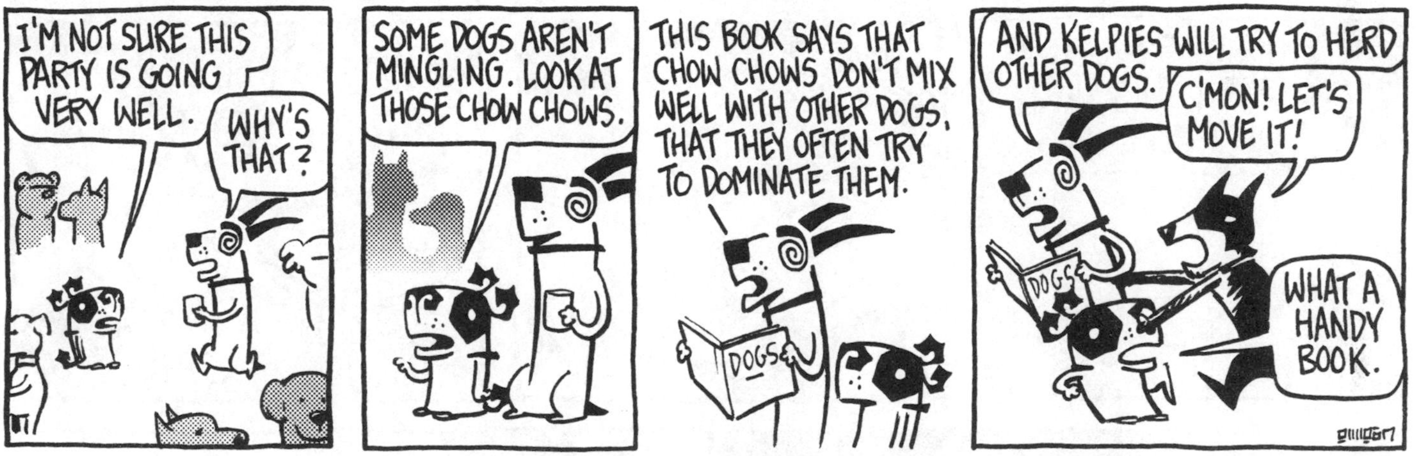
I'M NOT SURE THIS PARTY IS GOING VERY WELL.
WHY'S THAT?
SOME DOGS AREN'T MINGLING. LOOK AT THOSE CHOW CHOWS.
THIS BOOK SAYS THAT CHOW CHOWS DON'T MIX WELL WITH OTHER DOGS, THAT THEY OFTEN TRY TO DOMINATE THEM.
DOGS
AND KELPIES WILL TRY TO HERD OTHER DOGS.
C'MON! LET'S MOVE IT!
DOGS
WHAT A HANDY BOOK.

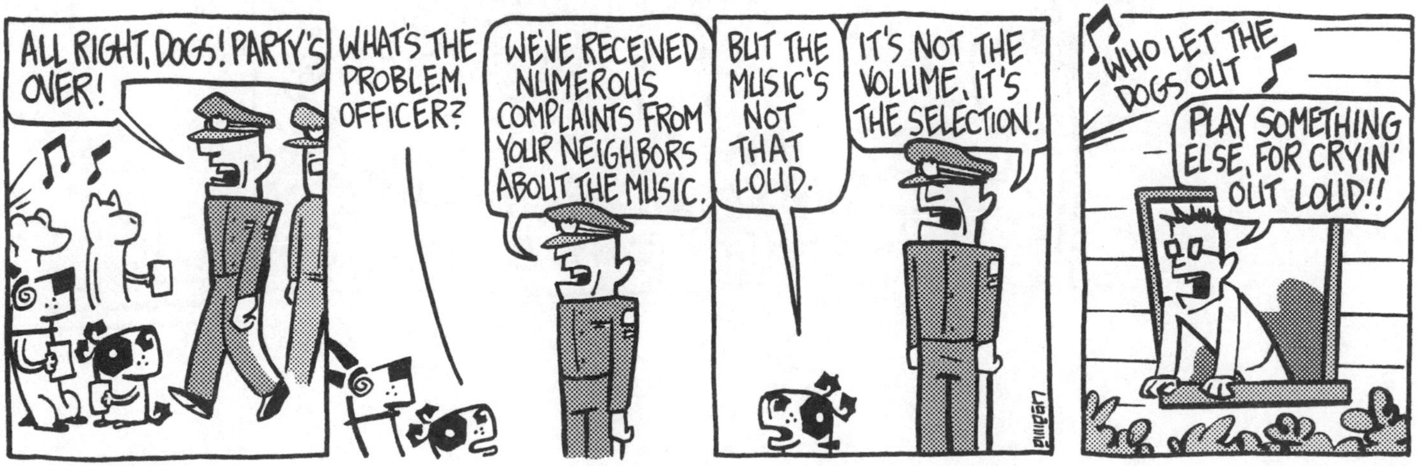
ALL RIGHT, DOGS! PARTY'S OVER!
WHAT'S THE PROBLEM, OFFICER?
WE'VE RECEIVED NUMEROUS COMPLAINTS FROM YOUR NEIGHBORS ABOUT THE MUSIC.
BUT THE MUSIC'S NOT THAT LOUD.
IT'S NOT THE VOLUME, IT'S THE SELECTION!
WHO LET THE DOGS OUT
PLAY SOMETHING ELSE, FOR CRYIN' OUT LOUD!!

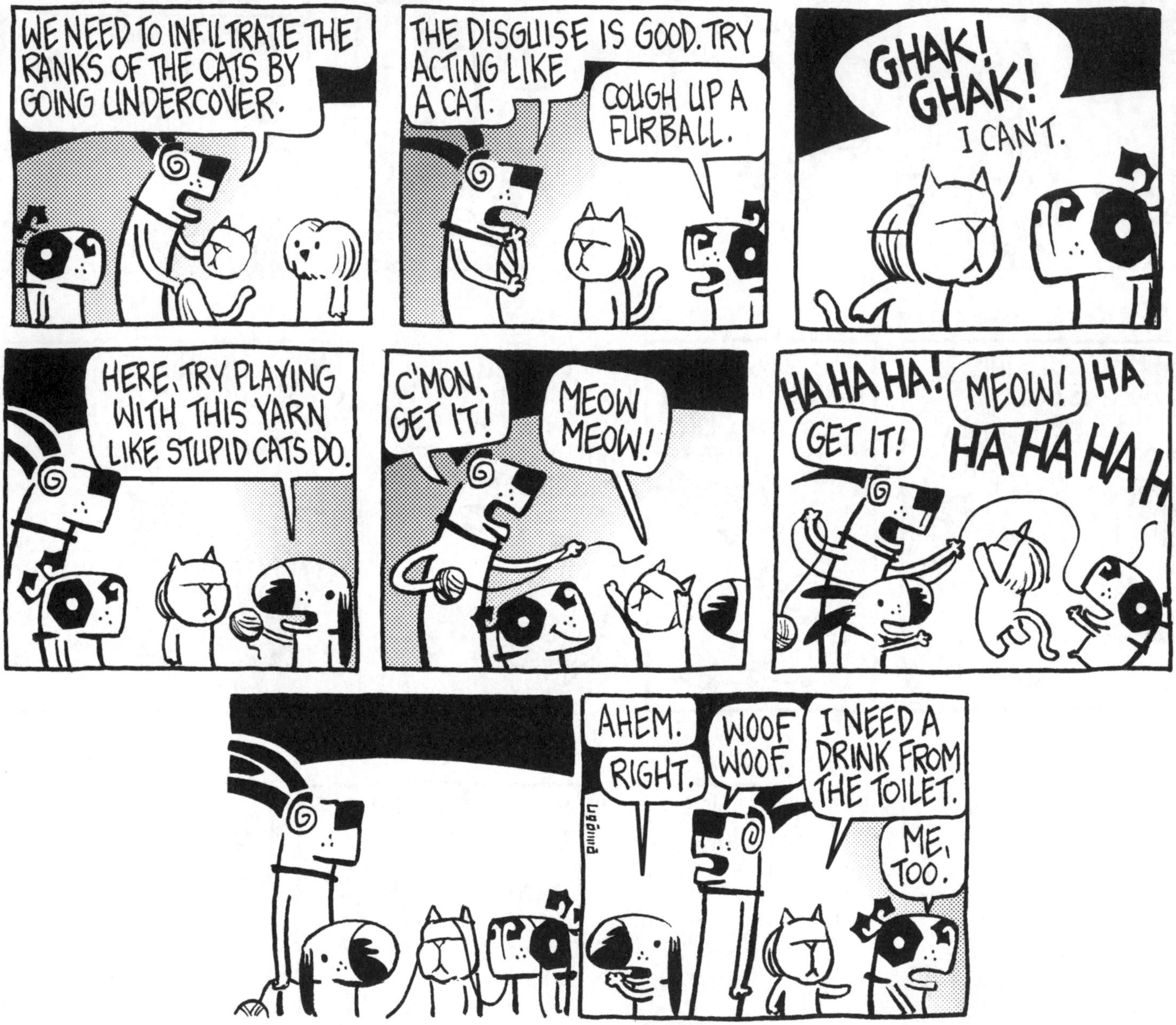
WE NEED TO INFILTRATE THE RANKS OF THE CATS BY GOING UNDERCOVER.
THE DISGUISE IS GOOD. TRY ACTING LIKE A CAT.
COUGH UP A FURBALL.
GHAK! GHAK!
I CAN'T.
HERE, TRY PLAYING WITH THIS YARN LIKE STUPID CATS DO.
C'MON, GET IT!
MEOW MEOW!
HA HA HA!
MEOW!
HA
GET IT!
HA HA HA HA H
AHEM.
RIGHT.
WOOF WOOF.
I NEED A DRINK FROM THE TOILET.
ME, TOO.

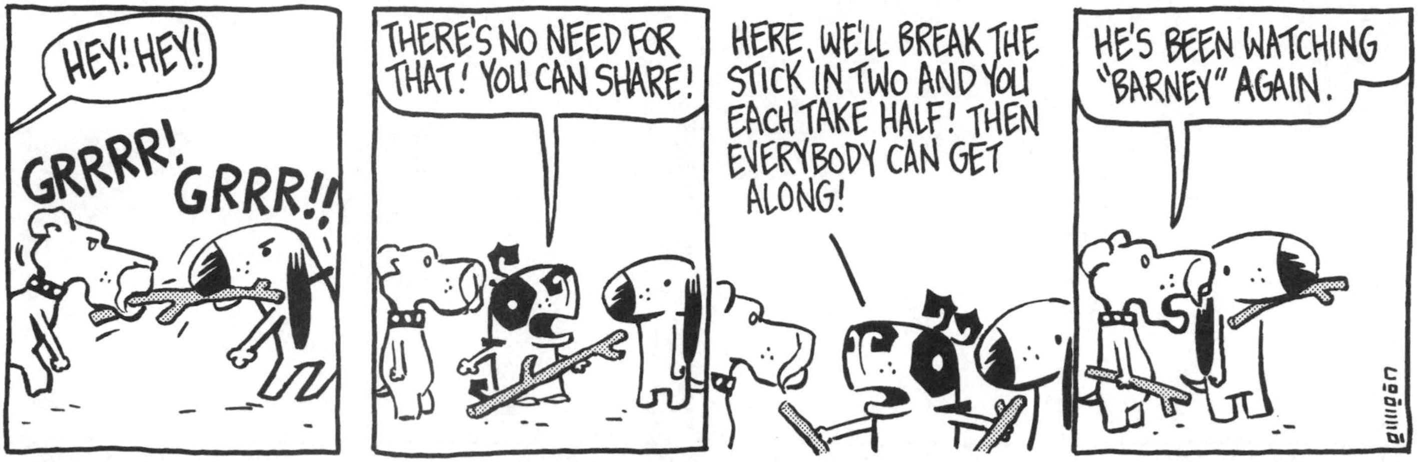
HEY! HEY!
GRRRR! GRRR!!
THERE'S NO NEED FOR THAT! YOU CAN SHARE!
HERE, WE'LL BREAK THE STICK IN TWO AND YOU EACH TAKE HALF! THEN EVERYBODY CAN GET ALONG!
HE'S BEEN WATCHING "BARNEY" AGAIN.

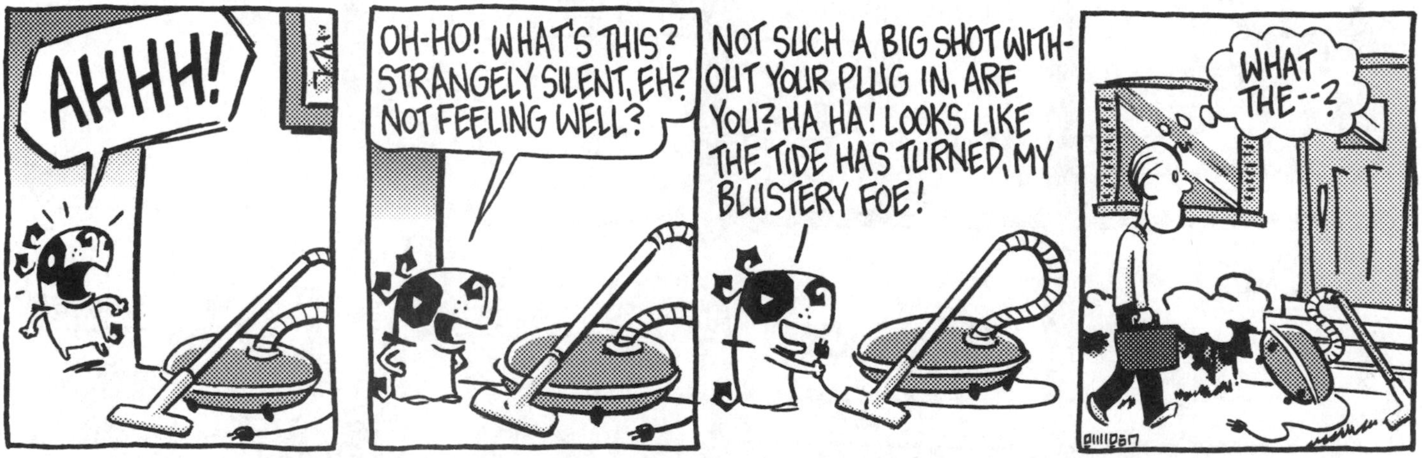
AHHH!
OH-HO! WHAT'S THIS? STRANGELY SILENT, EH? NOT FEELING WELL?
NOT SUCH A BIG SHOT WITH-OUT YOUR PLUG IN, ARE YOU? HA HA! LOOKS LIKE THE TIDE HAS TURNED, MY BLUSTERY FOE!
WHAT THE--?

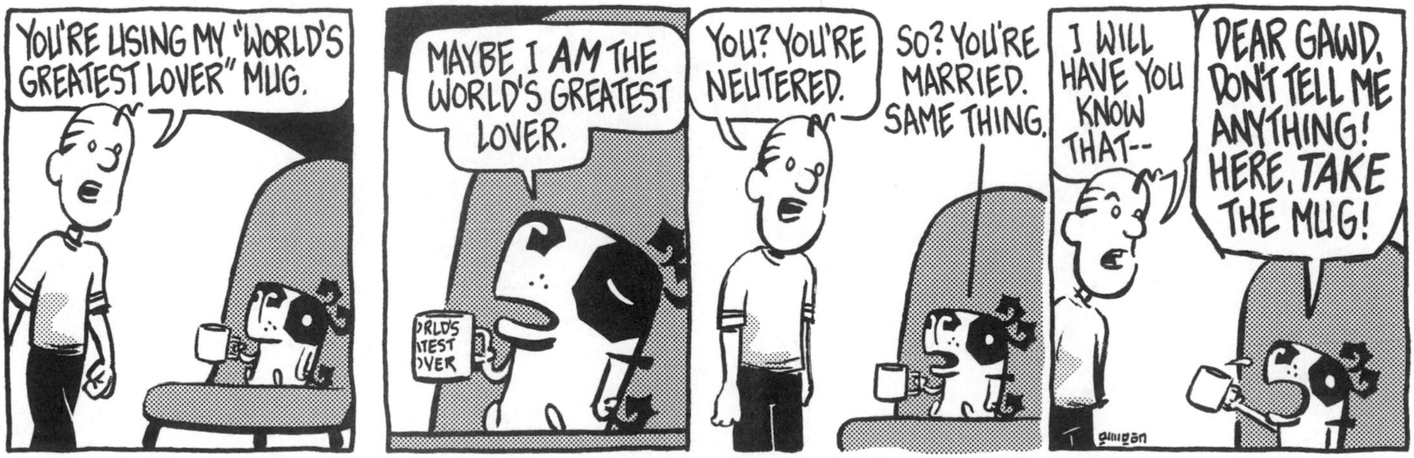
YOU'RE USING MY "WORLD'S GREATEST LOVER" MUG.
MAYBE I AM THE WORLD'S GREATEST LOVER.
YOU? YOU'RE NEUTERED.
SO? YOU'RE MARRIED. SAME THING.
I WILL HAVE YOU KNOW THAT--
DEAR GAWD, DON'T TELL ME ANYTHING! HERE, TAKE THE MUG!

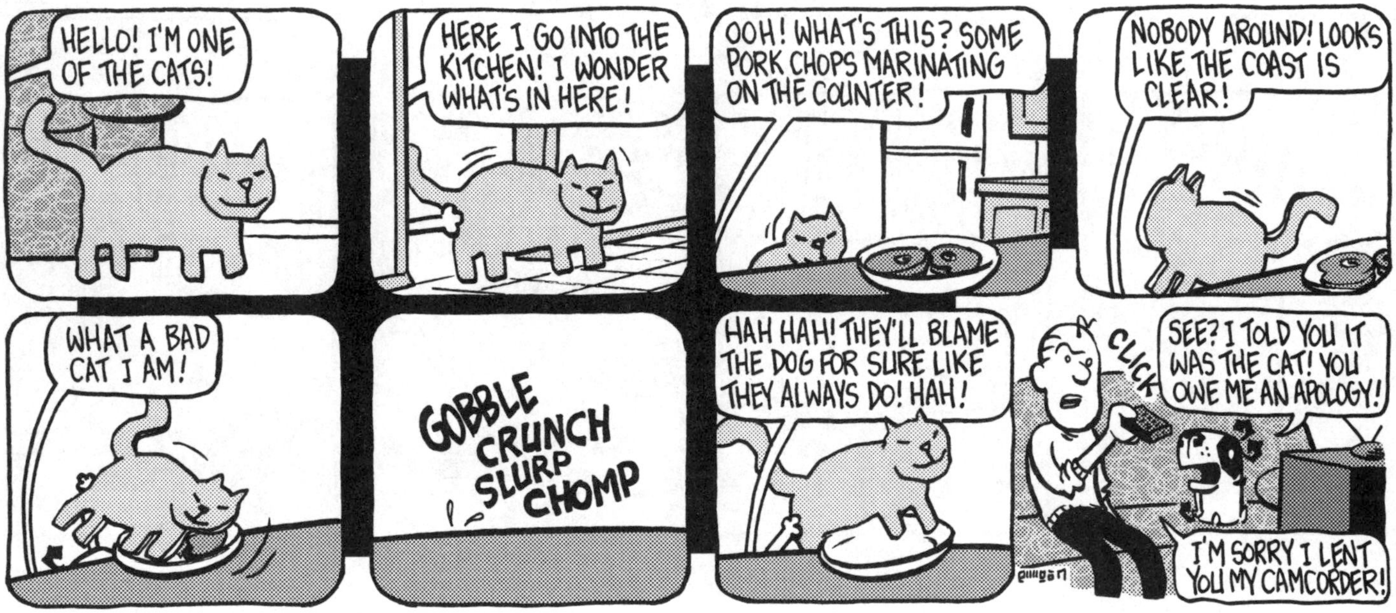
HELLO! I'M ONE OF THE CATS!
HERE I GO INTO THE KITCHEN! I WONDER WHAT'S IN HERE!
OOH! WHAT'S THIS? SOME PORK CHOPS MARINATING ON THE COUNTER!
NOBODY AROUND! LOOKS LIKE THE COAST IS CLEAR!
WHAT A BAD CAT I AM!
GOBBLE
CRUNCH
SLURP
CHOMP
HAH HAH! THEY'LL BLAME THE DOG FOR SURE LIKE THEY ALWAYS DO! HAH!
CLICK
SEE? I TOLD YOU IT WAS THE CAT! YOU OWE ME AN APOLOGY!
I'M SORRY I LENT YOU MY CAMCORDER!

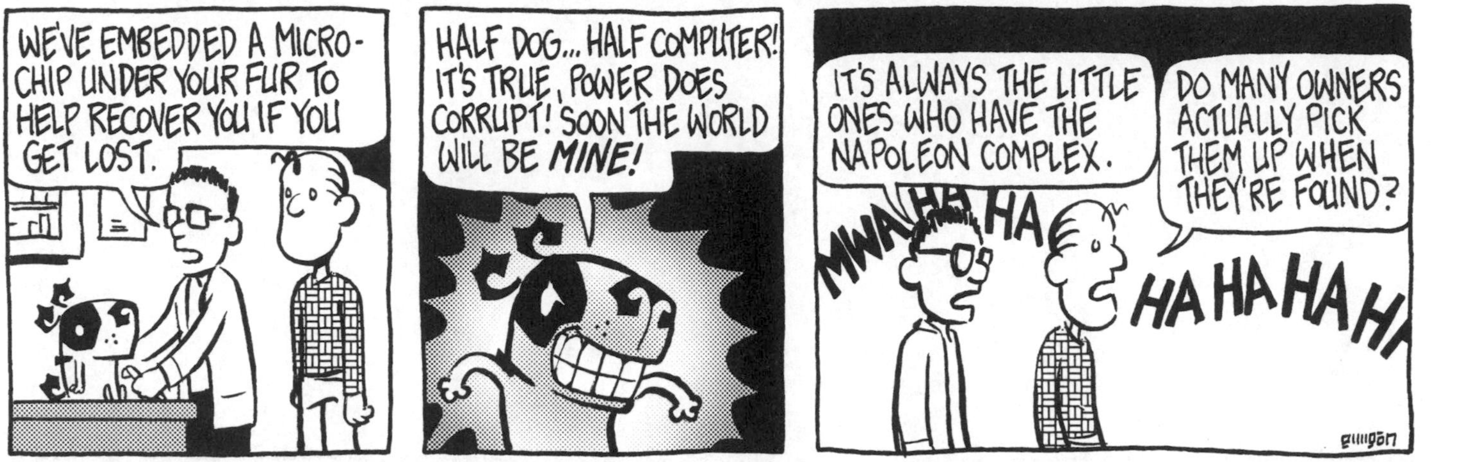
WE'VE EMBEDDED A MICRO-CHIP UNDER YOUR FUR TO HELP RECOVER YOU IF YOU GET LOST.
HALF DOG... HALF COMPUTER! IT'S TRUE, POWER DOES CORRUPT! SOON THE WORLD WILL BE MINE!
IT'S ALWAYS THE LITTLE ONES WHO HAVE THE NAPOLEON COMPLEX.
DO MANY OWNERS ACTUALLY PICK THEM UP WHEN THEY'RE FOUND?
MWAHAHAHA
HAHAHAHA

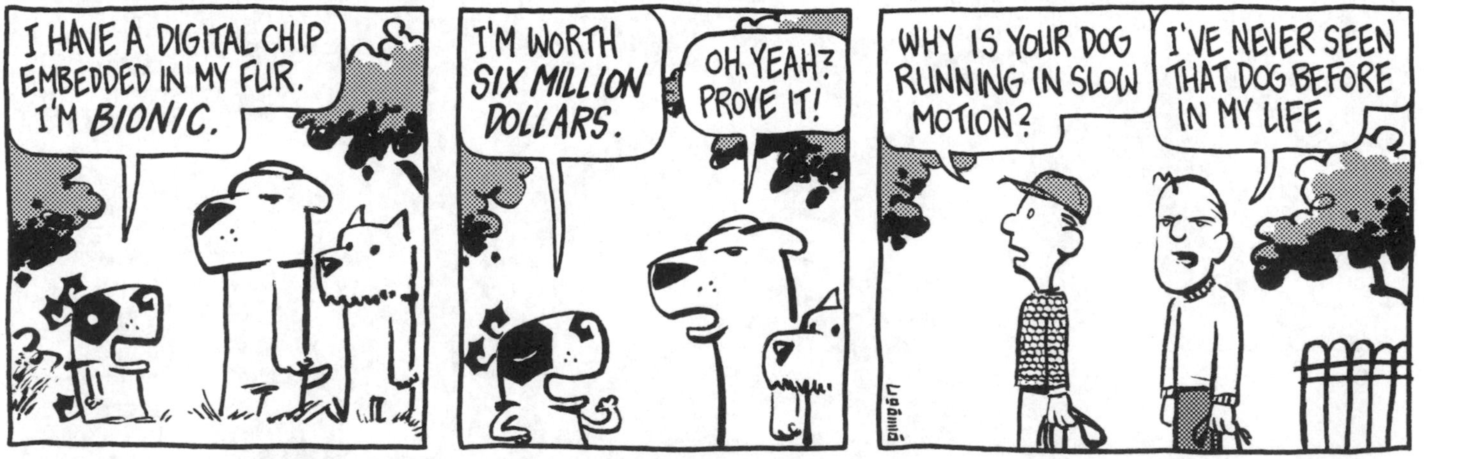
I HAVE A DIGITAL CHIP EMBEDDED IN MY FUR. I'M BIONIC.
I'M WORTH SIX MILLION DOLLARS.
OH, YEAH? PROVE IT!
WHY IS YOUR DOG RUNNING IN SLOW MOTION?
I'VE NEVER SEEN THAT DOG BEFORE IN MY LIFE.

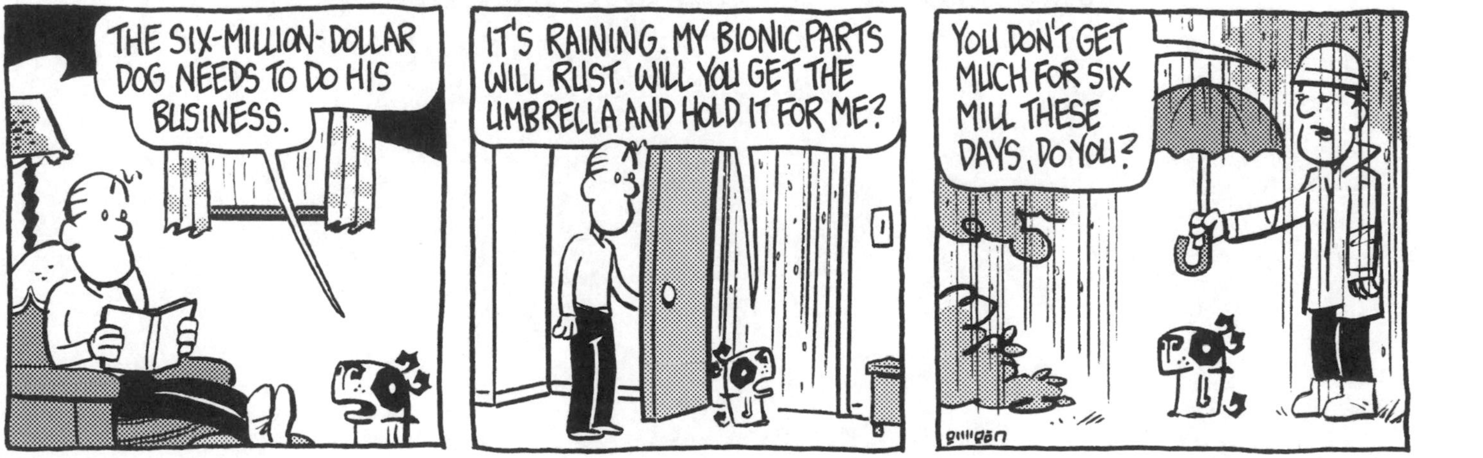
THE SIX-MILLION-DOLLAR DOG NEEDS TO DO HIS BUSINESS.
IT'S RAINING. MY BIONIC PARTS WILL RUST. WILL YOU GET THE UMBRELLA AND HOLD IT FOR ME?
YOU DON'T GET MUCH FOR SIX MILL THESE DAYS, DO YOU?

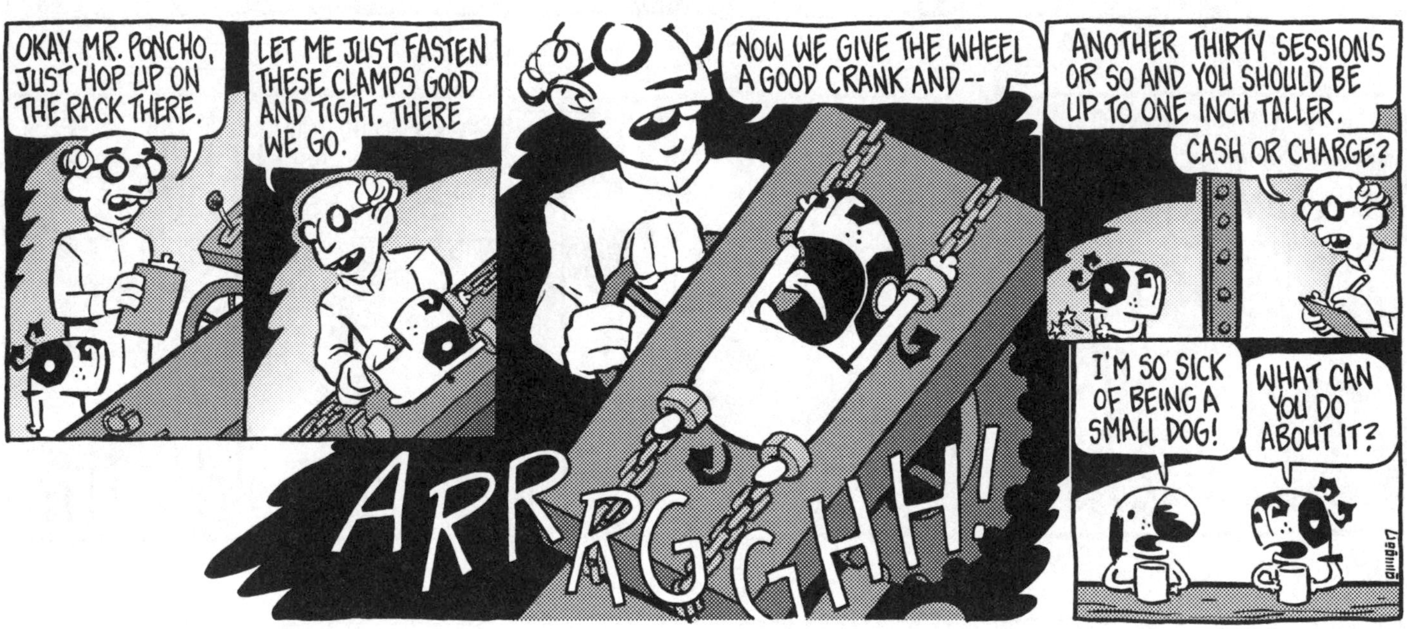
OKAY, MR. PONCHO, JUST HOP UP ON THE RACK THERE.
LET ME JUST FASTEN THESE CLAMPS GOOD AND TIGHT. THERE WE GO.
NOW WE GIVE THE WHEEL A GOOD CRANK AND--
ARRRGGHH!
ANOTHER THIRTY SESSIONS OR SO AND YOU SHOULD BE UP TO ONE INCH TALLER.
CASH OR CHARGE?
I'M SO SICK OF BEING A SMALL DOG!
WHAT CAN YOU DO ABOUT IT?

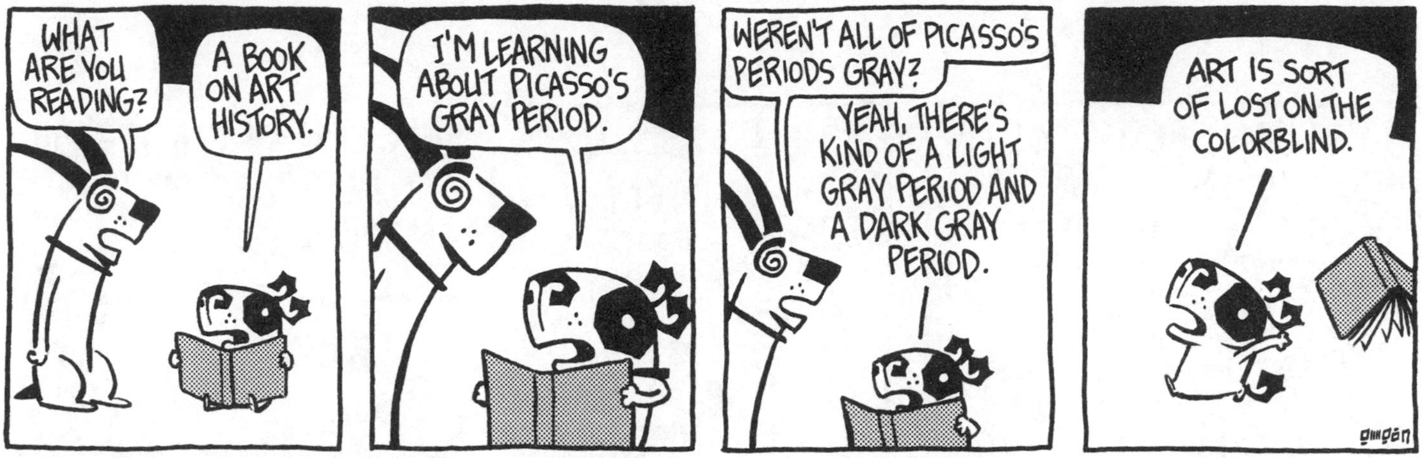
WHAT ARE YOU READING?
A BOOK ON ART HISTORY.
I'M LEARNING ABOUT PICASSO'S GRAY PERIOD.
WEREN'T ALL OF PICASSO'S PERIODS GRAY?
YEAH, THERE'S KIND OF A LIGHT GRAY PERIOD AND A DARK GRAY PERIOD.
ART IS SORT OF LOST ON THE COLORBLIND.

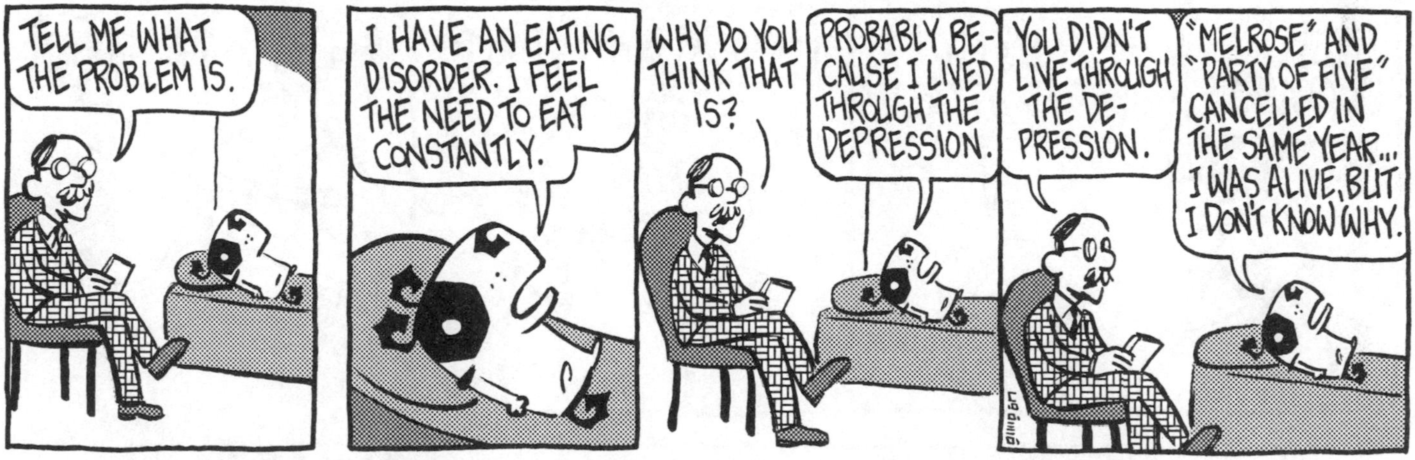
TELL ME WHAT THE PROBLEM IS.
I HAVE AN EATING DISORDER. I FEEL THE NEED TO EAT CONSTANTLY.
WHY DO YOU THINK THAT IS?
PROBABLY BE-CAUSE I LIVED THROUGH THE DEPRESSION.
YOU DIDN'T LIVE THROUGH THE DE-PRESSION.
"MELROSE" AND "PARTY OF FIVE" CANCELLED IN THE SAME YEAR... I WAS ALIVE, BUT I DON'T KNOW WHY.

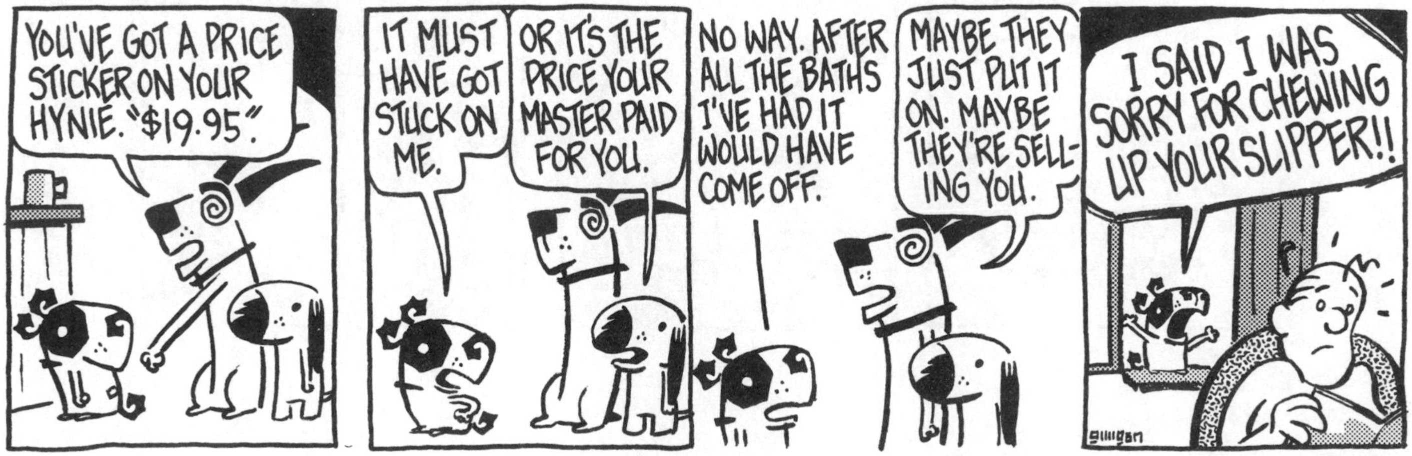
YOU'VE GOT A PRICE STICKER ON YOUR HYNIE. "$19.95".
IT MUST HAVE GOT STUCK ON ME.
OR IT'S THE PRICE YOUR MASTER PAID FOR YOU.
NO WAY. AFTER ALL THE BATHS I'VE HAD IT WOULD HAVE COME OFF.
MAYBE THEY JUST PUT IT ON. MAYBE THEY'RE SELL-ING YOU.
I SAID I WAS SORRY FOR CHEWING UP YOUR SLIPPER!!

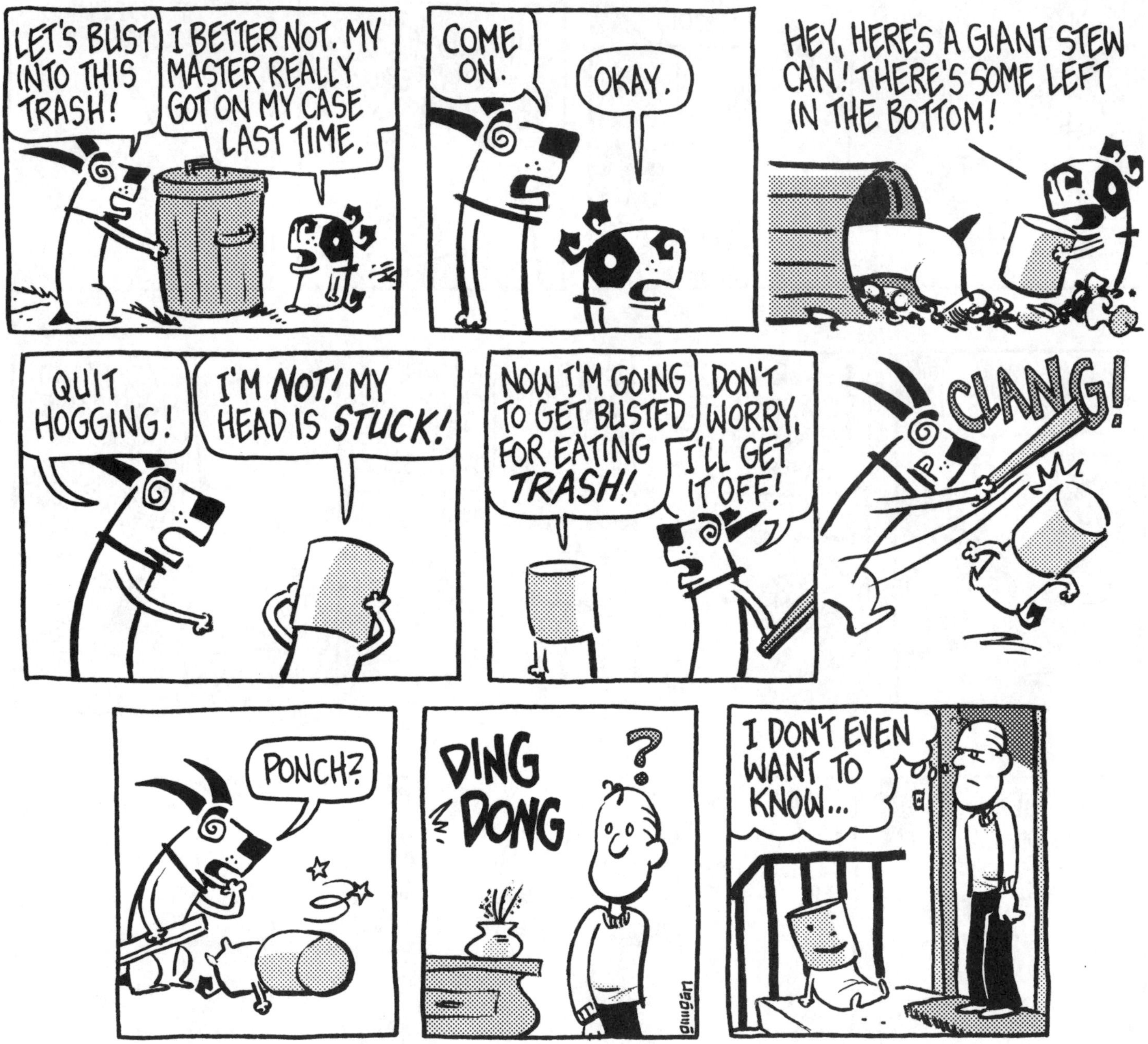
LET'S BUST INTO THIS TRASH!
I BETTER NOT. MY MASTER REALLY GOT ON MY CASE LAST TIME.
COME ON.
OKAY.
HEY, HERE'S A GIANT STEW CAN! THERE'S SOME LEFT IN THE BOTTOM!
QUIT HOGGING!
I'M NOT! MY HEAD IS STUCK!
NOW I'M GOING TO GET BUSTED FOR EATING TRASH!
DON'T WORRY, I'LL GET IT OFF!
CLANG!
PONCH?
DING DONG
?
I DON'T EVEN WANT TO KNOW...

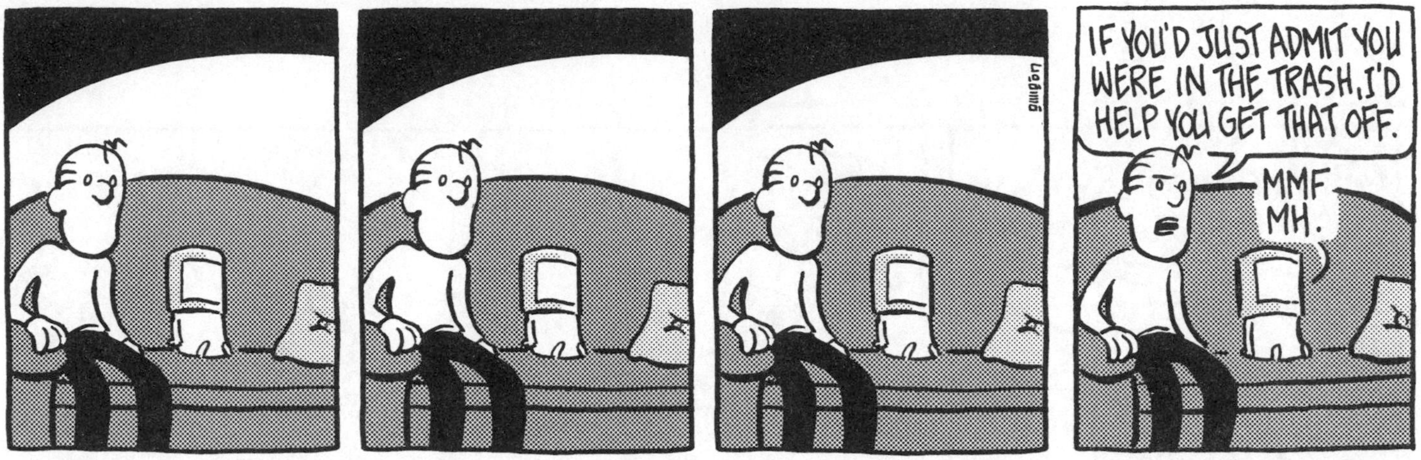
IF YOU'D JUST ADMIT YOU WERE IN THE TRASH, I'D HELP YOU GET THAT OFF.
MMF MH.

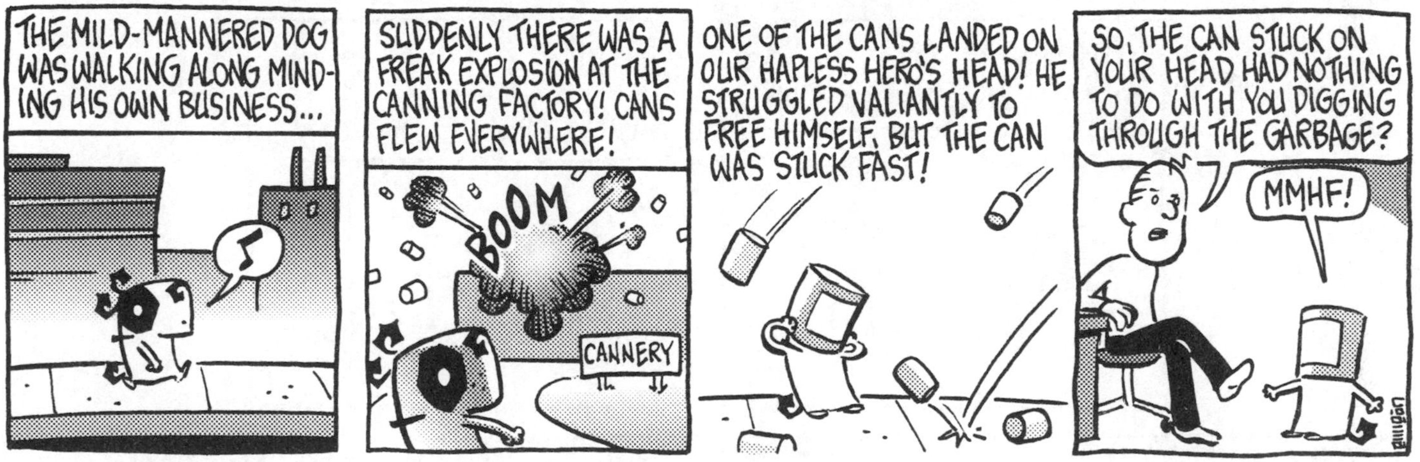
THE MILD-MANNERED DOG WAS WALKING ALONG MINDING HIS OWN BUSINESS...
SUDDENLY THERE WAS A FREAK EXPLOSION AT THE CANNING FACTORY! CANS FLEW EVERYWHERE!
BOOM
CANNERY
ONE OF THE CANS LANDED ON OUR HAPLESS HERO'S HEAD! HE STRUGGLED VALIANTLY TO FREE HIMSELF, BUT THE CAN WAS STUCK FAST!
SO, THE CAN STUCK ON YOUR HEAD HAD NOTHING TO DO WITH YOU DIGGING THROUGH THE GARBAGE?
MMHF!

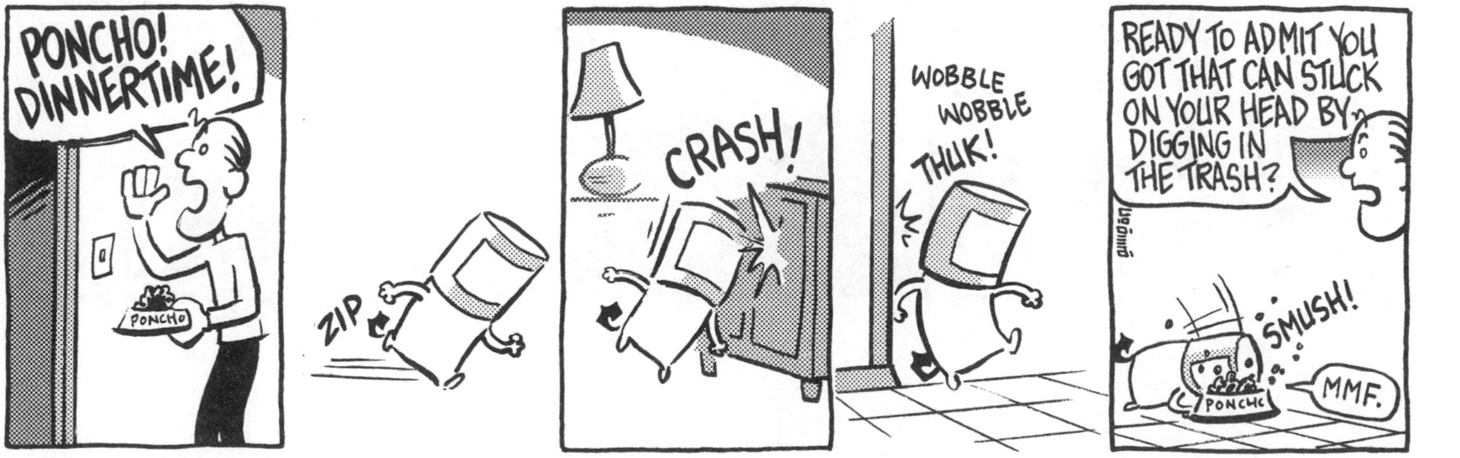
PONCHO! DINNERTIME!
PONCHO
ZIP
CRASH!
WOBBLE WOBBLE
THUK!
READY TO ADMIT YOU GOT THAT CAN STUCK ON YOUR HEAD BY DIGGING IN THE TRASH?
SMUSH!
MMF.
PONCHO

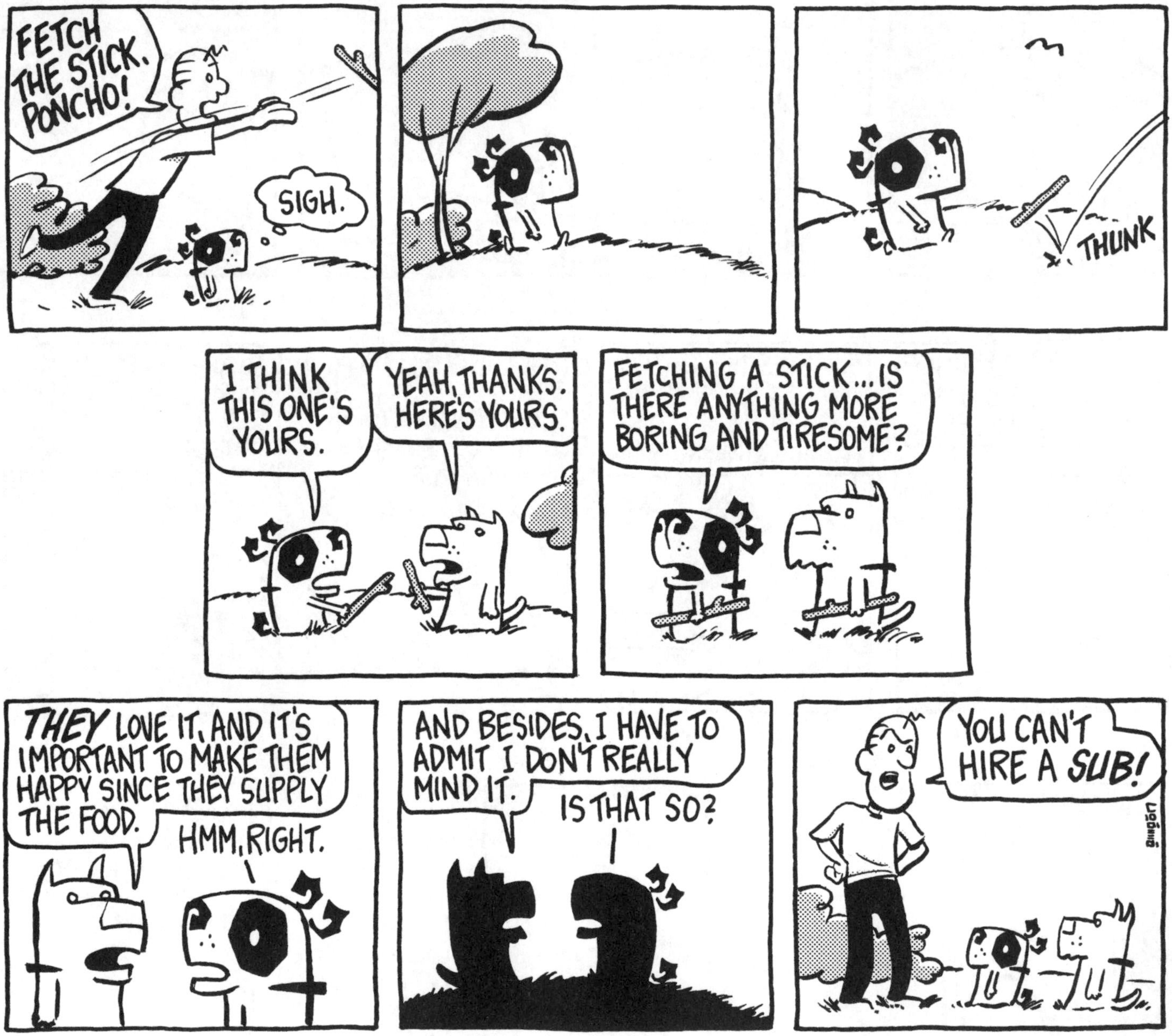
FETCH THE STICK, PONCHO!
SIGH.
THUNK
I THINK THIS ONE'S YOURS.
YEAH, THANKS. HERE'S YOURS.
FETCHING A STICK... IS THERE ANYTHING MORE BORING AND TIRESOME?
THEY LOVE IT, AND IT'S IMPORTANT TO MAKE THEM HAPPY SINCE THEY SUPPLY THE FOOD.
HMM, RIGHT.
AND BESIDES, I HAVE TO ADMIT I DON'T REALLY MIND IT.
IS THAT SO?
YOU CAN'T HIRE A *SUB*!

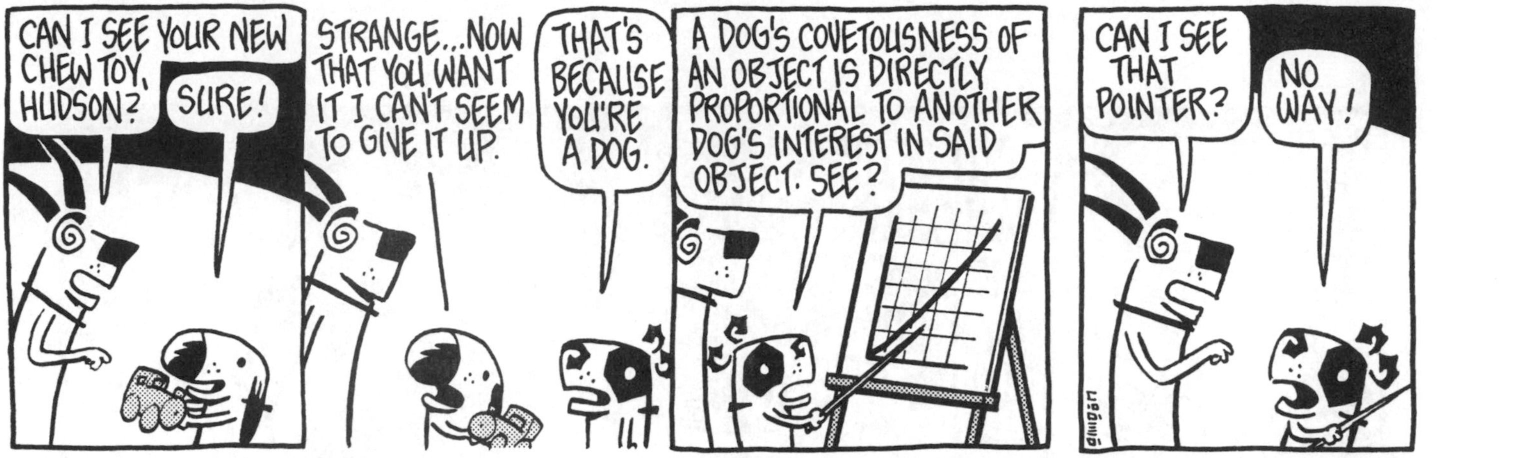
CAN I SEE YOUR NEW CHEW TOY, HUDSON?
SURE!
STRANGE...NOW THAT YOU WANT IT I CAN'T SEEM TO GIVE IT UP.
THAT'S BECAUSE YOU'RE A DOG.
A DOG'S COVETOUSNESS OF AN OBJECT IS DIRECTLY PROPORTIONAL TO ANOTHER DOG'S INTEREST IN SAID OBJECT. SEE?
CAN I SEE THAT POINTER?
NO WAY!

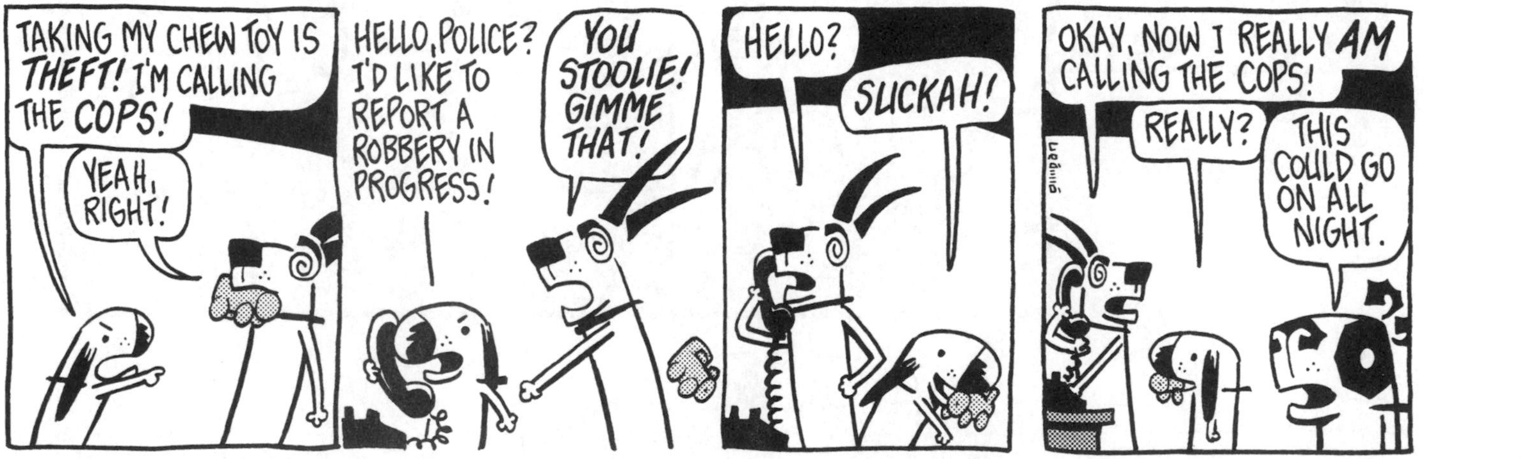
TAKING MY CHEW TOY IS *THEFT!* I'M CALLING THE *COPS!*
YEAH, RIGHT!
HELLO, POLICE? I'D LIKE TO REPORT A ROBBERY IN PROGRESS!
YOU STOOLIE! GIMME THAT!
HELLO?
SUCKAH!
OKAY, NOW I REALLY *AM* CALLING THE COPS!
REALLY?
THIS COULD GO ON ALL NIGHT.

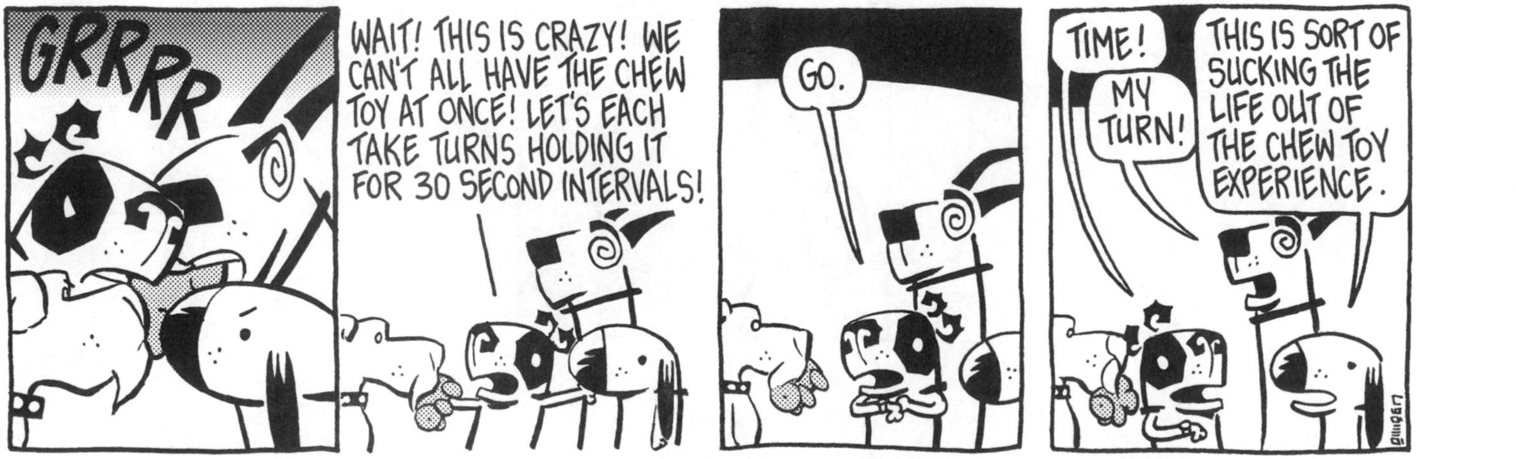
GRRRR
WAIT! THIS IS CRAZY! WE CAN'T ALL HAVE THE CHEW TOY AT ONCE! LET'S EACH TAKE TURNS HOLDING IT FOR 30 SECOND INTERVALS!
GO.
TIME!
MY TURN!
THIS IS SORT OF SUCKING THE LIFE OUT OF THE CHEW TOY EXPERIENCE.

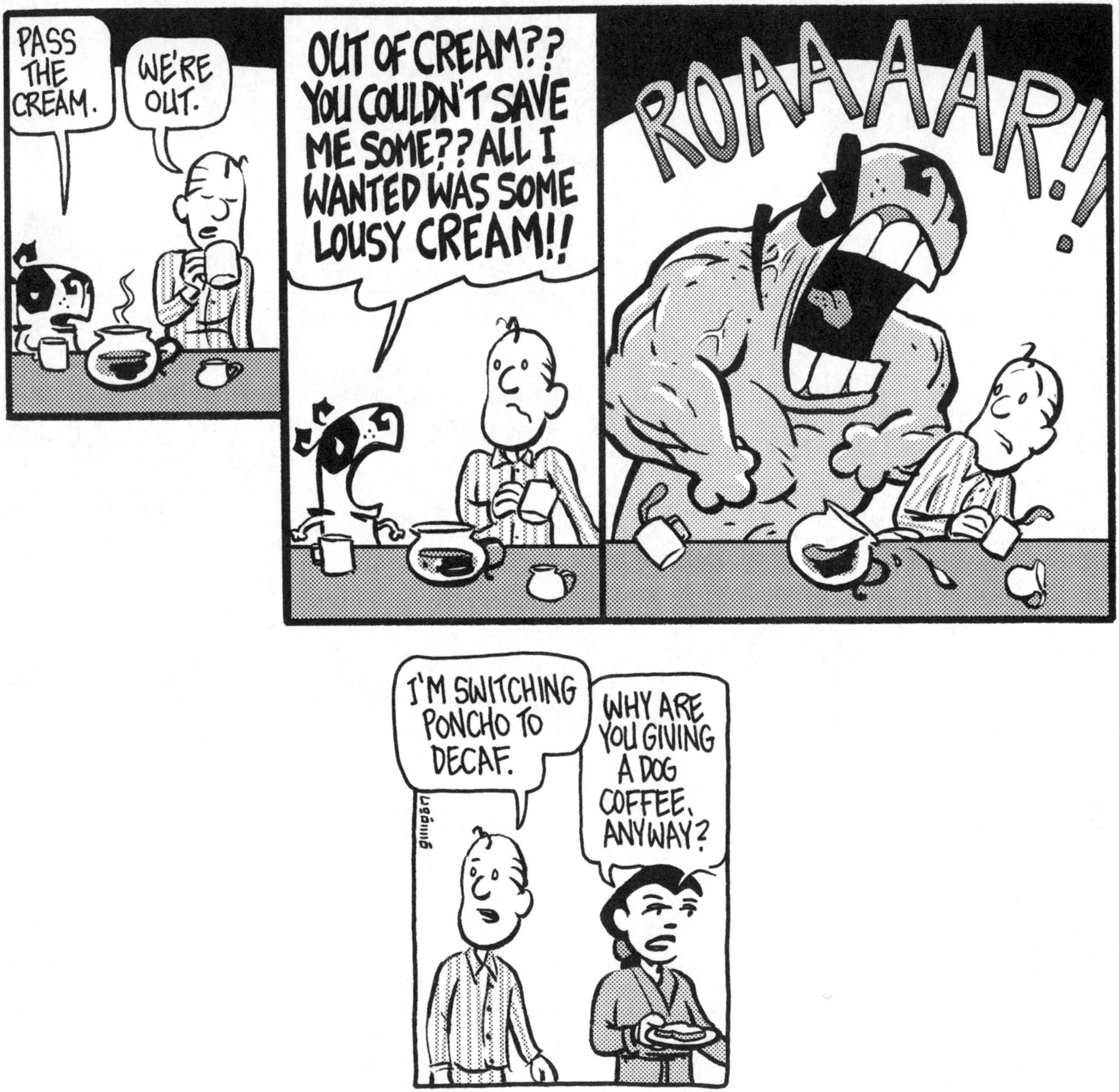
PASS THE CREAM.
WE'RE OUT.
OUT OF CREAM?? YOU COULDN'T SAVE ME SOME?? ALL I WANTED WAS SOME LOUSY CREAM!!
ROAAAAAR!!
I'M SWITCHING PONCHO TO DECAF.
WHY ARE YOU GIVING A DOG COFFEE, ANYWAY?
gilligan

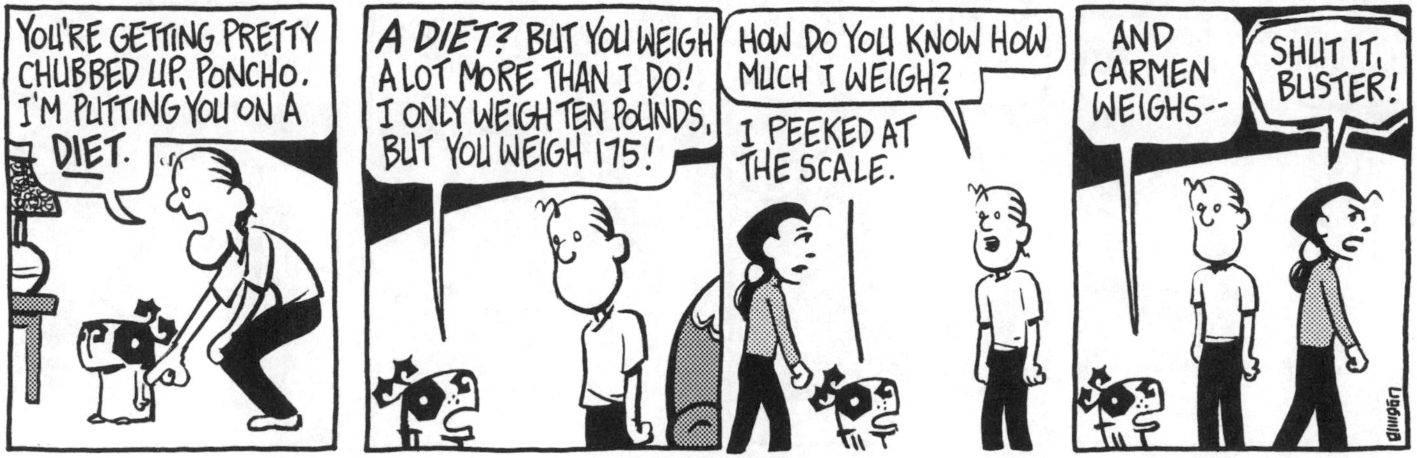
YOU'RE GETTING PRETTY CHUBBED UP, PONCHO. I'M PUTTING YOU ON A DIET.
A DIET? BUT YOU WEIGH A LOT MORE THAN I DO! I ONLY WEIGH TEN POUNDS, BUT YOU WEIGH 175!
HOW DO YOU KNOW HOW MUCH I WEIGH?
I PEEKED AT THE SCALE.
AND CARMEN WEIGHS--
SHUT IT, BUSTER!

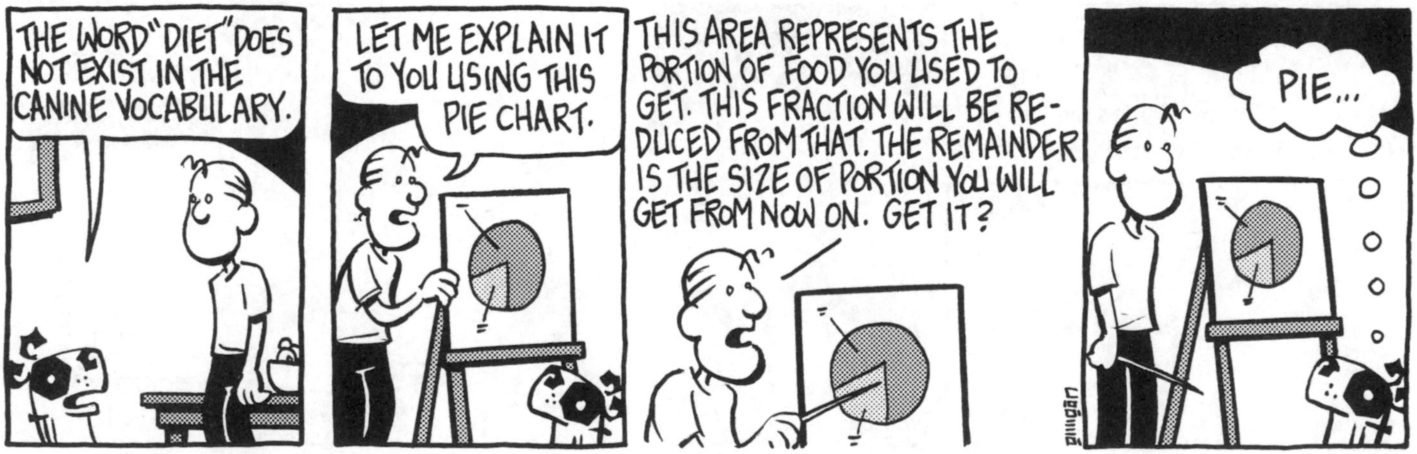
THE WORD "DIET" DOES NOT EXIST IN THE CANINE VOCABULARY.
LET ME EXPLAIN IT TO YOU USING THIS PIE CHART.
THIS AREA REPRESENTS THE PORTION OF FOOD YOU USED TO GET. THIS FRACTION WILL BE RE-DUCED FROM THAT. THE REMAINDER IS THE SIZE OF PORTION YOU WILL GET FROM NOW ON. GET IT?
PIE...

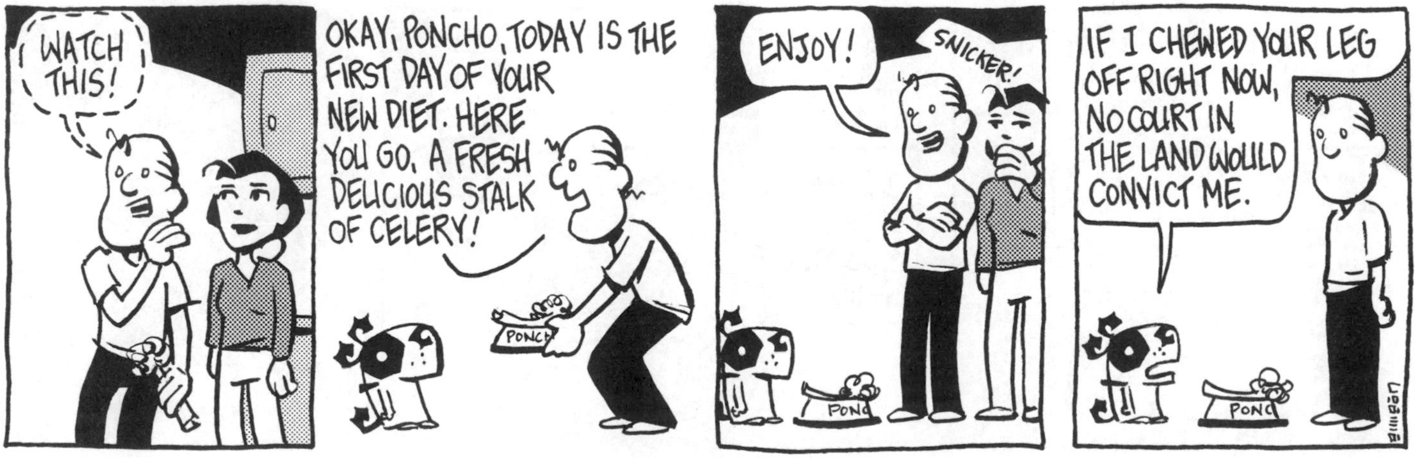
WATCH THIS!
OKAY, PONCHO, TODAY IS THE FIRST DAY OF YOUR NEW DIET. HERE YOU GO, A FRESH DELICIOUS STALK OF CELERY!
PONCH
ENJOY!
SNICKER!
PONC
IF I CHEWED YOUR LEG OFF RIGHT NOW, NO COURT IN THE LAND WOULD CONVICT ME.
PONC

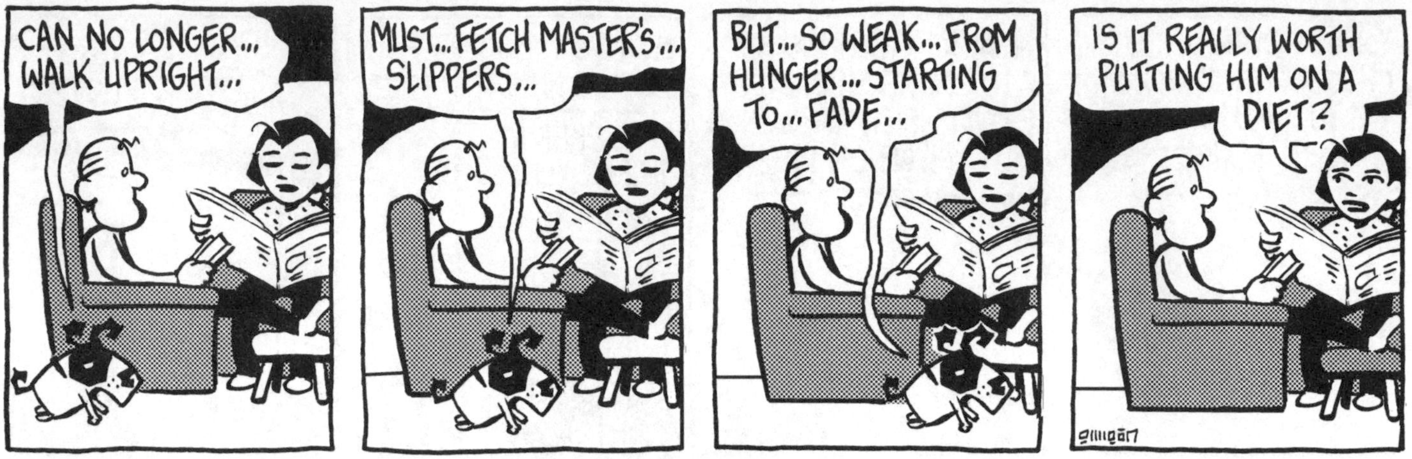
CAN NO LONGER... WALK UPRIGHT...
MUST... FETCH MASTER'S... SLIPPERS...
BUT... SO WEAK... FROM HUNGER... STARTING TO... FADE...
IS IT REALLY WORTH PUTTING HIM ON A DIET?

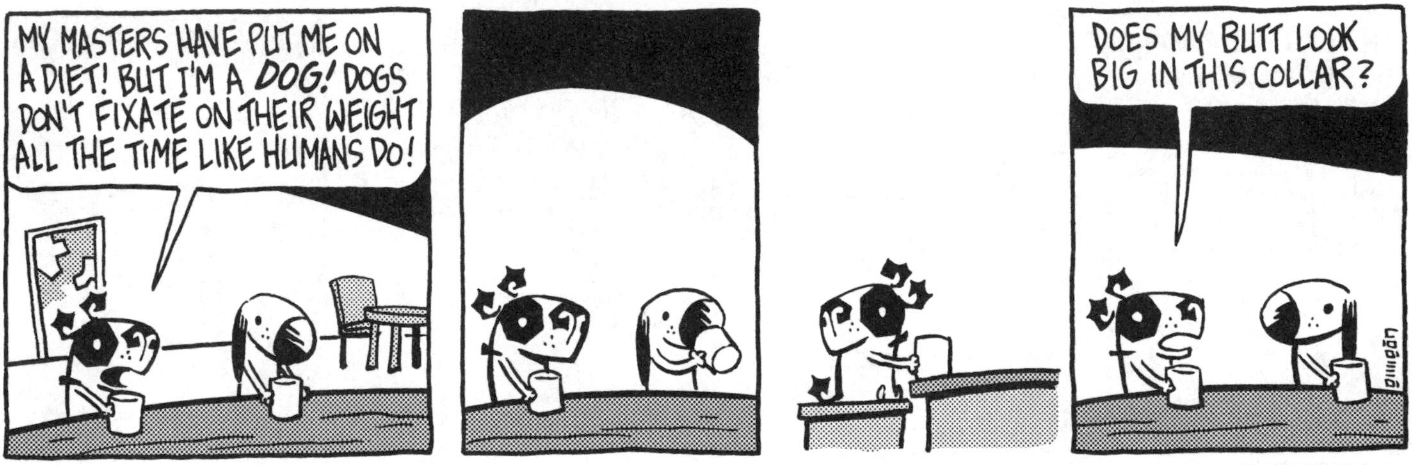
MY MASTERS HAVE PUT ME ON A DIET! BUT I'M A DOG! DOGS DON'T FIXATE ON THEIR WEIGHT ALL THE TIME LIKE HUMANS DO!
DOES MY BUTT LOOK BIG IN THIS COLLAR?

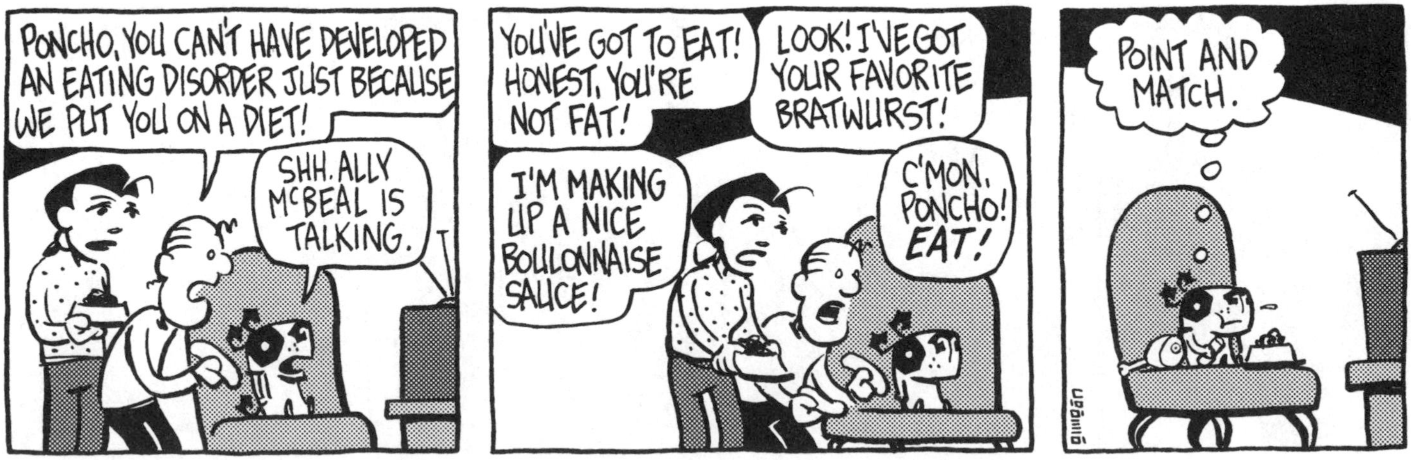
PONCHO, YOU CAN'T HAVE DEVELOPED AN EATING DISORDER JUST BECAUSE WE PUT YOU ON A DIET!
SHH. ALLY McBEAL IS TALKING.
YOU'VE GOT TO EAT! HONEST, YOU'RE NOT FAT!
LOOK! I'VE GOT YOUR FAVORITE BRATWURST!
I'M MAKING UP A NICE BOULONNAISE SAUCE!
C'MON, PONCHO! EAT!
POINT AND MATCH.

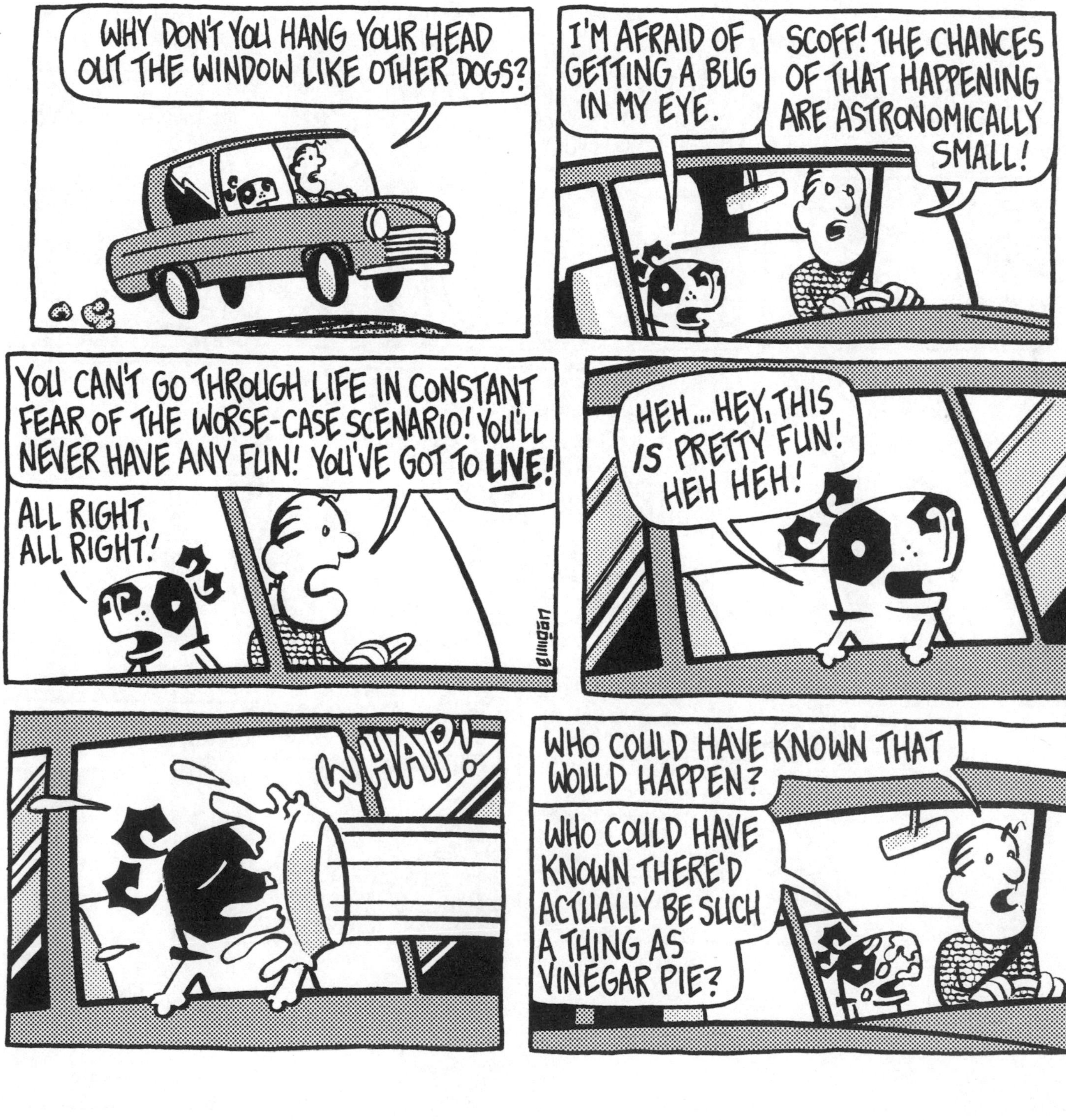
WHY DON'T YOU HANG YOUR HEAD OUT THE WINDOW LIKE OTHER DOGS?
I'M AFRAID OF GETTING A BUG IN MY EYE.
SCOFF! THE CHANCES OF THAT HAPPENING ARE ASTRONOMICALLY SMALL!
YOU CAN'T GO THROUGH LIFE IN CONSTANT FEAR OF THE WORSE-CASE SCENARIO! YOU'LL NEVER HAVE ANY FUN! YOU'VE GOT TO LIVE!
ALL RIGHT, ALL RIGHT!
gilligan
HEH... HEY, THIS IS PRETTY FUN! HEH HEH!
WHAP!
WHO COULD HAVE KNOWN THAT WOULD HAPPEN?
WHO COULD HAVE KNOWN THERE'D ACTUALLY BE SUCH A THING AS VINEGAR PIE?

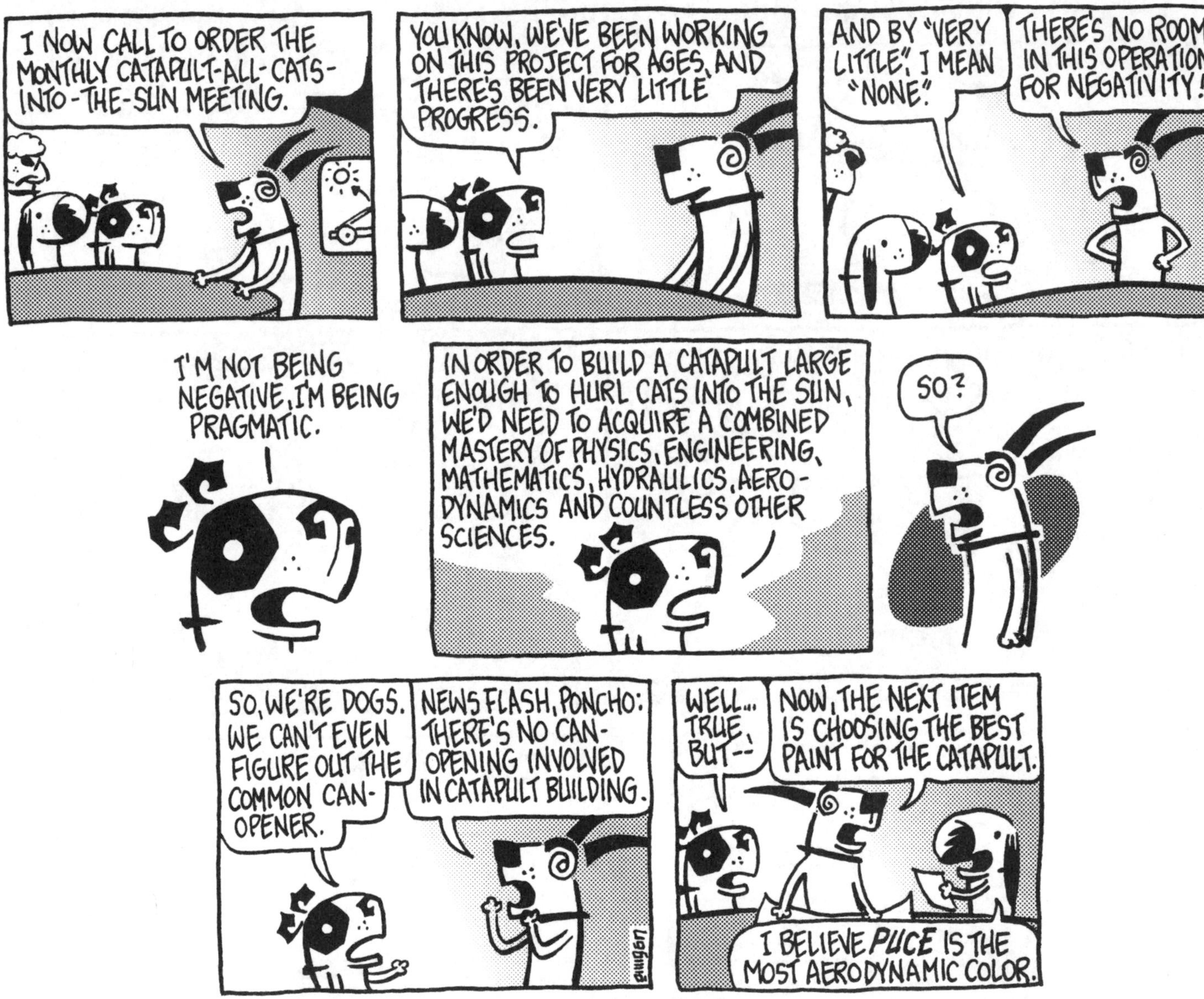
I NOW CALL TO ORDER THE MONTHLY CATAPULT-ALL-CATS-INTO-THE-SUN MEETING.
YOU KNOW, WE'VE BEEN WORKING ON THIS PROJECT FOR AGES, AND THERE'S BEEN VERY LITTLE PROGRESS.
AND BY "VERY LITTLE," I MEAN "NONE."
THERE'S NO ROOM IN THIS OPERATION FOR NEGATIVITY!
I'M NOT BEING NEGATIVE, I'M BEING PRAGMATIC.
IN ORDER TO BUILD A CATAPULT LARGE ENOUGH TO HURL CATS INTO THE SUN, WE'D NEED TO ACQUIRE A COMBINED MASTERY OF PHYSICS, ENGINEERING, MATHEMATICS, HYDRAULICS, AERO-DYNAMICS AND COUNTLESS OTHER SCIENCES.
SO?
SO, WE'RE DOGS. WE CAN'T EVEN FIGURE OUT THE COMMON CAN-OPENER.
NEWS FLASH, PONCHO: THERE'S NO CAN-OPENING INVOLVED IN CATAPULT BUILDING.
WELL... TRUE, BUT--!
NOW, THE NEXT ITEM IS CHOOSING THE BEST PAINT FOR THE CATAPULT.
I BELIEVE PUCE IS THE MOST AERODYNAMIC COLOR.

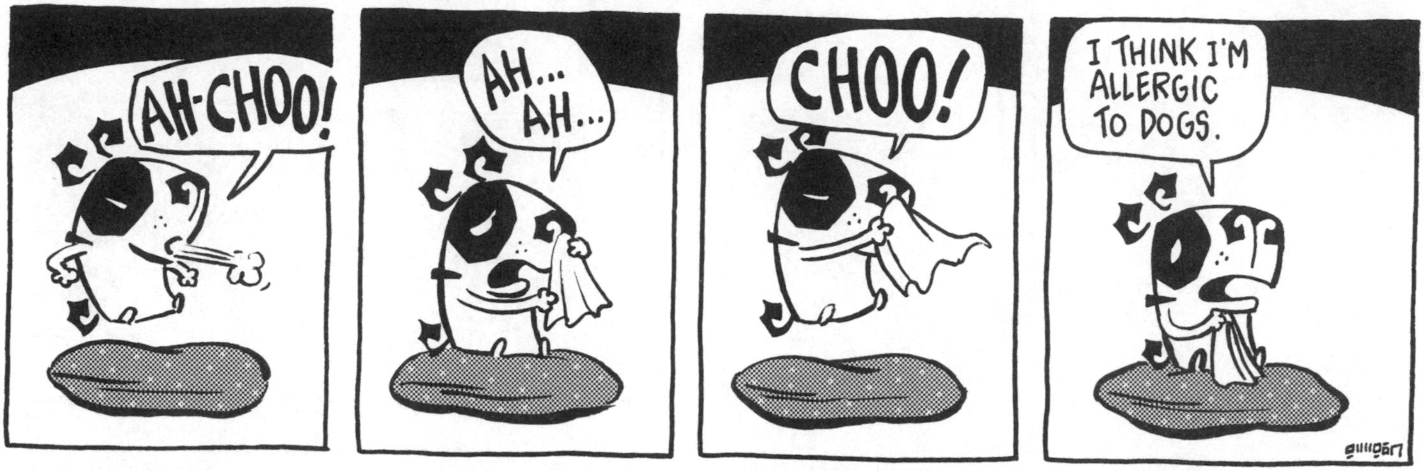
AH-CHOO!
AH... AH...
CHOO!
I THINK I'M ALLERGIC TO DOGS.

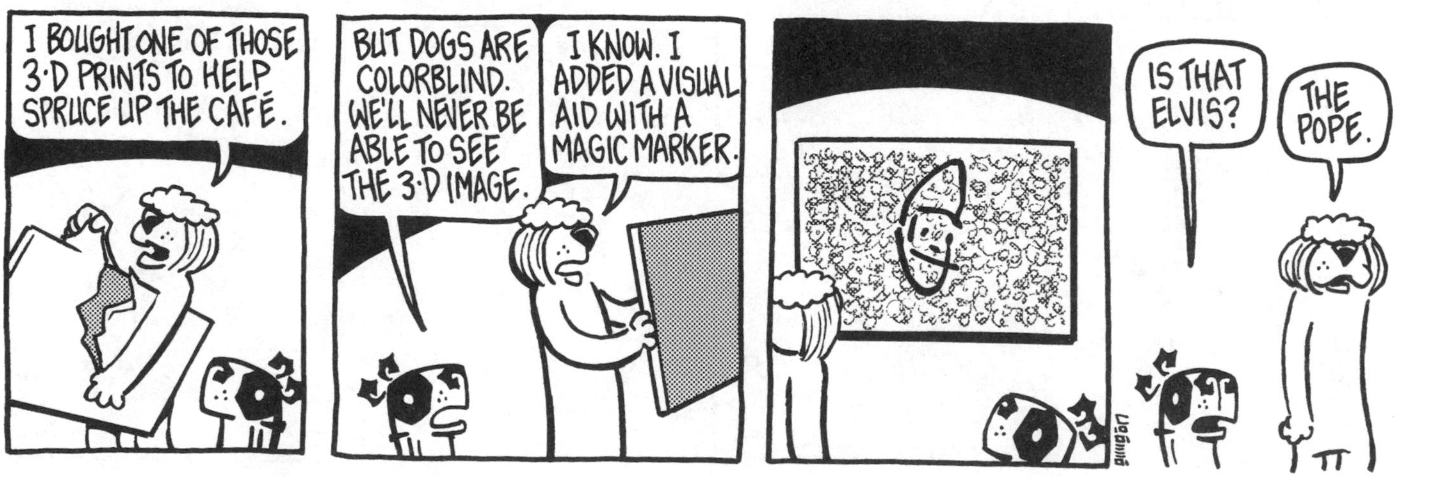
I BOUGHT ONE OF THOSE 3-D PRINTS TO HELP SPRUCE UP THE CAFÉ.
BUT DOGS ARE COLORBLIND. WE'LL NEVER BE ABLE TO SEE THE 3-D IMAGE.
I KNOW. I ADDED A VISUAL AID WITH A MAGIC MARKER.
IS THAT ELVIS?
THE POPE.

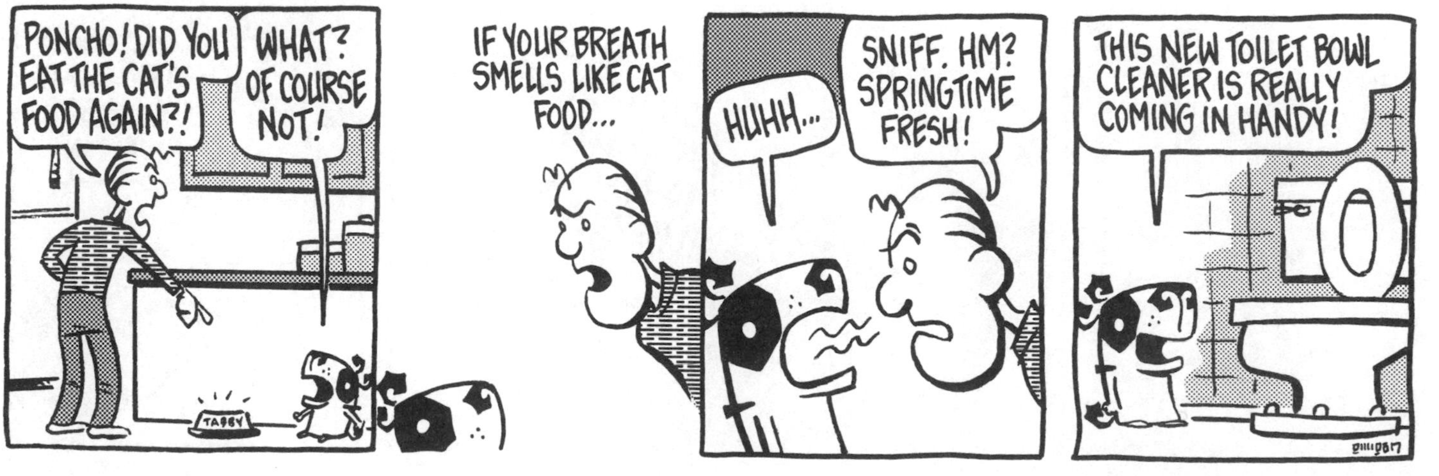
PONCHO! DID YOU EAT THE CAT'S FOOD AGAIN?!
WHAT? OF COURSE NOT!
TABBY
IF YOUR BREATH SMELLS LIKE CAT FOOD...
HUHH...
SNIFF. HM? SPRINGTIME FRESH!
THIS NEW TOILET BOWL CLEANER IS REALLY COMING IN HANDY!

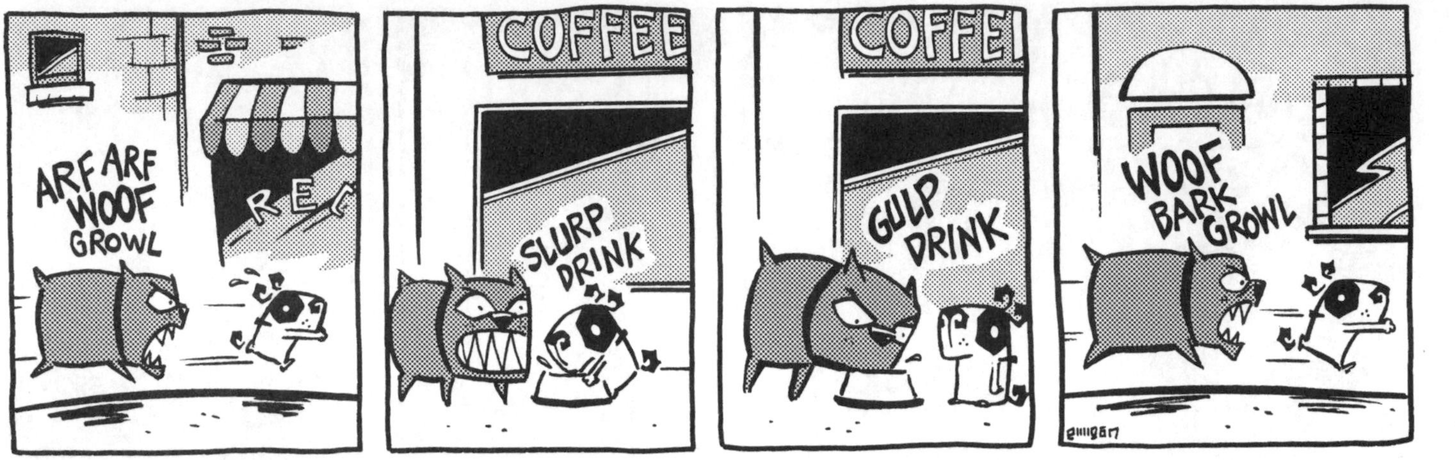
ARF ARF
WOOF
GROWL
COFFEE
SLURP
DRINK
COFFE
GULP
DRINK
WOOF
BARK
GROWL

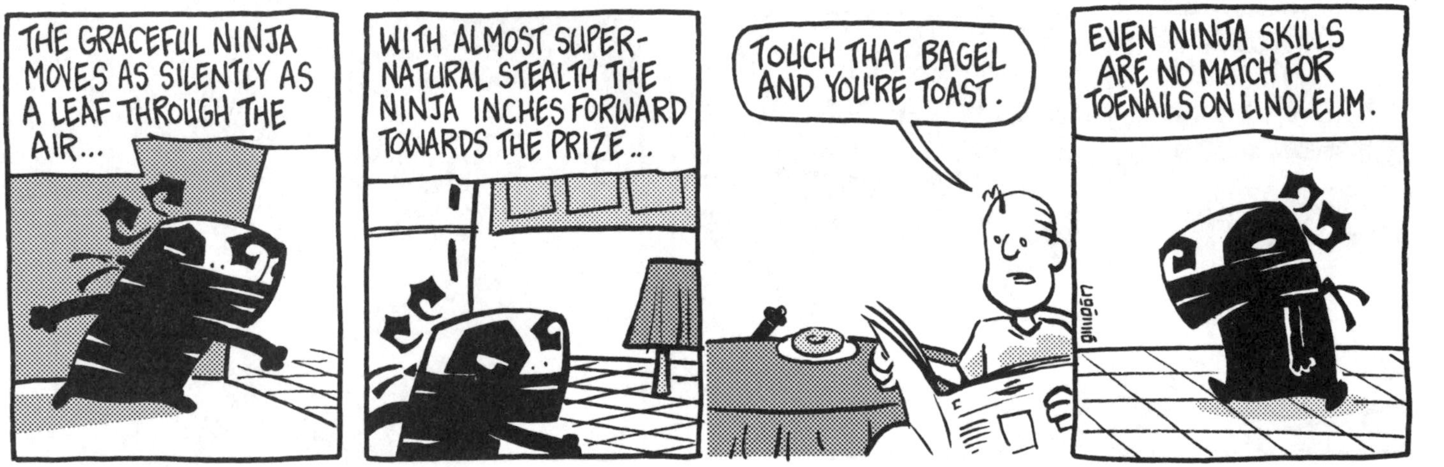
THE GRACEFUL NINJA MOVES AS SILENTLY AS A LEAF THROUGH THE AIR...
WITH ALMOST SUPER-NATURAL STEALTH THE NINJA INCHES FORWARD TOWARDS THE PRIZE...
TOUCH THAT BAGEL AND YOU'RE TOAST.
EVEN NINJA SKILLS ARE NO MATCH FOR TOENAILS ON LINOLEUM.

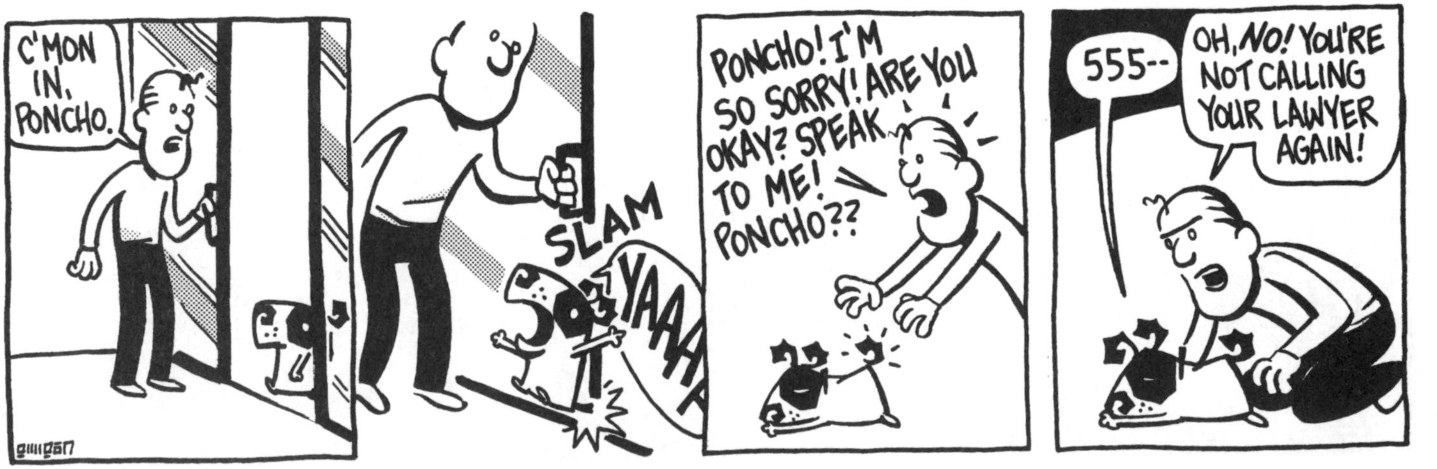
C'MON IN, PONCHO.
SLAM
YAAAAA
PONCHO! I'M SO SORRY! ARE YOU OKAY? SPEAK TO ME! PONCHO??
555--
OH, NO! YOU'RE NOT CALLING YOUR LAWYER AGAIN!

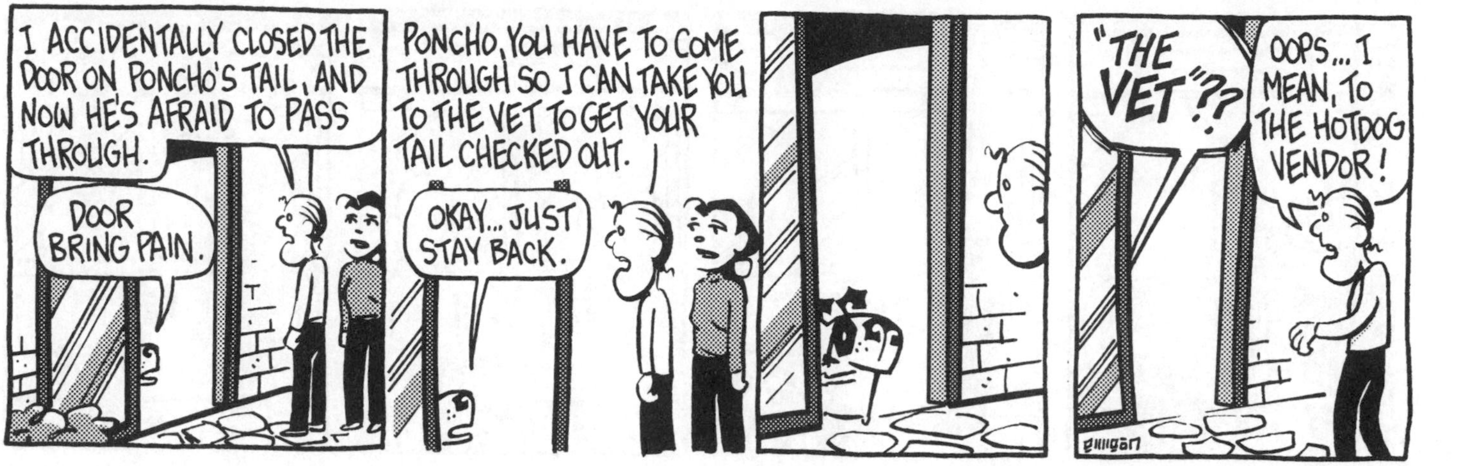
I ACCIDENTALLY CLOSED THE DOOR ON PONCHO'S TAIL, AND NOW HE'S AFRAID TO PASS THROUGH.
DOOR BRING PAIN.
PONCHO, YOU HAVE TO COME THROUGH SO I CAN TAKE YOU TO THE VET TO GET YOUR TAIL CHECKED OUT.
OKAY... JUST STAY BACK.
"THE VET"??
OOPS... I MEAN, TO THE HOTDOG VENDOR!
gilligan

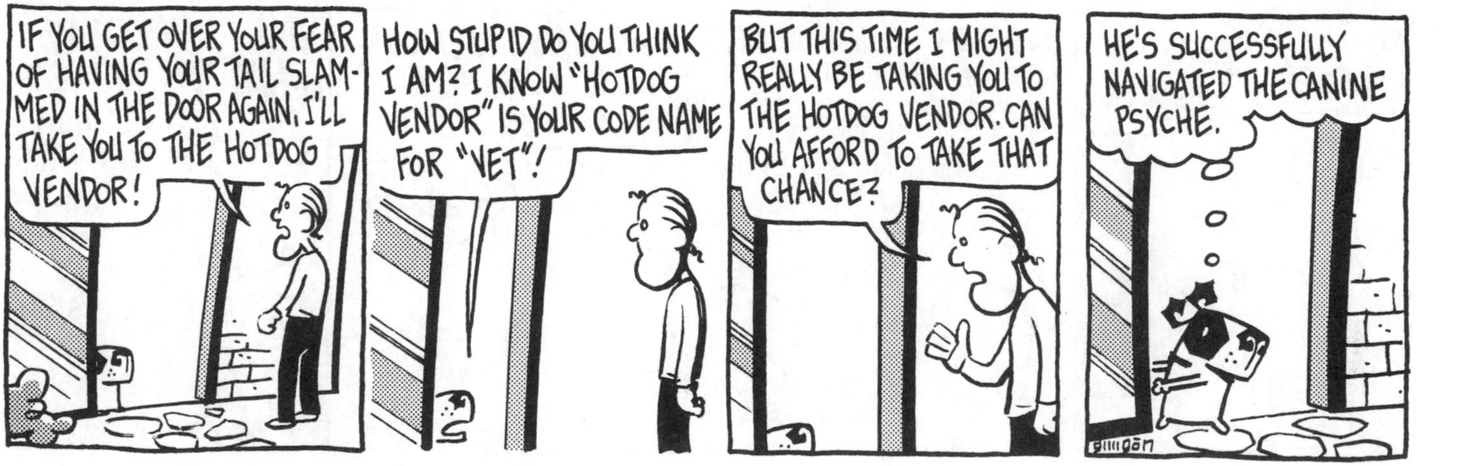
IF YOU GET OVER YOUR FEAR OF HAVING YOUR TAIL SLAMMED IN THE DOOR AGAIN, I'LL TAKE YOU TO THE HOTDOG VENDOR!
HOW STUPID DO YOU THINK I AM? I KNOW "HOTDOG VENDOR" IS YOUR CODE NAME FOR "VET"!
BUT THIS TIME I MIGHT REALLY BE TAKING YOU TO THE HOTDOG VENDOR. CAN YOU AFFORD TO TAKE THAT CHANCE?
HE'S SUCCESSFULLY NAVIGATED THE CANINE PSYCHE.
gilligan

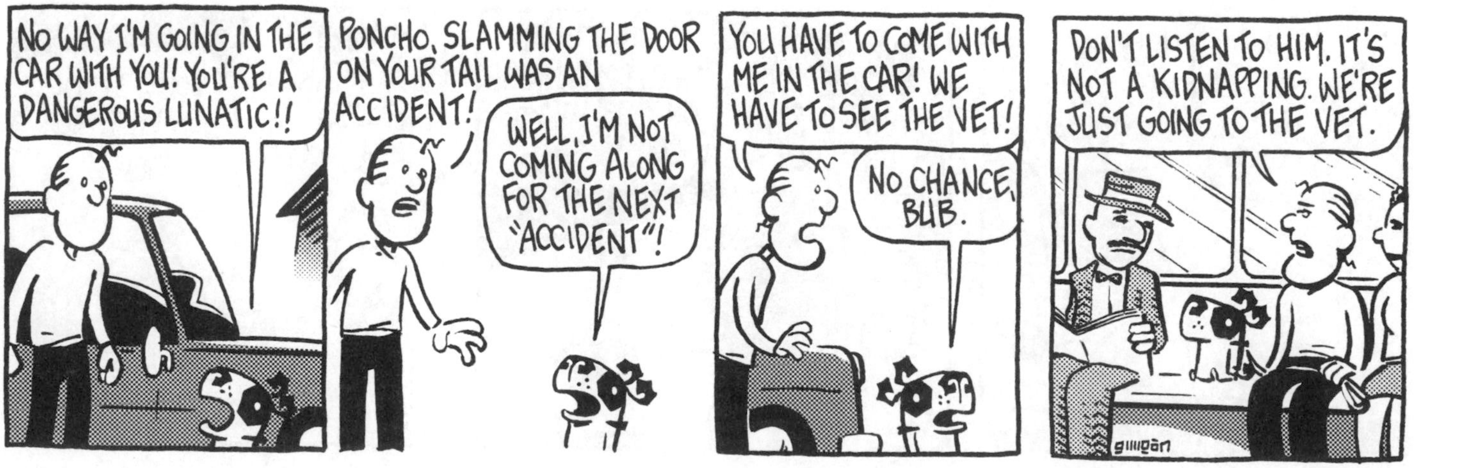
NO WAY I'M GOING IN THE CAR WITH YOU! YOU'RE A DANGEROUS LUNATIC!!
PONCHO, SLAMMING THE DOOR ON YOUR TAIL WAS AN ACCIDENT!
WELL, I'M NOT COMING ALONG FOR THE NEXT "ACCIDENT"!
YOU HAVE TO COME WITH ME IN THE CAR! WE HAVE TO SEE THE VET!
NO CHANCE, BUB.
DON'T LISTEN TO HIM. IT'S NOT A KIDNAPPING. WE'RE JUST GOING TO THE VET.
gilligan

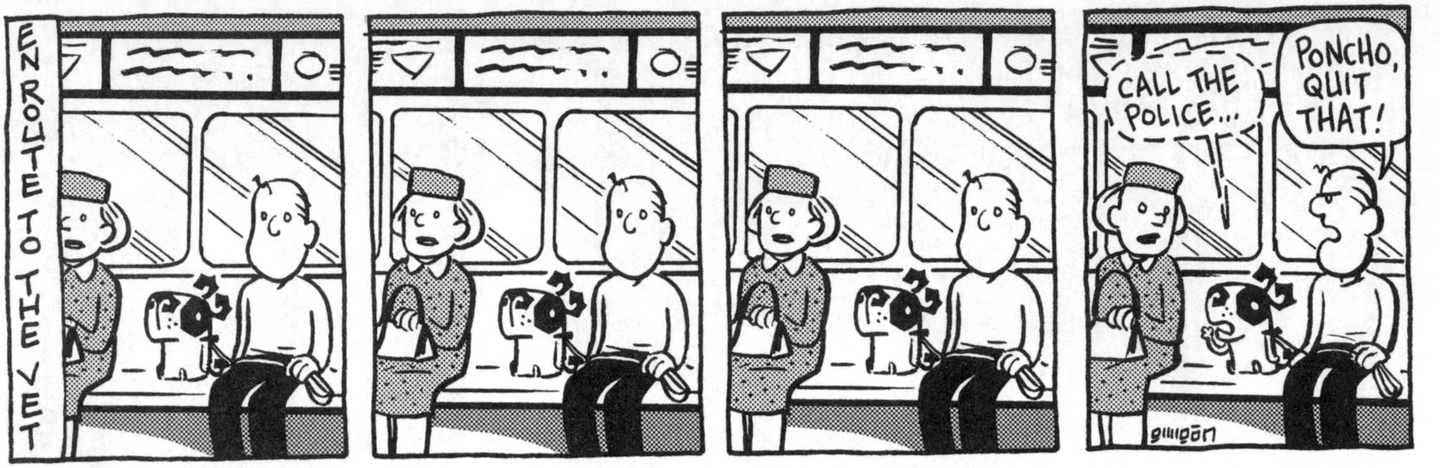
EN ROUTE TO THE VET
CALL THE POLICE...
PONCHO, QUIT THAT!

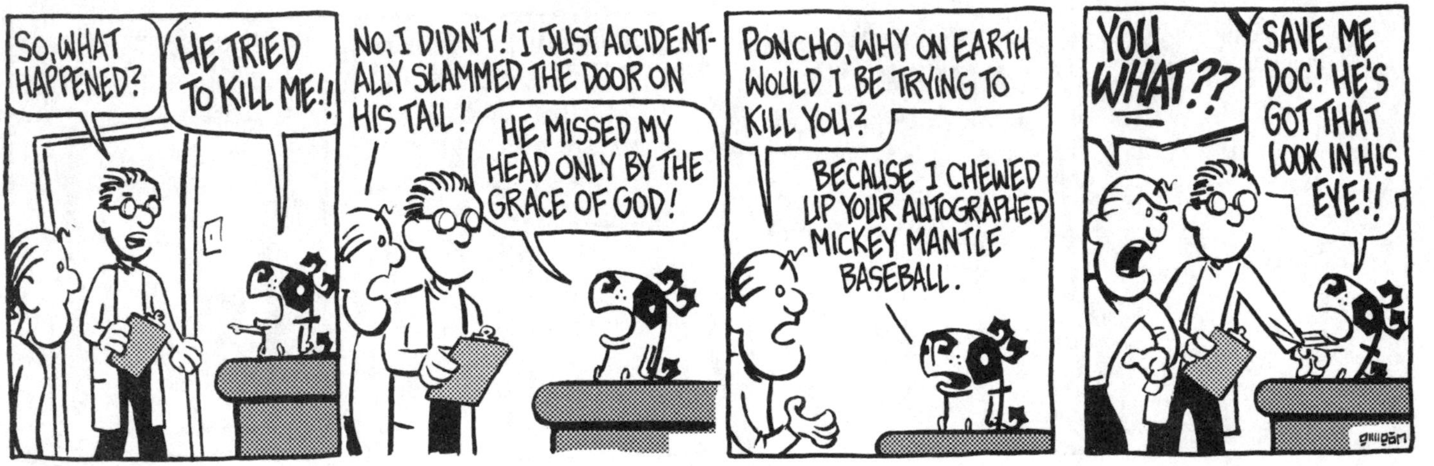
SO, WHAT HAPPENED?
HE TRIED TO KILL ME!!
NO, I DIDN'T! I JUST ACCIDENT-ALLY SLAMMED THE DOOR ON HIS TAIL!
HE MISSED MY HEAD ONLY BY THE GRACE OF GOD!
PONCHO, WHY ON EARTH WOULD I BE TRYING TO KILL YOU?
BECAUSE I CHEWED UP YOUR AUTOGRAPHED MICKEY MANTLE BASEBALL.
YOU WHAT??
SAVE ME DOC! HE'S GOT THAT LOOK IN HIS EYE!!

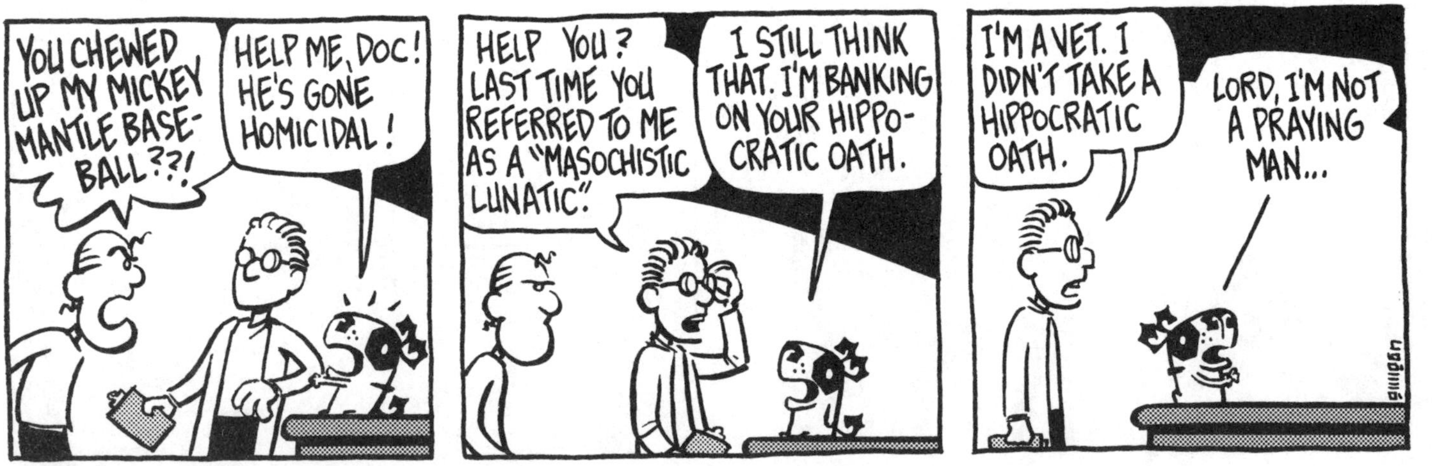
YOU CHEWED UP MY MICKEY MANTLE BASE-BALL??!
HELP ME, DOC! HE'S GONE HOMICIDAL!
HELP YOU? LAST TIME YOU REFERRED TO ME AS A "MASOCHISTIC LUNATIC."
I STILL THINK THAT. I'M BANKING ON YOUR HIPPO-CRATIC OATH.
I'M A VET. I DIDN'T TAKE A HIPPOCRATIC OATH.
LORD, I'M NOT A PRAYING MAN...

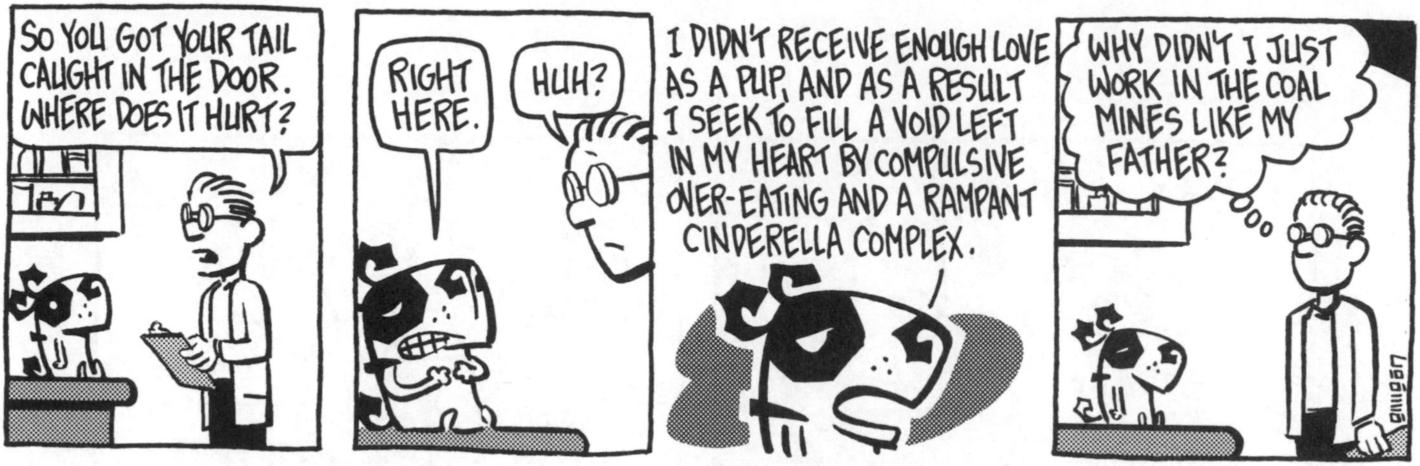
SO YOU GOT YOUR TAIL CAUGHT IN THE DOOR. WHERE DOES IT HURT?
RIGHT HERE.
HUH?
I DIDN'T RECEIVE ENOUGH LOVE AS A PUP, AND AS A RESULT I SEEK TO FILL A VOID LEFT IN MY HEART BY COMPULSIVE OVER-EATING AND A RAMPANT CINDERELLA COMPLEX.
WHY DIDN'T I JUST WORK IN THE COAL MINES LIKE MY FATHER?

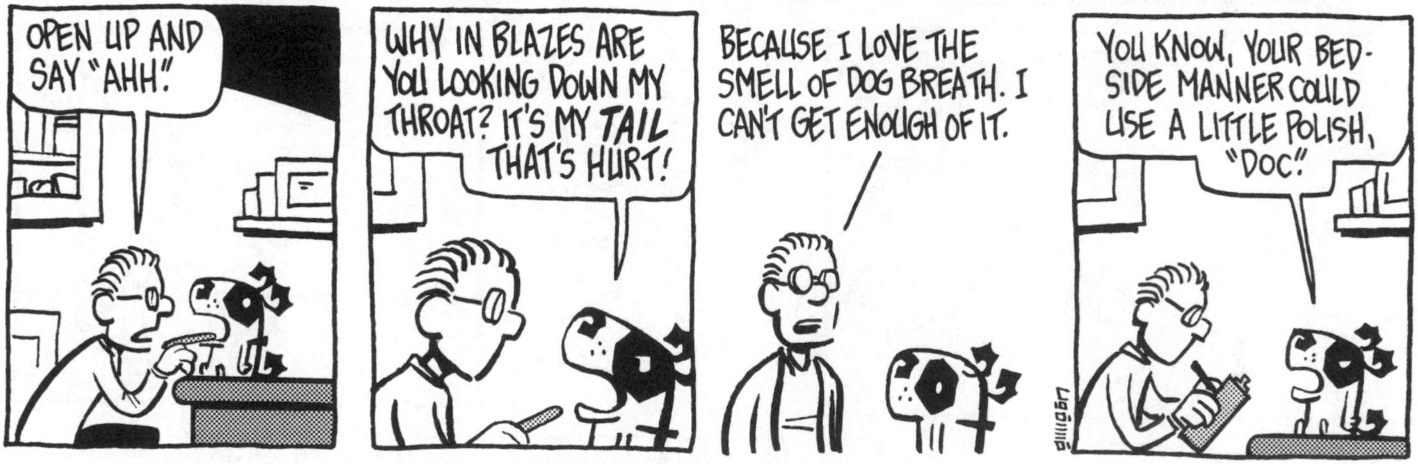
OPEN UP AND SAY "AHH."
WHY IN BLAZES ARE YOU LOOKING DOWN MY THROAT? IT'S MY TAIL THAT'S HURT!
BECAUSE I LOVE THE SMELL OF DOG BREATH. I CAN'T GET ENOUGH OF IT.
YOU KNOW, YOUR BED-SIDE MANNER COULD USE A LITTLE POLISH, "DOC."

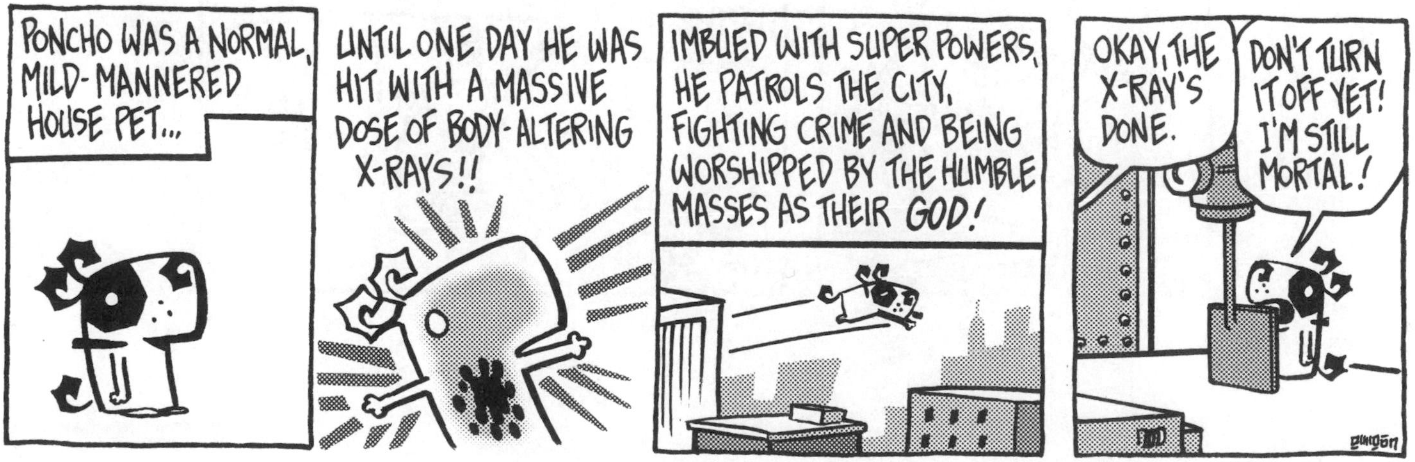
PONCHO WAS A NORMAL, MILD-MANNERED HOUSE PET...
UNTIL ONE DAY HE WAS HIT WITH A MASSIVE DOSE OF BODY-ALTERING X-RAYS!!
IMBUED WITH SUPER POWERS, HE PATROLS THE CITY, FIGHTING CRIME AND BEING WORSHIPPED BY THE HUMBLE MASSES AS THEIR GOD!
OKAY, THE X-RAY'S DONE.
DON'T TURN IT OFF YET! I'M STILL MORTAL!

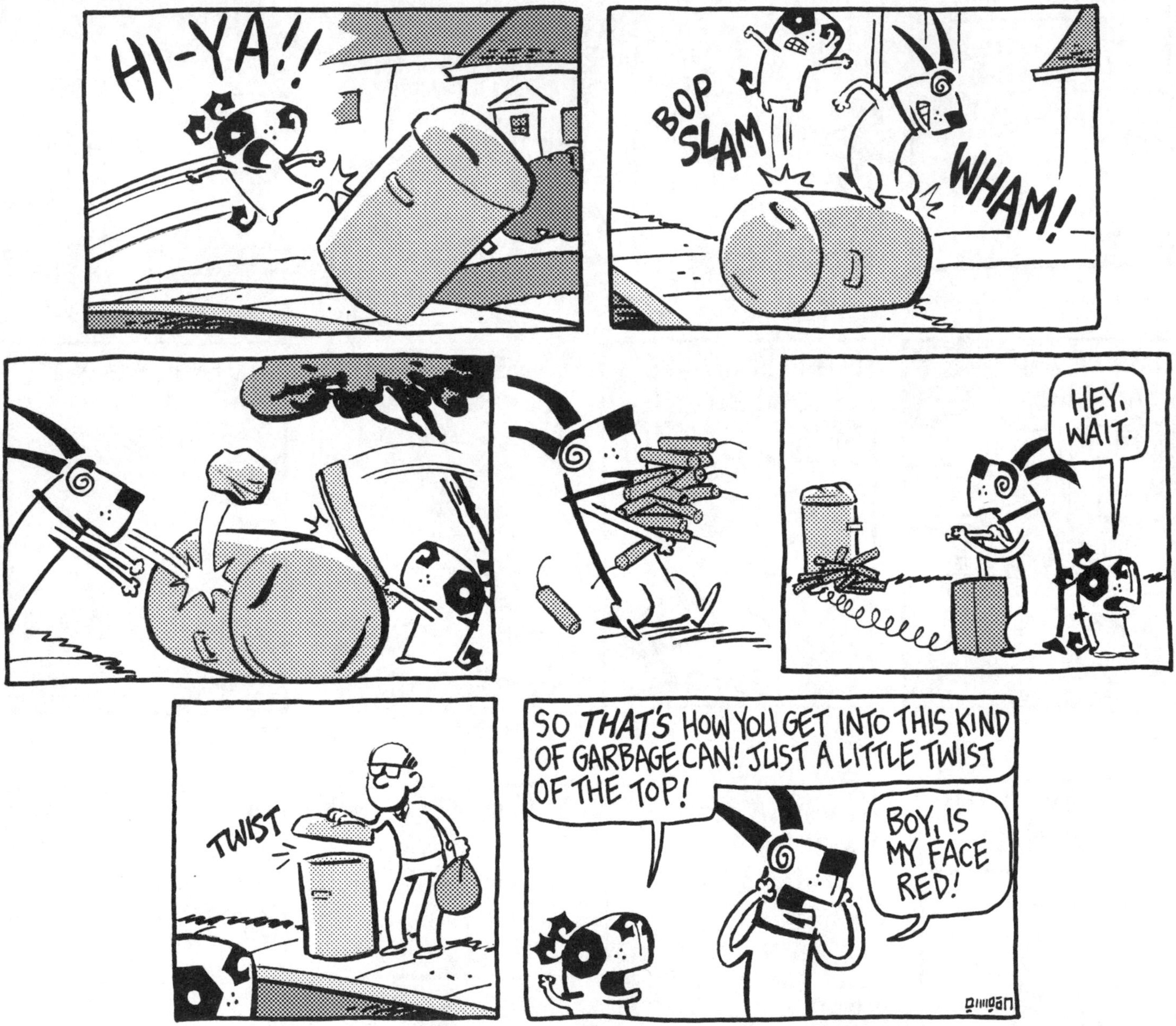
HI-YA!!!
BOP
SLAM
WHAM!
HEY, WAIT.
TWIST
SO *THAT'S* HOW YOU GET INTO THIS KIND OF GARBAGE CAN! JUST A LITTLE TWIST OF THE TOP!
BOY, IS MY FACE RED!
DILLIGAN

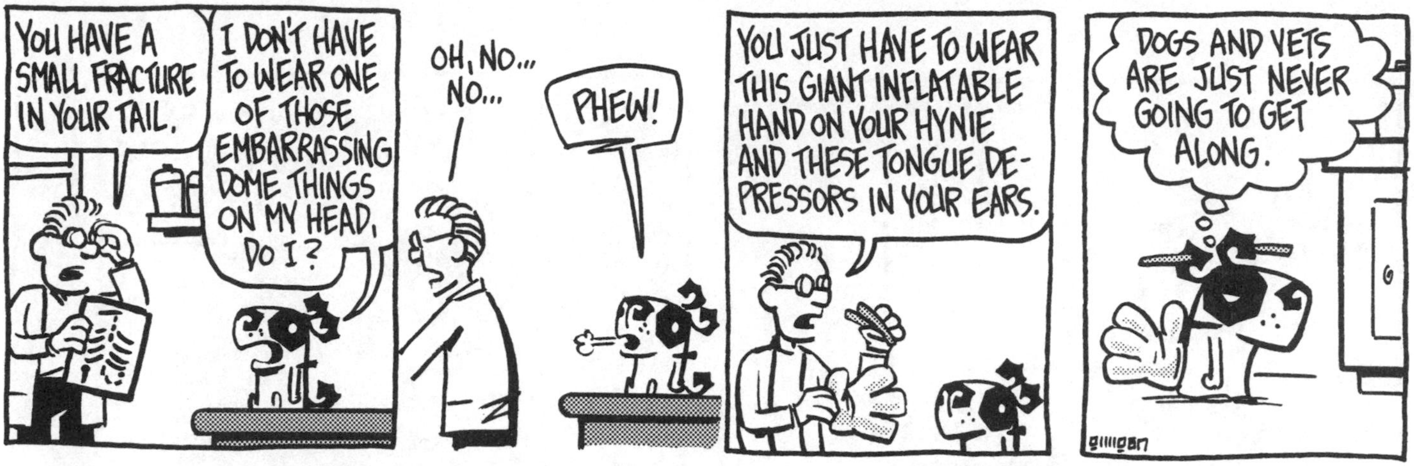
YOU HAVE A SMALL FRACTURE IN YOUR TAIL.
I DON'T HAVE TO WEAR ONE OF THOSE EMBARRASSING DOME THINGS ON MY HEAD, DO I?
OH, NO... NO...
PHEW!
YOU JUST HAVE TO WEAR THIS GIANT INFLATABLE HAND ON YOUR HYNIE AND THESE TONGUE DEPRESSORS IN YOUR EARS.
DOGS AND VETS ARE JUST NEVER GOING TO GET ALONG.
gilligan

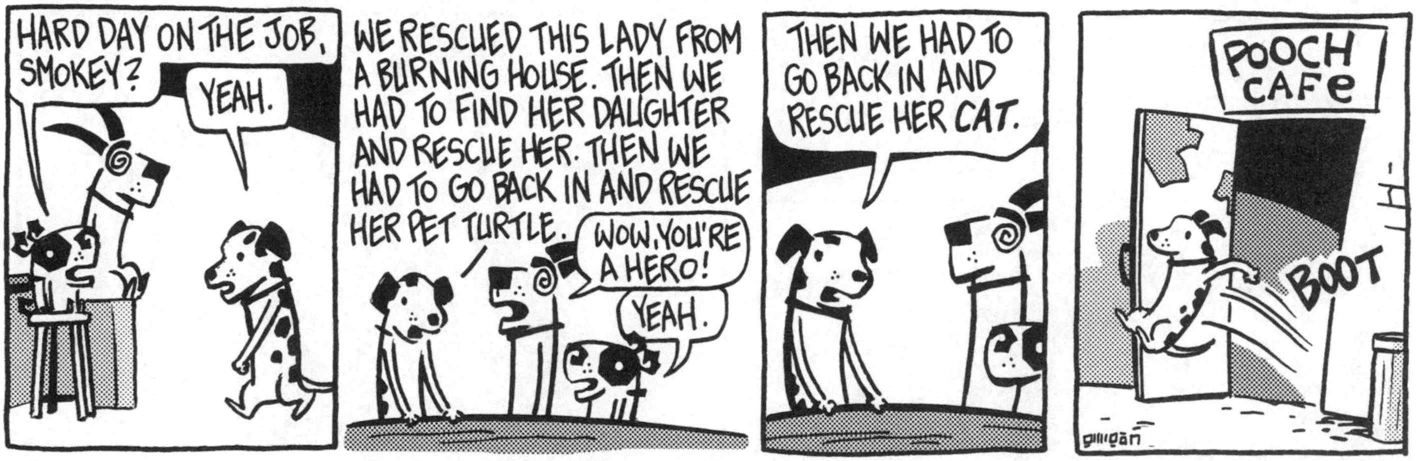
HARD DAY ON THE JOB, SMOKEY?
YEAH.
WE RESCUED THIS LADY FROM A BURNING HOUSE. THEN WE HAD TO FIND HER DAUGHTER AND RESCUE HER. THEN WE HAD TO GO BACK IN AND RESCUE HER PET TURTLE.
WOW, YOU'RE A HERO!
YEAH.
THEN WE HAD TO GO BACK IN AND RESCUE HER CAT.
POOCH CAFE
BOOT
gilligan

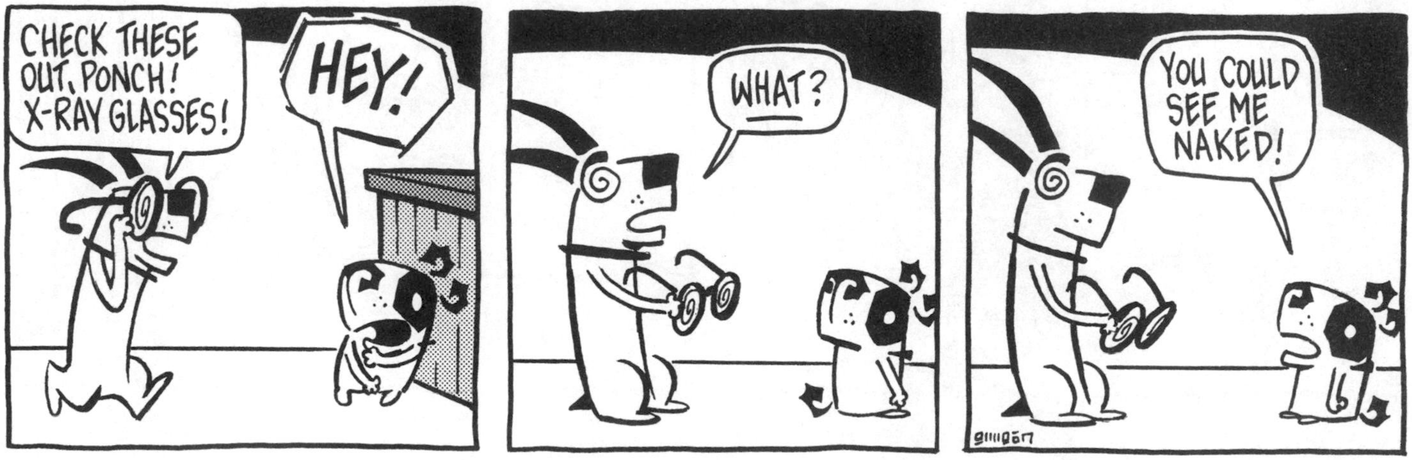
CHECK THESE OUT, PONCH! X-RAY GLASSES!
HEY!
WHAT?
YOU COULD SEE ME NAKED!
gilligan

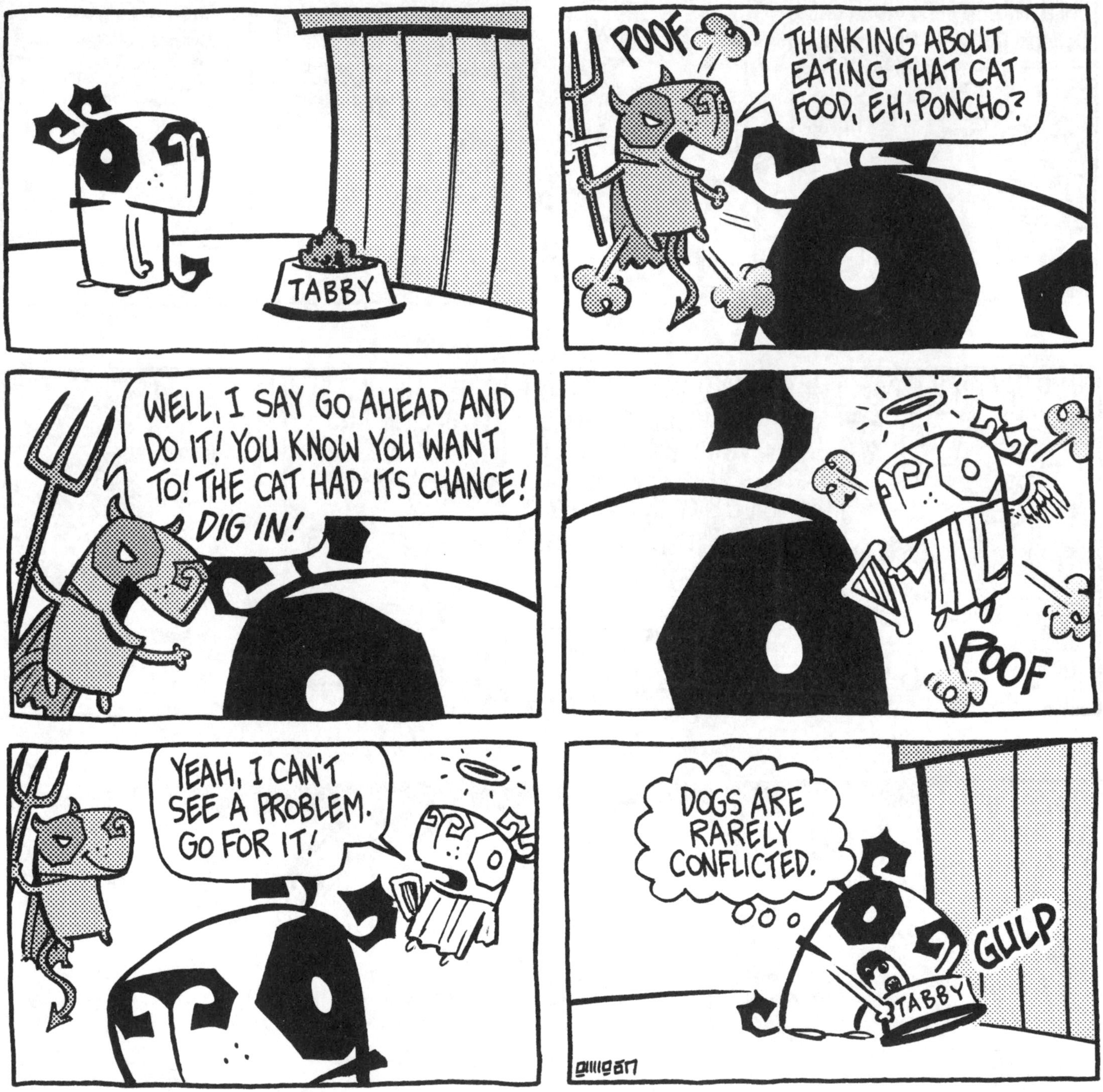
TABBY
POOF
THINKING ABOUT EATING THAT CAT FOOD, EH, PONCHO?
WELL, I SAY GO AHEAD AND DO IT! YOU KNOW YOU WANT TO! THE CAT HAD ITS CHANCE! DIG IN!
POOF
YEAH, I CAN'T SEE A PROBLEM. GO FOR IT!
DOGS ARE RARELY CONFLICTED.
GULP
TABBY

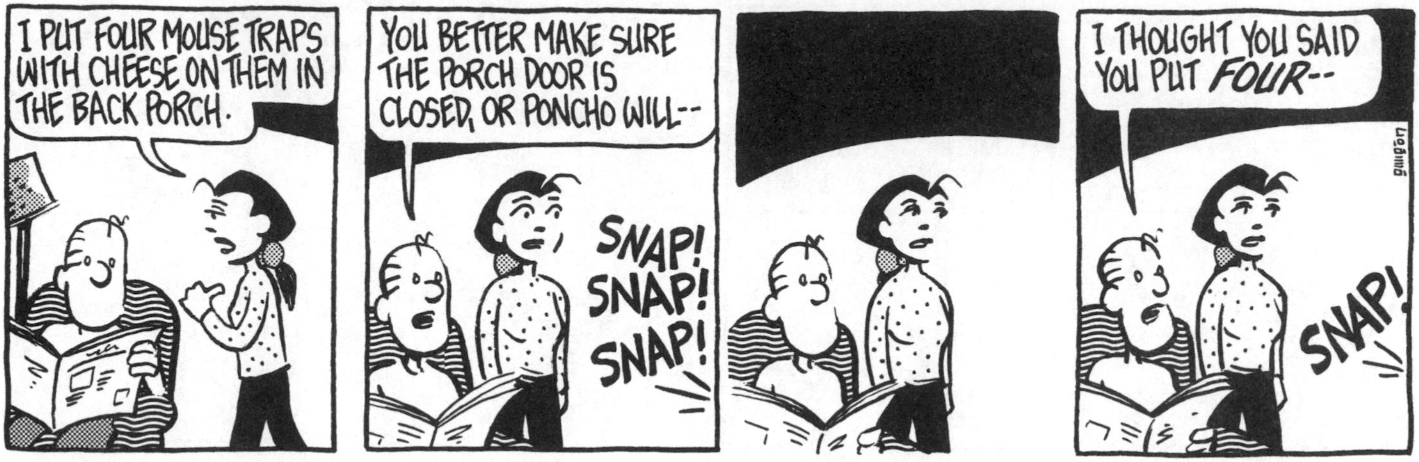
I PUT FOUR MOUSE TRAPS WITH CHEESE ON THEM IN THE BACK PORCH.
YOU BETTER MAKE SURE THE PORCH DOOR IS CLOSED, OR PONCHO WILL--
SNAP! SNAP! SNAP!
I THOUGHT YOU SAID YOU PUT *FOUR*--
SNAP!
GILLIGAN

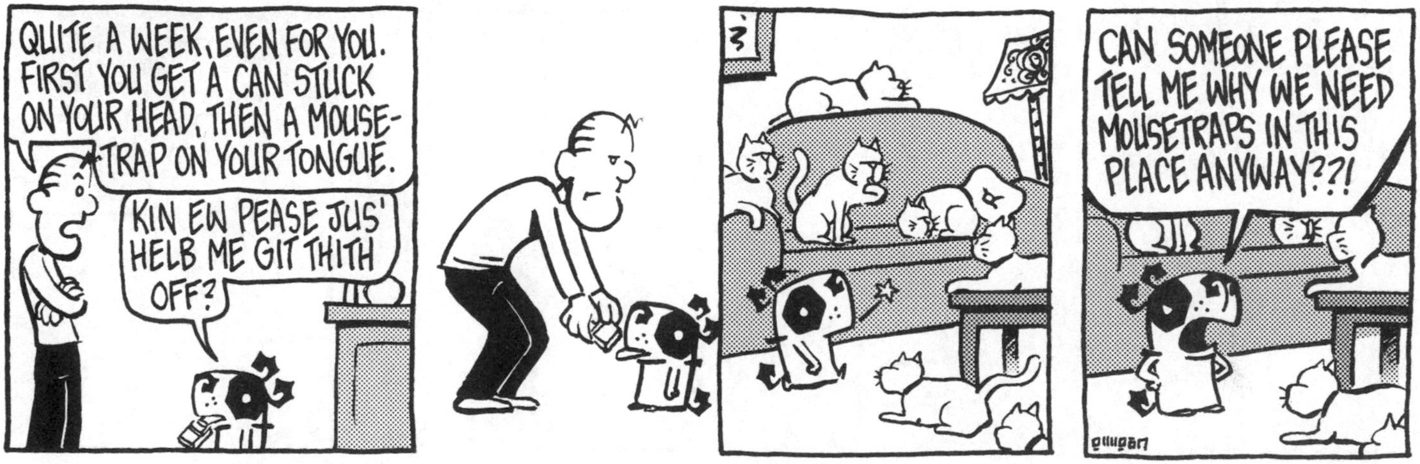
QUITE A WEEK, EVEN FOR YOU. FIRST YOU GET A CAN STUCK ON YOUR HEAD, THEN A MOUSE-TRAP ON YOUR TONGUE.
KIN EW PEASE JUS' HELB ME GIT THITH OFF?
CAN SOMEONE PLEASE TELL ME WHY WE NEED MOUSETRAPS IN THIS PLACE ANYWAY??!
GILLIGAN

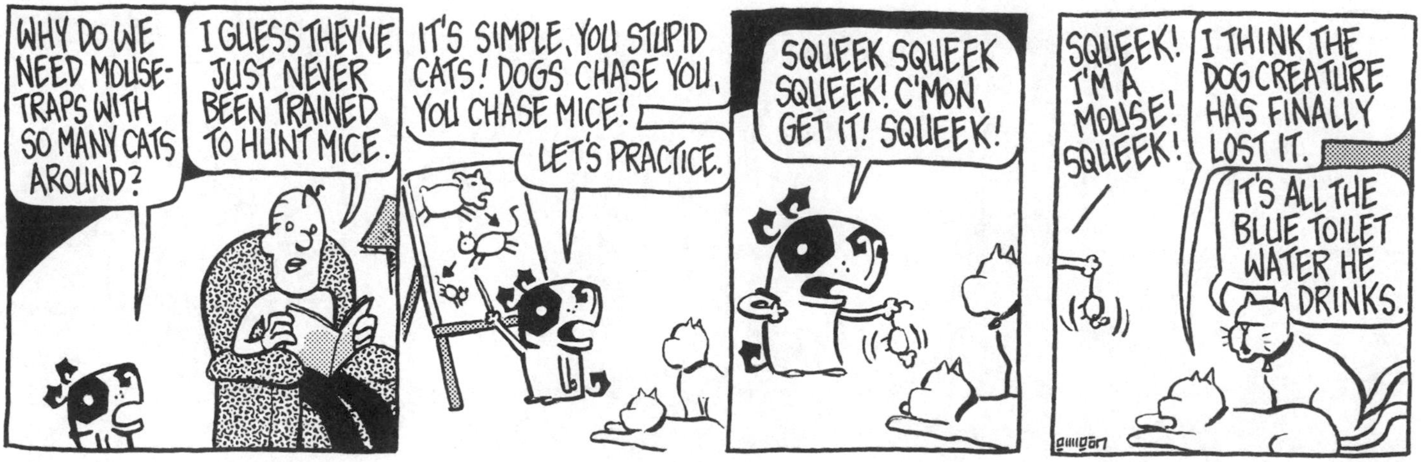
WHY DO WE NEED MOUSE-TRAPS WITH SO MANY CATS AROUND?
I GUESS THEY'VE JUST NEVER BEEN TRAINED TO HUNT MICE.
IT'S SIMPLE, YOU STUPID CATS! DOGS CHASE YOU, YOU CHASE MICE!
LET'S PRACTICE.
SQUEEK SQUEEK SQUEEK! C'MON, GET IT! SQUEEK!
SQUEEK! I'M A MOUSE! SQUEEK!
I THINK THE DOG CREATURE HAS FINALLY LOST IT.
IT'S ALL THE BLUE TOILET WATER HE DRINKS.
GILLIGAN

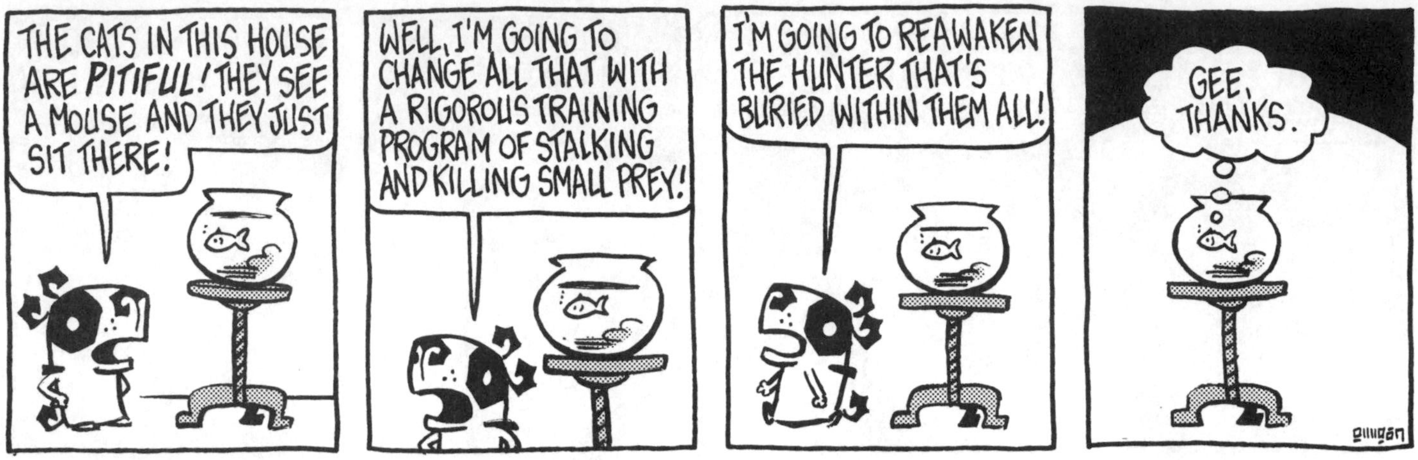
THE CATS IN THIS HOUSE ARE *PITIFUL!* THEY SEE A MOUSE AND THEY JUST SIT THERE!
WELL, I'M GOING TO CHANGE ALL THAT WITH A RIGOROUS TRAINING PROGRAM OF STALKING AND KILLING SMALL PREY!
I'M GOING TO REAWAKEN THE HUNTER THAT'S BURIED WITHIN THEM ALL!
GEE, THANKS.

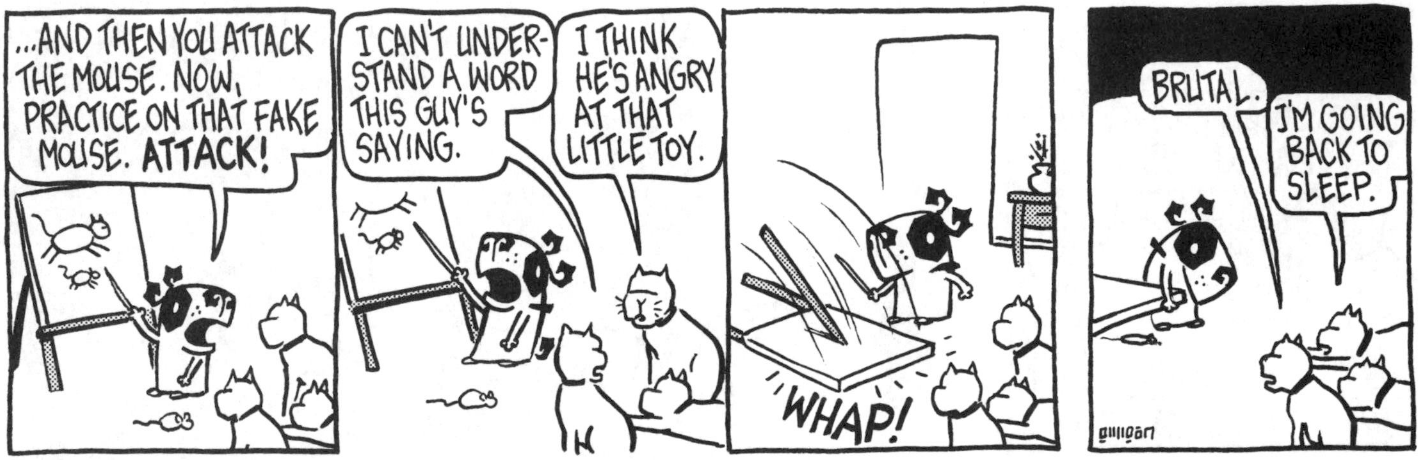
...AND THEN YOU ATTACK THE MOUSE. NOW, PRACTICE ON THAT FAKE MOUSE. **ATTACK!**
I CAN'T UNDERSTAND A WORD THIS GUY'S SAYING.
I THINK HE'S ANGRY AT THAT LITTLE TOY.
WHAP!
BRUTAL.
I'M GOING BACK TO SLEEP.

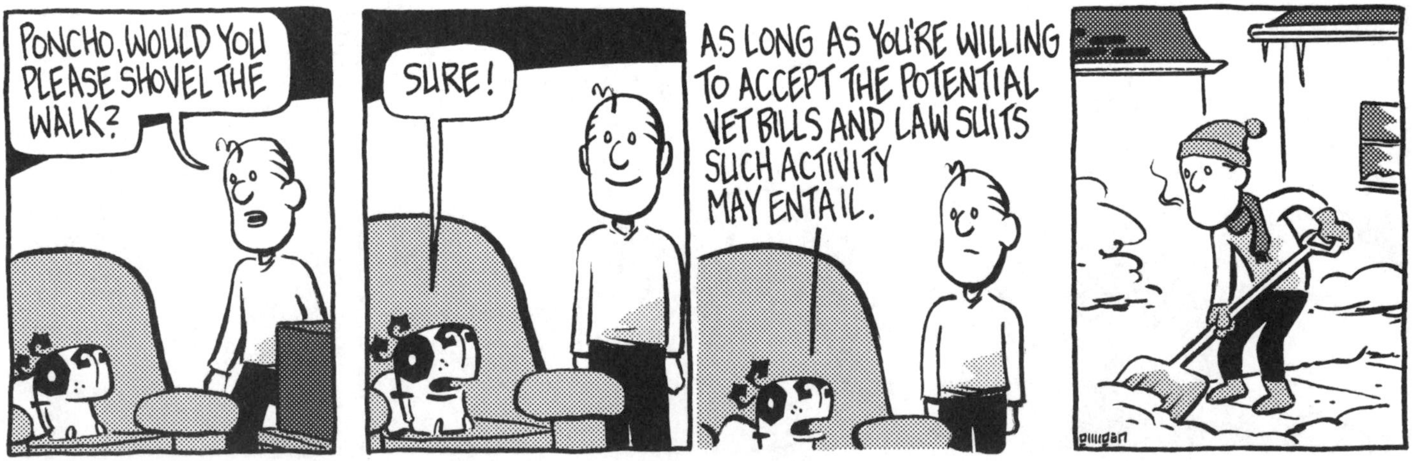
PONCHO, WOULD YOU PLEASE SHOVEL THE WALK?
SURE!
AS LONG AS YOU'RE WILLING TO ACCEPT THE POTENTIAL VET BILLS AND LAW SUITS SUCH ACTIVITY MAY ENTAIL.

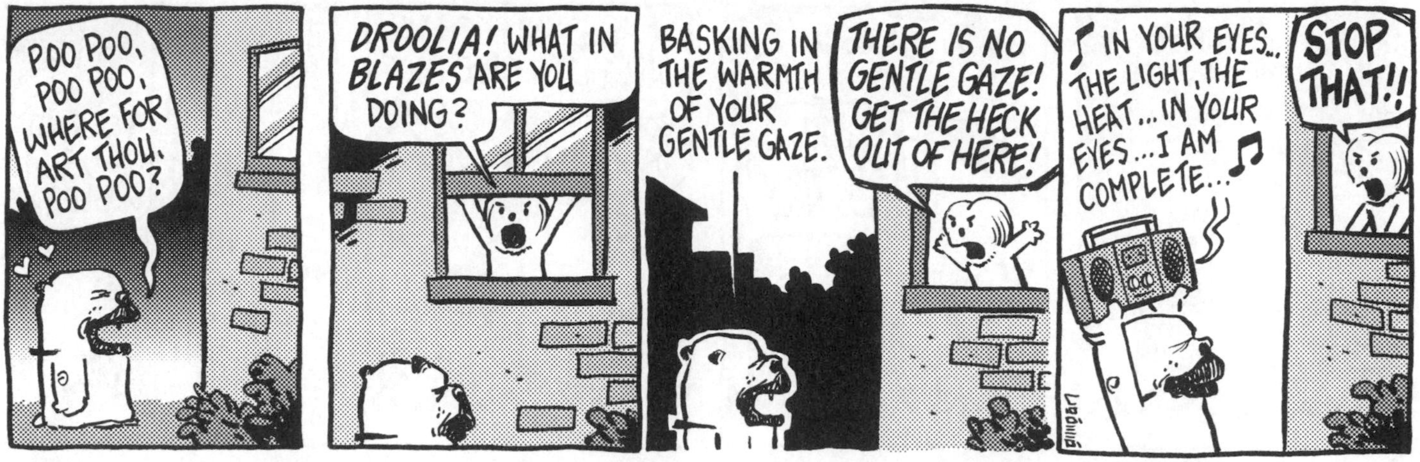

POO POO, POO POO, WHERE FOR ART THOU, POO POO?
DROOLIA! WHAT IN BLAZES ARE YOU DOING?
BASKING IN THE WARMTH OF YOUR GENTLE GAZE.
THERE IS NO GENTLE GAZE! GET THE HECK OUT OF HERE!
♪ IN YOUR EYES... THE LIGHT, THE HEAT... IN YOUR EYES... I AM COMPLETE... ♫
STOP THAT!!

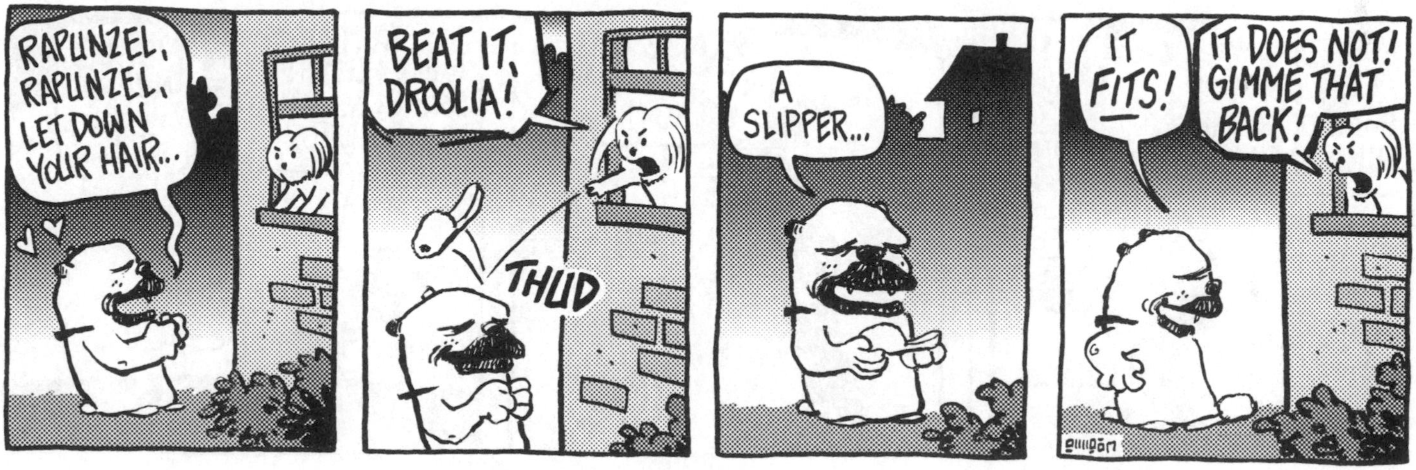

RAPUNZEL, RAPUNZEL, LET DOWN YOUR HAIR...
BEAT IT, DROOLIA!
THUD
A SLIPPER...
IT FITS!
IT DOES NOT! GIMME THAT BACK!

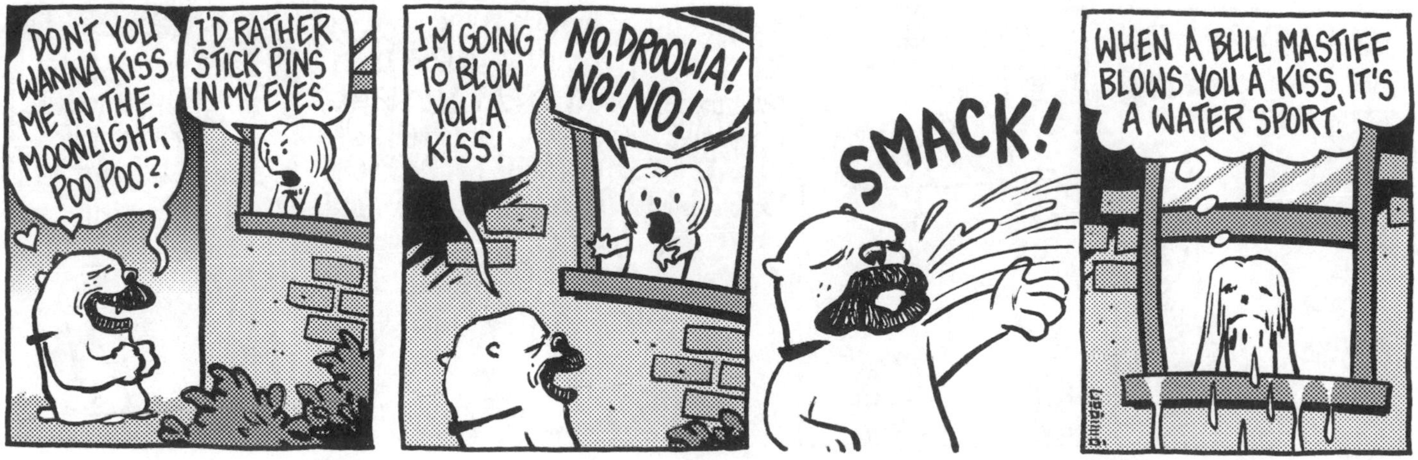

DON'T YOU WANNA KISS ME IN THE MOONLIGHT, POO POO?
I'D RATHER STICK PINS IN MY EYES.
I'M GOING TO BLOW YOU A KISS!
NO, DROOLIA! NO! NO!
SMACK!
WHEN A BULL MASTIFF BLOWS YOU A KISS, IT'S A WATER SPORT.

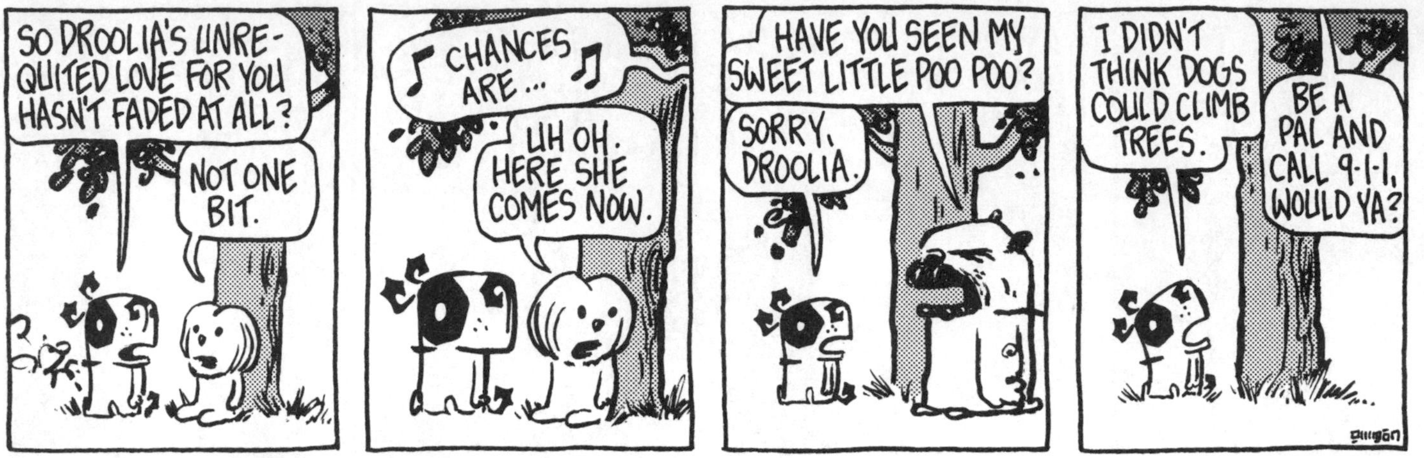
SO DROOLIA'S UNRE-QUITED LOVE FOR YOU HASN'T FADED AT ALL?
NOT ONE BIT.
♪ CHANCES ARE ... ♫
UH OH. HERE SHE COMES NOW.
HAVE YOU SEEN MY SWEET LITTLE POO POO?
SORRY, DROOLIA.
I DIDN'T THINK DOGS COULD CLIMB TREES.
BE A PAL AND CALL 9-1-1, WOULD YA?

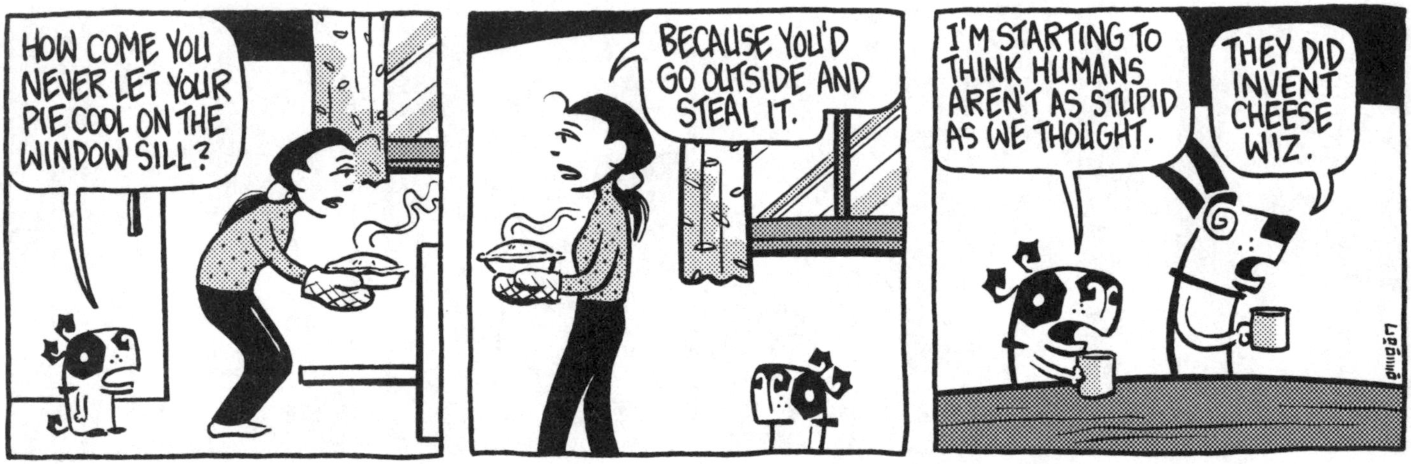
HOW COME YOU NEVER LET YOUR PIE COOL ON THE WINDOW SILL?
BECAUSE YOU'D GO OUTSIDE AND STEAL IT.
I'M STARTING TO THINK HUMANS AREN'T AS STUPID AS WE THOUGHT.
THEY DID INVENT CHEESE WIZ.

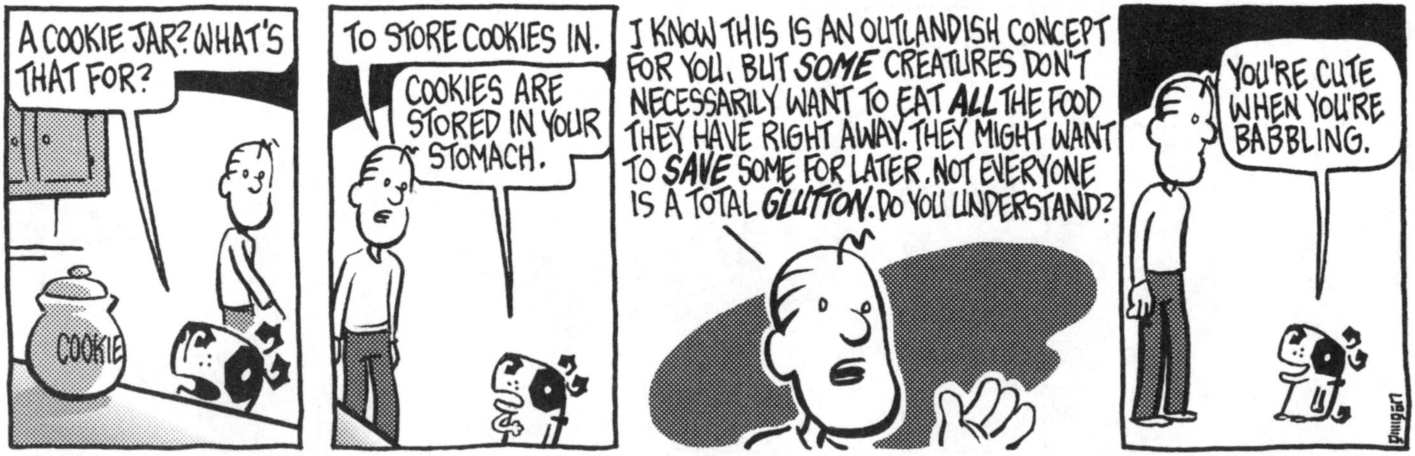
A COOKIE JAR? WHAT'S THAT FOR?
COOKIE
TO STORE COOKIES IN.
COOKIES ARE STORED IN YOUR STOMACH.
I KNOW THIS IS AN OUTLANDISH CONCEPT FOR YOU, BUT SOME CREATURES DON'T NECESSARILY WANT TO EAT ALL THE FOOD THEY HAVE RIGHT AWAY. THEY MIGHT WANT TO SAVE SOME FOR LATER. NOT EVERYONE IS A TOTAL GLUTTON. DO YOU UNDERSTAND?
YOU'RE CUTE WHEN YOU'RE BABBLING.

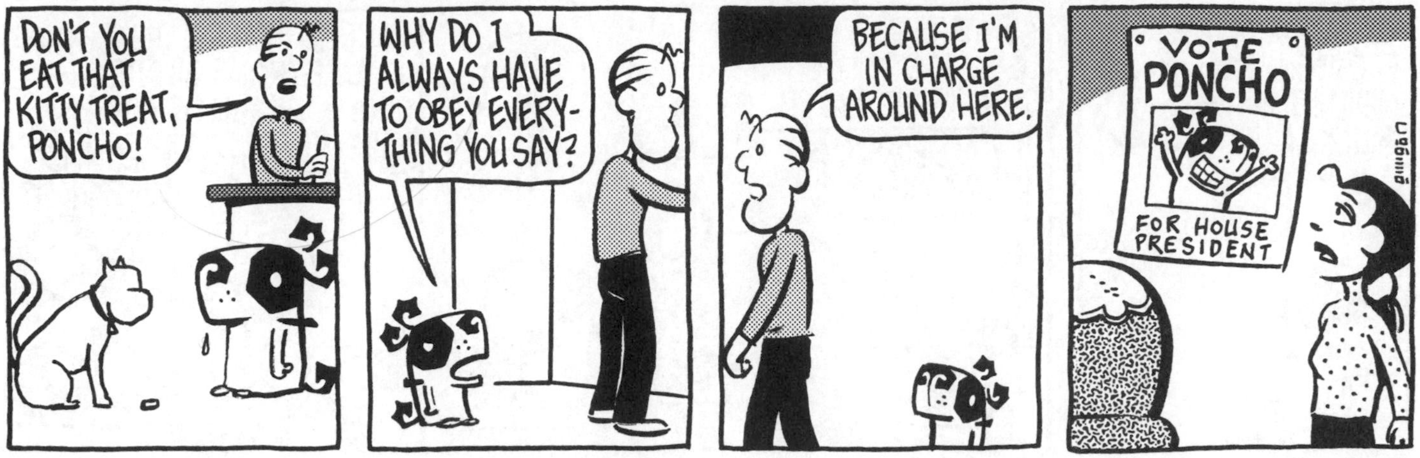
DON'T YOU EAT THAT KITTY TREAT, PONCHO!
WHY DO I ALWAYS HAVE TO OBEY EVERY-THING YOU SAY?
BECAUSE I'M IN CHARGE AROUND HERE.
VOTE PONCHO
FOR HOUSE PRESIDENT

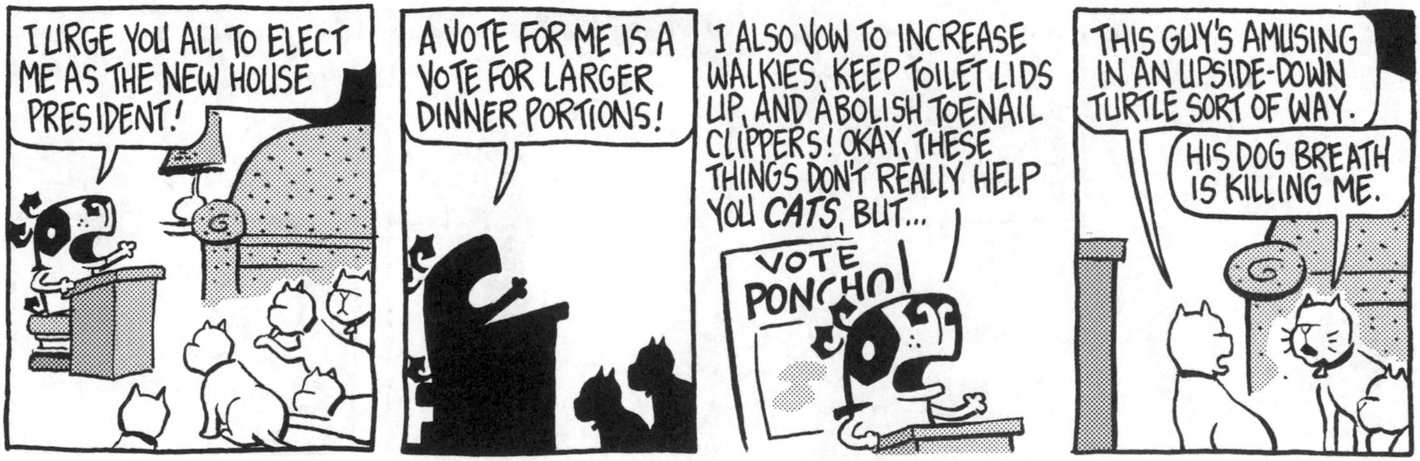
I URGE YOU ALL TO ELECT ME AS THE NEW HOUSE PRESIDENT!
A VOTE FOR ME IS A VOTE FOR LARGER DINNER PORTIONS!
I ALSO VOW TO INCREASE WALKIES, KEEP TOILET LIDS UP, AND ABOLISH TOENAIL CLIPPERS! OKAY, THESE THINGS DON'T REALLY HELP YOU CATS, BUT...
VOTE PONCHO
THIS GUY'S AMUSING IN AN UPSIDE-DOWN TURTLE SORT OF WAY.
HIS DOG BREATH IS KILLING ME.

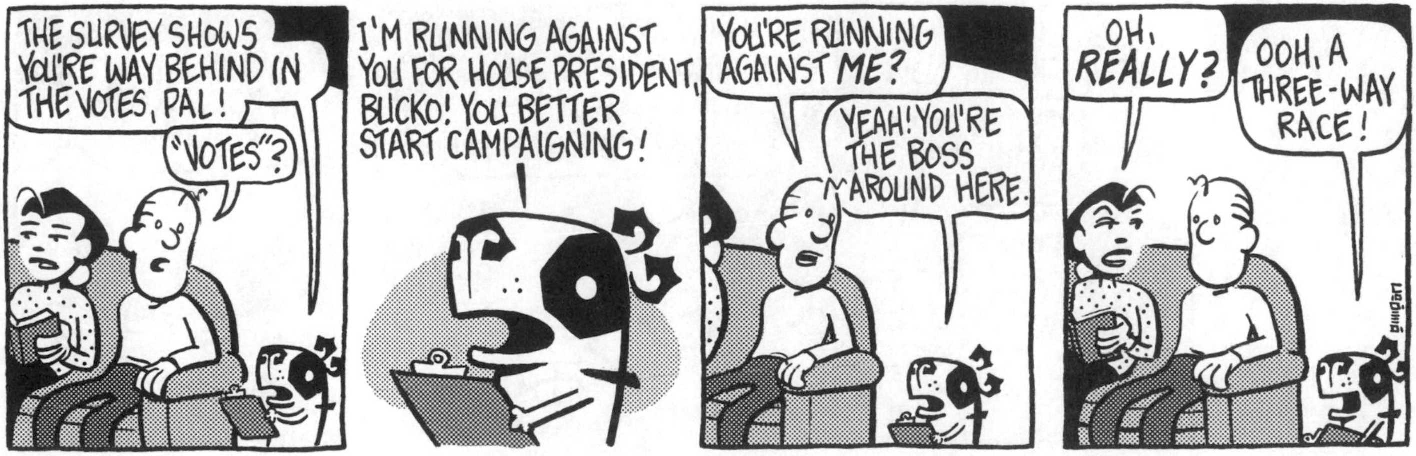
THE SURVEY SHOWS YOU'RE WAY BEHIND IN THE VOTES, PAL!
"VOTES"?
I'M RUNNING AGAINST YOU FOR HOUSE PRESIDENT, BUCKO! YOU BETTER START CAMPAIGNING!
YOU'RE RUNNING AGAINST ME?
YEAH! YOU'RE THE BOSS AROUND HERE.
OH, REALLY?
OOH, A THREE-WAY RACE!

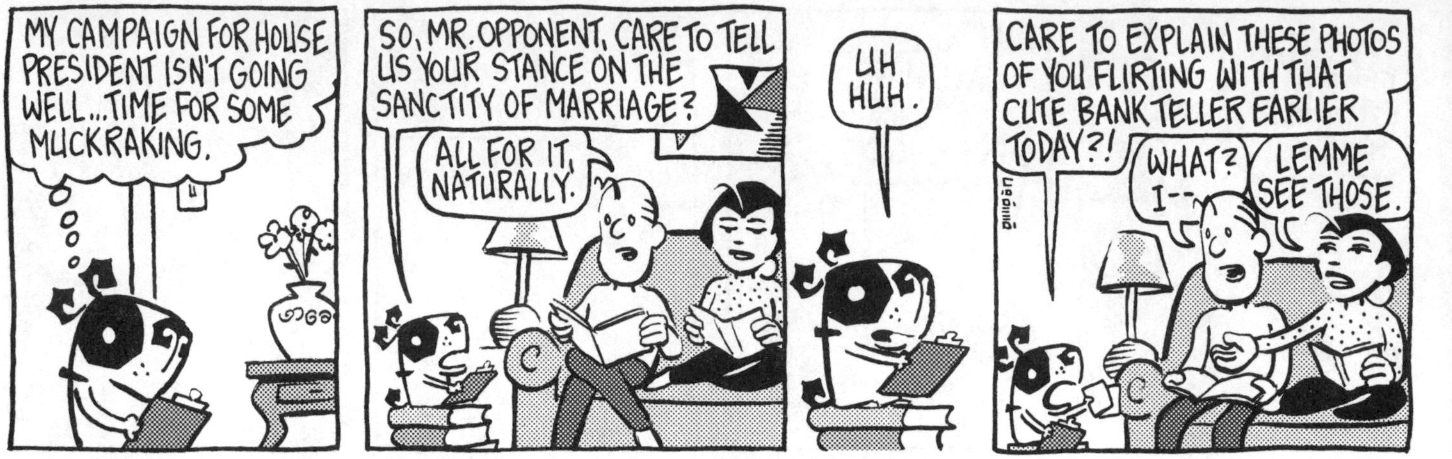
MY CAMPAIGN FOR HOUSE PRESIDENT ISN'T GOING WELL...TIME FOR SOME MUCKRAKING.
SO, MR. OPPONENT, CARE TO TELL US YOUR STANCE ON THE SANCTITY OF MARRIAGE?
ALL FOR IT, NATURALLY.
UH HUH.
CARE TO EXPLAIN THESE PHOTOS OF YOU FLIRTING WITH THAT CUTE BANK TELLER EARLIER TODAY?!
WHAT? I--
LEMME SEE THOSE.

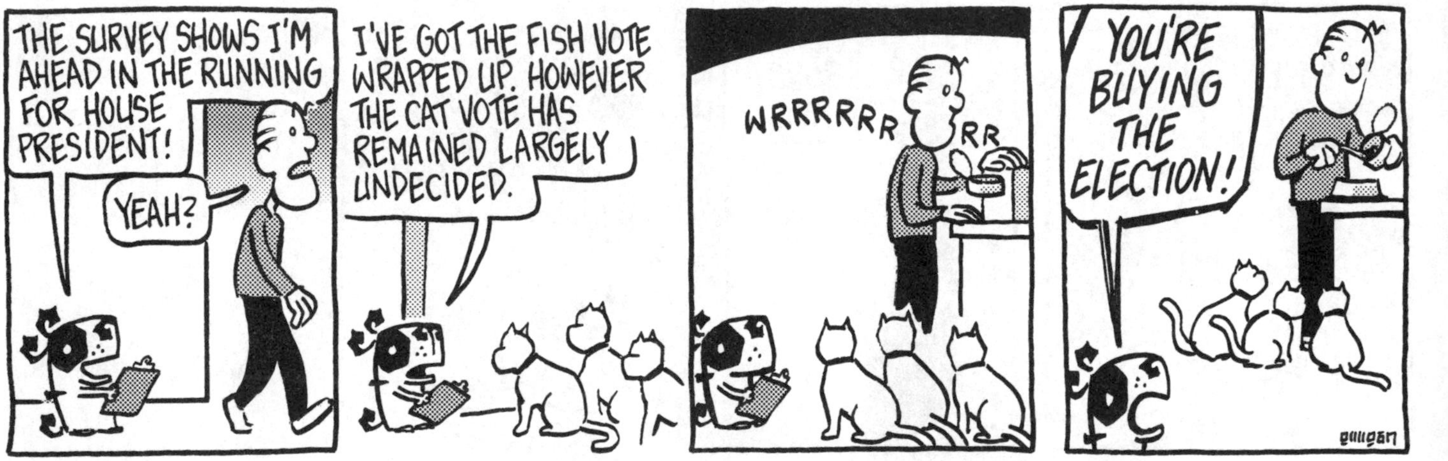
THE SURVEY SHOWS I'M AHEAD IN THE RUNNING FOR HOUSE PRESIDENT!
YEAH?
I'VE GOT THE FISH VOTE WRAPPED UP. HOWEVER THE CAT VOTE HAS REMAINED LARGELY UNDECIDED.
WRRRRRRRRR
YOU'RE BUYING THE ELECTION!

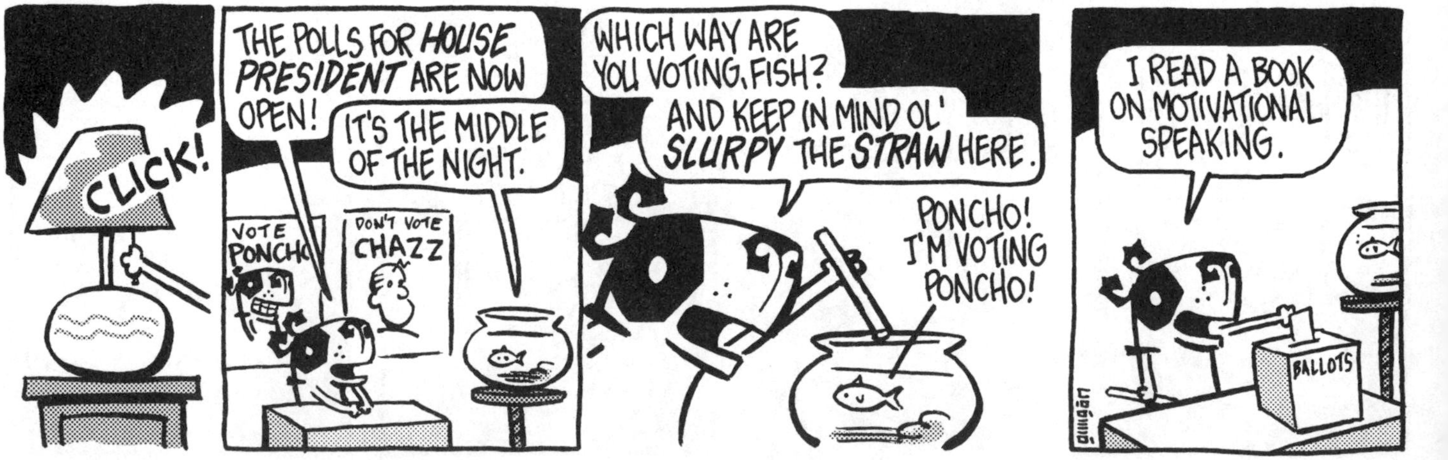
CLICK!
THE POLLS FOR HOUSE PRESIDENT ARE NOW OPEN!
IT'S THE MIDDLE OF THE NIGHT.
VOTE PONCHO
DON'T VOTE CHAZZ
WHICH WAY ARE YOU VOTING, FISH?
AND KEEP IN MIND OL' SLURPY THE STRAW HERE.
PONCHO! I'M VOTING PONCHO!
I READ A BOOK ON MOTIVATIONAL SPEAKING.
BALLOTS

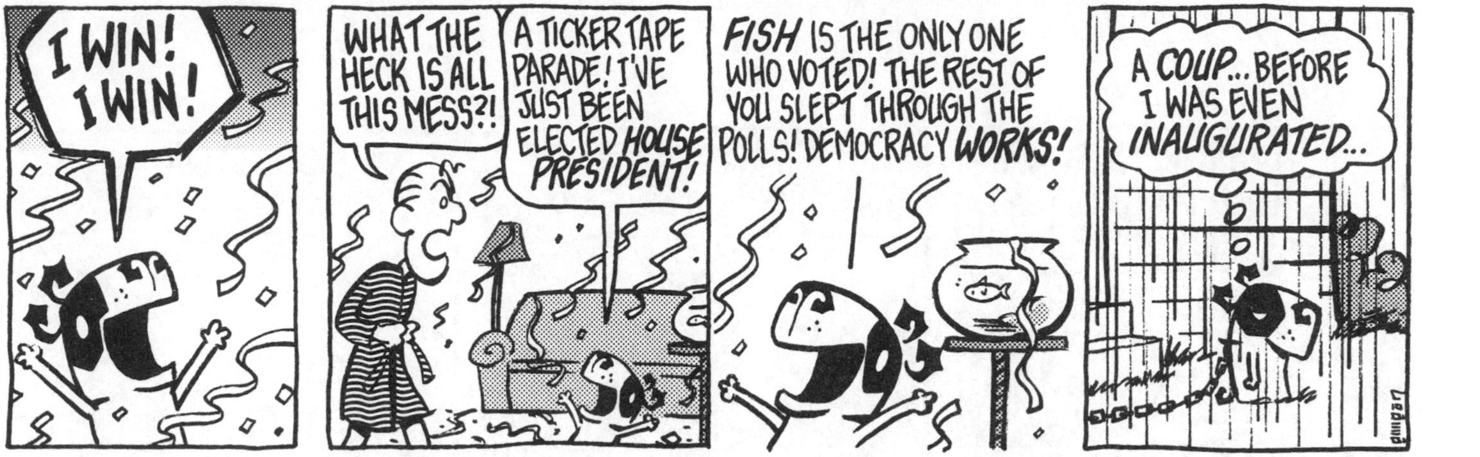
I WIN! I WIN!
WHAT THE HECK IS ALL THIS MESS?!
A TICKER TAPE PARADE! I'VE JUST BEEN ELECTED HOUSE PRESIDENT!
FISH IS THE ONLY ONE WHO VOTED! THE REST OF YOU SLEPT THROUGH THE POLLS! DEMOCRACY WORKS!
A COUP... BEFORE I WAS EVEN INAUGURATED...

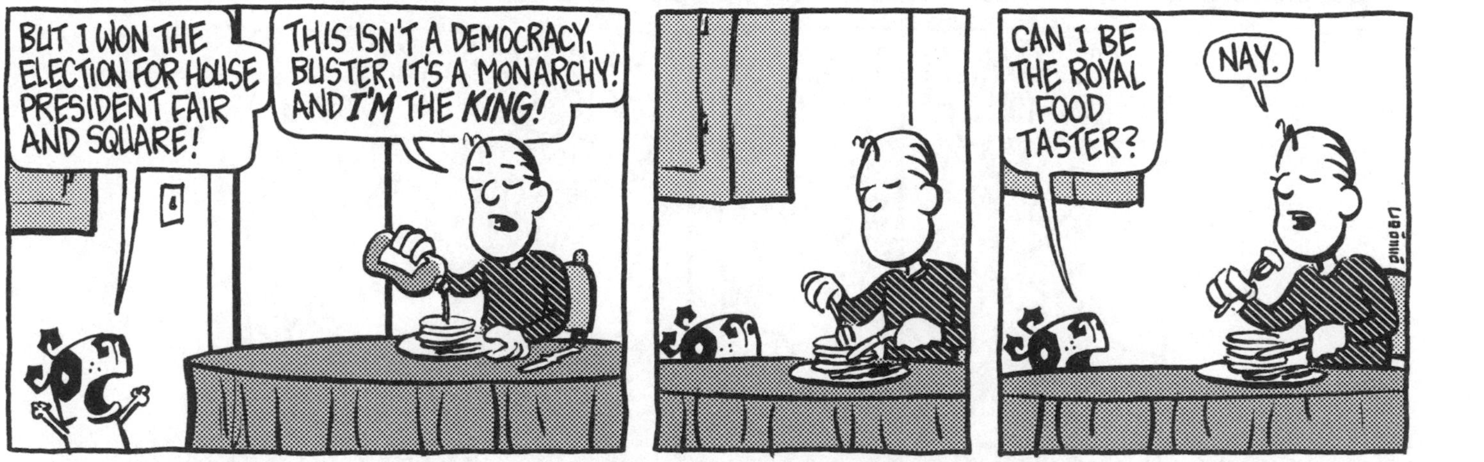
BUT I WON THE ELECTION FOR HOUSE PRESIDENT FAIR AND SQUARE!
THIS ISN'T A DEMOCRACY, BUSTER, IT'S A MONARCHY! AND I'M THE KING!
CAN I BE THE ROYAL FOOD TASTER?
NAY.

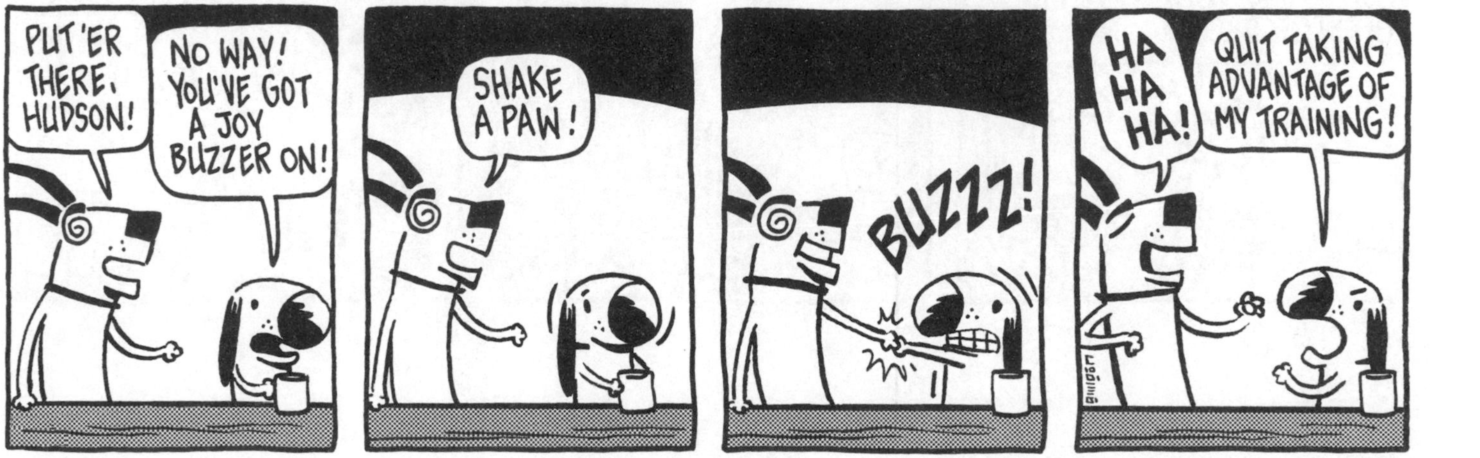
PUT 'ER THERE, HUDSON!
NO WAY! YOU'VE GOT A JOY BUZZER ON!
SHAKE A PAW!
BUZZZ!
HA HA HA!
QUIT TAKING ADVANTAGE OF MY TRAINING!

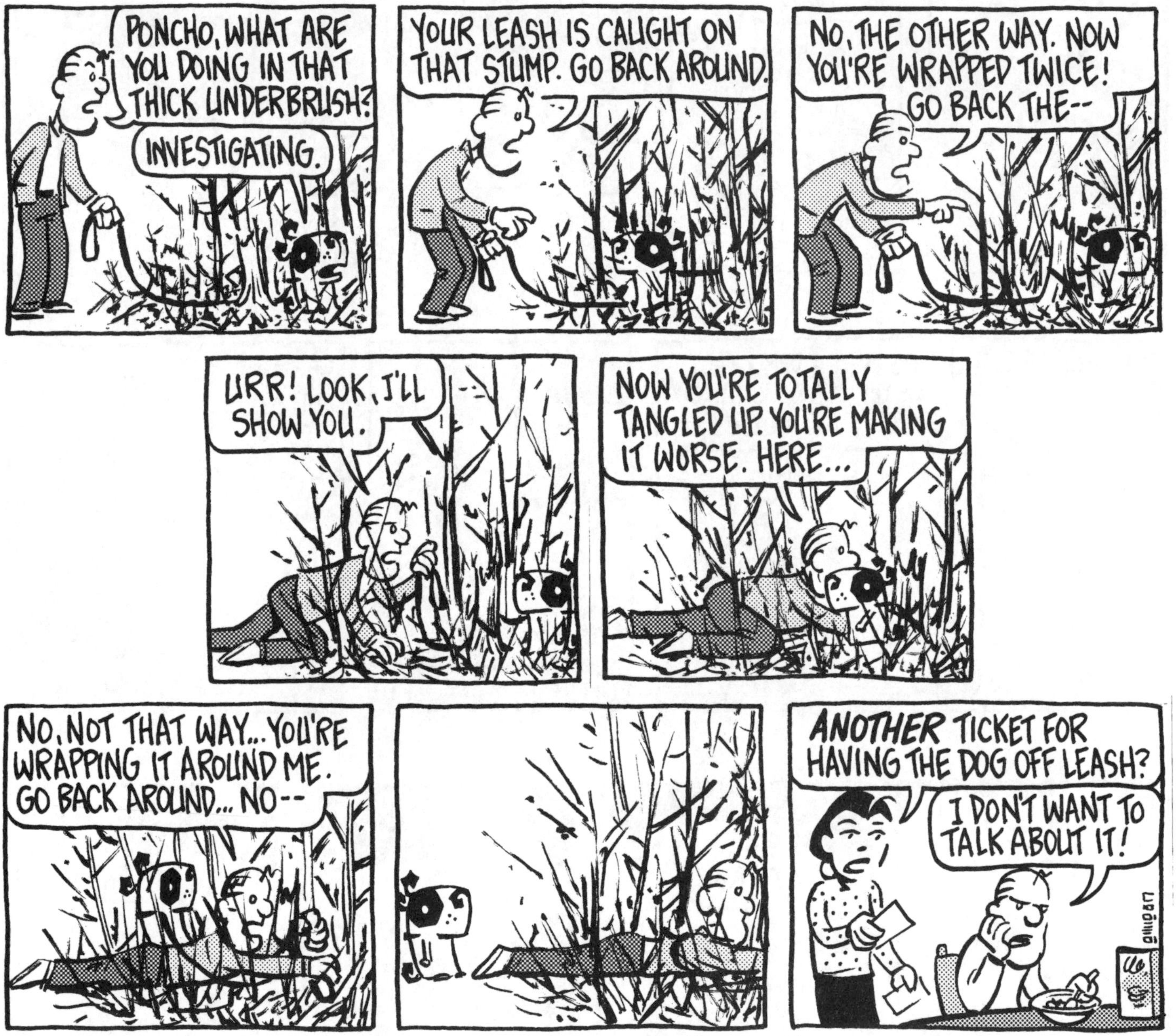
PONCHO, WHAT ARE YOU DOING IN THAT THICK UNDERBRUSH?
INVESTIGATING.
YOUR LEASH IS CAUGHT ON THAT STUMP. GO BACK AROUND.
NO, THE OTHER WAY. NOW YOU'RE WRAPPED TWICE! GO BACK THE--
URR! LOOK, I'LL SHOW YOU.
NOW YOU'RE TOTALLY TANGLED UP. YOU'RE MAKING IT WORSE. HERE...
NO, NOT THAT WAY... YOU'RE WRAPPING IT AROUND ME. GO BACK AROUND... NO--
ANOTHER TICKET FOR HAVING THE DOG OFF LEASH?
I DON'T WANT TO TALK ABOUT IT!

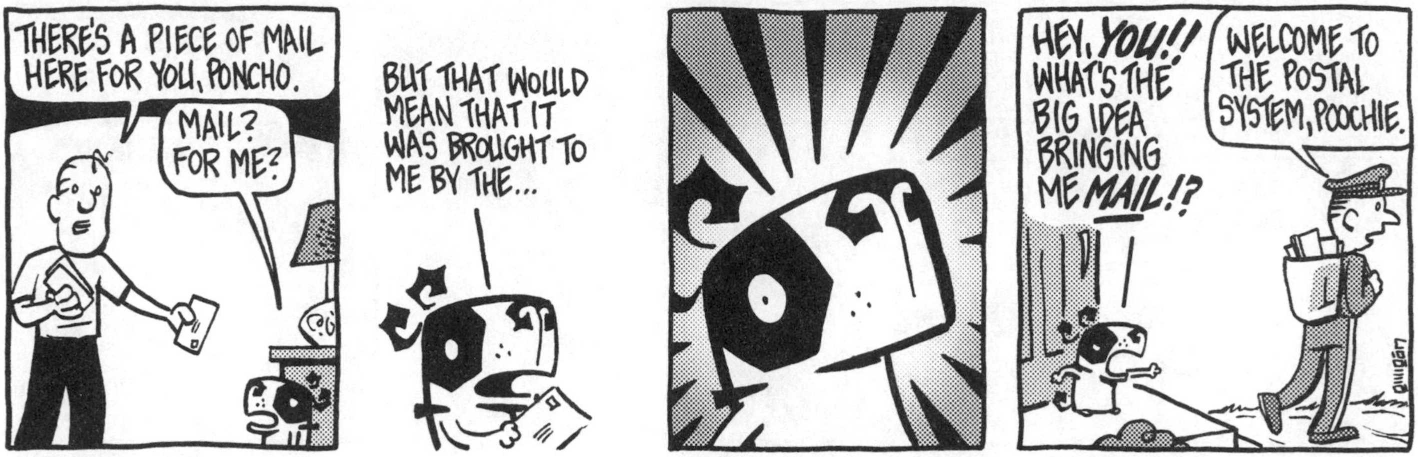
THERE'S A PIECE OF MAIL HERE FOR YOU, PONCHO.
MAIL? FOR ME?
BUT THAT WOULD MEAN THAT IT WAS BROUGHT TO ME BY THE...
HEY, YOU!! WHAT'S THE BIG IDEA BRINGING ME MAIL!?
WELCOME TO THE POSTAL SYSTEM, POOCHIE.

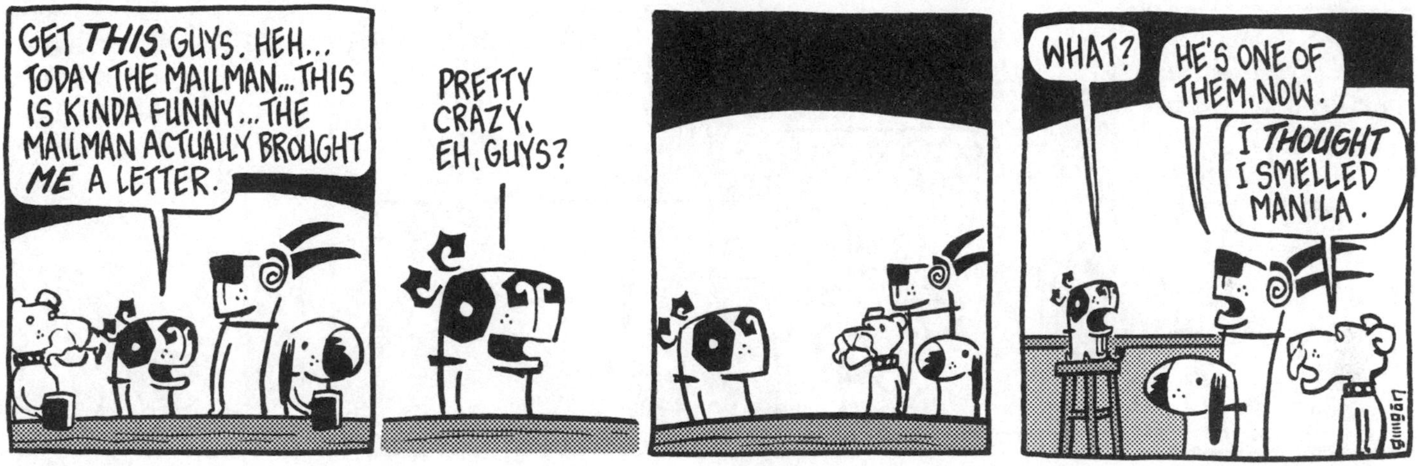
GET THIS, GUYS. HEH... TODAY THE MAILMAN...THIS IS KINDA FUNNY...THE MAILMAN ACTUALLY BROUGHT ME A LETTER.
PRETTY CRAZY, EH, GUYS?
WHAT?
HE'S ONE OF THEM, NOW.
I THOUGHT I SMELLED MANILA.

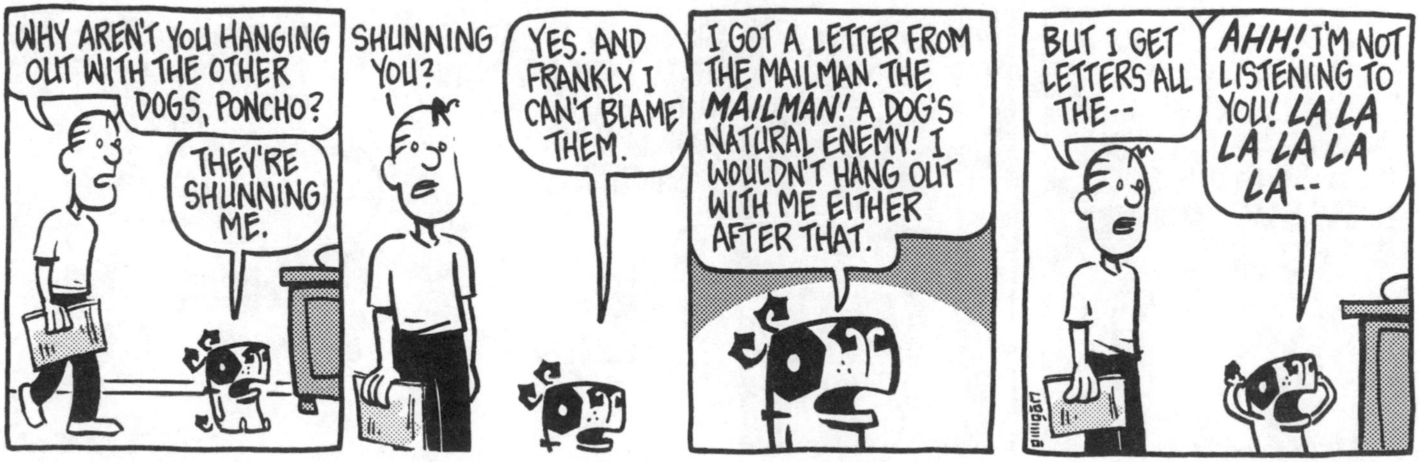
WHY AREN'T YOU HANGING OUT WITH THE OTHER DOGS, PONCHO?
THEY'RE SHUNNING ME.
SHUNNING YOU?
YES. AND FRANKLY I CAN'T BLAME THEM.
I GOT A LETTER FROM THE MAILMAN. THE MAILMAN! A DOG'S NATURAL ENEMY! I WOULDN'T HANG OUT WITH ME EITHER AFTER THAT.
BUT I GET LETTERS ALL THE--
AHH! I'M NOT LISTENING TO YOU! LA LA LA LA LA LA--

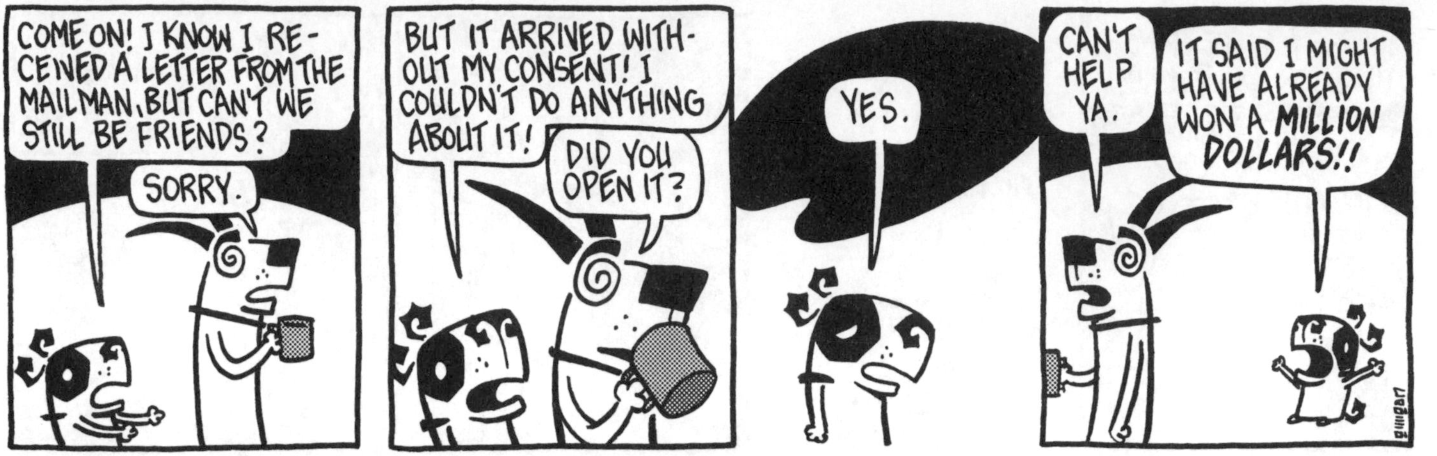
COME ON! I KNOW I RECEIVED A LETTER FROM THE MAILMAN, BUT CAN'T WE STILL BE FRIENDS?
SORRY.
BUT IT ARRIVED WITHOUT MY CONSENT! I COULDN'T DO ANYTHING ABOUT IT!
DID YOU OPEN IT?
YES.
CAN'T HELP YA.
IT SAID I MIGHT HAVE ALREADY WON A **MILLION DOLLARS!!**

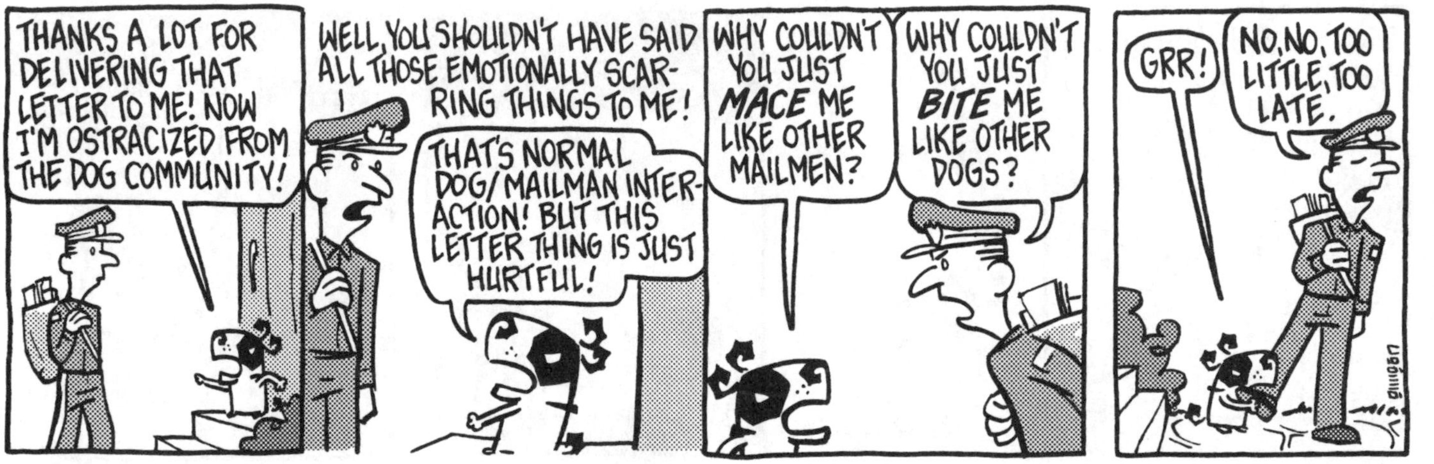
THANKS A LOT FOR DELIVERING THAT LETTER TO ME! NOW I'M OSTRACIZED FROM THE DOG COMMUNITY!
WELL, YOU SHOULDN'T HAVE SAID ALL THOSE EMOTIONALLY SCARRING THINGS TO ME!
THAT'S NORMAL DOG/MAILMAN INTERACTION! BUT THIS LETTER THING IS JUST HURTFUL!
WHY COULDN'T YOU JUST *MACE* ME LIKE OTHER MAILMEN?
WHY COULDN'T YOU JUST *BITE* ME LIKE OTHER DOGS?
GRR!
NO, NO, TOO LITTLE, TOO LATE.

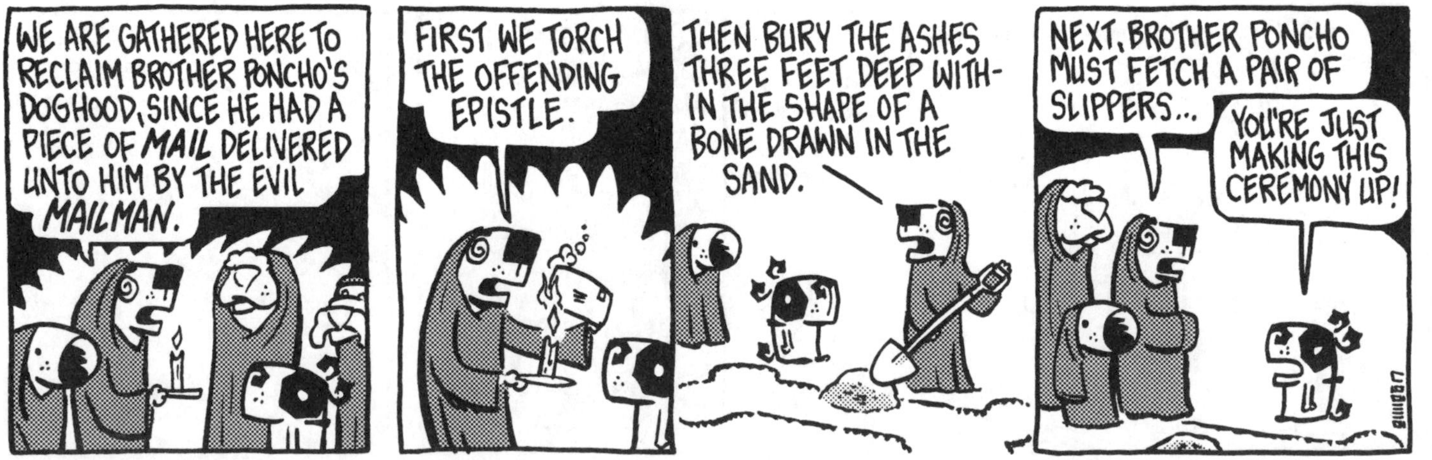
WE ARE GATHERED HERE TO RECLAIM BROTHER PONCHO'S DOGHOOD, SINCE HE HAD A PIECE OF *MAIL* DELIVERED UNTO HIM BY THE EVIL *MAILMAN*.
FIRST WE TORCH THE OFFENDING EPISTLE.
THEN BURY THE ASHES THREE FEET DEEP WITHIN THE SHAPE OF A BONE DRAWN IN THE SAND.
NEXT, BROTHER PONCHO MUST FETCH A PAIR OF SLIPPERS...
YOU'RE JUST MAKING THIS CEREMONY UP!

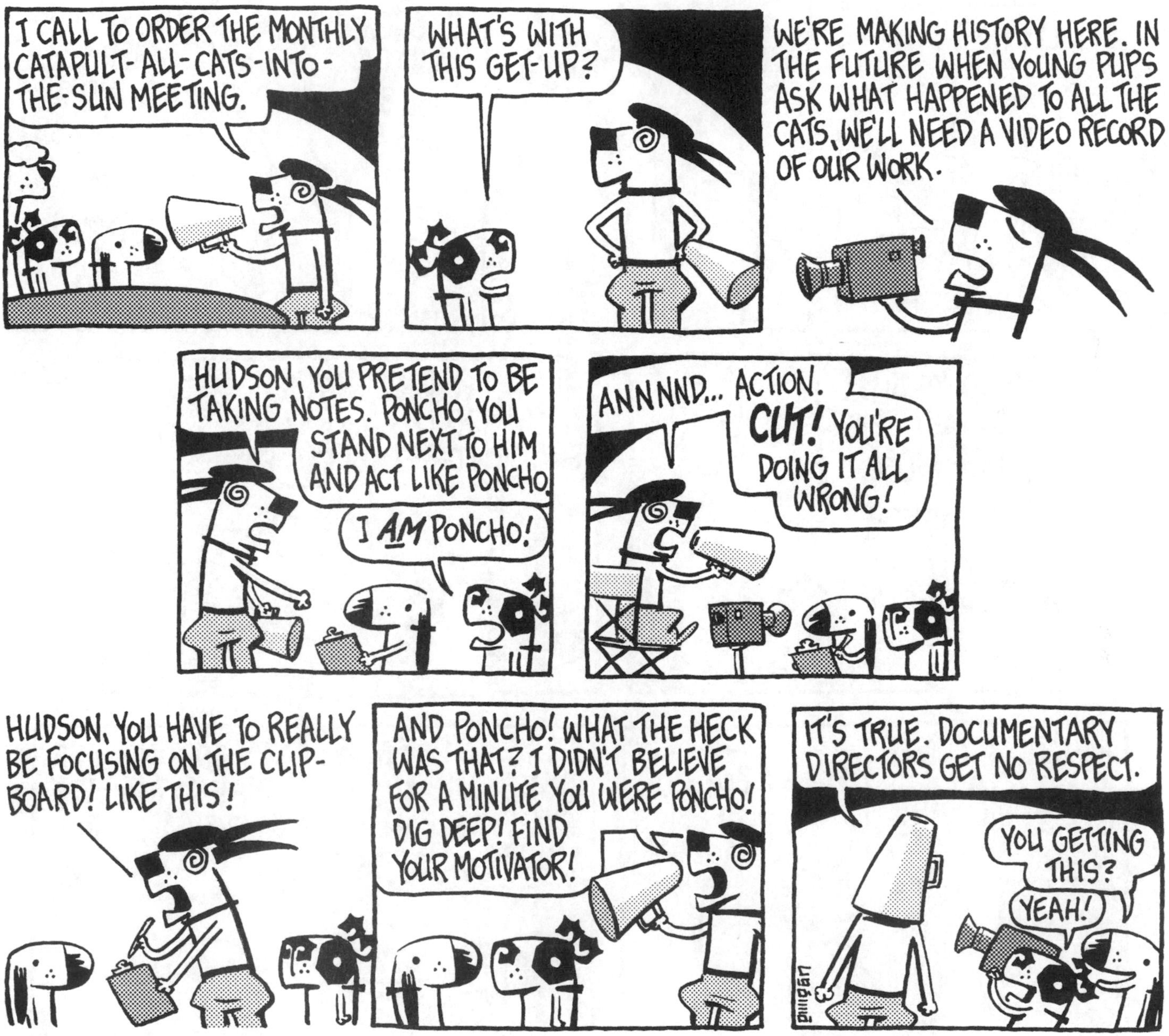
I CALL TO ORDER THE MONTHLY CATAPULT-ALL-CATS-INTO-THE-SUN MEETING.
WHAT'S WITH THIS GET-UP?
WE'RE MAKING HISTORY HERE. IN THE FUTURE WHEN YOUNG PUPS ASK WHAT HAPPENED TO ALL THE CATS, WE'LL NEED A VIDEO RECORD OF OUR WORK.
HUDSON, YOU PRETEND TO BE TAKING NOTES. PONCHO, YOU STAND NEXT TO HIM AND ACT LIKE PONCHO.
I *AM* PONCHO!
ANNNND... ACTION.
CUT! YOU'RE DOING IT ALL WRONG!
HUDSON, YOU HAVE TO REALLY BE FOCUSING ON THE CLIP-BOARD! LIKE THIS!
AND PONCHO! WHAT THE HECK WAS THAT? I DIDN'T BELIEVE FOR A MINUTE YOU WERE PONCHO! DIG DEEP! FIND YOUR MOTIVATOR!
IT'S TRUE. DOCUMENTARY DIRECTORS GET NO RESPECT.
YOU GETTING THIS?
YEAH!
DILLIGAN

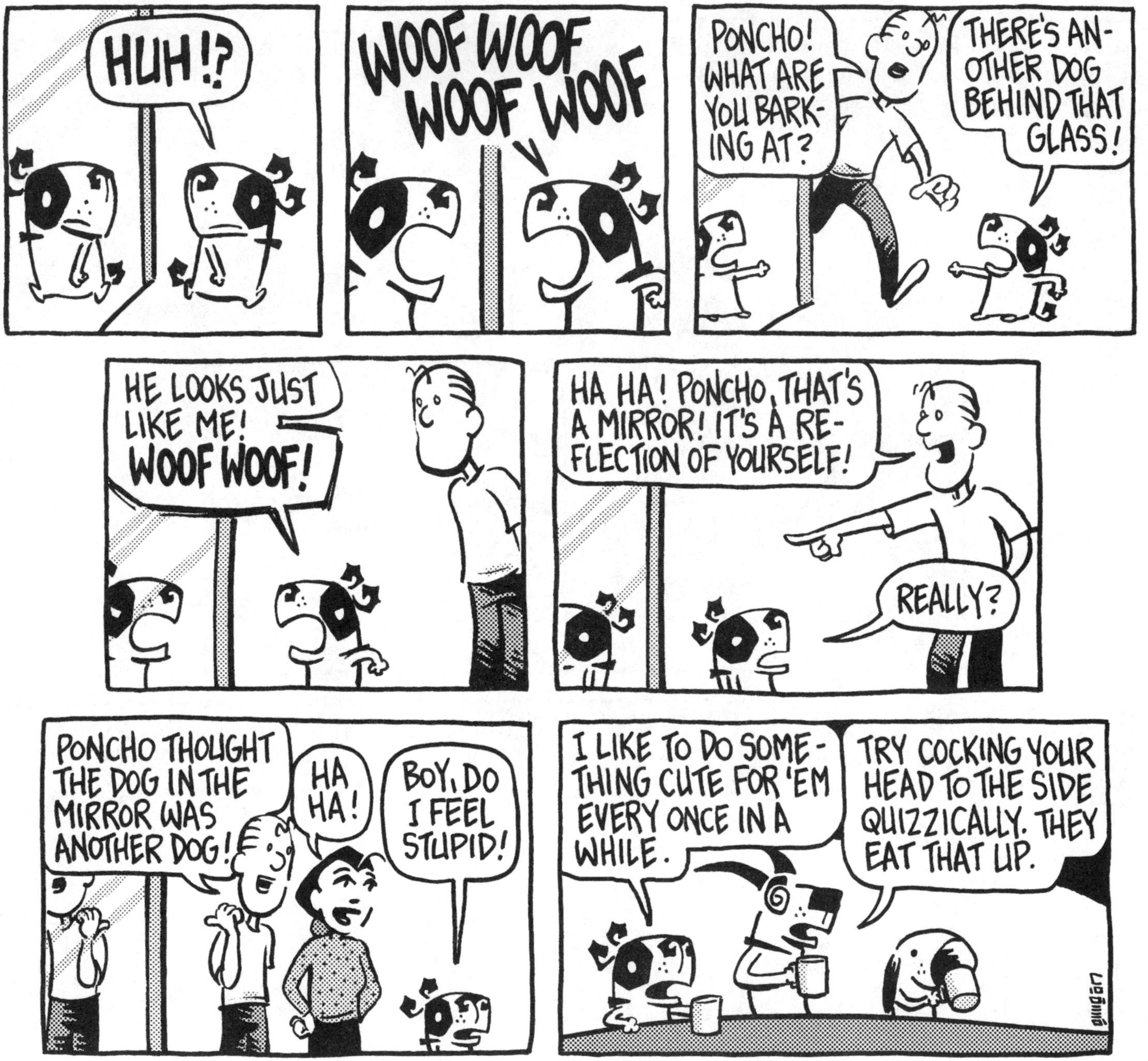
HUH!?
WOOF WOOF WOOF WOOF
PONCHO! WHAT ARE YOU BARKING AT?
THERE'S ANOTHER DOG BEHIND THAT GLASS!
HE LOOKS JUST LIKE ME! WOOF WOOF!
HA HA! PONCHO, THAT'S A MIRROR! IT'S A REFLECTION OF YOURSELF!
REALLY?
PONCHO THOUGHT THE DOG IN THE MIRROR WAS ANOTHER DOG!
HA HA!
BOY, DO I FEEL STUPID!
I LIKE TO DO SOMETHING CUTE FOR 'EM EVERY ONCE IN A WHILE.
TRY COCKING YOUR HEAD TO THE SIDE QUIZZICALLY. THEY EAT THAT UP.

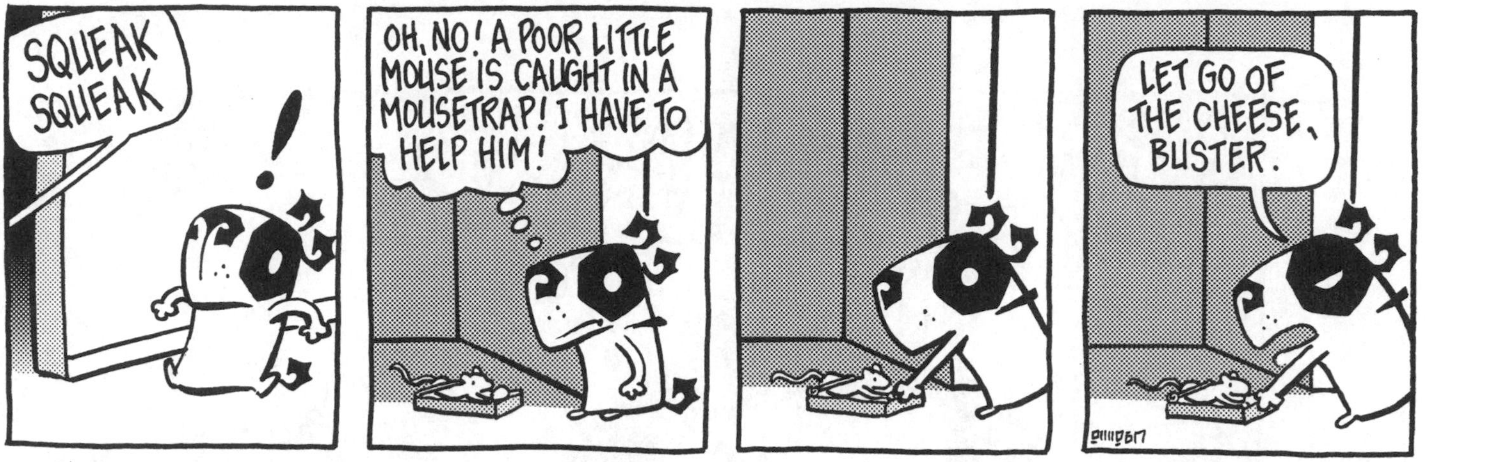
SQUEAK SQUEAK
!
OH, NO! A POOR LITTLE MOUSE IS CAUGHT IN A MOUSETRAP! I HAVE TO HELP HIM!
LET GO OF THE CHEESE, BUSTER.

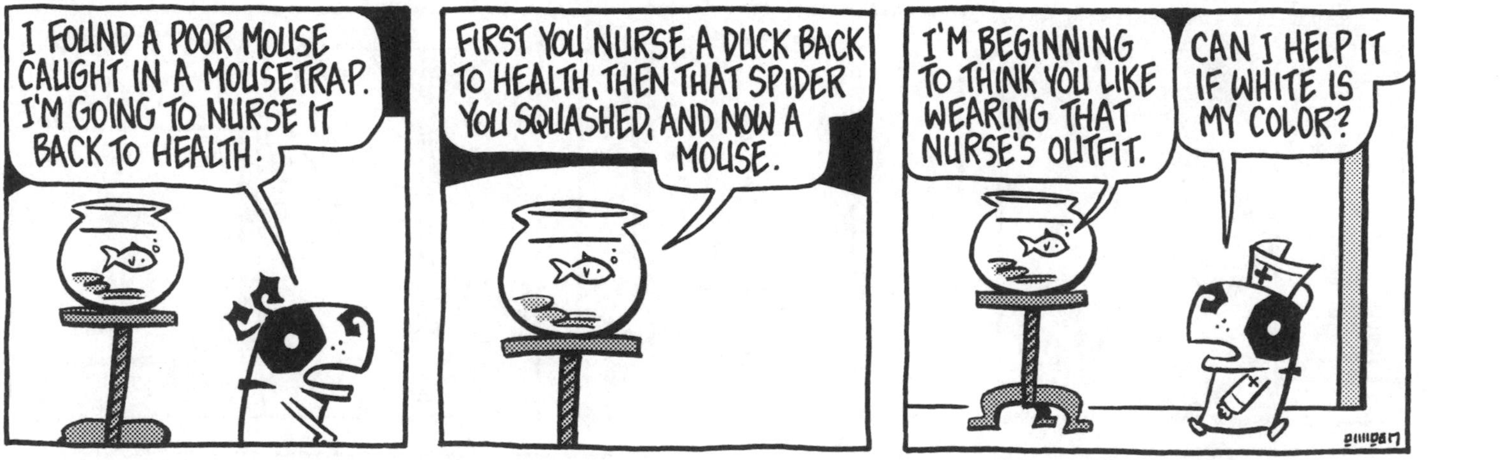
I FOUND A POOR MOUSE CAUGHT IN A MOUSETRAP. I'M GOING TO NURSE IT BACK TO HEALTH.
FIRST YOU NURSE A DUCK BACK TO HEALTH, THEN THAT SPIDER YOU SQUASHED, AND NOW A MOUSE.
I'M BEGINNING TO THINK YOU LIKE WEARING THAT NURSE'S OUTFIT.
CAN I HELP IT IF WHITE IS MY COLOR?

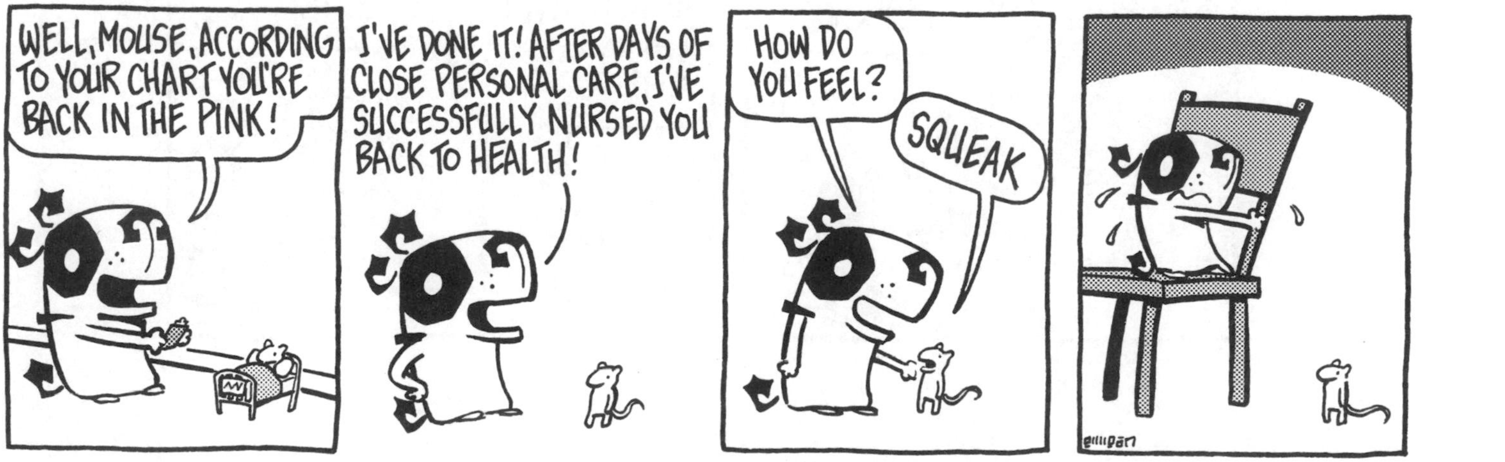
WELL, MOUSE, ACCORDING TO YOUR CHART YOU'RE BACK IN THE PINK!
I'VE DONE IT! AFTER DAYS OF CLOSE PERSONAL CARE, I'VE SUCCESSFULLY NURSED YOU BACK TO HEALTH!
HOW DO YOU FEEL?
SQUEAK

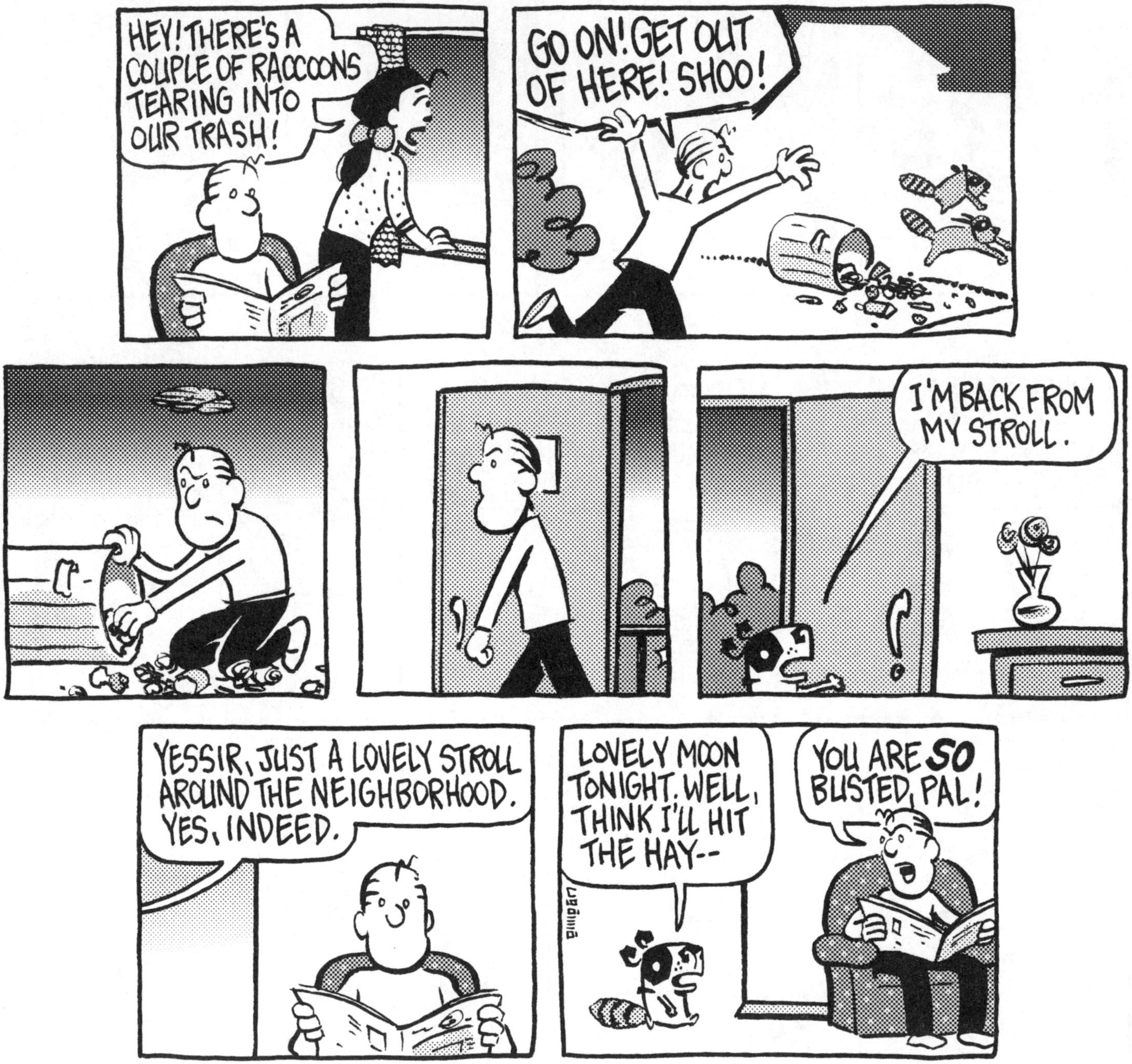
HEY! THERE'S A COUPLE OF RACCOONS TEARING INTO OUR TRASH!
GO ON! GET OUT OF HERE! SHOO!
I'M BACK FROM MY STROLL.
YESSIR, JUST A LOVELY STROLL AROUND THE NEIGHBORHOOD. YES, INDEED.
LOVELY MOON TONIGHT. WELL, THINK I'LL HIT THE HAY--
YOU ARE **SO** BUSTED, PAL!

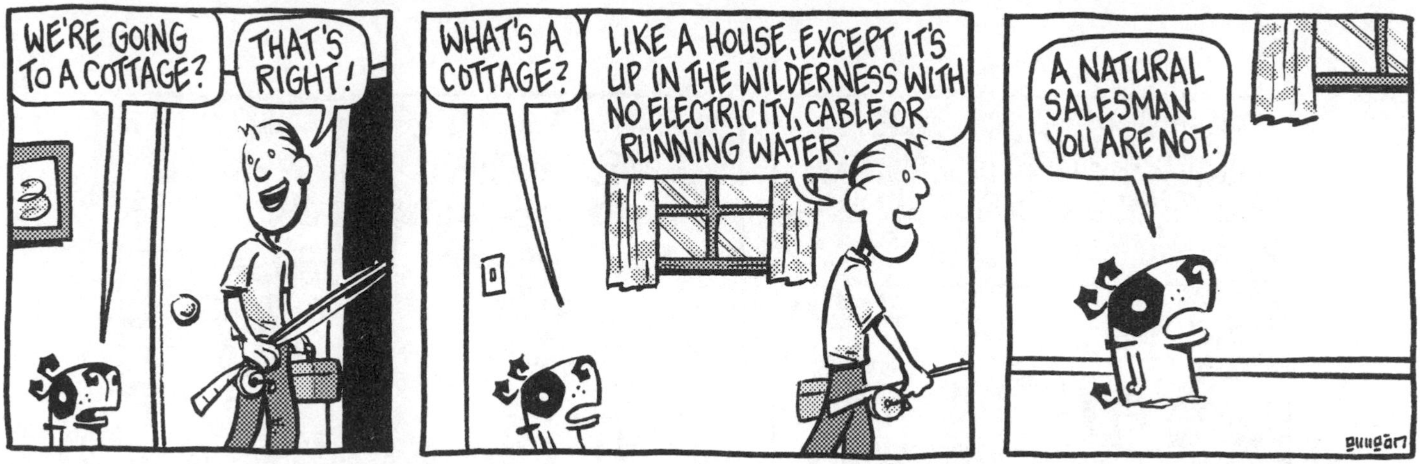
WE'RE GOING TO A COTTAGE?
THAT'S RIGHT!
WHAT'S A COTTAGE?
LIKE A HOUSE, EXCEPT IT'S UP IN THE WILDERNESS WITH NO ELECTRICITY, CABLE OR RUNNING WATER.
A NATURAL SALESMAN YOU ARE NOT.

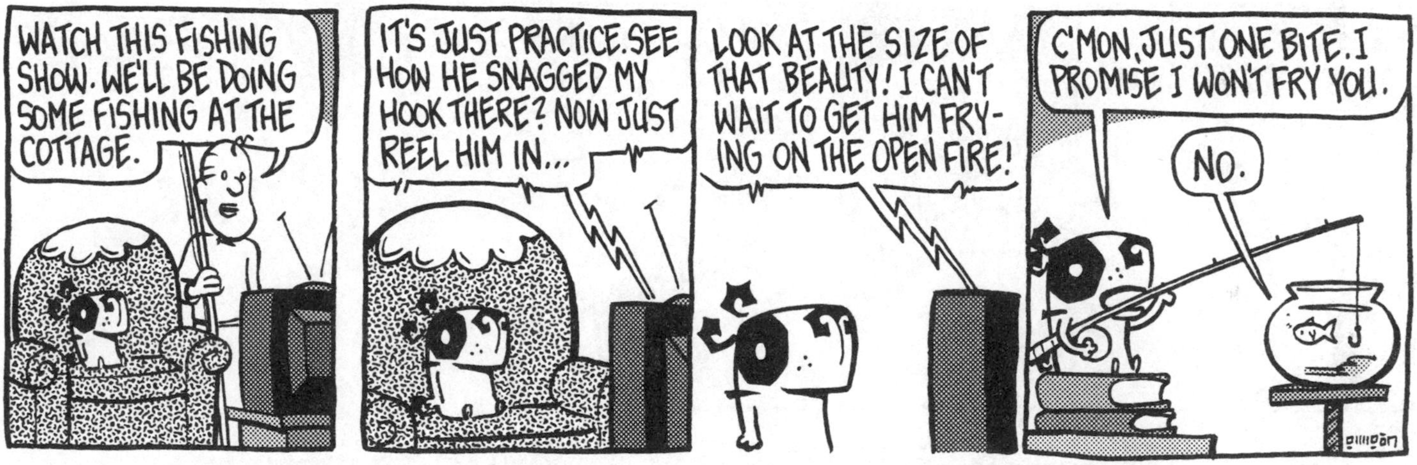
WATCH THIS FISHING SHOW. WE'LL BE DOING SOME FISHING AT THE COTTAGE.
IT'S JUST PRACTICE. SEE HOW HE SNAGGED MY HOOK THERE? NOW JUST REEL HIM IN...
LOOK AT THE SIZE OF THAT BEAUTY! I CAN'T WAIT TO GET HIM FRY-ING ON THE OPEN FIRE!
C'MON, JUST ONE BITE. I PROMISE I WON'T FRY YOU.
NO.

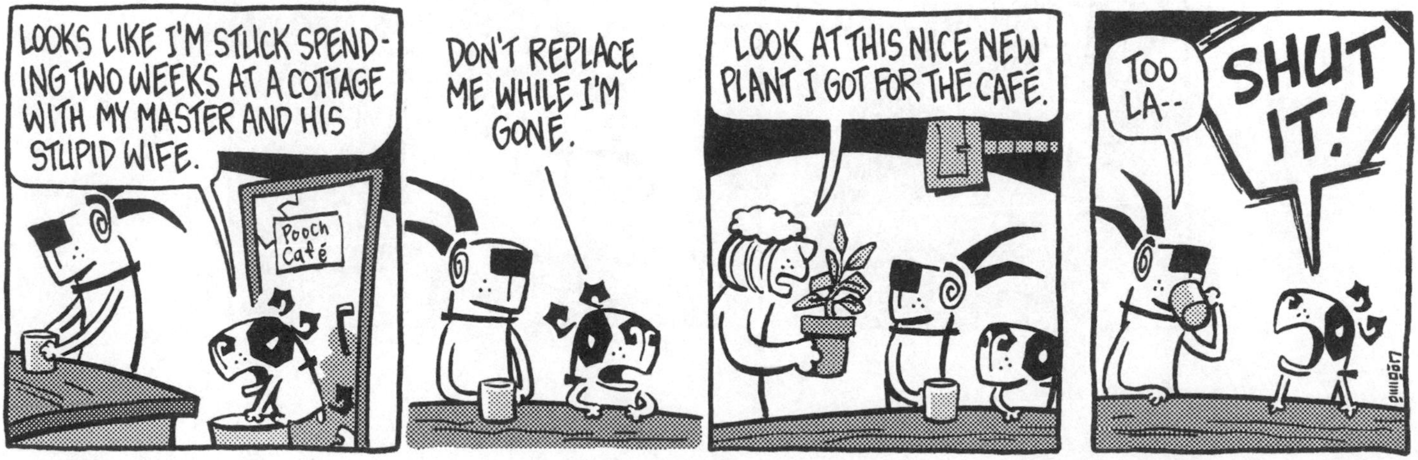
LOOKS LIKE I'M STUCK SPEND-ING TWO WEEKS AT A COTTAGE WITH MY MASTER AND HIS STUPID WIFE.
Pooch Café
DON'T REPLACE ME WHILE I'M GONE.
LOOK AT THIS NICE NEW PLANT I GOT FOR THE CAFÉ.
TOO LA--
SHUT IT!

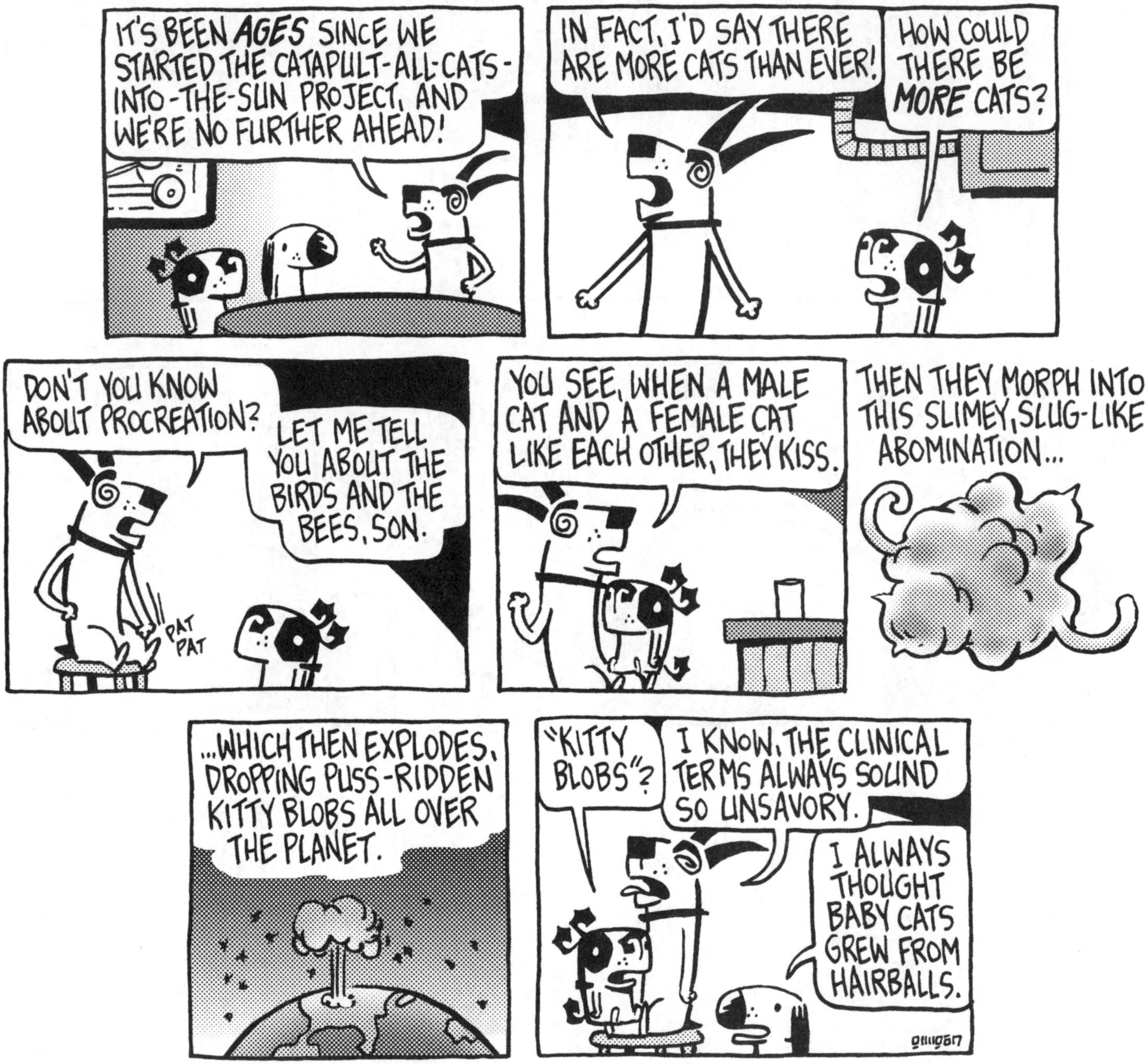
IT'S BEEN AGES SINCE WE STARTED THE CATAPULT-ALL-CATS-INTO-THE-SUN PROJECT, AND WE'RE NO FURTHER AHEAD!
IN FACT, I'D SAY THERE ARE MORE CATS THAN EVER!
HOW COULD THERE BE MORE CATS?
DON'T YOU KNOW ABOUT PROCREATION?
LET ME TELL YOU ABOUT THE BIRDS AND THE BEES, SON.
PAT PAT
YOU SEE, WHEN A MALE CAT AND A FEMALE CAT LIKE EACH OTHER, THEY KISS.
THEN THEY MORPH INTO THIS SLIMEY, SLUG-LIKE ABOMINATION...
...WHICH THEN EXPLODES, DROPPING PUSS-RIDDEN KITTY BLOBS ALL OVER THE PLANET.
"KITTY BLOBS"?
I KNOW, THE CLINICAL TERMS ALWAYS SOUND SO UNSAVORY.
I ALWAYS THOUGHT BABY CATS GREW FROM HAIRBALLS.
gilligan

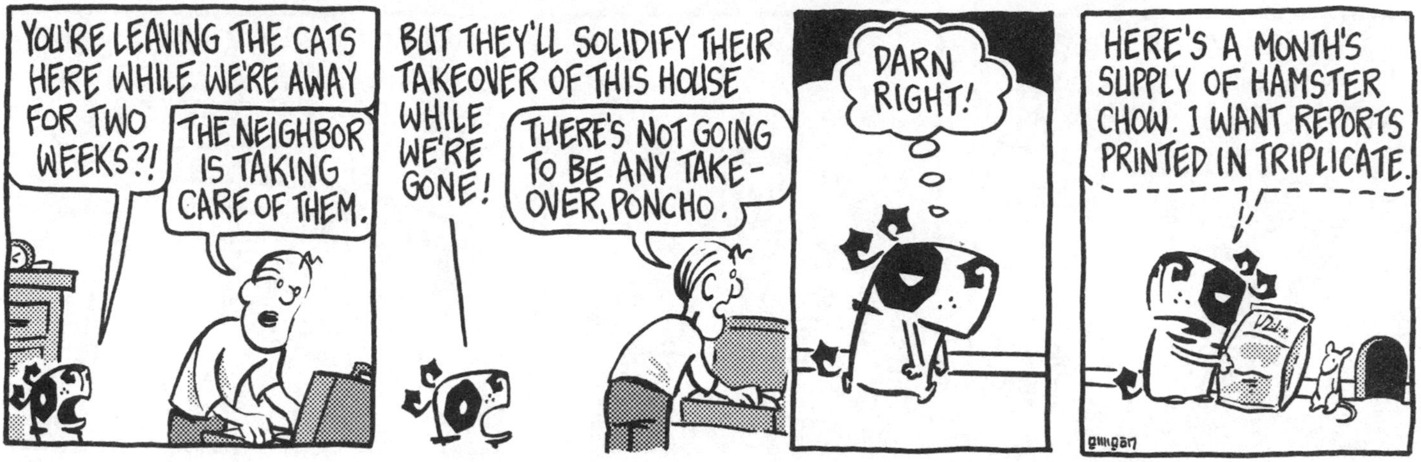
YOU'RE LEAVING THE CATS HERE WHILE WE'RE AWAY FOR TWO WEEKS?!
THE NEIGHBOR IS TAKING CARE OF THEM.
BUT THEY'LL SOLIDIFY THEIR TAKEOVER OF THIS HOUSE WHILE WE'RE GONE!
THERE'S NOT GOING TO BE ANY TAKE-OVER, PONCHO.
DARN RIGHT!
HERE'S A MONTH'S SUPPLY OF HAMSTER CHOW. I WANT REPORTS PRINTED IN TRIPLICATE.

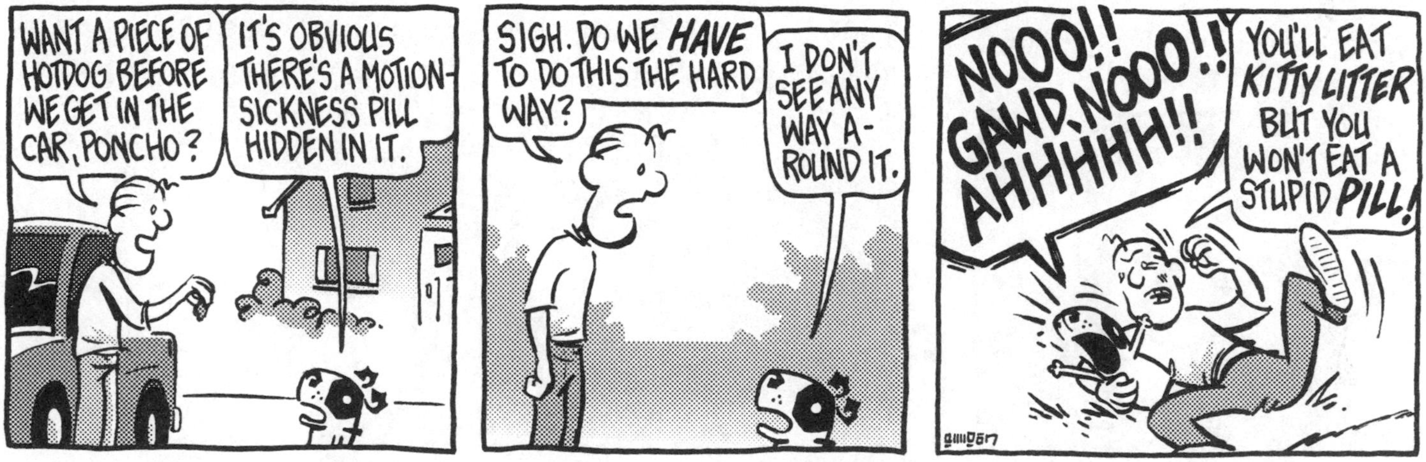
WANT A PIECE OF HOTDOG BEFORE WE GET IN THE CAR, PONCHO?
IT'S OBVIOUS THERE'S A MOTION-SICKNESS PILL HIDDEN IN IT.
SIGH. DO WE HAVE TO DO THIS THE HARD WAY?
I DON'T SEE ANY WAY A-ROUND IT.
NOOO!! GAWD, NOOO!! AHHHHH!!
YOU'LL EAT KITTY LITTER BUT YOU WON'T EAT A STUPID PILL!

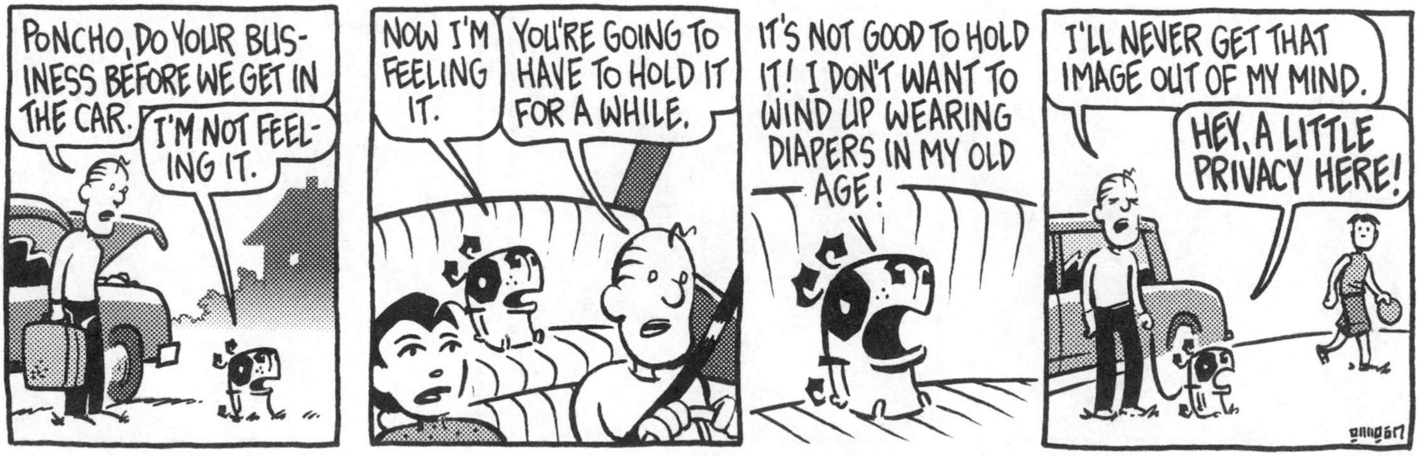
PONCHO, DO YOUR BUS-INESS BEFORE WE GET IN THE CAR.
I'M NOT FEEL-ING IT.
NOW I'M FEELING IT.
YOU'RE GOING TO HAVE TO HOLD IT FOR A WHILE.
IT'S NOT GOOD TO HOLD IT! I DON'T WANT TO WIND UP WEARING DIAPERS IN MY OLD AGE!
I'LL NEVER GET THAT IMAGE OUT OF MY MIND.
HEY, A LITTLE PRIVACY HERE!

Panel 1: SO, THERE'S NO RUNNING WATER AT THIS COTTAGE? — THAT'S RIGHT, PONCHO.

Panel 3: JUST SO YOU GUYS KNOW, THE JOYS OF DOING YOUR BUSINESS OUTSIDE WEAR OFF SURPRISINGLY FAST.

Panel 4: WE'RE CHECKING TO MAKE SURE EVERYONE IS BUCKLED UP FOR SAFTY.

Panel 5: UH OH! I'M NOT WEARING MY SEAT BELT! — THAT'S OKAY. WE ONLY REQUIRE HUMANS TO WEAR THEIR BELTS, NOT DOGS.

Panel 6: WELL, ISN'T THAT HEARTWARMING. YOUR CONCERN IS OVERWHELMING. MAN'S BEST FRIEND, INDEED... — THAT'S ENOUGH, PONCHO.

Panel 7: BOY, AM I STARVED! — THERE'S NOTHING TO EAT AROUND HERE FOR MILES. YEAH.

Panel 8: HERE WE ARE AT THE COTTAGE AT LAST, EVERYONE!

Panel 9: ♪ CELEBRATE GOOD TIMES, COME ON! ♪

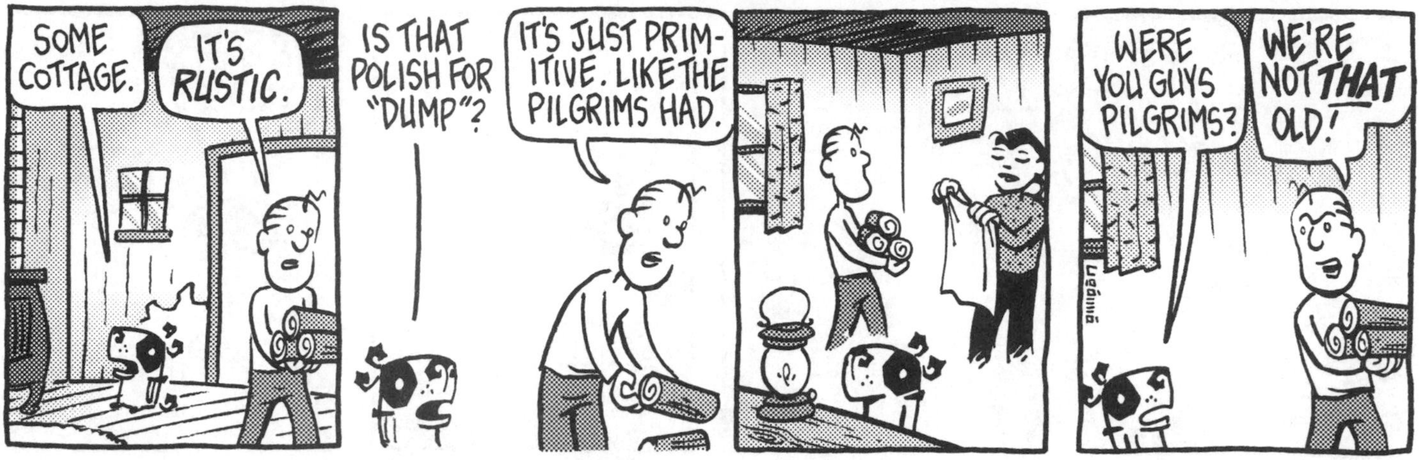
SOME COTTAGE.
IT'S RUSTIC.
IS THAT POLISH FOR "DUMP"?
IT'S JUST PRIMITIVE. LIKE THE PILGRIMS HAD.
WERE YOU GUYS PILGRIMS?
WE'RE NOT THAT OLD!

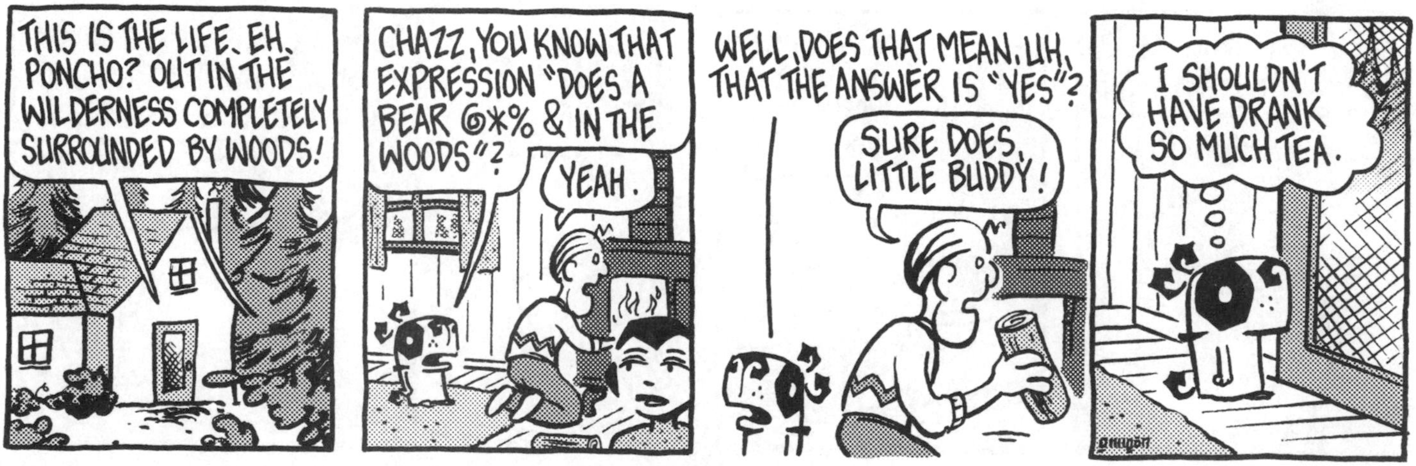
THIS IS THE LIFE, EH, PONCHO? OUT IN THE WILDERNESS COMPLETELY SURROUNDED BY WOODS!
CHAZZ, YOU KNOW THAT EXPRESSION "DOES A BEAR @*% & IN THE WOODS"?
YEAH.
WELL, DOES THAT MEAN, UH, THAT THE ANSWER IS "YES"?
SURE DOES, LITTLE BUDDY!
I SHOULDN'T HAVE DRANK SO MUCH TEA.

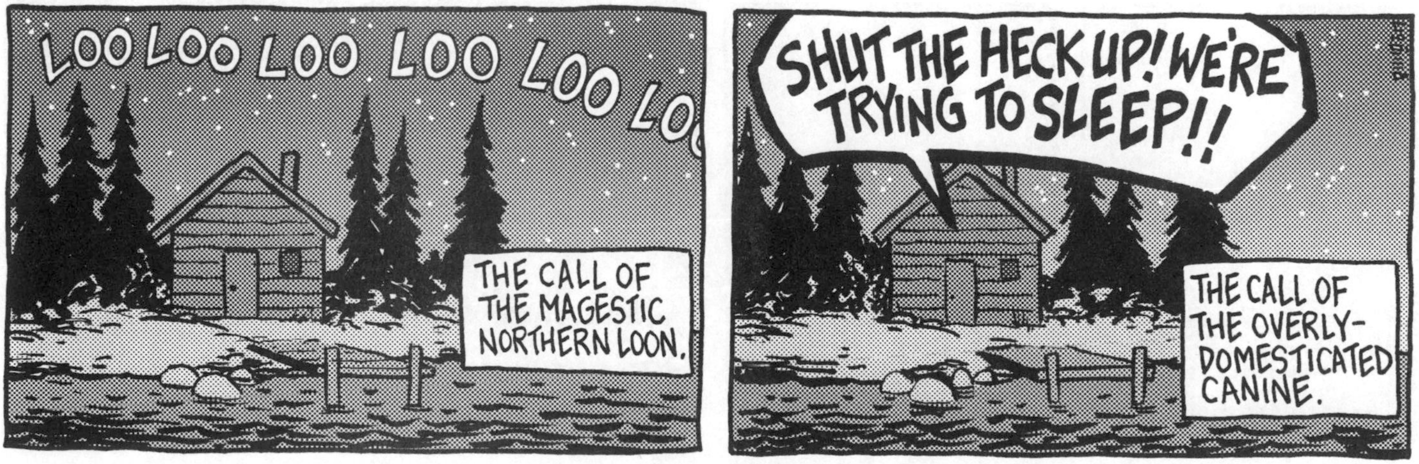
LOO LOO LOO LOO LOO LOO
THE CALL OF THE MAGESTIC NORTHERN LOON.
SHUT THE HECK UP! WE'RE TRYING TO SLEEP!!
THE CALL OF THE OVERLY-DOMESTICATED CANINE.

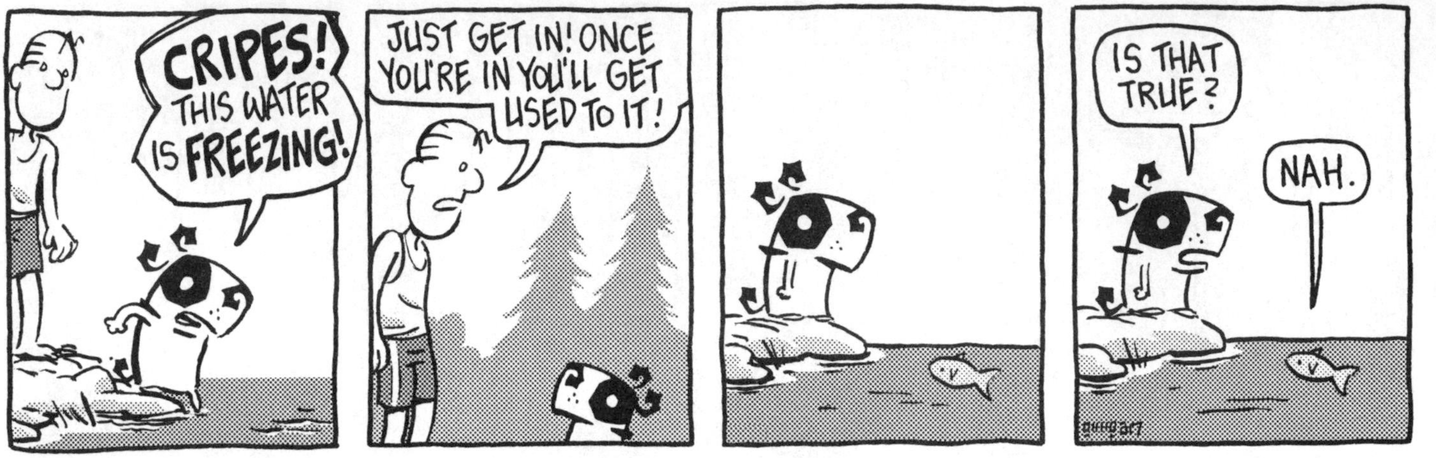
CRIPES! THIS WATER IS FREEZING!
JUST GET IN! ONCE YOU'RE IN YOU'LL GET USED TO IT!
IS THAT TRUE?
NAH.

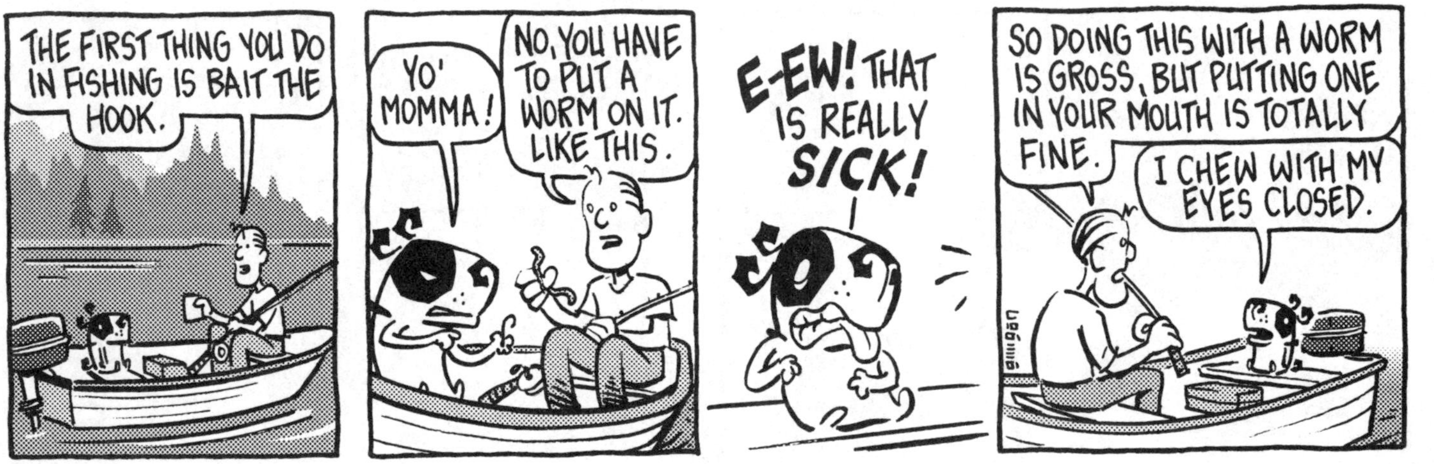
THE FIRST THING YOU DO IN FISHING IS BAIT THE HOOK.
YO' MOMMA!
NO, YOU HAVE TO PUT A WORM ON IT. LIKE THIS.
E-EW! THAT IS REALLY SICK!
SO DOING THIS WITH A WORM IS GROSS, BUT PUTTING ONE IN YOUR MOUTH IS TOTALLY FINE.
I CHEW WITH MY EYES CLOSED.

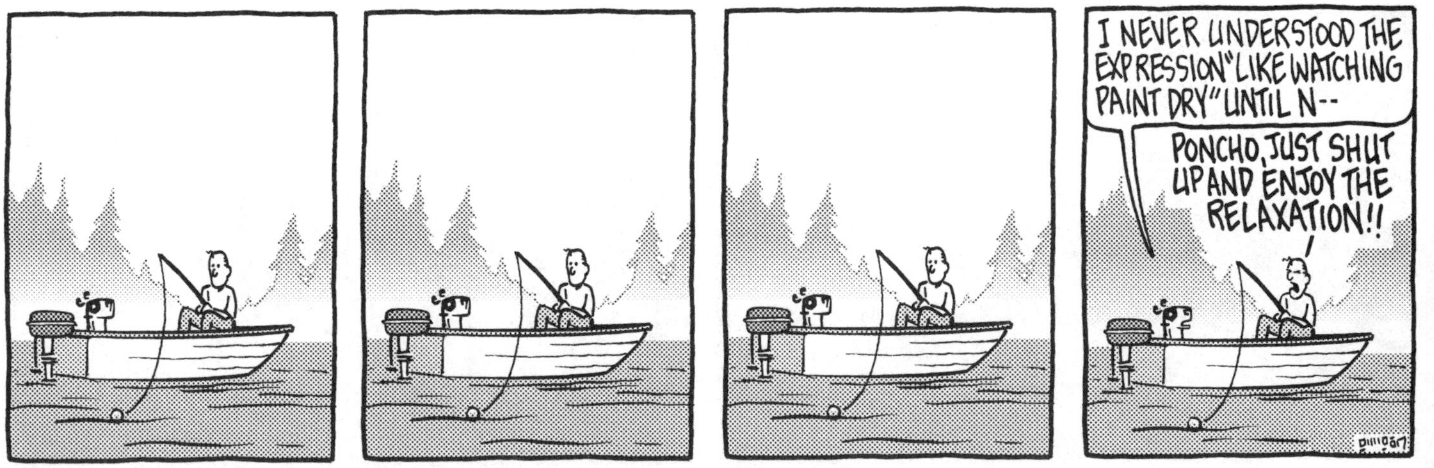
I NEVER UNDERSTOOD THE EXPRESSION "LIKE WATCHING PAINT DRY" UNTIL N--
PONCHO, JUST SHUT UP AND ENJOY THE RELAXATION!!

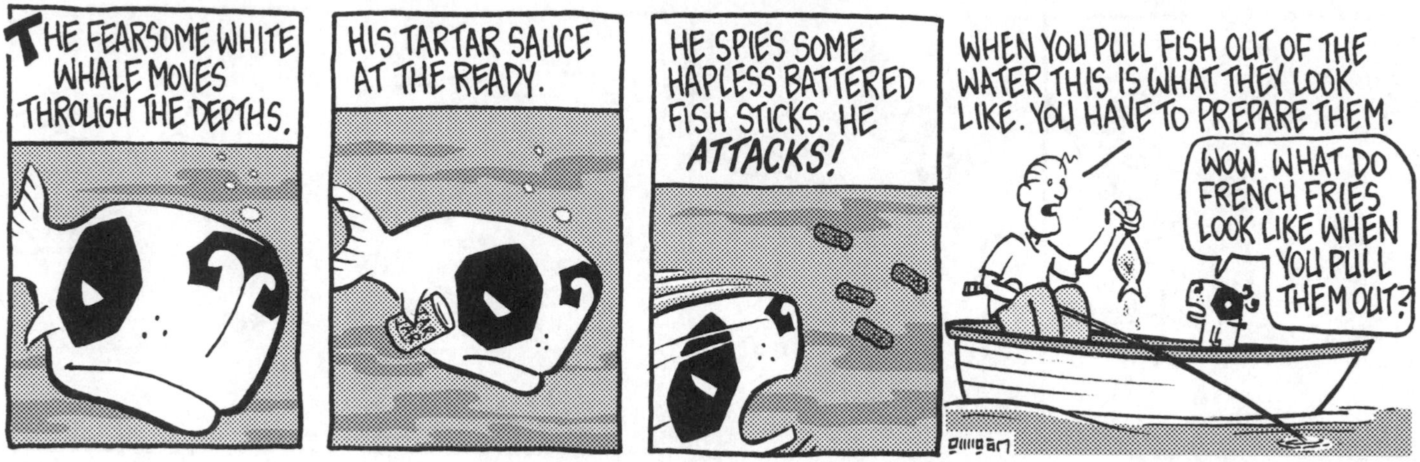
THE FEARSOME WHITE WHALE MOVES THROUGH THE DEPTHS.
HIS TARTAR SAUCE AT THE READY.
HE SPIES SOME HAPLESS BATTERED FISH STICKS. HE *ATTACKS!*
WHEN YOU PULL FISH OUT OF THE WATER THIS IS WHAT THEY LOOK LIKE. YOU HAVE TO PREPARE THEM.
WOW. WHAT DO FRENCH FRIES LOOK LIKE WHEN YOU PULL THEM OUT?
gilligan

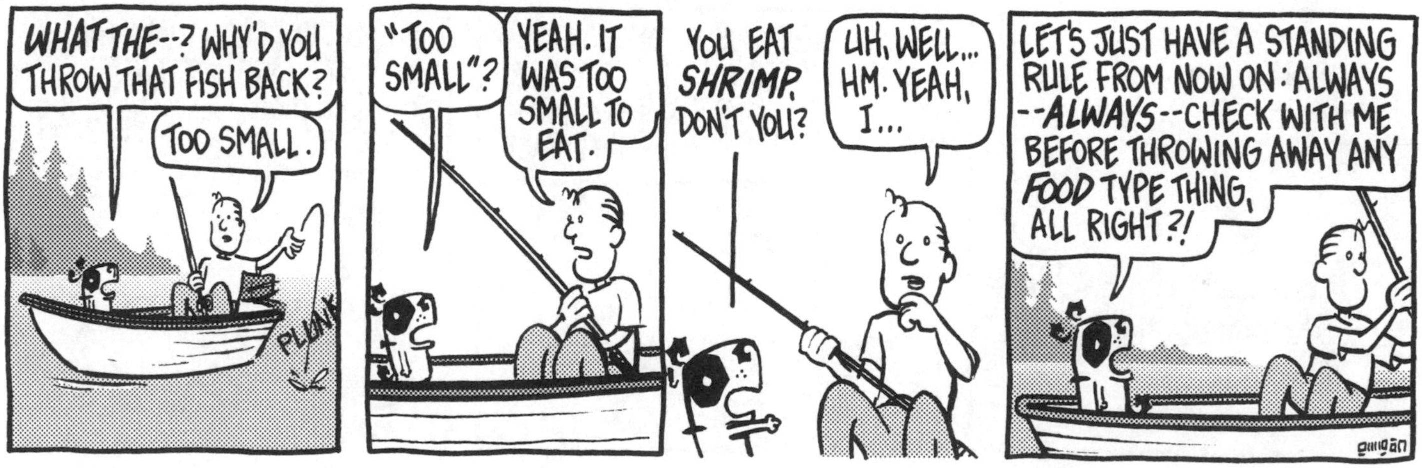
WHAT THE--? WHY'D YOU THROW THAT FISH BACK?
TOO SMALL.
PLUNK
"TOO SMALL"?
YEAH. IT WAS TOO SMALL TO EAT.
YOU EAT *SHRIMP*. DON'T YOU?
UH, WELL... HM. YEAH, I...
LET'S JUST HAVE A STANDING RULE FROM NOW ON: ALWAYS --*ALWAYS*--CHECK WITH ME BEFORE THROWING AWAY ANY *FOOD* TYPE THING, ALL RIGHT?!
gilligan

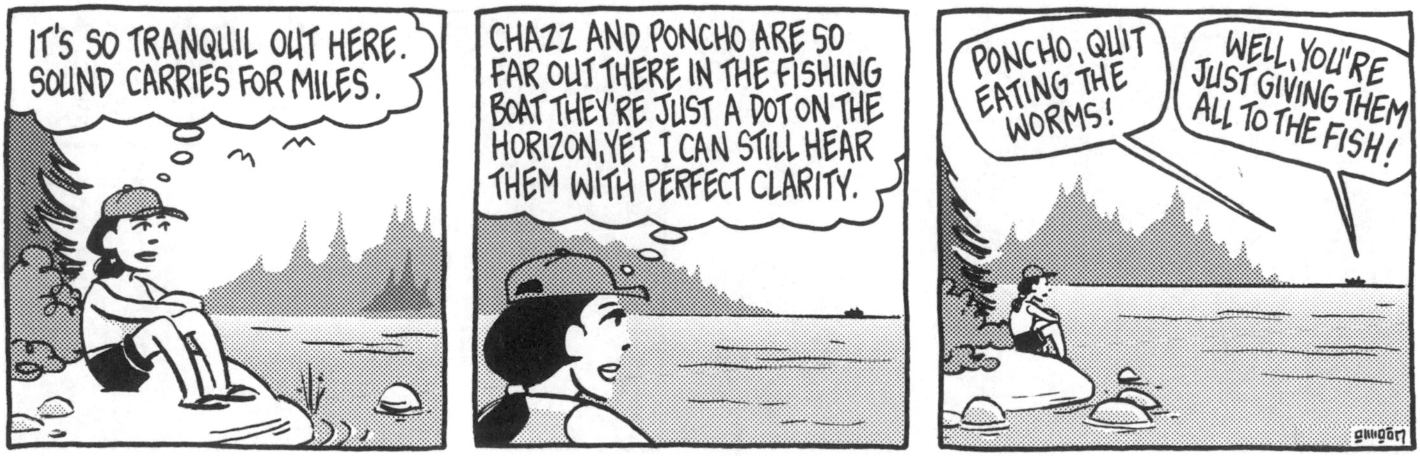
IT'S SO TRANQUIL OUT HERE. SOUND CARRIES FOR MILES.
CHAZZ AND PONCHO ARE SO FAR OUT THERE IN THE FISHING BOAT THEY'RE JUST A DOT ON THE HORIZON, YET I CAN STILL HEAR THEM WITH PERFECT CLARITY.
PONCHO, QUIT EATING THE WORMS!
WELL, YOU'RE JUST GIVING THEM ALL TO THE FISH!
gilligan

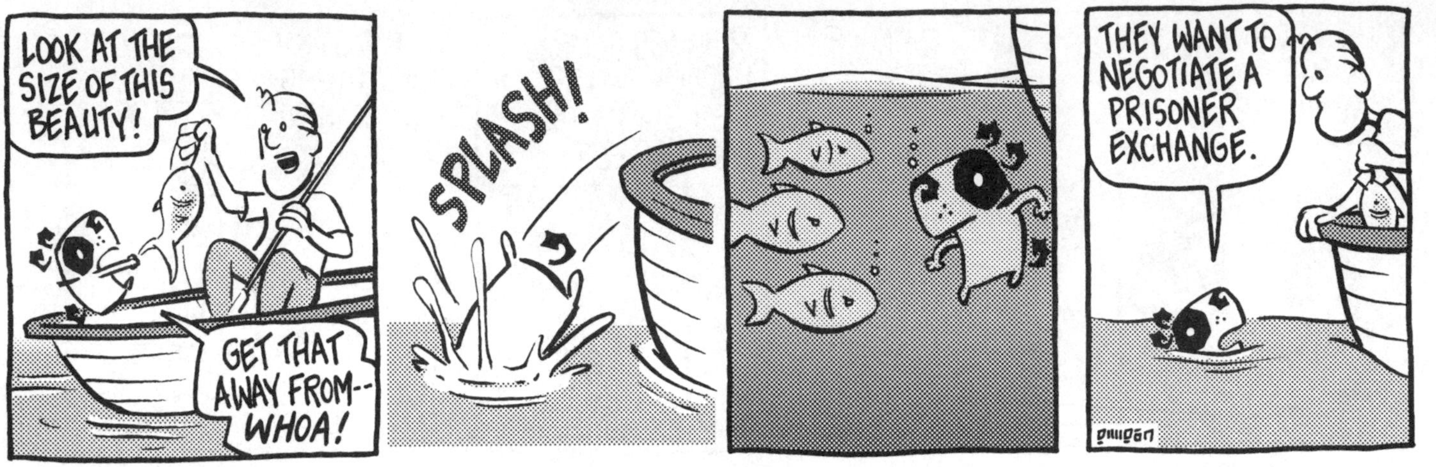
LOOK AT THE SIZE OF THIS BEAUTY!
GET THAT AWAY FROM-- WHOA!
SPLASH!
THEY WANT TO NEGOTIATE A PRISONER EXCHANGE.

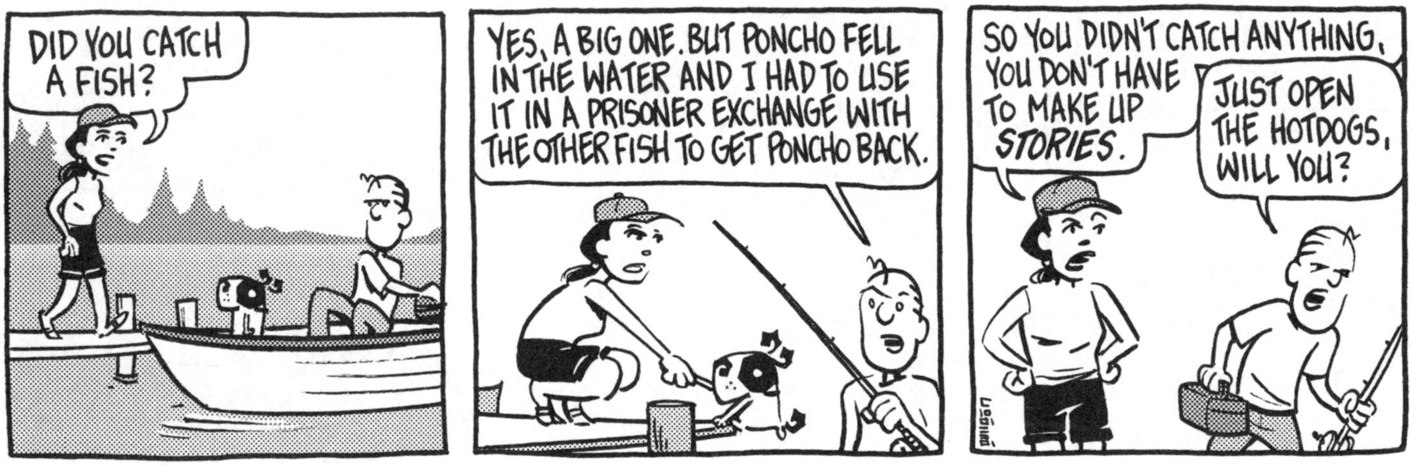
DID YOU CATCH A FISH?
YES, A BIG ONE. BUT PONCHO FELL IN THE WATER AND I HAD TO USE IT IN A PRISONER EXCHANGE WITH THE OTHER FISH TO GET PONCHO BACK.
SO YOU DIDN'T CATCH ANYTHING, YOU DON'T HAVE TO MAKE UP STORIES.
JUST OPEN THE HOTDOGS, WILL YOU?

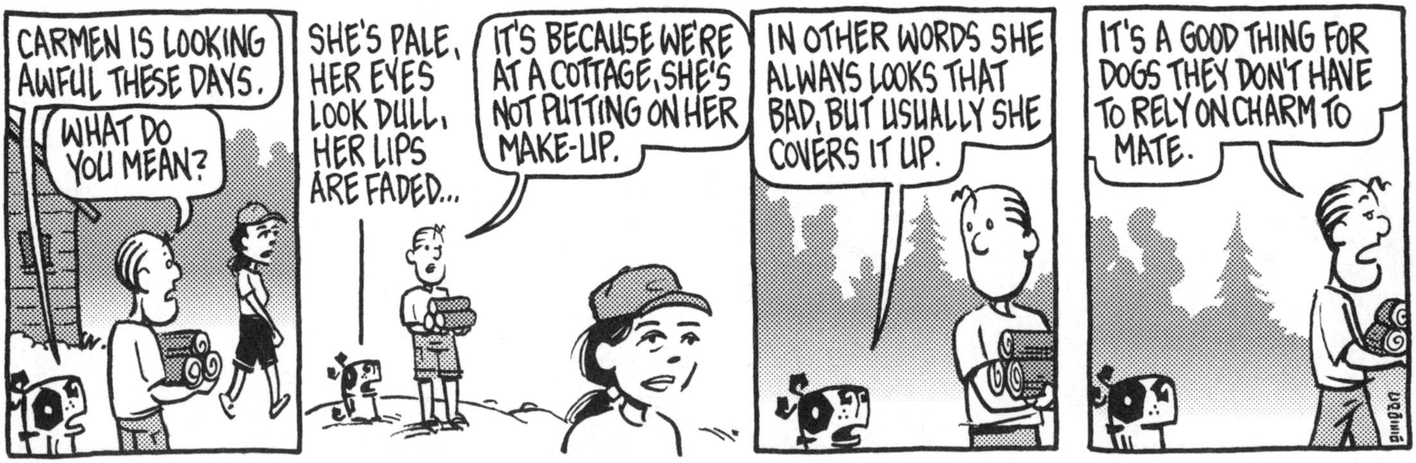
CARMEN IS LOOKING AWFUL THESE DAYS.
WHAT DO YOU MEAN?
SHE'S PALE, HER EYES LOOK DULL, HER LIPS ARE FADED...
IT'S BECAUSE WE'RE AT A COTTAGE, SHE'S NOT PUTTING ON HER MAKE-UP.
IN OTHER WORDS SHE ALWAYS LOOKS THAT BAD, BUT USUALLY SHE COVERS IT UP.
IT'S A GOOD THING FOR DOGS THEY DON'T HAVE TO RELY ON CHARM TO MATE.

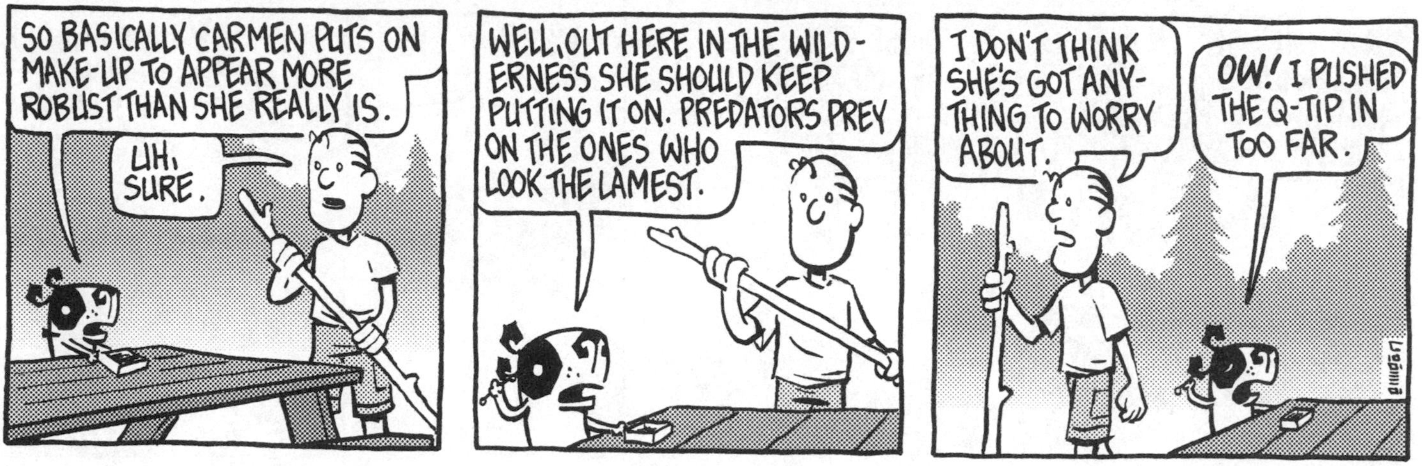
SO BASICALLY CARMEN PUTS ON MAKE-UP TO APPEAR MORE ROBUST THAN SHE REALLY IS.
UH, SURE.
WELL, OUT HERE IN THE WILDERNESS SHE SHOULD KEEP PUTTING IT ON. PREDATORS PREY ON THE ONES WHO LOOK THE LAMEST.
I DON'T THINK SHE'S GOT ANYTHING TO WORRY ABOUT.
OW! I PUSHED THE Q-TIP IN TOO FAR.

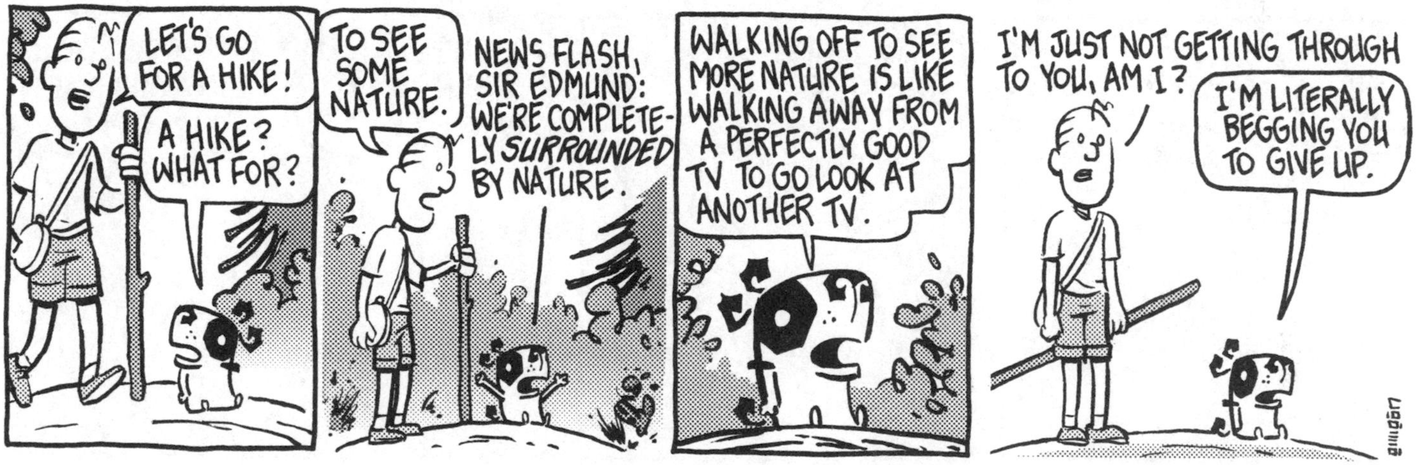
LET'S GO FOR A HIKE!
A HIKE? WHAT FOR?
TO SEE SOME NATURE.
NEWS FLASH, SIR EDMUND: WE'RE COMPLETELY *SURROUNDED* BY NATURE.
WALKING OFF TO SEE MORE NATURE IS LIKE WALKING AWAY FROM A PERFECTLY GOOD TV TO GO LOOK AT ANOTHER TV.
I'M JUST NOT GETTING THROUGH TO YOU, AM I?
I'M LITERALLY BEGGING YOU TO GIVE UP.

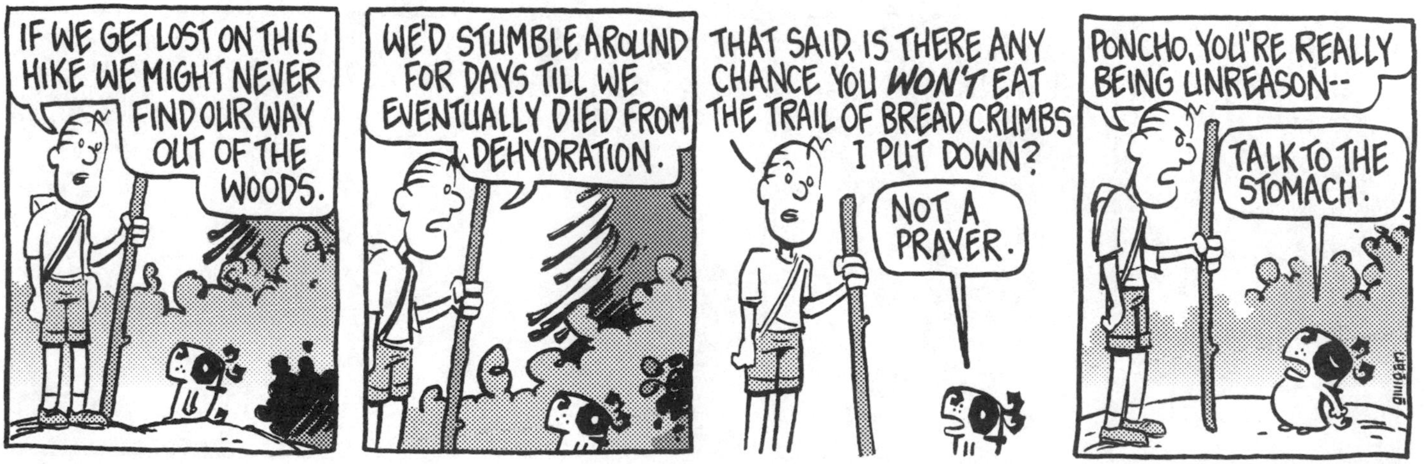
IF WE GET LOST ON THIS HIKE WE MIGHT NEVER FIND OUR WAY OUT OF THE WOODS.
WE'D STUMBLE AROUND FOR DAYS TILL WE EVENTUALLY DIED FROM DEHYDRATION.
THAT SAID, IS THERE ANY CHANCE YOU *WON'T* EAT THE TRAIL OF BREAD CRUMBS I PUT DOWN?
NOT A PRAYER.
PONCHO, YOU'RE REALLY BEING UNREASON--
TALK TO THE STOMACH.

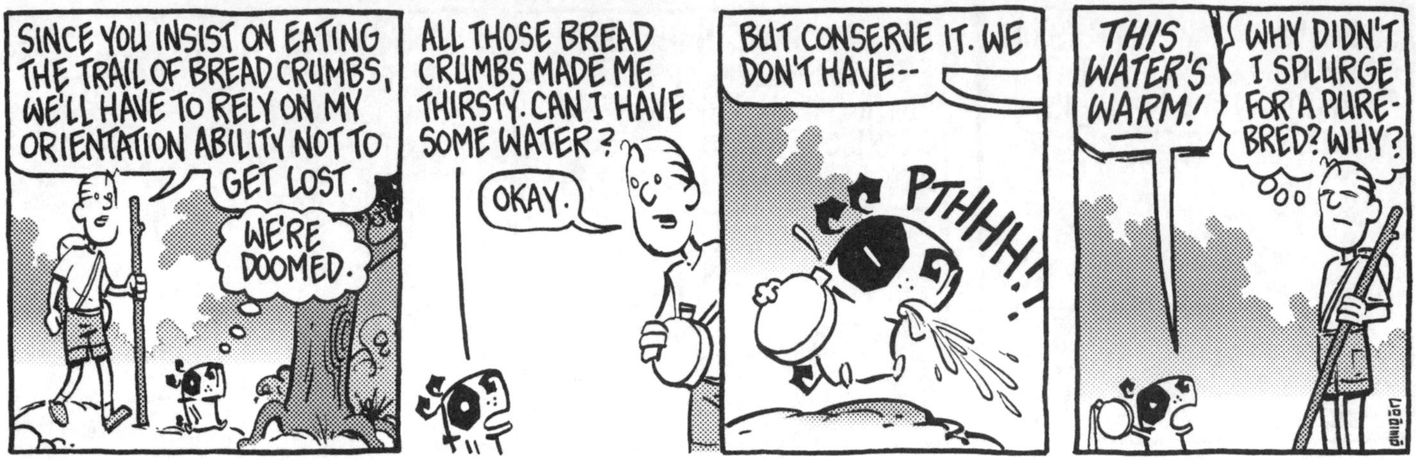
SINCE YOU INSIST ON EATING THE TRAIL OF BREAD CRUMBS, WE'LL HAVE TO RELY ON MY ORIENTATION ABILITY NOT TO GET LOST.
WE'RE DOOMED.
ALL THOSE BREAD CRUMBS MADE ME THIRSTY. CAN I HAVE SOME WATER?
OKAY.
BUT CONSERVE IT. WE DON'T HAVE--
PTHHHH!!
THIS WATER'S WARM!
WHY DIDN'T I SPLURGE FOR A PURE-BRED? WHY?

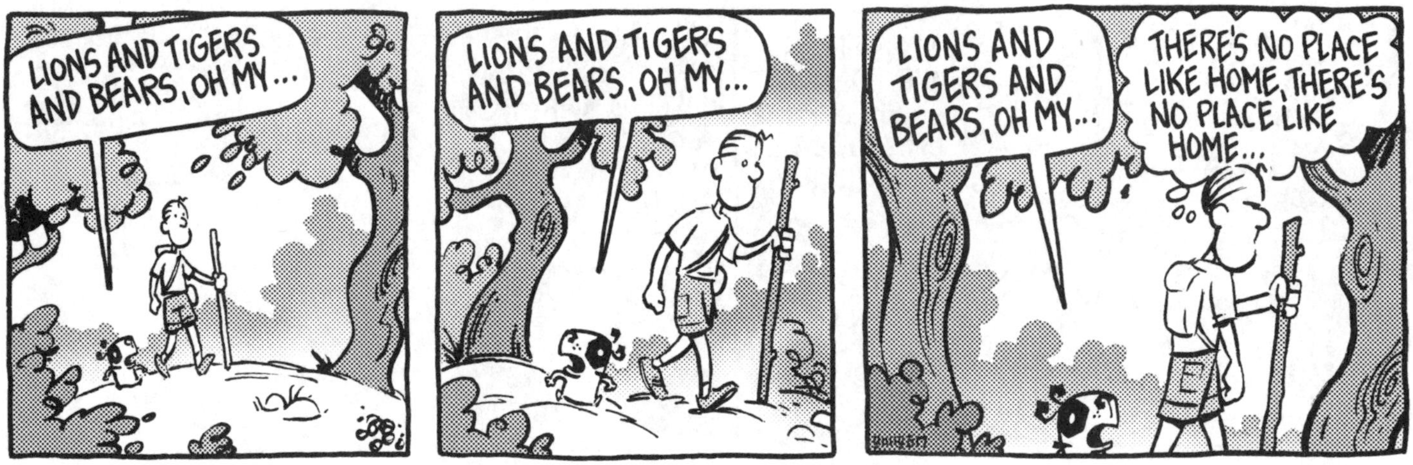
LIONS AND TIGERS AND BEARS, OH MY...
LIONS AND TIGERS AND BEARS, OH MY...
LIONS AND TIGERS AND BEARS, OH MY...
THERE'S NO PLACE LIKE HOME, THERE'S NO PLACE LIKE HOME...

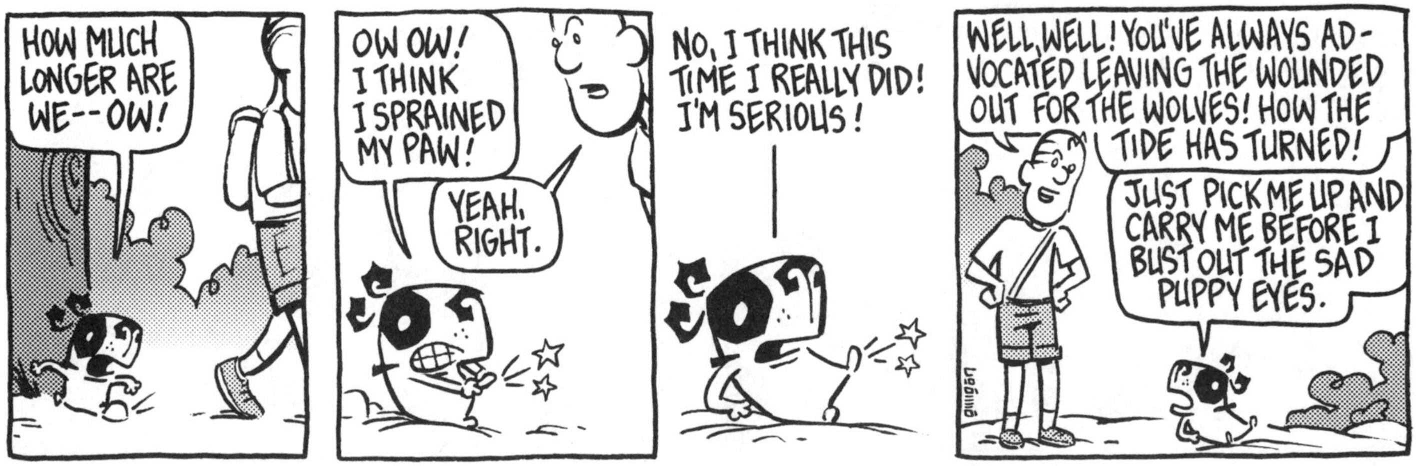
HOW MUCH LONGER ARE WE--OW!
OW OW! I THINK I SPRAINED MY PAW!
YEAH, RIGHT.
NO, I THINK THIS TIME I REALLY DID! I'M SERIOUS!
WELL, WELL! YOU'VE ALWAYS AD-VOCATED LEAVING THE WOUNDED OUT FOR THE WOLVES! HOW THE TIDE HAS TURNED!
JUST PICK ME UP AND CARRY ME BEFORE I BUST OUT THE SAD PUPPY EYES.

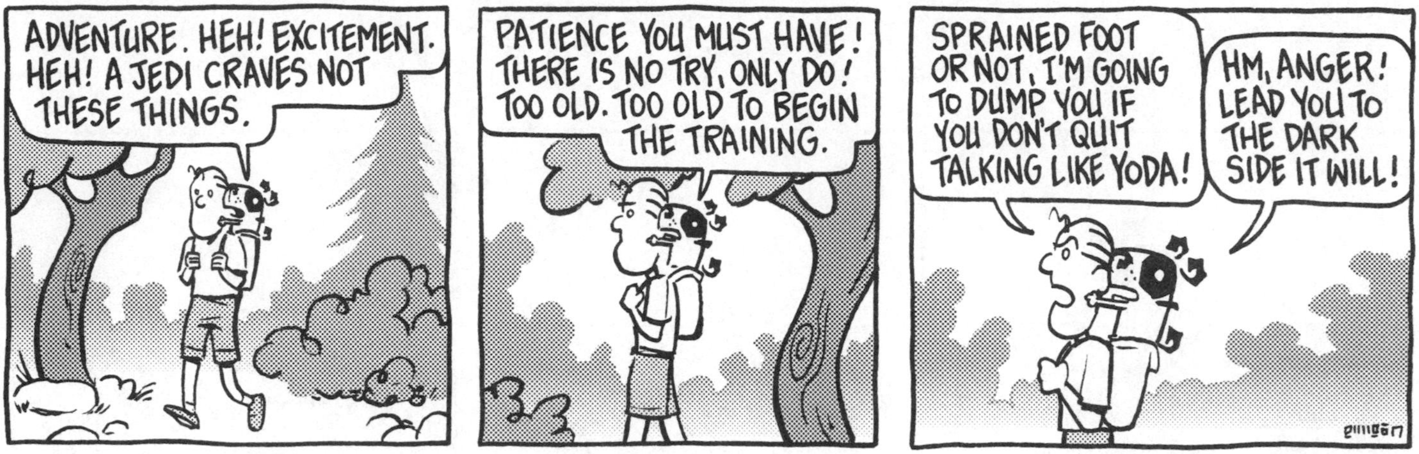
ADVENTURE. HEH! EXCITEMENT. HEH! A JEDI CRAVES NOT THESE THINGS.
PATIENCE YOU MUST HAVE! THERE IS NO TRY, ONLY DO! TOO OLD. TOO OLD TO BEGIN THE TRAINING.
SPRAINED FOOT OR NOT, I'M GOING TO DUMP YOU IF YOU DON'T QUIT TALKING LIKE YODA!
HM, ANGER! LEAD YOU TO THE DARK SIDE IT WILL!

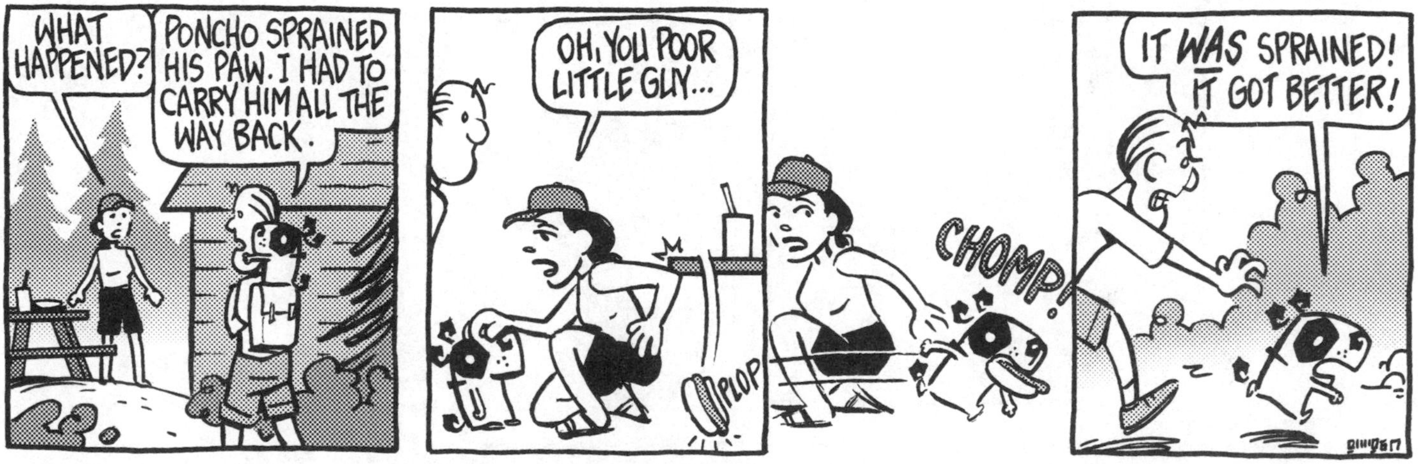
WHAT HAPPENED?
PONCHO SPRAINED HIS PAW. I HAD TO CARRY HIM ALL THE WAY BACK.
OH, YOU POOR LITTLE GUY...
PLOP
CHOMP!
IT WAS SPRAINED! IT GOT BETTER!

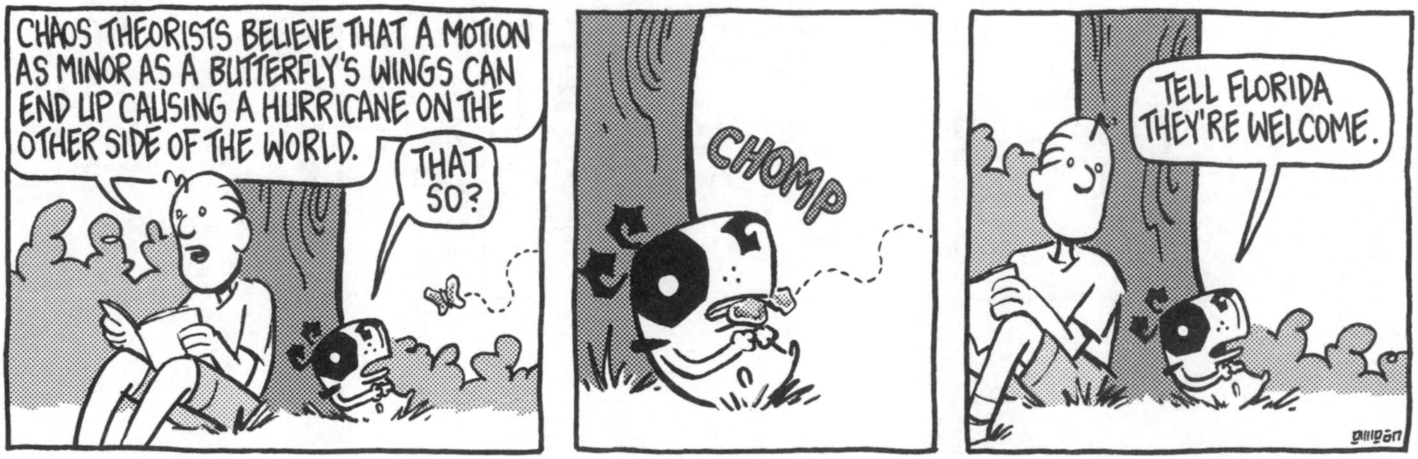
CHAOS THEORISTS BELIEVE THAT A MOTION AS MINOR AS A BUTTERFLY'S WINGS CAN END UP CAUSING A HURRICANE ON THE OTHER SIDE OF THE WORLD.
THAT SO?
CHOMP
TELL FLORIDA THEY'RE WELCOME.

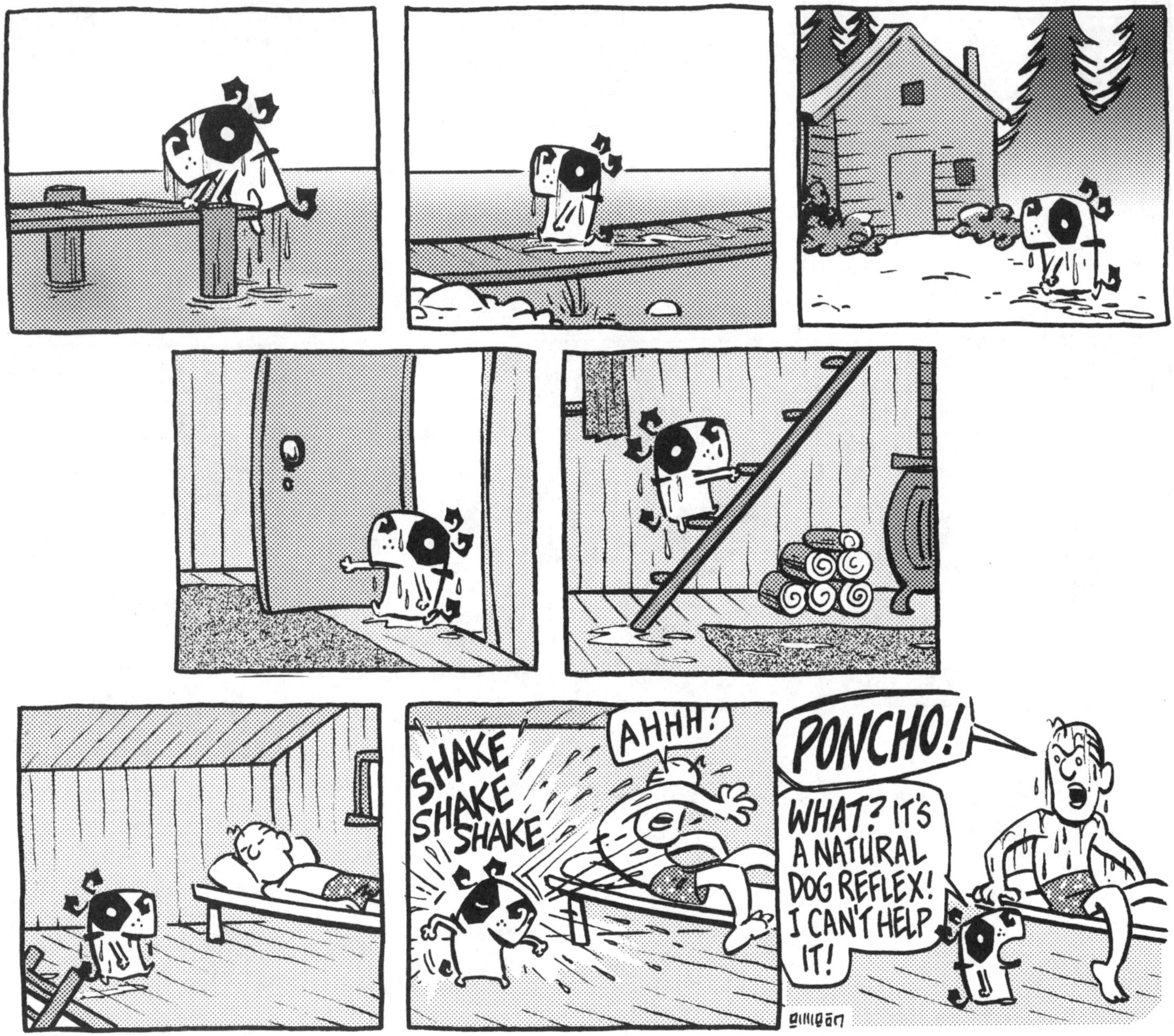
SHAKE
SHAKE
SHAKE
AHHH!
PONCHO!
WHAT? IT'S A NATURAL DOG REFLEX! I CAN'T HELP IT!
gilligan

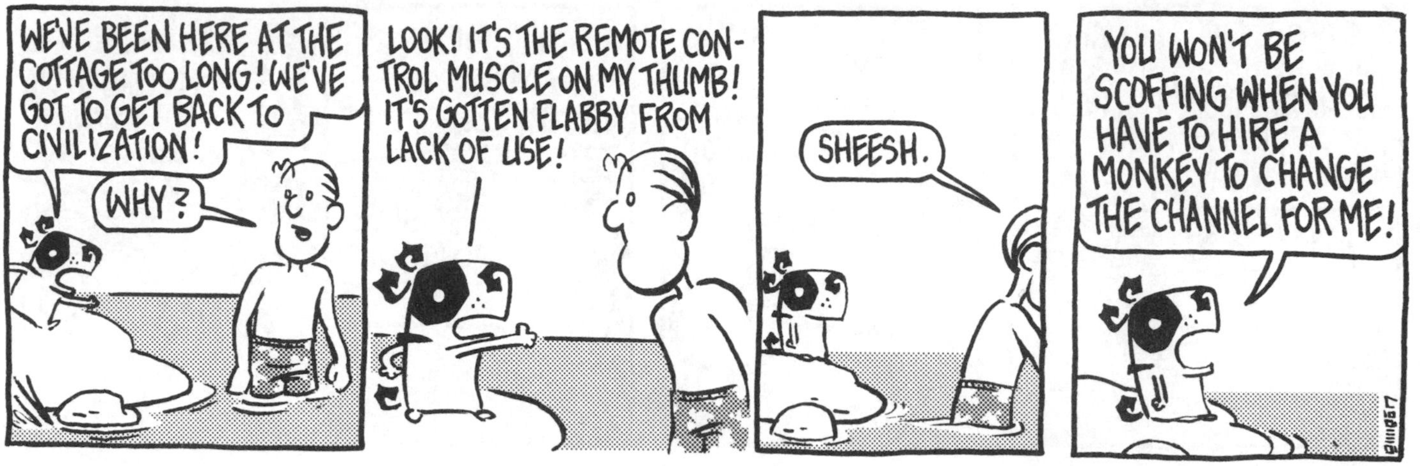
WE'VE BEEN HERE AT THE COTTAGE TOO LONG! WE'VE GOT TO GET BACK TO CIVILIZATION!
WHY?
LOOK! IT'S THE REMOTE CONTROL MUSCLE ON MY THUMB! IT'S GOTTEN FLABBY FROM LACK OF USE!
SHEESH.
YOU WON'T BE SCOFFING WHEN YOU HAVE TO HIRE A MONKEY TO CHANGE THE CHANNEL FOR ME!

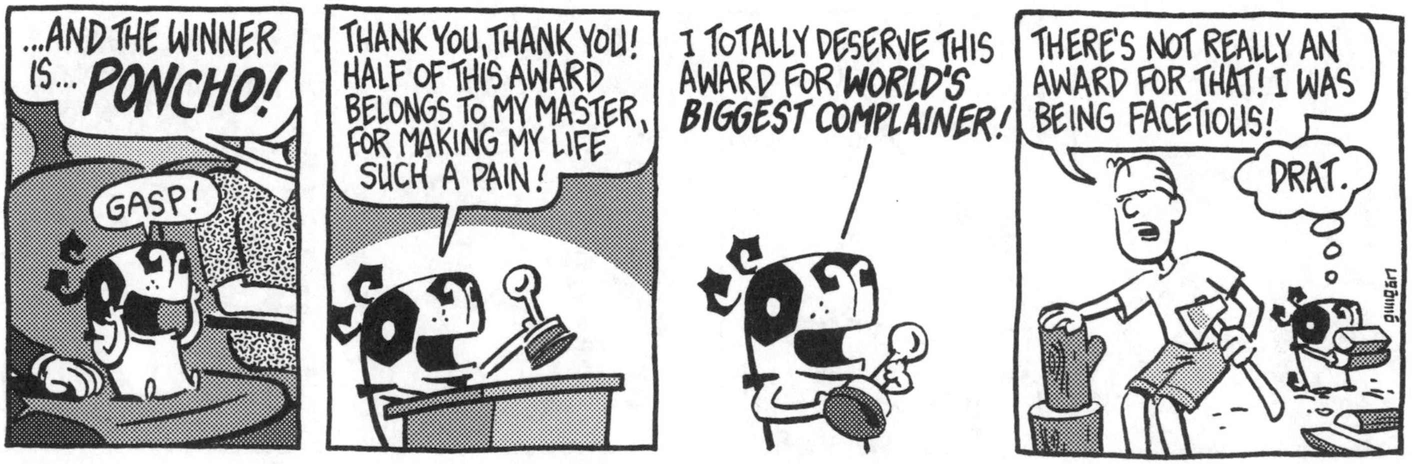
...AND THE WINNER IS... PONCHO!
GASP!
THANK YOU, THANK YOU! HALF OF THIS AWARD BELONGS TO MY MASTER, FOR MAKING MY LIFE SUCH A PAIN!
I TOTALLY DESERVE THIS AWARD FOR WORLD'S BIGGEST COMPLAINER!
THERE'S NOT REALLY AN AWARD FOR THAT! I WAS BEING FACETIOUS!
DRAT.

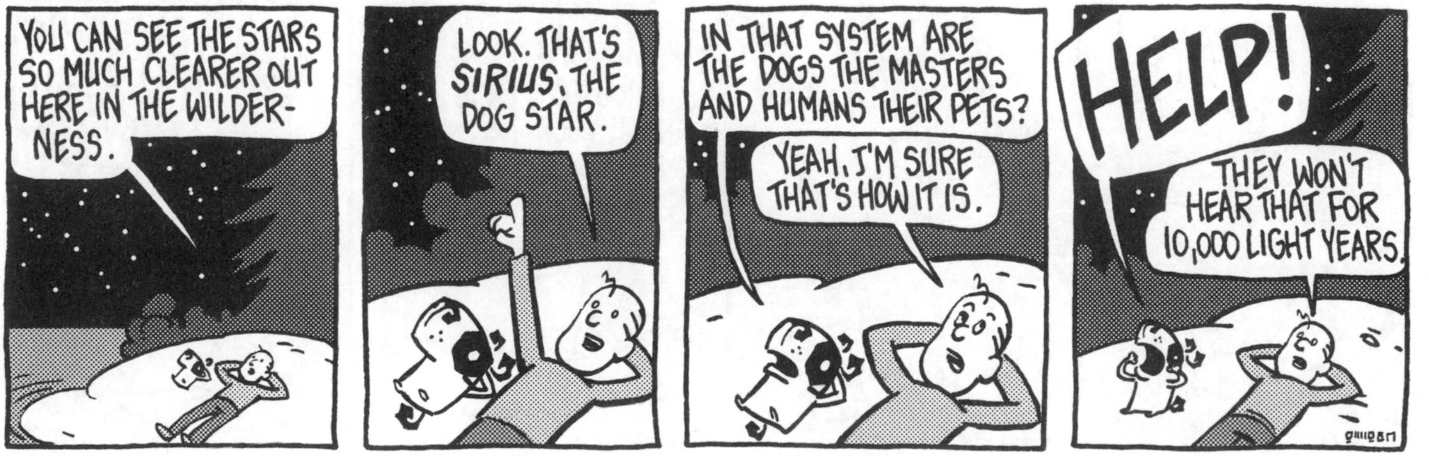
YOU CAN SEE THE STARS SO MUCH CLEARER OUT HERE IN THE WILDERNESS.
LOOK. THAT'S SIRIUS, THE DOG STAR.
IN THAT SYSTEM ARE THE DOGS THE MASTERS AND HUMANS THEIR PETS?
YEAH, I'M SURE THAT'S HOW IT IS.
HELP!
THEY WON'T HEAR THAT FOR 10,000 LIGHT YEARS.

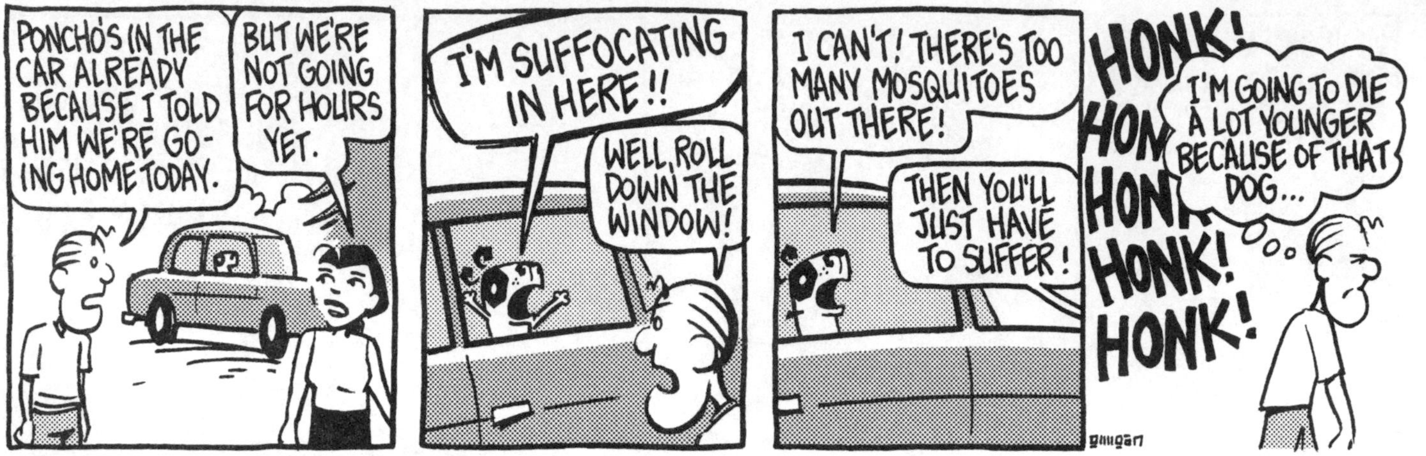
PONCHO'S IN THE CAR ALREADY BECAUSE I TOLD HIM WE'RE GO-ING HOME TODAY.
BUT WE'RE NOT GOING FOR HOURS YET.
I'M SUFFOCATING IN HERE!!
WELL, ROLL DOWN THE WINDOW!
I CAN'T! THERE'S TOO MANY MOSQUITOES OUT THERE!
THEN YOU'LL JUST HAVE TO SUFFER!
HONK!
HON
HON
HONK!
HONK!
I'M GOING TO DIE A LOT YOUNGER BECAUSE OF THAT DOG...
gilligan

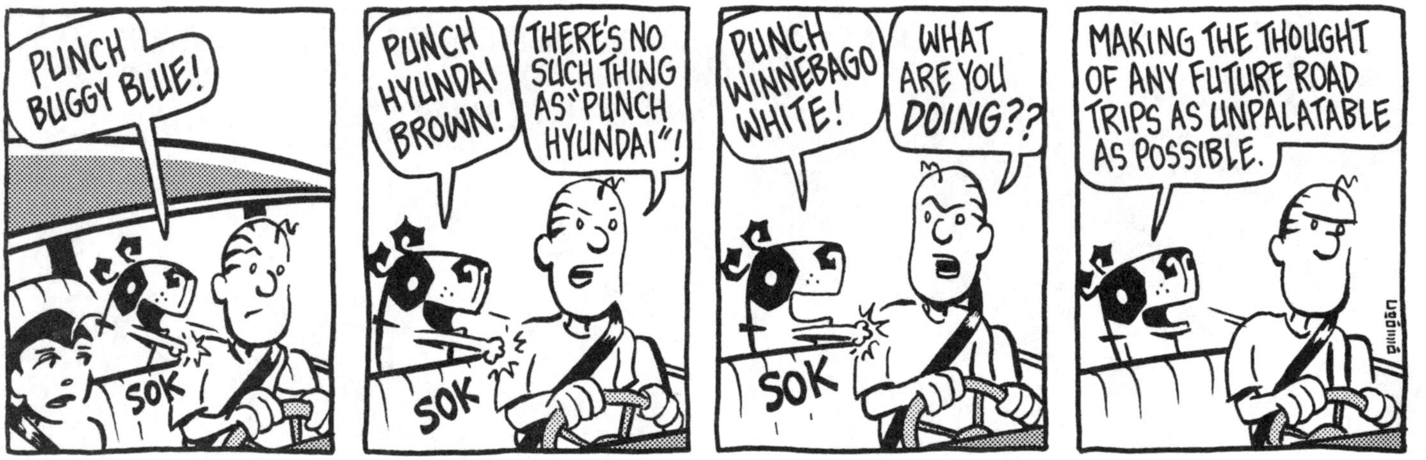
PUNCH BUGGY BLUE!
SOK
PUNCH HYUNDAI BROWN!
THERE'S NO SUCH THING AS "PUNCH HYUNDAI"!
SOK
PUNCH WINNEBAGO WHITE!
WHAT ARE YOU DOING??
SOK
MAKING THE THOUGHT OF ANY FUTURE ROAD TRIPS AS UNPALATABLE AS POSSIBLE.
gilligan

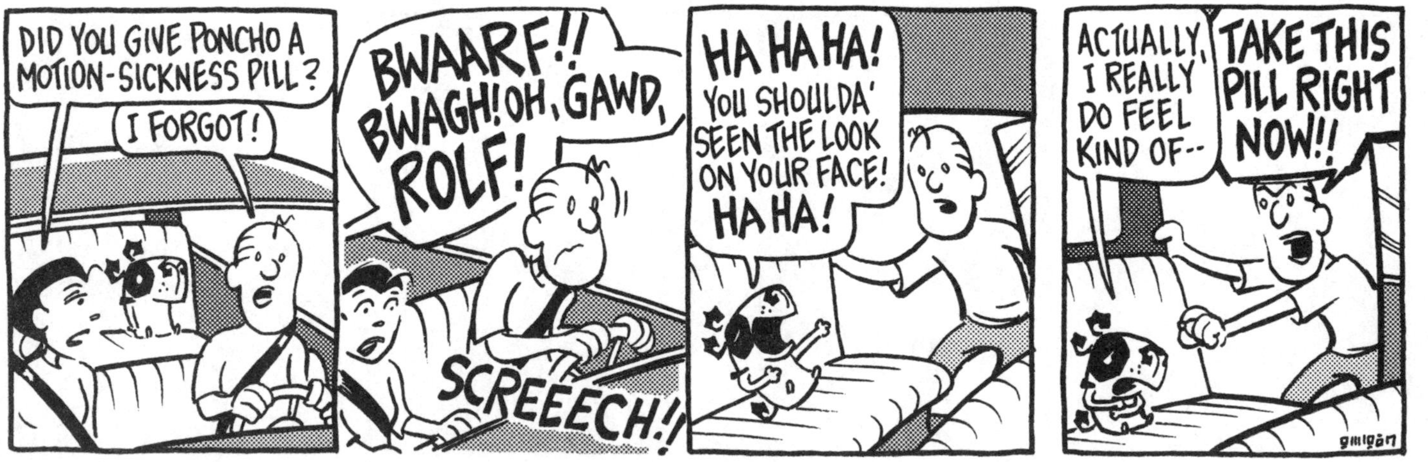
DID YOU GIVE PONCHO A MOTION-SICKNESS PILL?
I FORGOT!
BWAARF!! BWAGH! OH, GAWD, ROLF!
SCREEECH!!
HA HA HA! YOU SHOULDA' SEEN THE LOOK ON YOUR FACE! HA HA!
ACTUALLY, I REALLY DO FEEL KIND OF--
TAKE THIS PILL RIGHT NOW!!
gilligan

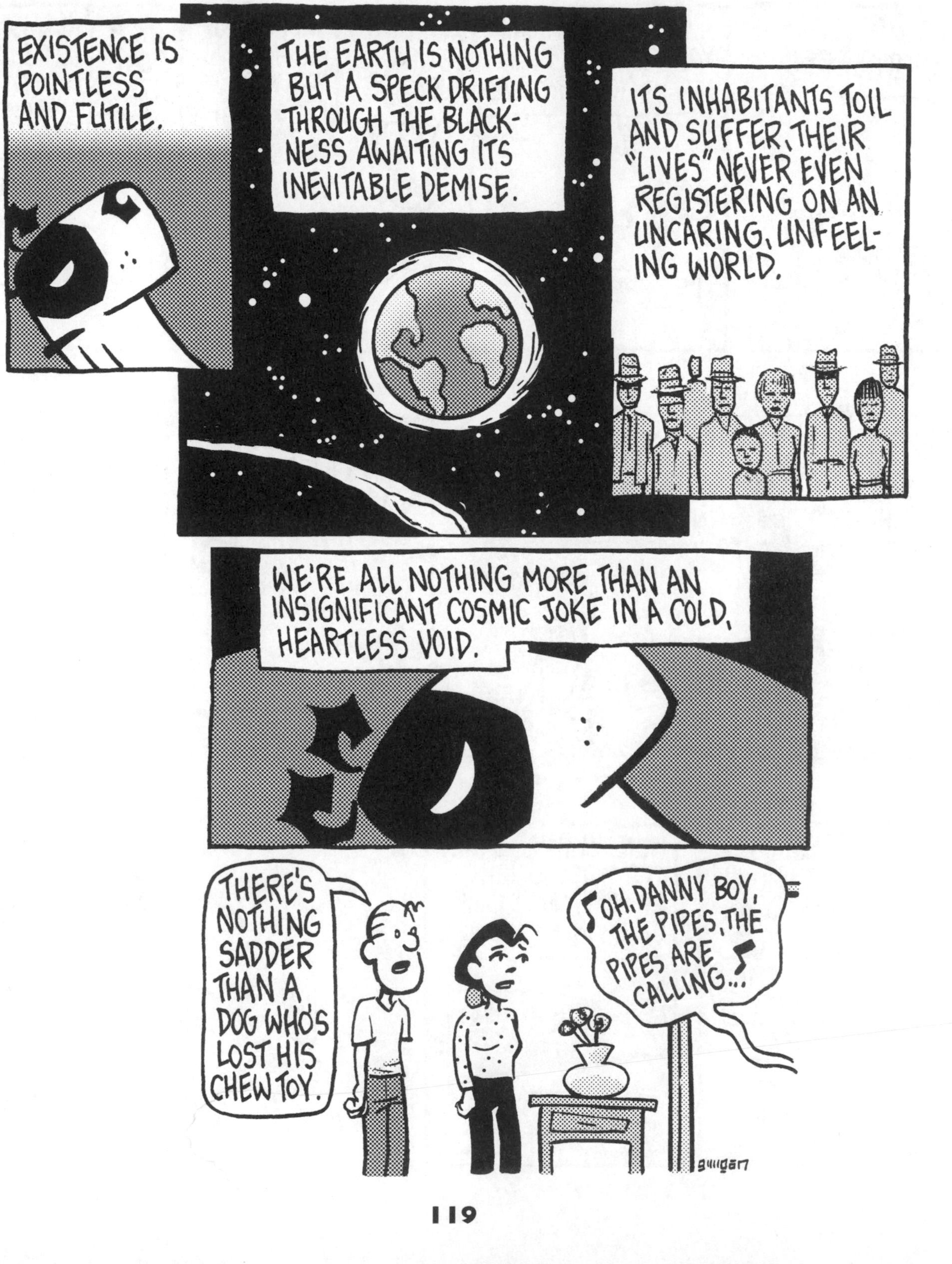
EXISTENCE IS POINTLESS AND FUTILE.
THE EARTH IS NOTHING BUT A SPECK DRIFTING THROUGH THE BLACKNESS AWAITING ITS INEVITABLE DEMISE.
ITS INHABITANTS TOIL AND SUFFER, THEIR "LIVES" NEVER EVEN REGISTERING ON AN UNCARING, UNFEELING WORLD.
WE'RE ALL NOTHING MORE THAN AN INSIGNIFICANT COSMIC JOKE IN A COLD, HEARTLESS VOID.
THERE'S NOTHING SADDER THAN A DOG WHO'S LOST HIS CHEW TOY.
♪ OH, DANNY BOY, THE PIPES, THE PIPES ARE ♪ CALLING...
gulligan

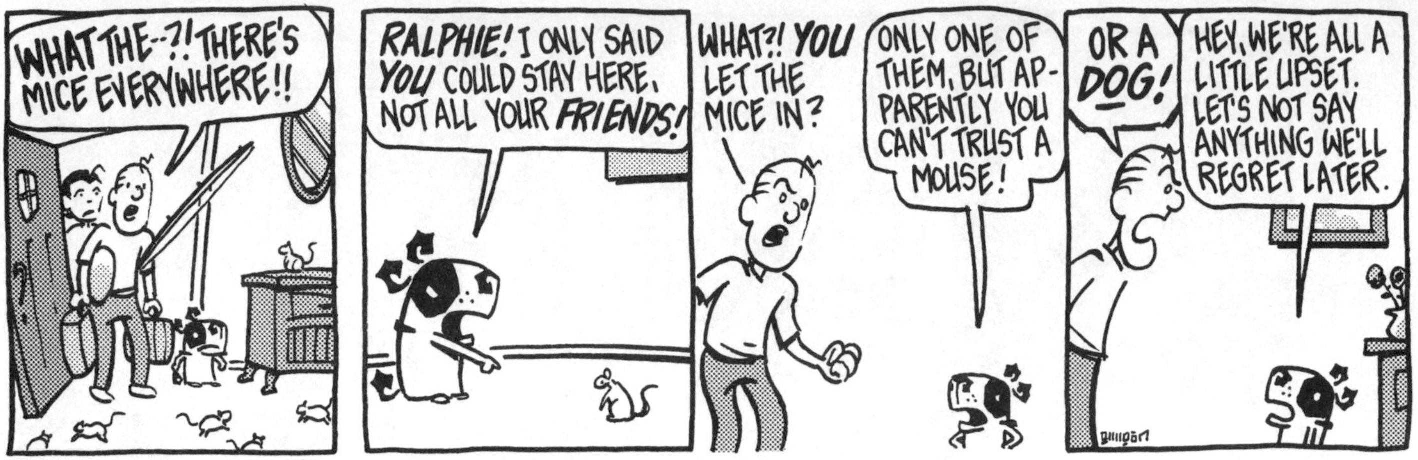
WHAT THE--?! THERE'S MICE EVERYWHERE!!
RALPHIE! I ONLY SAID YOU COULD STAY HERE, NOT ALL YOUR FRIENDS!
WHAT?! YOU LET THE MICE IN?
ONLY ONE OF THEM, BUT APPARENTLY YOU CAN'T TRUST A MOUSE!
OR A DOG!
HEY, WE'RE ALL A LITTLE UPSET. LET'S NOT SAY ANYTHING WE'LL REGRET LATER.

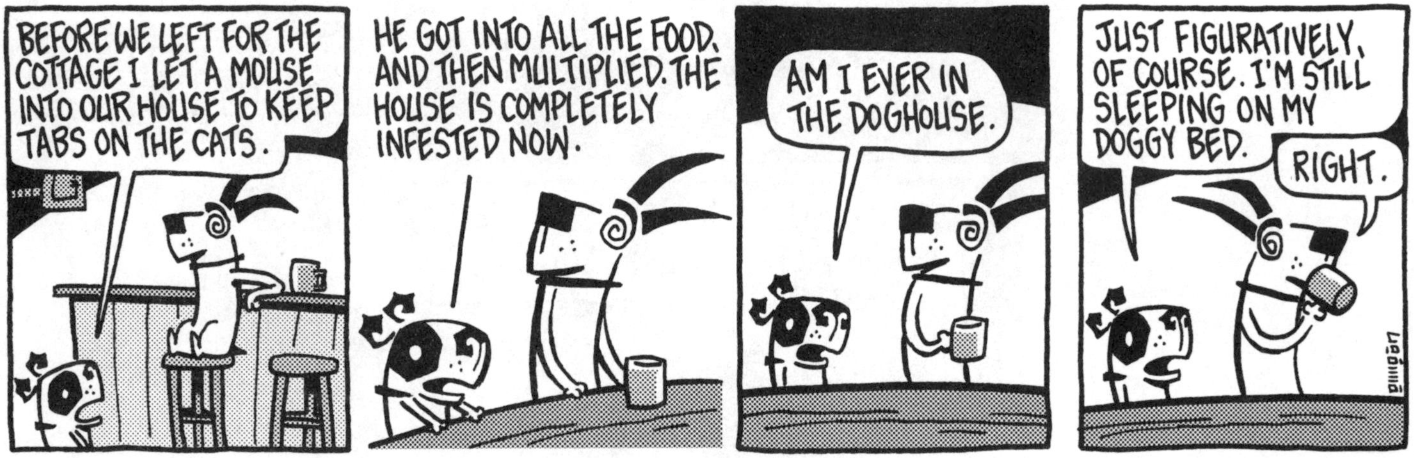
BEFORE WE LEFT FOR THE COTTAGE I LET A MOUSE INTO OUR HOUSE TO KEEP TABS ON THE CATS.
HE GOT INTO ALL THE FOOD, AND THEN MULTIPLIED. THE HOUSE IS COMPLETELY INFESTED NOW.
AM I EVER IN THE DOGHOUSE.
JUST FIGURATIVELY, OF COURSE. I'M STILL SLEEPING ON MY DOGGY BED.
RIGHT.

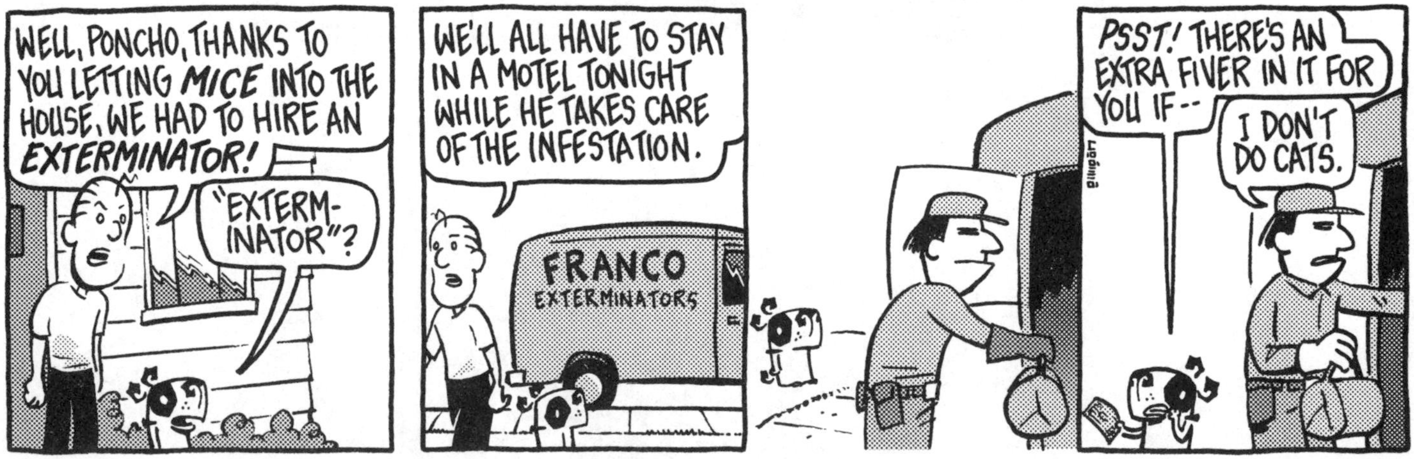
WELL, PONCHO, THANKS TO YOU LETTING MICE INTO THE HOUSE, WE HAD TO HIRE AN EXTERMINATOR!
"EXTERMINATOR"?
WE'LL ALL HAVE TO STAY IN A MOTEL TONIGHT WHILE HE TAKES CARE OF THE INFESTATION.
FRANCO EXTERMINATORS
PSST! THERE'S AN EXTRA FIVER IN IT FOR YOU IF--
I DON'T DO CATS.

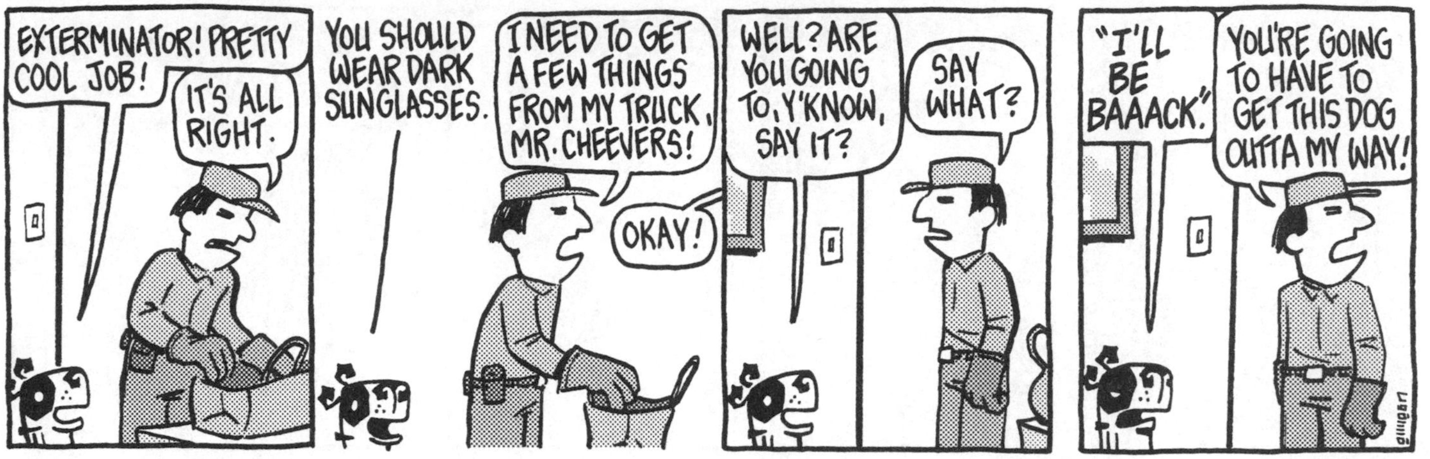
EXTERMINATOR! PRETTY COOL JOB!
IT'S ALL RIGHT.
YOU SHOULD WEAR DARK SUNGLASSES.
I NEED TO GET A FEW THINGS FROM MY TRUCK, MR. CHEEVERS!
OKAY!
WELL? ARE YOU GOING TO, Y'KNOW, SAY IT?
SAY WHAT?
"I'LL BE BAAACK."
YOU'RE GOING TO HAVE TO GET THIS DOG OUTTA MY WAY!

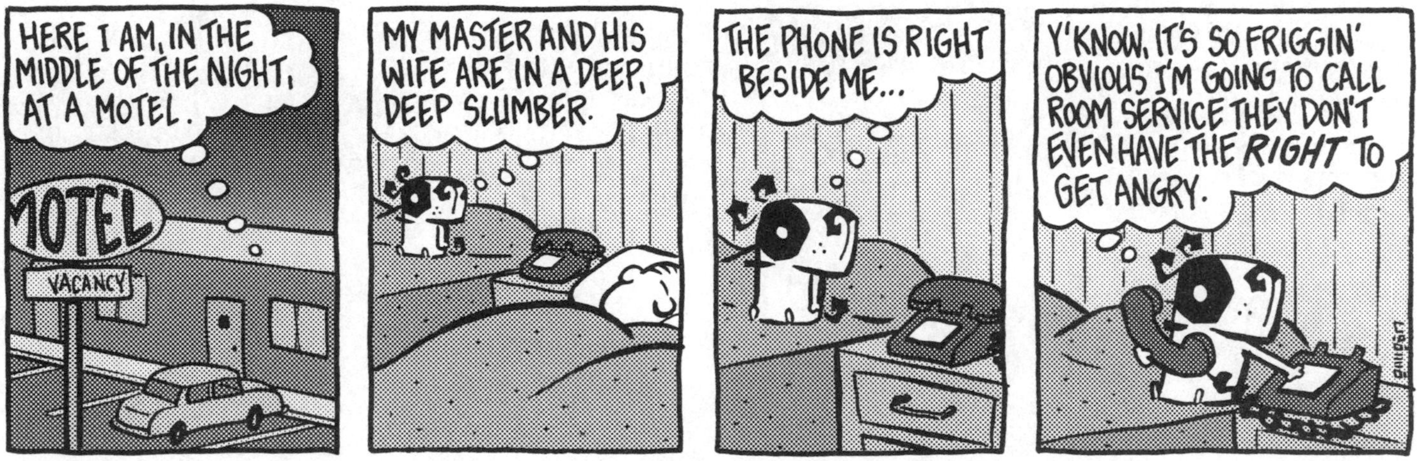
HERE I AM, IN THE MIDDLE OF THE NIGHT, AT A MOTEL.
MOTEL
VACANCY
MY MASTER AND HIS WIFE ARE IN A DEEP, DEEP SLUMBER.
THE PHONE IS RIGHT BESIDE ME...
Y'KNOW, IT'S SO FRIGGIN' OBVIOUS I'M GOING TO CALL ROOM SERVICE THEY DON'T EVEN HAVE THE *RIGHT* TO GET ANGRY.

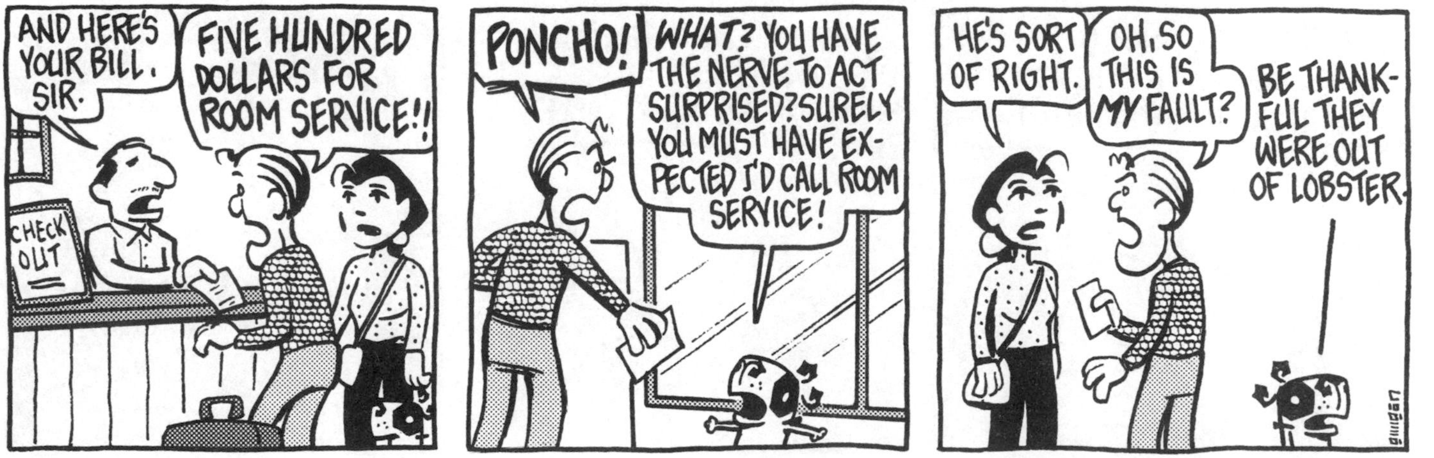
AND HERE'S YOUR BILL, SIR.
FIVE HUNDRED DOLLARS FOR ROOM SERVICE!!
CHECK OUT
PONCHO!
WHAT? YOU HAVE THE NERVE TO ACT SURPRISED? SURELY YOU MUST HAVE EXPECTED I'D CALL ROOM SERVICE!
HE'S SORT OF RIGHT.
OH, SO THIS IS *MY* FAULT?
BE THANKFUL THEY WERE OUT OF LOBSTER.

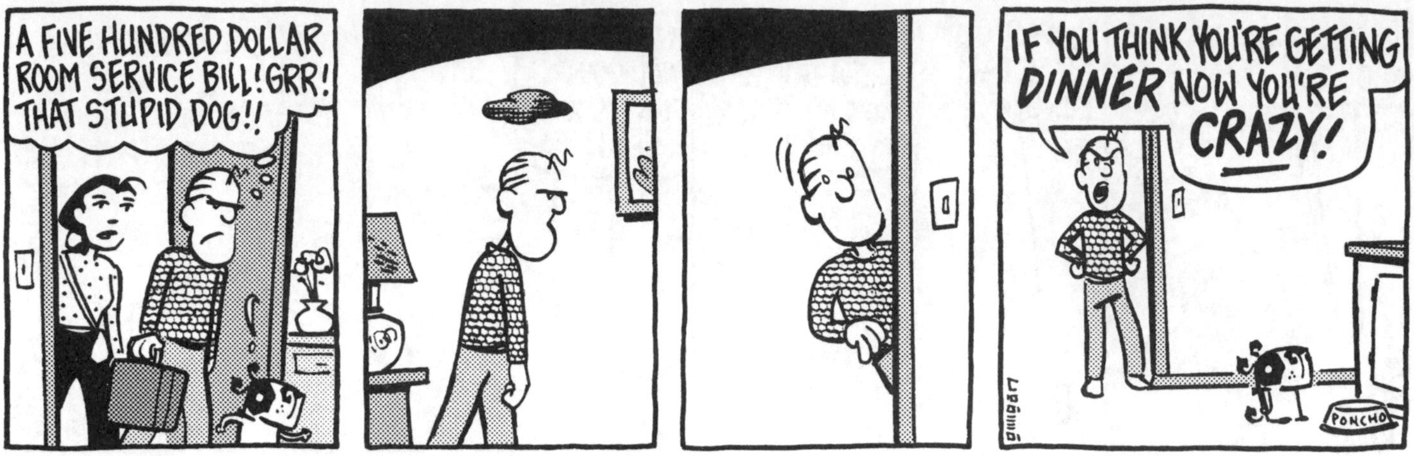
A FIVE HUNDRED DOLLAR ROOM SERVICE BILL! GRR! THAT STUPID DOG!!
IF YOU THINK YOU'RE GETTING DINNER NOW YOU'RE CRAZY!
PONCHO

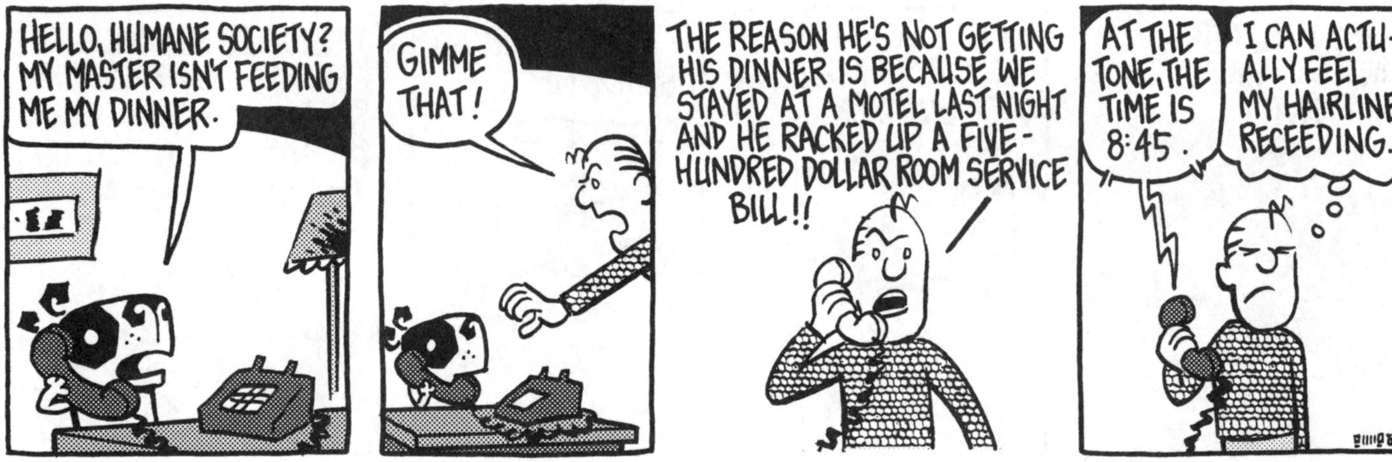
HELLO, HUMANE SOCIETY? MY MASTER ISN'T FEEDING ME MY DINNER.
GIMME THAT!
THE REASON HE'S NOT GETTING HIS DINNER IS BECAUSE WE STAYED AT A MOTEL LAST NIGHT AND HE RACKED UP A FIVE-HUNDRED DOLLAR ROOM SERVICE BILL!!
AT THE TONE, THE TIME IS 8:45.
I CAN ACTUALLY FEEL MY HAIRLINE RECEEDING.

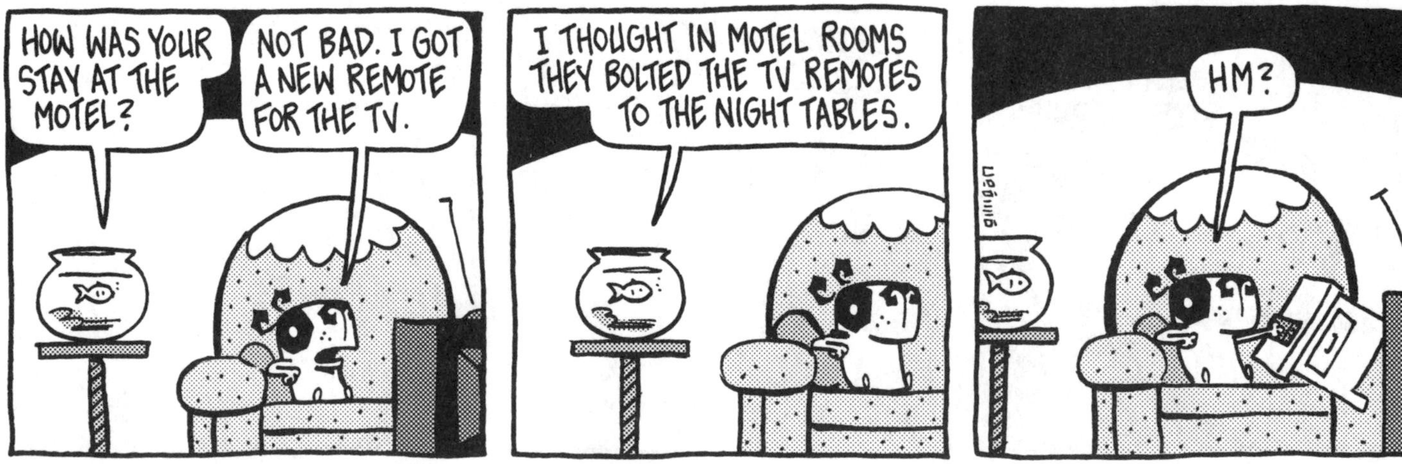
HOW WAS YOUR STAY AT THE MOTEL?
NOT BAD. I GOT A NEW REMOTE FOR THE TV.
I THOUGHT IN MOTEL ROOMS THEY BOLTED THE TV REMOTES TO THE NIGHT TABLES.
HM?

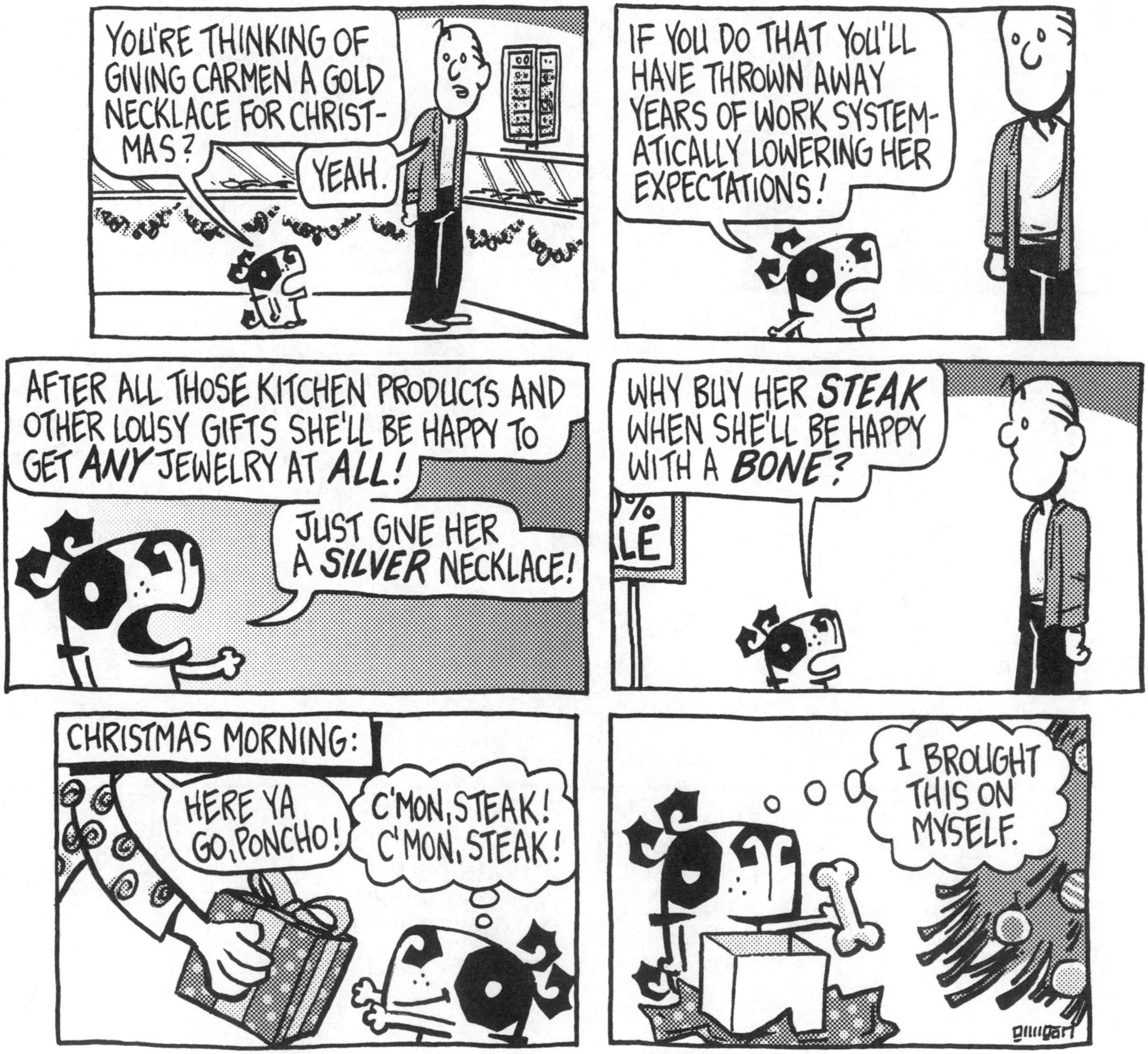
YOU'RE THINKING OF GIVING CARMEN A GOLD NECKLACE FOR CHRIST-MAS?
YEAH.
IF YOU DO THAT YOU'LL HAVE THROWN AWAY YEARS OF WORK SYSTEM-ATICALLY LOWERING HER EXPECTATIONS!
AFTER ALL THOSE KITCHEN PRODUCTS AND OTHER LOUSY GIFTS SHE'LL BE HAPPY TO GET *ANY* JEWELRY AT *ALL*!
JUST GIVE HER A *SILVER* NECKLACE!
WHY BUY HER *STEAK* WHEN SHE'LL BE HAPPY WITH A *BONE*?
CHRISTMAS MORNING:
HERE YA GO, PONCHO!
C'MON, STEAK! C'MON, STEAK!
I BROUGHT THIS ON MYSELF.
GILLIGAN

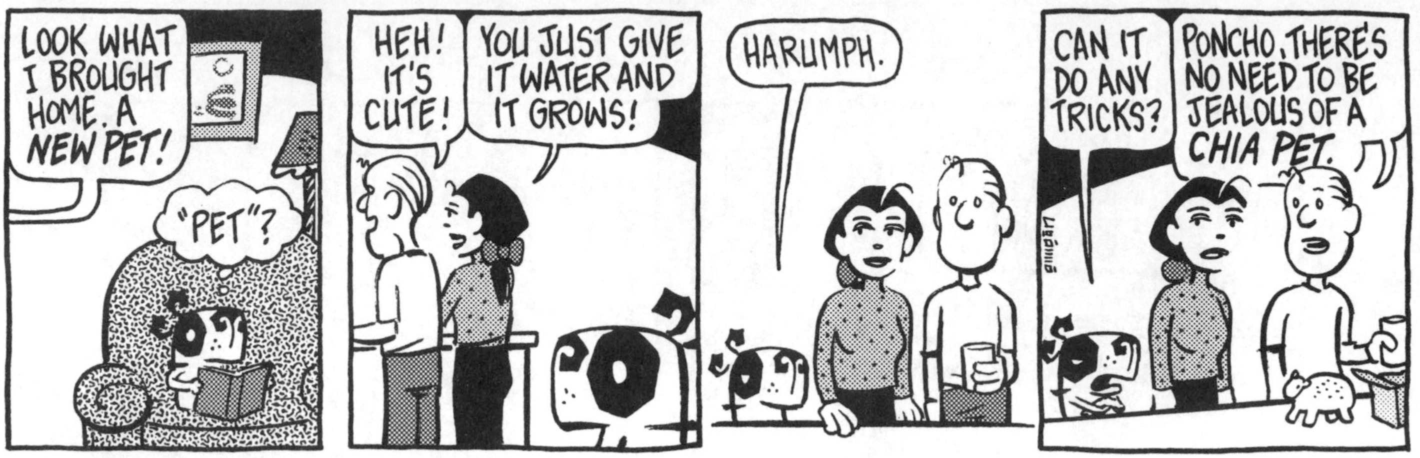
LOOK WHAT I BROUGHT HOME. A NEW PET!
"PET"?
HEH! IT'S CUTE!
YOU JUST GIVE IT WATER AND IT GROWS!
HARUMPH.
CAN IT DO ANY TRICKS?
PONCHO, THERE'S NO NEED TO BE JEALOUS OF A CHIA PET.

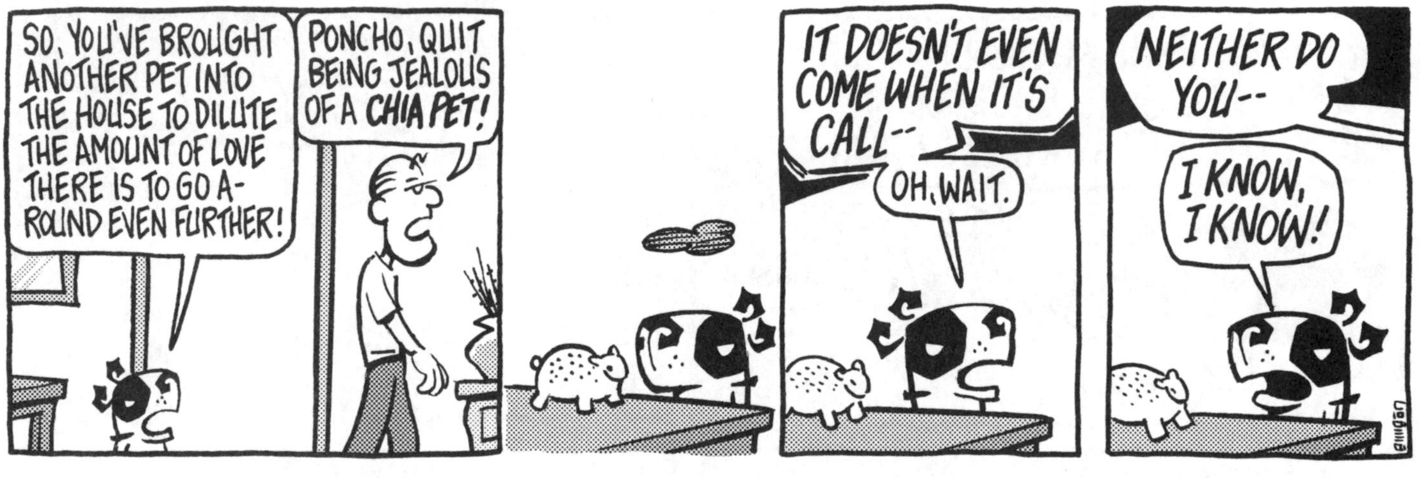
SO, YOU'VE BROUGHT ANOTHER PET INTO THE HOUSE TO DILUTE THE AMOUNT OF LOVE THERE IS TO GO A-ROUND EVEN FURTHER!
PONCHO, QUIT BEING JEALOUS OF A CHIA PET!
IT DOESN'T EVEN COME WHEN IT'S CALL--
OH, WAIT.
NEITHER DO YOU--
I KNOW, I KNOW!

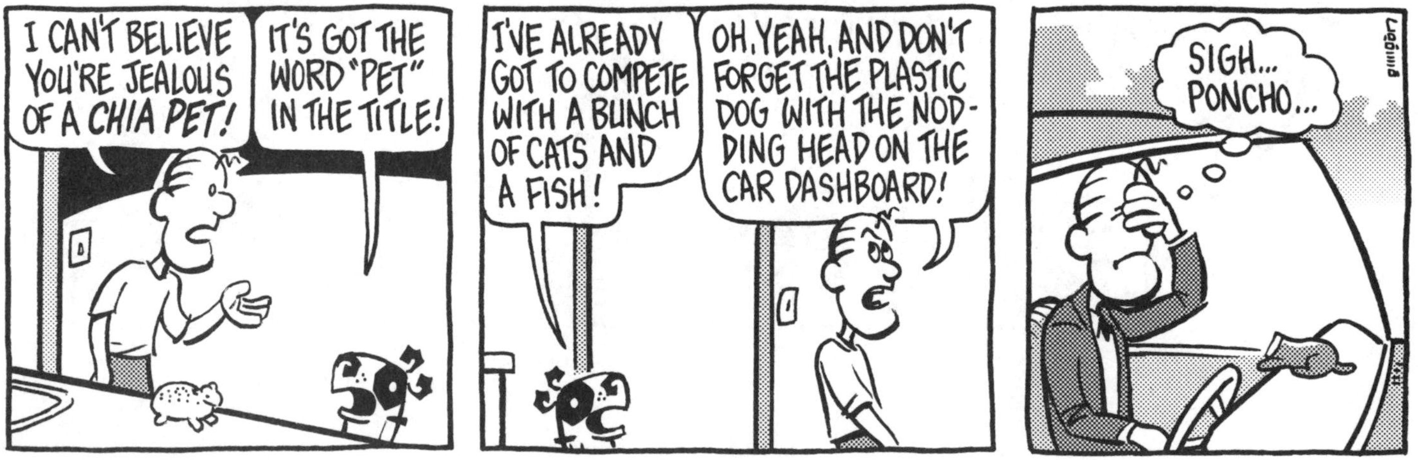
I CAN'T BELIEVE YOU'RE JEALOUS OF A CHIA PET!
IT'S GOT THE WORD "PET" IN THE TITLE!
I'VE ALREADY GOT TO COMPETE WITH A BUNCH OF CATS AND A FISH!
OH, YEAH, AND DON'T FORGET THE PLASTIC DOG WITH THE NOD-DING HEAD ON THE CAR DASHBOARD!
SIGH... PONCHO...

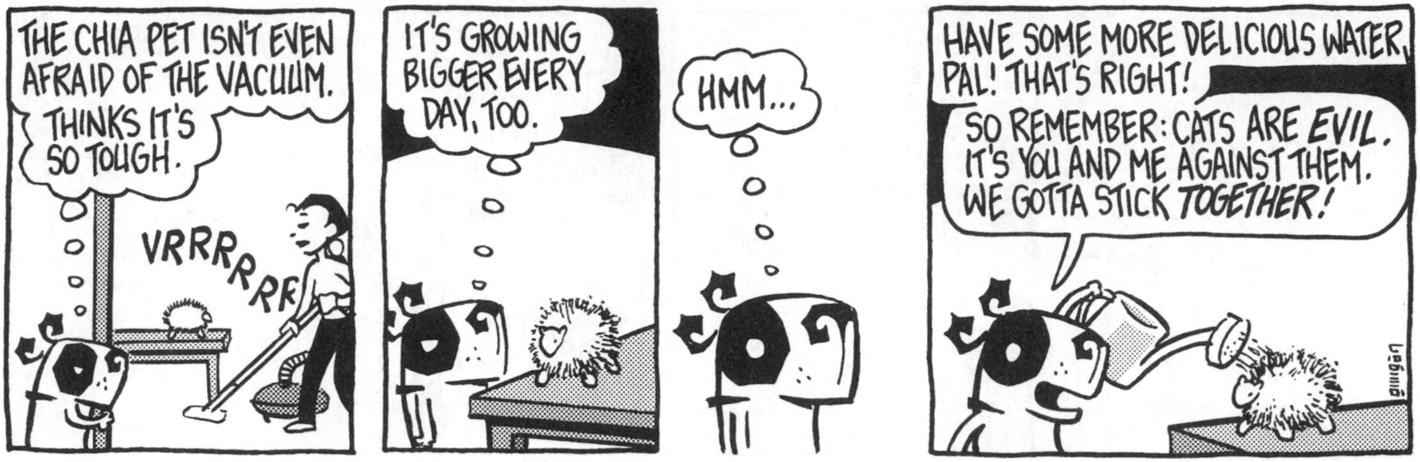
THE CHIA PET ISN'T EVEN AFRAID OF THE VACUUM.
THINKS IT'S SO TOUGH.
VRRRRRRR
IT'S GROWING BIGGER EVERY DAY, TOO.
HMM...
HAVE SOME MORE DELICIOUS WATER, PAL! THAT'S RIGHT!
SO REMEMBER: CATS ARE *EVIL*. IT'S YOU AND ME AGAINST THEM. WE GOTTA STICK *TOGETHER*!

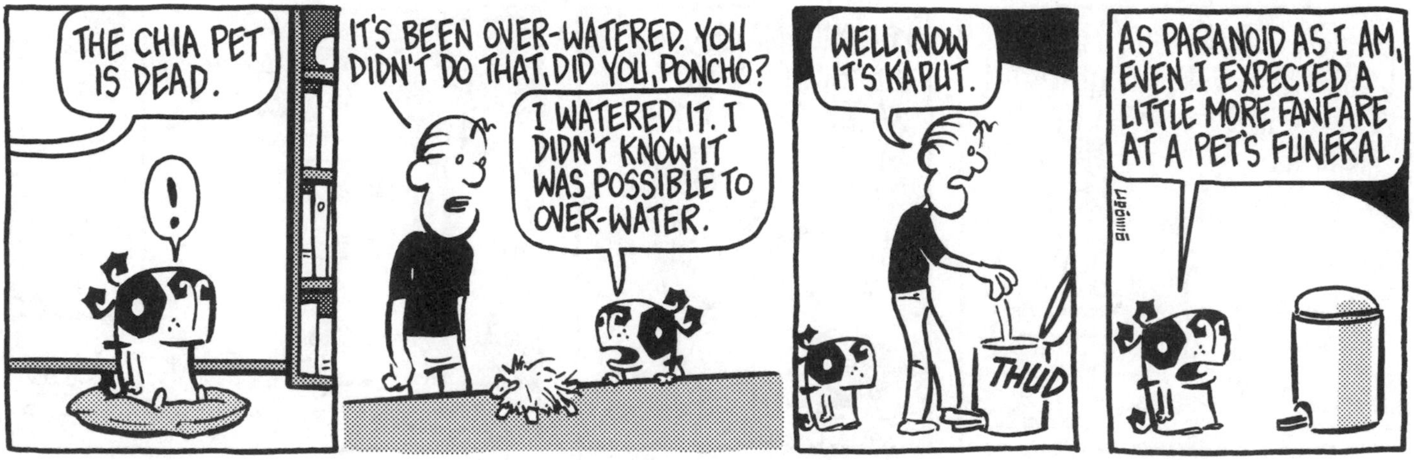
THE CHIA PET IS DEAD.
!
IT'S BEEN OVER-WATERED. YOU DIDN'T DO THAT, DID YOU, PONCHO?
I WATERED IT. I DIDN'T KNOW IT WAS POSSIBLE TO OVER-WATER.
WELL, NOW IT'S KAPUT.
THUD
AS PARANOID AS I AM, EVEN I EXPECTED A LITTLE MORE FANFARE AT A PET'S FUNERAL.

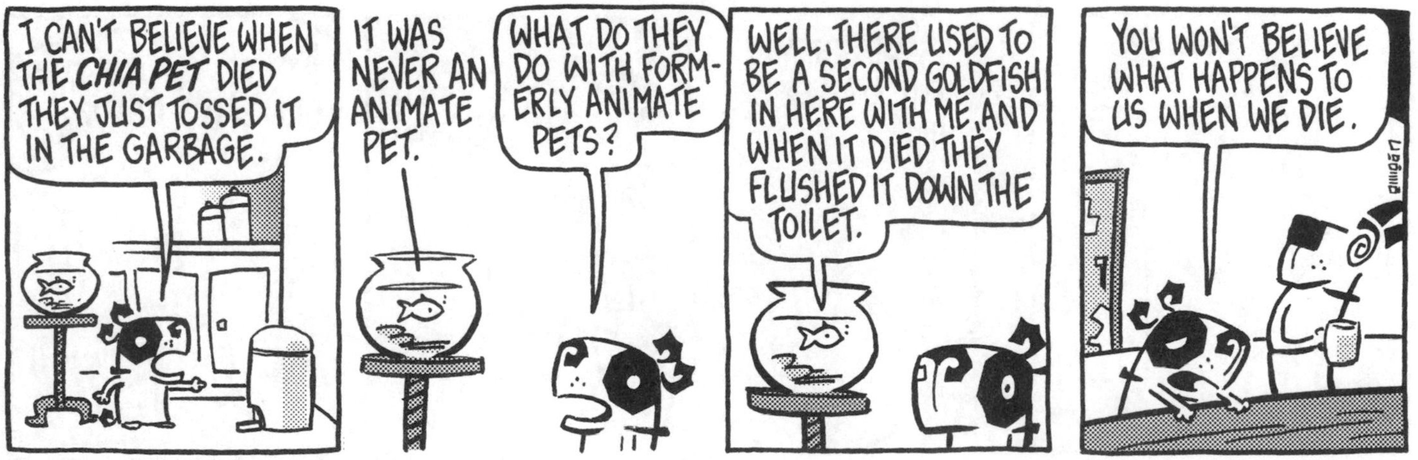
I CAN'T BELIEVE WHEN THE *CHIA PET* DIED THEY JUST TOSSED IT IN THE GARBAGE.
IT WAS NEVER AN ANIMATE PET.
WHAT DO THEY DO WITH FORMERLY ANIMATE PETS?
WELL, THERE USED TO BE A SECOND GOLDFISH IN HERE WITH ME, AND WHEN IT DIED THEY FLUSHED IT DOWN THE TOILET.
YOU WON'T BELIEVE WHAT HAPPENS TO US WHEN WE DIE.

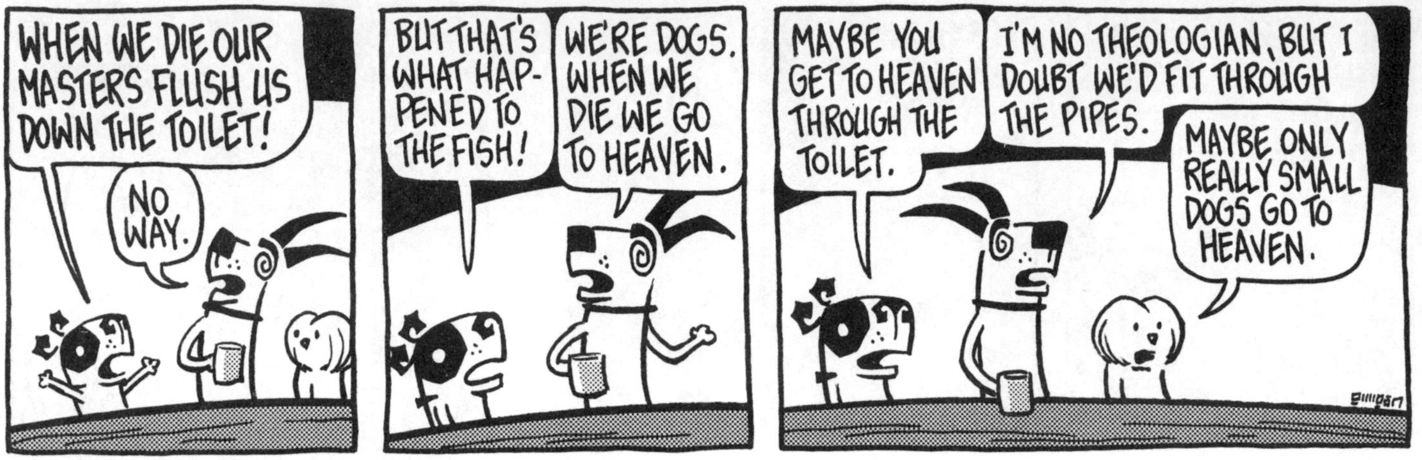
WHEN WE DIE OUR MASTERS FLUSH US DOWN THE TOILET!
NO WAY.
BUT THAT'S WHAT HAPPENED TO THE FISH!
WE'RE DOGS. WHEN WE DIE WE GO TO HEAVEN.
MAYBE YOU GET TO HEAVEN THROUGH THE TOILET.
I'M NO THEOLOGIAN, BUT I DOUBT WE'D FIT THROUGH THE PIPES.
MAYBE ONLY REALLY SMALL DOGS GO TO HEAVEN.

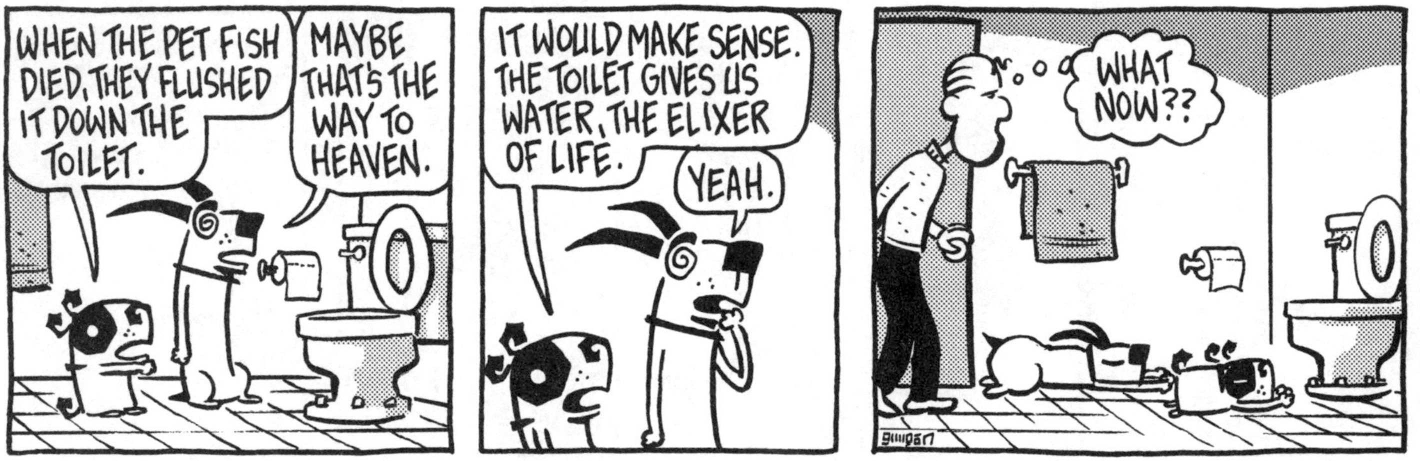
WHEN THE PET FISH DIED, THEY FLUSHED IT DOWN THE TOILET.
MAYBE THAT'S THE WAY TO HEAVEN.
IT WOULD MAKE SENSE. THE TOILET GIVES US WATER, THE ELIXER OF LIFE.
YEAH.
WHAT NOW??

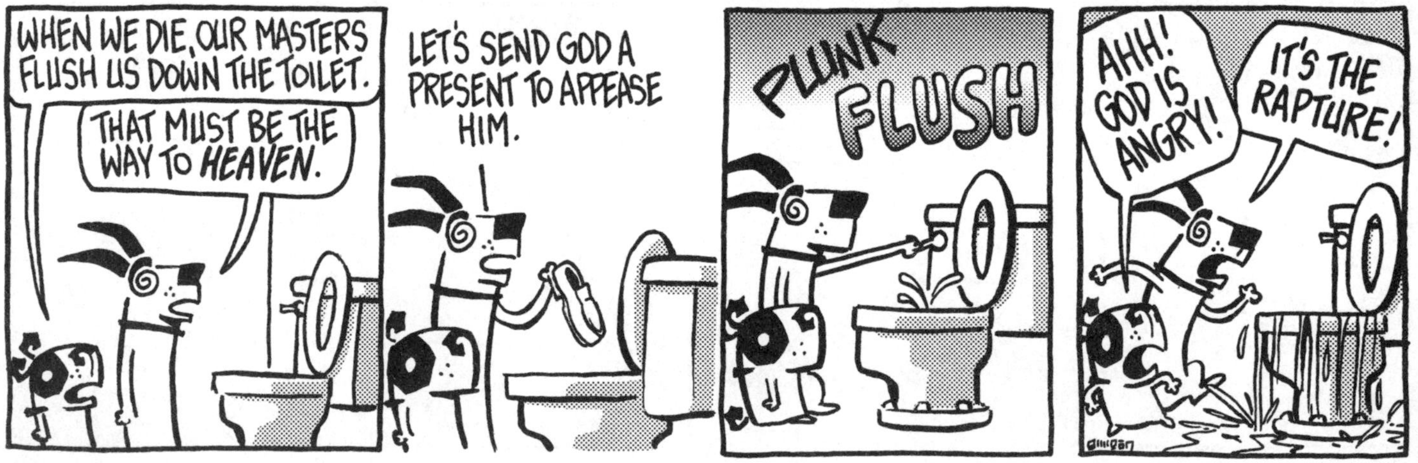
WHEN WE DIE, OUR MASTERS FLUSH US DOWN THE TOILET.
THAT MUST BE THE WAY TO HEAVEN.
LET'S SEND GOD A PRESENT TO APPEASE HIM.
PLUNK
FLUSH
AHH! GOD IS ANGRY!
IT'S THE RAPTURE!

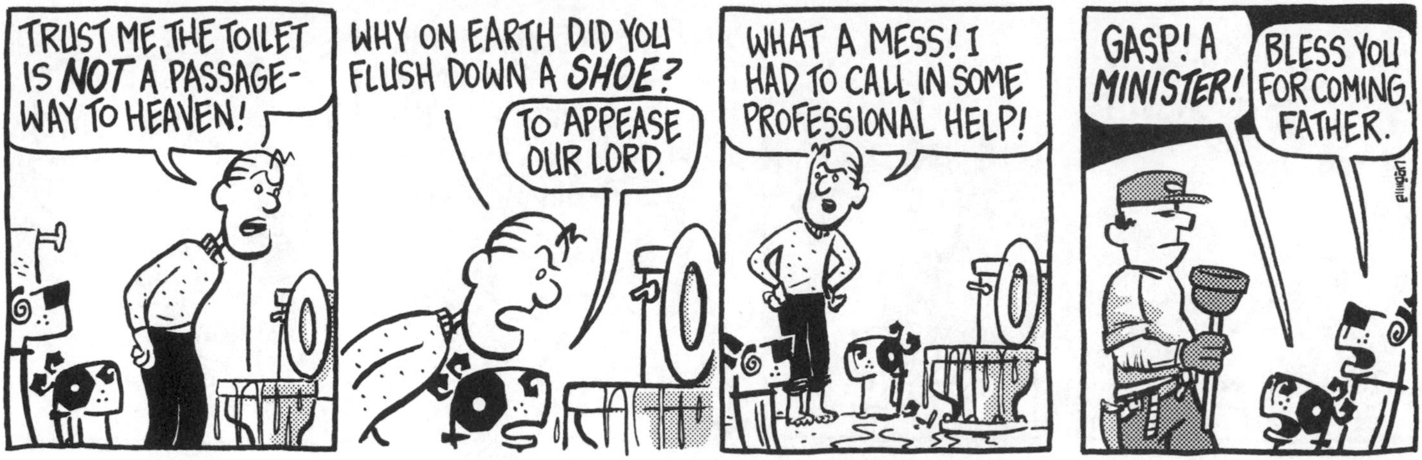
TRUST ME, THE TOILET IS NOT A PASSAGE-WAY TO HEAVEN!
WHY ON EARTH DID YOU FLUSH DOWN A SHOE?
TO APPEASE OUR LORD.
WHAT A MESS! I HAD TO CALL IN SOME PROFESSIONAL HELP!
GASP! A MINISTER!
BLESS YOU FOR COMING, FATHER.

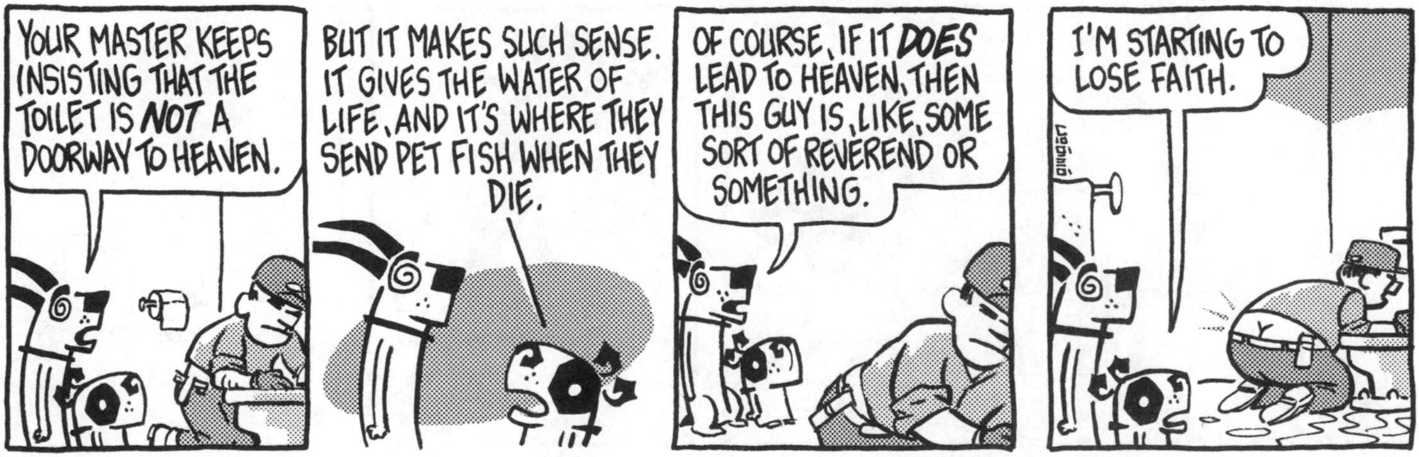
YOUR MASTER KEEPS INSISTING THAT THE TOILET IS NOT A DOORWAY TO HEAVEN.
BUT IT MAKES SUCH SENSE. IT GIVES THE WATER OF LIFE, AND IT'S WHERE THEY SEND PET FISH WHEN THEY DIE.
OF COURSE, IF IT DOES LEAD TO HEAVEN, THEN THIS GUY IS, LIKE, SOME SORT OF REVEREND OR SOMETHING.
I'M STARTING TO LOSE FAITH.

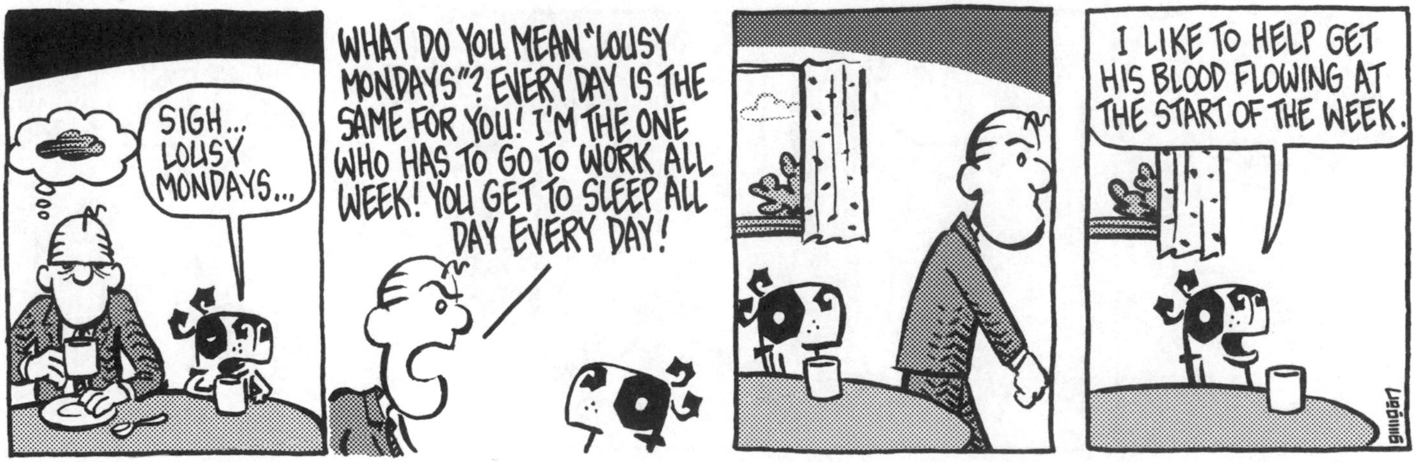
SIGH... LOUSY MONDAYS...
WHAT DO YOU MEAN "LOUSY MONDAYS"? EVERY DAY IS THE SAME FOR YOU! I'M THE ONE WHO HAS TO GO TO WORK ALL WEEK! YOU GET TO SLEEP ALL DAY EVERY DAY!
I LIKE TO HELP GET HIS BLOOD FLOWING AT THE START OF THE WEEK.

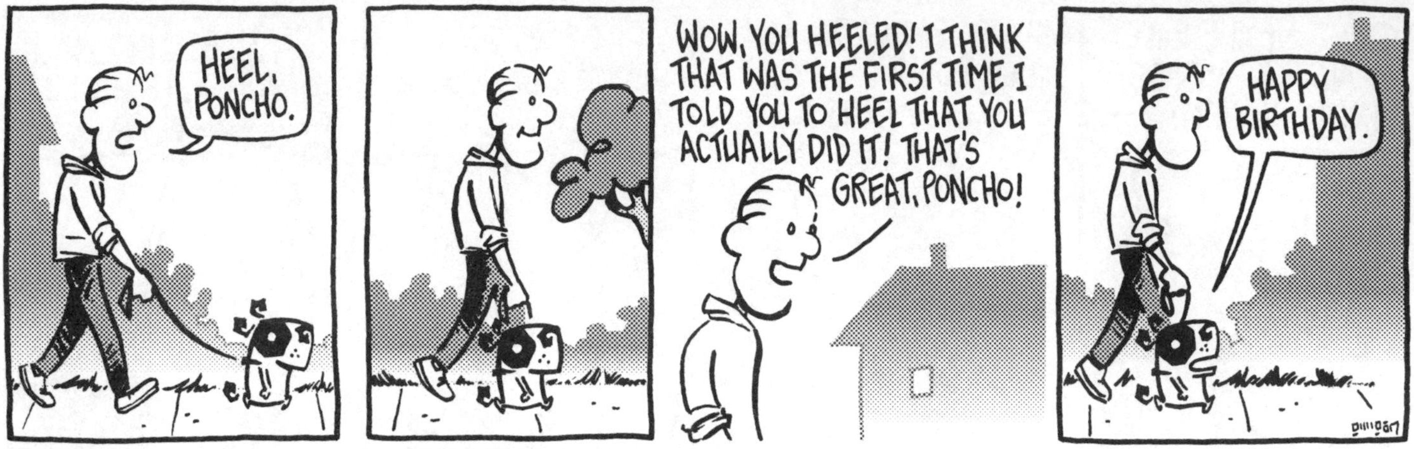
HEEL, PONCHO.
WOW, YOU HEELED! I THINK THAT WAS THE FIRST TIME I TOLD YOU TO HEEL THAT YOU ACTUALLY DID IT! THAT'S GREAT, PONCHO!
HAPPY BIRTHDAY.

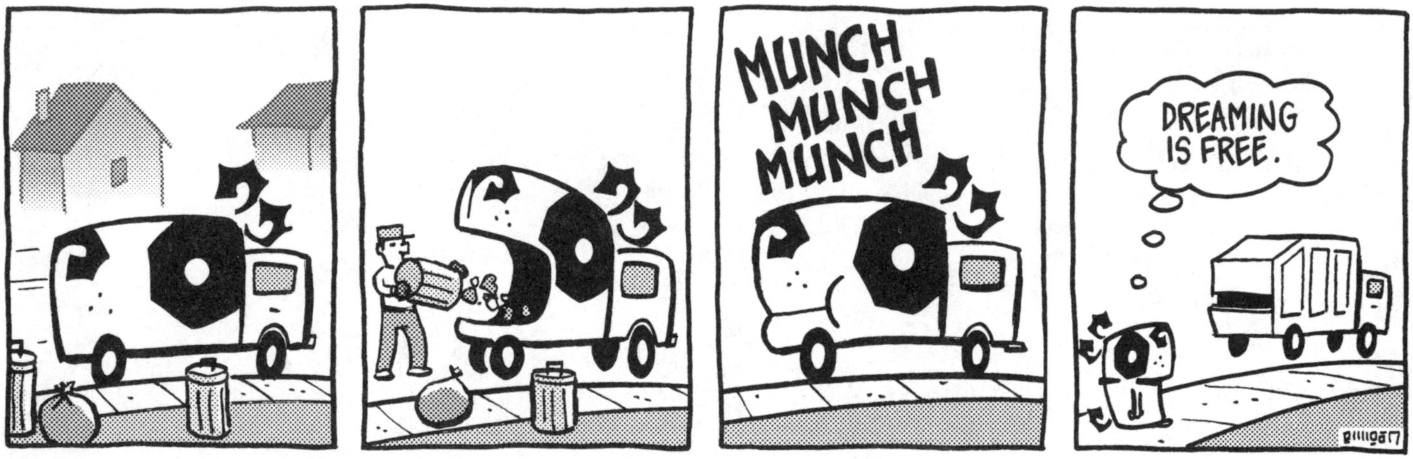
MUNCH MUNCH MUNCH
DREAMING IS FREE.

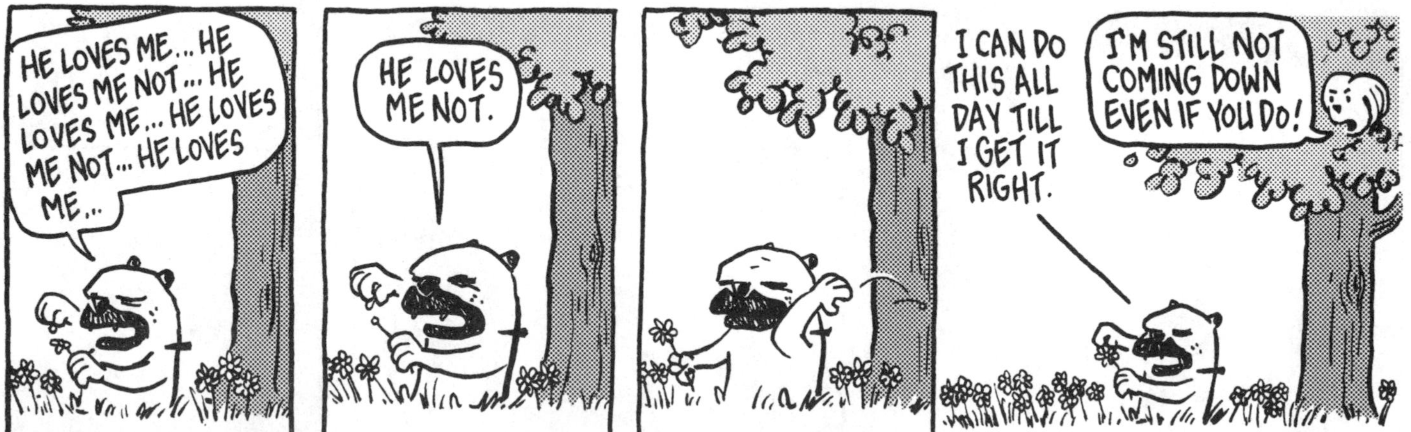
HE LOVES ME... HE LOVES ME NOT... HE LOVES ME... HE LOVES ME NOT... HE LOVES ME...
HE LOVES ME NOT.
I CAN DO THIS ALL DAY TILL I GET IT RIGHT.
I'M STILL NOT COMING DOWN EVEN IF YOU DO!